D0930510

Transport Networks in Europe

MGEN
MR907

Transport Networks in Europe

Concepts, Analysis and Policies

Edited by

Kenneth Button
Professor of Public Policy,
George Mason University, Virginia, USA

Peter Nijkamp
Professor in Regional, Urban and Environmental Economics,
Free University, Amsterdam, The Netherlands

Hugo Priemus
Managing Director of OTB Research Institute for Housing,
Urban and Mobility Studies,
Delft University of Technology, The Netherlands

Université d'Ottawa
BIBLIOTHÈQUES
LIBRARIES
University of Ottawa

Edward Elgar
Cheltenham, UK • Northampton, MA, USA

b24926280

© Kenneth J. Button, Peter Nijkamp and Hugo Priemus 1998

All rights reserved. No part of this publication may be reproduced, stored in a retrieval system or transmitted in any form or by any means, electronic, mechanical or photocopying, recording, or otherwise without the prior permission of the publisher.

Published by
Edward Elgar Publishing Limited
8 Lansdown Place
Cheltenham
Glos GL50 2HU
UK

Edward Elgar Publishing, Inc.
6 Market Street
Northampton
Massachusetts 01060
USA

HE
242
.T73
1998

A catalogue record for this book
is available from the British Library

Library of Congress Cataloguing in Publication Data
Transport networks in Europe: concepts, analysis and policies /
    edited by Kenneth J. Button, Peter Nijkamp, Hugo Priemus.
        Revision of papers presented at a European research conference in
1995.
        Includes bibliographical references.
        1. Transportation—Europe—Congresses. 2. Infrastructure
(Economics)—Europe—Congresses. 3. Transportation and state–
–Europe—Congresses. I. Button, Kenneth John. II. Nijkamp, Peter.
III. Priemus, Hugo.
HE242.A2T73 1998
388'.094—dc21
                                                                97-35406
                                                                    CIP

ISBN 1 85898 582 X

Printed and bound in Great Britain by Bookcraft (Bath) Ltd, Midsomer Norton, Somerset

Contents

Tables

Figures

Contributors

David Banister, University College London, UK

Joseph Berechman, Faculty of Social Sciences, Tel Aviv University, Israel

Piet H.L. Bovy, Faculty of Civil Engineering, Delft University of Technology, The Netherlands

Kenneth Button, Institute of Public Policy, George Mason University, Virginia, USA

Cristina Capineri, Dipartimento di Storia-Sezione Geografia, University of Siena, Italy

Roberta Capello, Department of Economics, Politecnico of Milan, Italy

Álvaro Costa, Faculdade de Engenharia da Universidade do Porto, Portugal

Fabienne Corvers, Maastricht Economics Research Institute on Innovation and Technology (MERIT), Maastricht, The Netherlands

Daniele Fabbri, Department of Economics, University of Bologna, Italy

Michel Frybourg, Groupe ENOES, Paris, France

Bernard Gérardin, 6, Chemin du Bois d'Haucourt, Pierrefonds - 60350, France

Marina van Geenhuizen, Department of Technology Policy Management, Delft University of Technology, The Netherlands

Maria Giaoutzi, Geography and Regional Planning, National Technical University, Athens, Greece

Dirk-Jan F. Kamann, Faculty of Economics, University of Groningen, The Netherlands

Heli Koski, University of Oulu, Department of Economics, Oulu, Finland

Dino Martellato, Department of Economics, University of Venice, Italy

Peter Nijkamp, Department of Economics, Free University, Amsterdam, The Netherlands

Hugo Priemus, OTB Institute of Technology Policy Management, Delft University of Technology, The Netherlands

Remigio Ratti, Centre for Economic Research, Cantone Ticino, Bellinzona, Switzerland

Aura Reggiani, Department of Economics, University of Bologna, Italy

Aisling J. Reynolds-Feighan, Department of Economics, University College Dublin, Dublin, Ireland

Sytze A. Rienstra, Department of Economics, Free University, Amsterdam, The Netherlands

Odette van de Riet, School of Systems Engineering, Delft University of Technology, The Netherlands

Piet Rietveld, Department of Economics, Free University, Amsterdam, The Netherlands

Eliahu Stern, Department of Geography, Ben Gurion University of the Negev, Beer Sheba, Israel

Mart Tacken, OSPA Research Institute, Delft University of Technology, The Netherlands

Patricia Twaalfhoven, School of Systems Engineering, Delft University of Technology, The Netherlands

Erik T. Verhoef, Department of Economics, Free University, Amsterdam, The Netherlands

José Viegas, CESUR, Instituto Superior Tecnico, Lisbon, Portugal

Jaap M. Vleugel, Department of Economics, Free University, De Boelelaan, Amsterdam, The Netherlands

Preface

Europe is in a transitional stage, from both an economic and political perspective. Free trade, open access, more competition and more market orientation have become the fundamentals for the current restructuring process of European countries, not only in the traditional economic heartland of Europe, but also in Central and Eastern European countries.

The former political-geographical dividing lines in Europe were also reflected in fragmented international infrastructure networks. In light of current transformation processes, it is no surprise that infrastructure networks are regarded as some of the strategic key forces through which more openness and free transport and communications can be induced and materialized. Consequently, interest in infrastructure issues is at present very high in Europe, a process which is even accelerated and reoriented due to the need to operate a sustainable development in Europe.

This volume gives an overview of the current concepts, analyses and policies related to European transport networks. The collection brings together revised versions of papers presented to, and discussed during, the European Research Conference entitled 'Policies on European Networks' held under the auspices of the Network on European Communications and Transport Activity Research (NECTAR) in Espinho (Portugal) from 17 to 23 April 1995. This conference was co-sponsored by the European Science Foundation and the Euroconferences Activity as part of the Human Capital and Mobility Programme of the European Union. The conference was chaired by Kenneth Button (Fairfax) and Peter Nijkamp (Amsterdam); the vice chair was Michael Wegener (Dortmund). The Organizing Committee consisted of Joseph (Yossi) Berechman (Tel Aviv), Roberto Camagni (Milan) and David Banister (London). We expect that the contributions in this book will offer a more profound insight into network concepts (Part One of the book) and network policies (Part Two of the book), as they are emerging in Europe.

The editors wish to acknowledge editing assistance offered by Dianne Biederberg (Contact Europe).

Kenneth Button
Peter Nijkamp
Hugo Priemus

1. European Transport Networks: A Strategic View

Hugo Priemus, Kenneth Button and Peter Nijkamp

1. INTRODUCTION

Diversity has traditionally been the trademark of European countries. However, at present, Europe is rapidly evolving from an aggregation of strongly fragmented market areas into an undivided and uniform market with an unprecedented scope (Commission of the European Communities 1991). This development is proceeding along several lines. For one thing, more countries are joining the European Union (EU). Sweden, Austria and Finland joined up in January 1995, and the EU is now being approached for admission by a large number of countries in Central and Eastern Europe. At the same time, steps are being taken within the EU to remove any obstacles to effective competition that prevailing national borders may represent.

As fiscal and bureaucratic obstacles to improved competition are removed, however, and as legislation through the EU is better harmonized, new bottlenecks to effective trade and communications will appear. The significance of transport networks in the EU is growing. In the transport of people, goods, services and information, there is a crucial need for well functioning infrastructure networks. The European Commission promotes the liberalization of transport markets and the privatization of transport services. At the same time, there is growing concern with priorities and bottlenecks in European transport networks which go beyond the scope of private firms and national governments.

2. TRANS EUROPEAN NETWORKS

An important strategic policy initiative in Europe has been the decision to construct and/or improve Trans European Networks (TENs). They consist of 54,000 kilometres of road: 40,000 kilometres in current use, and 14,000 under construction, to be completed by 2002 (Commission of the European Communities 1993). A further important element is the development of a 30,000 kilometre European network of high speed railways. Incredibly high financial cost figures are involved, but this needs to be set in the context that this must be achieved at a time when the share of public investment in transport infrastructure has actually fallen from 1.5 percent of Europe's GDP in 1975 to about 0.8 percent in 1990.

Transport and infrastructure policies are expected to meet economic, social and environmental goals. The European transport network should improve the accessibility of all parts of the European Union, internally and externally, while simultaneously being consistent with environmentally sustainable outcomes. This has to do with the contribution that transport makes to economic growth and employment opportunities: how can production and consumption be facilitated by transport, infrastructure and logistics? But transport has also an intricate linkage with the environmental quality of consumption and production.

Transport can promote sustainable patterns of production and consumption, but it can also obstruct them. The environmental effects of transport itself must also be taken into consideration. We know that trucks, cars, trains and aeroplanes have detrimental environmental effects. Although significant efforts are being made to improve the environmental quality of these means of transport, it is felt by many that the environment would benefit if a larger share of goods transport were to take place by sea, inland waterways, pipelines and rail. An even more strategic approach would be one which would work towards limiting the need for physical transport itself: substituting telecommunications for physical mobility, and reducing transport distances to levels that people can travel by bicycle or on foot. At first glance, however, these efforts might seem to be rather at odds with the desire for improved accessibility, the improved use of existing infrastructure, improved transport quality, and rising transport speeds.

Transport is becoming increasingly complex, and one possible solution to meeting the diverse demands placed on it lies in the promotion of multimodal transport in the movement of both people and goods. By this is meant – to adopt current 'Euro jargon' – the interconnectivity and the interoperability of networks using various kinds of infrastructure (road, rail, inland waterways, sea, air). For this reason it sometimes involves the construction of new infrastructure, especially with regard to any 'missing links' in networks and to the provision of suitable interchange points (Nijkamp et al. 1994). In exceptional cases, it also implies the creation of entirely new networks, such as a European high speed train system. More often it concerns the expansion of the scale or of the carrying capacity of existing infrastructure, by means of traffic management and the use of telecommunications technologies. Finally, having opted for a given infrastructure use, proper measures can then be taken directly to limit environmental damage.

The various chapters in this volume provide insights into various key issues which confront transport policy makers in Europe during the last period of the twentieth century. The contributions included here put particular emphasis on network issues, both from a theoretical and an applied perspective. For the sake of illustration, they draw upon a wide range of contemporary European experiences. They also range from broad strategic contributions to more micro analyses of particular issues which confront those responsible for specific elements in European transport networks. These issues will now concisely be introduced.

3. EVALUATING THE WHOLE

Considerable effort has been expended over the years on developing cost-benefit and a variety of related partial equilibrium techniques to assess the justification for building a new or extending an existing link to a network. Less has been done on seeking ways to evaluate strategic options across an entire network or system of networks. In their contribution, Frybourg and Nijkamp examine this border question and, in particular, look at the potential policy distortions which may arise if incomplete or inappropriate strategic analysis is conducted. They focus particularly on the role which transport plays in economic, political and social systems as well as on the narrower perspective of direct user and operator effects put in the particular context of developments taking place within Europe. From this an analysis framework is developed for evaluating European transport networks.

4. SYNERGY IN NETWORKS

The chapters by Capineri and Kamann, and Capello and Rietveld both deal with the issue of synergies in networks albeit from different perspectives. The existence and quantification of positive synergy effects is important to ensure that network infrastructure investment, both in nodes and links, is taken to its optimal level. Capineri and Kamann take a broad view of synergy effects, discuss definitions and consider the managerial and institutional problems of fully realizing potential synergy gains. The analysis focuses in particular on how one can develop a synthesis of the various ideas concerning network synergies by initially considering physical and territorial networks, then non-physical interactor networks and, finally, incorporating the territorial dimension into interactor networks.

Capello and Rietveld look at networks from a strictly economic perspective and focus on the externalities which exist within networks. They take care to carefully define what synergy effects in networks actually are in the micro, meso and macro contexts and review the literature at each of these areas of spatial aggregation. Significant differences in meaning emerge and, in addition, the exact nature of any externality component is often difficult to define or quantify. They find that the concept is not a simple one, but can embrace externality considerations and complementarity in economic actions as well as that of cooperative behaviour. While most synergy effects are internalized, there may be instances where they are external to the market. Government policy, it is argued, needs to be carefully devised to ensure that it is not counterproductive in wasting potential synergy benefits.

5.   TRANSPORT AND REGIONAL DEVELOPMENT

There is a longstanding debate concerning the links between transport and economic development. The direction of causation is still far from clear and the implications of different forms of transport policy for spatial development are even less certain. The so called active space approach to the topic is explored by Marina van Geenhuizen and Remigio Ratti in the context of European case studies of Rotterdam and the Chiasso region of Switzerland. The approach pays particular attention to exploring the links between transport supply, the resultant openness of a region and the ability of a region to manage this system in a long term sustainable way. The contribution highlights the usefulness and flexibility of the activity space approach in terms of its ability to identify the implications of alternative transport policy trajectories.

6.   CONGESTION PROBLEMS

Efficient use of any transport network inevitably means a degree of congestion, at least for part of the time, and policy questions relate to optimizing this level of physical interaction. Stern, Bovy and Tacken focus on one aspect of this problem, namely the behavioural response to road traffic congestion. A fuller understanding of this behavioural response is needed not only to consider how congestion should best be handled in the short run in terms of measures such as traffic management and public transport policy, but is important if longer term investment strategies are to follow efficient paths and if land use plans are to conform to social requirements.

There are numerous possible short and long term responses individuals and firms may have when confronted with traffic congestion. The study takes data, mainly at the individual level, from the Netherlands to examine how individuals may react to congested situations, both in the short and long term. Adjusting trip times emerges as a preferred option, but importantly, the chapter also points to the fact that excessive attention in the past may have been paid to reactions to changes in average trip times, whereas differences in the variability in travel time may often be a very important factor influencing travellers' behaviour.

7. STRATEGIES FOR FREIGHT

Van de Riet and Twaalfhoven contribute a chapter concerned with the design of strategies for freight transport in the Netherlands embracing road, water and rail modes to lessen the overall impact of freight transport on the physical environment. In particular, it describes the potential of the PACE-FORWARD model, a hybrid model drawing on existing and robust Dutch transport models, for gaining insights into the implications of various policies on a range of environmental factors including emissions and safety as well as economic measures such as national income. One important conclusion drawn from simulations using the model is that highly cost-effective solutions can be attained by making better use of existing systems and networks rather than constructing large new ones.

8. NETWORKS, RISK, UNCERTAINTY AND REACTIVE BEHAVIOUR

Improved information networks and enhanced access to them can lead to both increased industrial efficiency and improved regional economic performance. In part, this results from the positive synergy effects discussed above which can enhance any simple economic gains from network provision. There may, however, also be indirect costs involved as indicated in the contribution by Koski. One element of these costs is that associated with various aspects of risk and uncertainty inherent in joining a new network. Such risks include the probability of the network growing to maximize synergy effects, the prospect of alternative technologies or information channels emerging and willingness of others to participate in the information network. The problem, however, is often a circular one in that without optimal level of risk aversion, there can emerge suboptimal involvement, or lack of critical mass, in the network and hence a loss in synergy benefits.

The model developed to explore this issue is a simple one involving a single manager/owner of a firm. It allows, however, the consideration of such issues as the importance of the separation of ownership from management, the motivation of owners and the implications of certain types of inertia.

The conclusions drawn by Koski are that policies may be needed to reduce the levels of uncertainty in the introduction of new networks and that there is a role for a proactive policy with regard to the fostering of advanced communications technology.

9. NETWORK ACCESSIBILITY

Europe has extensive transport and communications networks which have been developed over many centuries. There is an accepted need that they should be continually improved, updated and, where appropriate, expanded. In some cases, links or nodes of particular networks may no longer serve a useful social function and need to be closed. A major issue, however, is the extent and nature of the access which should be allowed to these networks and from this the influence which such access has on land use and spatial development.

To analyse these types of questions initially requires a clear concept of accessibility, and this is part of the focus of the chapter by Martellato, Nijkamp and Reggiani. It reviews the literature on accessibility to transport and communications infrastructure networks. From the review, the conclusion is drawn that actual and variable accessibility are more useful concepts than potential and constant accessibility, mainly because from a practical perspective – although accessibility is a complex concept – the performance of the network is a key component.

10. THE PRIVATE-PUBLIC NEXUS

A recurring issue in this area is the degree to which public responsibilities should be involved and the extent to which private enterprises can be expected to produce the best possible outcome. The mixed economies of the EU generally hold that a certain combination of public and private decision making processes is the best answer. Nijkamp and Rienstra examine this issue in their contribution on the public–private nexus in financing infrastructure investment. Their analysis is concerned with roads and railways.

They argue that in this area the traditional arguments for government intervention have become less valid and that privatizing transport infrastructure may improve the competitive position of countries and regions.

They conclude that the privatization of infrastructure – firstly in its operation and secondly in its financing – may lead to economic efficiency gains, while other policy objectives (such as environmental goals) may be served at the same time. In practice, public–private partnerships may provide an interesting option in that they can combine the advantages of public and private regimes and reallocate the risks. The priorities formulated at a transport network level often lie outside the competencies and interests of private organizations, and in these cases, therefore, require a coordinated public policy, if possible at a pan-European level.

11. EUROPEAN AND URBAN POLICY PRIORITIES

In a subsequent chapter, Banister, Gérardin and Viegas also examine the question of the means by which transport infrastructure can be financed through new partnerships and the appropriate allocation of responsibilities between the private and public sectors. The authors argue that decision making must move away from national concerns and towards pan-European priorities, particularly if transport networks are at stake and the full benefits of the Single Internal Market are to be realized. Possibilities for public–private partnerships in both transport infrastructure networks and urban transport are explored.

Two basic types of partnership are next identified by Banister and his co-authors. At the European level, it concerns constructive or expansive partnerships and large scale investment priorities that involve putting together viable financial packages at considerable commercial risk. At the urban level, it concerns managerial partnerships often involving many actors, where the main concern is to manage access to the existing infrastructure in situations where there is excessive demand.

Banister and his co-authors provide an overview of the decisions taken at the meetings of the Edinburgh Council (1992), the Corfu Summit (1994) and the Essen European Council (1994). In 1992 the new European Investment Fund (EIF) was established and by 1994 this body had a priority list comprising fourteen projects, six of which were concerned with the high speed network. There is a particular interest in the full involvement of the private sector in these projects. Next, an overview is given of constructive private–public partnerships at the European level: the funding of the French TGV, the Birmingham Northern Relief Road, the Channel Tunnel Rail Link and the Channel Tunnel itself. The main problem with infrastructure investment at the European level appears to be the sharing of risk and the reduction of uncertainties for the private sector. At the urban level, new forms of partnership are being developed in terms of their systems management.

These partnerships involve most interested parties at the earliest stages in the development of projects and policies related to traffic generation. The EU can play a crucial role here, both in setting up the appropriate financing mechanisms for large scale projects and in promoting new forms of partnership.

12. PUBLIC INTERVENTION IN URBAN TRANSPORT

At the interface where the free market and the public sectors meet, the transport world has long experience of enjoying subsidies. Public intervention in public transit supply is often defended on the grounds of market shortcomings, such as the existence of economies of scale or the potential divergence between social and private costs. As always, such remedies for market failures should be set against the government's own failures. Fabbri has analysed mechanisms such as auctioning, yardstick competition, incentive schemes, auditing and regulation through competition within the theoretical framework of incentives theory. The problem of the definition of operational incentive contracts is discussed with reference to past and recent experiments with performance based subsidization programmes.

Incentives theory provides a solution to so called 'principal/agent' problems which emerge whenever a principal wants to induce an agent to take some action which is costly to the agent, which requires some effort or runs counter to the agent's own interests. The main problem is to design an incentive payment for the agent that induces the latter to make the optimal decision from the principal's viewpoint. Fabbri provides an example of this theory that is related to the problem of transit subsidy. Deregulation does not necessarily mean that transit subsidies are completely eliminated. Moreover, in a privatized transit market a local government may still decide to give direct subsidies in return for a socially superior transit service. The author gives some general guidelines for the adoption of incentive schemes for adopting performance based public transit subsidies.

13. PUBLIC TRANSPORT EFFICIENCY

Next, Costa analyses urban public transport efficiency and effectiveness in a contribution which examines the Madrid metro system. The focus is particularly on the implications of changes in the institutional structure of the system. He applies Data Envelopment Analysis (DEA) to provide a relative measure of economic performance in terms of the extent to which effective use is made of physical inputs by public transport operators in

Madrid. Costa also uses the Efficiency/Effectiveness Matrix (EEM) as a new methodology for evaluating the performance and resource allocation of a public transport operator.

At the technical level, the results of this evaluation confirm a greater discretionary power associated with the EEM methodology when compared with the use of the DEA technique. The number of passengers on the Madrid metro has increased since 1985 due to a lowering of transport fares resulting from the intensive use of travel permits and the improved coordination of travel modes. The formation of networks at an urban and regional level can, indeed, make an important contribution to the efficiency of urban public transport.

14. HUB AND SPOKE NETWORKS

The aviation sector will most probably also exhibit drastic changes. Reynolds-Feighan and Berechman examine the impact of liberalization in the European aviation industry. This liberalization is not a specifically European phenomenon, but rather a worldwide development having far-reaching consequences for competitive relationships, cooperative ventures and amalgamations between air travel companies, and the formation of hub and spoke networks. Regarding air freight transport, it seems to be difficult for new competitors to gain entry into intra-European routes.

Deregulation of aviation markets will likely be followed by an intensified use of hub and spoke networks in which different European airports compete for a mainport status. Nevertheless, the air freight sector is faced with several constraints to its growth. Environmental constraints, in particular, reduce the ability of the air freight sector to benefit fully from market liberalization.

15. BORDERS AS BARRIERS IN TRANSPORT NETWORKS

The creation of a single European market means that the borders between member countries will gradually lose significance, but this has proved to be a slow moving process to date and many borders are still barriers to effective competition.

Corvers and Giaoutzi analyse the changing opportunities for border region development as a result of European integration. Border regions are faced with new economic development possibilities which were previously unknown. Borders region barriers have traditionally induced a fragmentation of market areas along with a duplication of services, resulting in diseconomies of scale and scope that reduce the region's development potential and efficiency. Borders thus tend to disrupt transport networks.

In many cases, borders have acted as barriers to communications, hindering the opportunities for the regional actors involved in innovation processes to get in touch, start linkages and set up networks with their counterparts just across the border. The scope for government intervention, at national and also at regional levels, to facilitate the cross-border diffusion of knowledge is explored. For firms having a high technological capacity, cross-border networking in border regions means better economic performance. The main goals of public intervention, it is argued, should be the removal of network barriers by providing information on how to obtain access to sources of knowledge and favouring of a process that enables actors to initiate and augment linkages. These guidelines apply not only to European-wide and national policies but also to policy making at the regional level.

16. SUSTAINABLE TRANSPORT NETWORKS: PREDICTED AND DESIRED SCENARIOS

In the short and medium term, European integration will lead to increased mobility, and this will include a greater use of polluting transport modes. The improvement and expansion of European transport networks would therefore seem to be at odds with environmental criteria (World Commission on Environment and Development 1987). However, Nijkamp, Rienstra and Vleugel show how long term sustainable transport system scenarios can be designed and assessed. The authors conclude that major changes in technology, public policy and individual behaviour will be necessary if the transport system is to be made compatible with environmental sustainability. In their contribution, experts were asked to give their views on characteristics of future transport, while next, predicted and desired scenarios were constructed on the basis of these opinions. The predicted scenario is one in which many current trends continue and the transport system remains largely as it is today. The desired scenario presents a more collective transport system which includes new modes of transport, such as high speed trains, light rail systems and people-movers.

Spatial planning policy seems to be of major importance for the future of transport. Concentrated and compact spatial planning development may well be an important factor in the success of collective transport modes. The authors conclude that it would be possible, if difficult, to achieve a transport system which is more consistent with ideas of sustainability. Such a system depends on major societal changes and is correspondingly difficult to implement.

Finally, Button and Verhoef investigate the interdependencies between transport and spatial economies in the context of policies having a global environmental aim. 'Environmental utilization space' is introduced as a prerequisite tool for global sustainability. A binding environmental utilization space results in a positive, system wide, social 'shadow price of sustainability'. The application of system wide marginal tax rules based on this shadow price leads to the most cost-effective way of achieving global environmental targets.

Such first-best policies will probably not be applied, however. Optimal second-best policies seem feasible, taking into account the likely sectoral and spatial spinoffs that such policies may bring about. Environmental transport policies have indirect side effects which can be investigated.

17. TRANSPORT NETWORKS: THE LONG ROAD TO SUSTAINABILITY

The contributions to this collection make it clear that the area of tension between the demands of material growth and environmental sustainability is still to be bridged. The highest current priority in integrating Europe is being given to the expansion and improvement of the EU's transport networks; this emphasis will almost inevitably increase overall mobility but at the cost of significantly higher pollution caused by the resultant increase in traffic volumes.

Politicians will almost inevitably have to develop a more strategic view of European transport networks in the future, one in which more emphasis is laid on fostering the use of less environmentally damaging patterns and modes of transport. In many cases this will mean the increased application of cleaner technologies to vehicles, but it will almost certainly also mean more use of modes such as the train, metro and shipping and changes in overall travel behaviour. Within urban areas, the use of bicycles and walking is also likely to receive more encouragement.

We possess many of the intellectual tools with which the tradeoff between mobility and sustainability can be analysed. On the face of it, today's increasing market orientation in European transport might appear to be at odds with a shift towards less environmentally intrusive modes, but on closer examination this problem turns out to be an illusion. When a firm and appropriate public policy is carried out at European, national, and regional levels; when market oriented policy instruments (such as road pricing and tradable permits) are employed to meet overall economic efficiency targets; and when technological research and development are directed towards the closer attunement of transport and the environment, then at last we shall be able to limit transport's adverse external effects and develop transport networks consistent with overall sustainable development. The route to these sustainable transport networks at European and urban levels remains, alas, a long and difficult one.

REFERENCES

Commission of the European Communities (1991), *Europe 2000, Outlook for the Development of a Community's Territory*, Brussels: DG XVI.

Commission of the European Communities (1993), *Trans European Networks – Towards a Masterplan for a Road Network and Road Traffic*, CEC Directorate General for Transport, Report of the Motorway Working Group, Brussels.

Nijkamp, P., J.M. Vleugel, R. Maggi and I. Masser (1994), *Missing Transport Networks in Europe*, Aldershot: Avebury.

World Commission of Environment and Development (1987), *Our Common Future*, Oxford/New York: Oxford University Press.

PART ONE

Networks: New Concepts, Analysis and
Modelling

2. Assessing Changes in Integrated European Transport Network Operations

Michel Frybourg and Peter Nijkamp

1. NEW ROLES IN TRANSPORT: MULTIPLE ACTORS AND SUSTAINABLE CHAINS

Transport policy in Europe is in a state of flux. There is a need to develop an assessment methodology for new transport developments against the background of structural changes that are taking place at present. Based on a broad inventory of driving forces, this contribution aims to identify a frame of reference for investigating the economic synergy created by the new logic in European transport operations.

Transport is often regarded as a *derived* demand, which serves to bridge the distance between origins (for example, places of production, household residences) and destination (for example, markets, places of work). This means that transport is part of a *long logistic chain* on which many actors impact: collection, production, transportation and distribution are closely intertwined phenomena. This holds for commodities, but also for passengers (see Bayliss 1992). In recent years this chain has been influenced by various factors or trends (see also Banister el al. 1995):

- *Intensification* of transport; commodity transport in tonmiles tends to grow faster than the economic growth rate in Europe.
- Increase in *competition* in freight transport; the open character of the European market has generated intense competition leading to falling profit rates in the transport sector.
- The main competitive factor is the *price-quality ratio*; this means the need for an efficient organization of commodity transport, supported by advanced logistics.
- The *quality of logistic services* (internal and external) is a sine qua non; as a consequence, there is development towards a spatial concentration of

15

logistic services which would ensure economies of scale and scope (in terms of punctuality, reliability, flexibility, customer orientation, information provision, and packaging of services).

- The trend toward *logistic ports* seems inevitable; this means that regions which offer favourable opportunities for such logistic services may become dominant actors in the form of logistic mainports (supported by sophisticated telecommunication services).

- *Increase in intermodal competition and complementarity*; the result will be that the control functions of freight transport will gain importance, especially in transshipment points, so that most likely a new landscape of hierarchically organized and functionally specialized logistic centres will arise.

- *A decline in regulatory regimes* on transport markets; this will create an increasing opportunity for private sector initiatives in transport chains.

In this context, it is clear that European integration will never come into being if there is not an *efficiently operating network* connecting all nodes of the European network economy. A network is not just a sum of links and nodes, but an infrastructure configuration that is operated to provide services through one or several *operators*. A network is thus a value added configuration taking active advantage of an essentially passive infrastructure. The positive impacts of infrastructure do not only derive from the mere creation of physical facilities, but from the services generated by operators. This evidence has sometimes been neglected because of the self-operated private car, but as far as freight road transport is concerned (or most other modes) the operator is a prerequisite to any value added network. This also means that infrastructure investment cannot create economic potential, but only develop it. Thus, a network employs passive infrastructure whose amount of added value is related to the efficiency of operators.

It is also clear that a physical network has a geographic meaning and covers a given area: no network without territory and no territory without networks. A network is related to a territory and has to be adopted by a *territorial authority* (which can be local, regional, national or European) whose position will be conditioned by the spatial impact of the network. It has long been recognized in economic development theory that growth in economic activity is enhanced by trade and hence by physical access to ever larger markets for products and raw materials. Infrastructure network weaknesses limit the realization of this development potential and therefore territorial authorities are in general sensitive to the impact of infrastructure on spatial, regional and economic area development. So any strategic or political change in the territorial organization has a managerial consequence at the level of the infrastructure network. In this respect, Article XII of the Maastricht Treaty is the natural consequence of the single market and heralds the birth of the European Union characterized by Trans European Networks.

In light of the strategic importance of networks, it is also clear that the evaluation of investment programmes in a transport network should not be based on individual projects, but on the economic *synergy* created by network operators in an interconnected infrastructure. This means that an infrastructure network is a cohesive set of links (edges) between population concentrations or economic activity centres (the so called nodes), which serve to provide all services (transportation, communication) that are necessary for an efficient transport of persons, goods or information between nodes. The assessment and the evaluation of a network should therefore take account of the way such a network can be designed, developed and *operated* (see also EC 1994).

Internationalization, reflected inter alia in global sourcing, has created interwoven networks of international trading and industrial relations, in which firms in several countries produce different goods and service components of the same final product. In the last two decades, globalization and intensified competition in world trade has not only emerged from the liberalization of trade policies in many countries, but also from major advances in communication, transport and storage technologies. The 'extended' firm – or the network firm – incorporating several formal and informal links (for example, mergers or partnerships) with other firms is mainly economically oriented and reflects prevailing market forces. It falls short, however, in including and considering environmental effects and sociocultural impacts. Therefore, it is also necessary to introduce sustainable development criteria.

It should be stressed that infrastructure activities which create the most significant and durable benefits in terms of both production and consumption provide a degree of reliability and quality that is required by *paying users*. User charges should thus be based on economic prices reflecting both costs of supply and demand considerations (willingness to pay) as well as externalities. This means that new policies on network operations should be based on customers' preferences (and not mainly on modal interests), user charges and third party access. This approach is called *unbundling* by the World Bank in its *World Development Report 1994*. In this context much emphasis is placed on three principles: customer driven, user charges and third party access. Since public services are provided through a combination of capital and management, infrastructure is not only a matter of *investment* (or capital stock), but also a matter of *operation and management*. The weaknesses and deficiencies in the infrastructure sector are inherent in the weak incentives produced by the current institutional and organizational arrangements. Production inefficiency is consequently built into transport agencies, where outputs and inputs are not carefully measured, monitored and managed. Lack of maintenance is intertwined with political and institutional bias towards new investments. Traditionally, interest in networks was instigated by supply side motives, but it is increasingly recognized that new competitive behaviour of firms in Europe requires focusing policy interest much more directly on those actors who coordinate, manage and operate flows in this network. Consequently, due attention is needed for demand driven activities in the transport sector. But the way towards real value added networks based on interoperability, interconnectivity and integrated chains is still very long and full of obstacles, as it also requires a focus on private competitive actors in the transport market.

Infrastructure has unfortunately often been managed by means of a *bureaucracy*, not as a *service industry*. This traditional model is characterized by poor accounting for costs, little relationship between revenues and costs or between revenue and service performance, and thus lack of accountability to the ultimate users as the 'customers'. Apart from the poor service quality which has often resulted from this approach, bureaucratic systems of infrastructure provision have given little regard to good management of assets (for example, maintenance of roads, bridges, pipelines) which has often undermined their performance. Market instruments may therefore contribute to a greater extent to a more satisfactory provision of infrastructure. Market instruments are here conceived of as competition and pricing. A commercial orientation (for example, awareness of costs) and financial discipline are basic preconditions for the use of these market instruments. In many infrastructure activities, the potential for applying competition and pricing has moreover been enhanced by technological change, which has altered the nature of production and the services themselves.

For infrastructure activities which do not lend themselves to market instruments, other approaches may be needed to ensure a satisfactory performance. A corollary of this is that governments must focus on, and perform more effectively, the functions which should remain their responsibility, in particular certain well defined tasks of planning and regulation. The planning and financing of national highways, for example, remains a public responsibility in virtually all countries; on the other hand, many countries have adopted the goal of at least partially privatizing national railroads (for example, by privatizing railway operations).

As a result of various new market forces, the role of *public* (or semi-public) actors is declining and the importance of *private* operators is rising. Besides, in a long transport chain, the importance of transport and logistic costs may be rather significant, so that *cost improvement* in the transport sector is a necessary condition for reaping the fruits of an integrated European infrastructure network. This means that there is a need for a fresh look at European transport, particularly since transport chains tend to exhibit complex webs of ramifications and interactions. This is, for instance, reflected in the dual phenomenon of a simultaneous rise in standard packaging units (containers, pallets and so on) and in specialized handling services (for example, fast delivery services). Hub and spokes systems, new types of warehousing, just-in-time deliveries and many other phenomena illustrate the rich variety of modalities and configurations that are possible in modern transport activities. It is increasingly realized that the transport chain is increasingly governed by the wishes of the *customer*, so that ultimately the most important driving force in transport operations is executed by those integrators/actors who fulfil to a maximum degree the customers' wishes (in terms of costs, speed, reliability, and so on) (see OECD 1992).

In transportation planning relatively little attention is paid to the way the transport market is organized, and how this organization uses and shapes transport modalities. Especially the transaction theory of firms has shed new light on the interesting link between firm behaviour and network development (for example, hub and spokes systems). Even though transport systems may exhibit fragmented networks, various operators (for example, forwarding agencies, logistics suppliers) – through multimodal shipping, integral logistics and neo-Fordist customized delivery – are able to exploit transport networks for generating added value, not only in a local-regional but also in an international context. Globalization of markets, new forms of competition, more client orientation, integration of production, and warehousing, and transport innovations are shaping new opportunities for creative actors in the transport market reflected in joint ventures, 'filières', vertical integration etc. These new operators may to a large extent be considered as integrating actors in a spatial transport system which can be typified according to:

- the structure of the transport market (free competition, regulated market, and so on);
- the type of mode (road, rail, waterways, air, and so on);
- the geographical coverage (from local to global);
- the quality of service (including scale and scope), and the tariff system;
- the sophistication of transportation technology (for example, logistic platforms, telematics, information systems);
- the structure of the network (for example, hierarchy, hub and spokes, and so on);
- the territorial and modal policy competence on networks;
- the barriers to a full performance of networks (for example, regulations, conflict of competence, and so on);
- the integration with telecommunication (EDI, and so on).

Thus the transport market is in full motion as a result of new technology, new governance and worldwide mobility drift.

2. VALUE ADDED AND IMPEDIMENTS IN EUROPEAN TRANSPORT

2.1 Transport as a Value Added Logistics Process

It is clear that the transport function is increasingly shifting away from a purely physical shipment of goods and persons to a *value added process* through which in each step of the transport chain new services and economic values are added (for instance, assembly in nodal points, service delivery to train passengers in railway stations). This often implies also a transformation into goods or services of a higher market value. An illustrative example is the modern component assembly industry, where components are produced in low wage or cheap resource countries (primary production) and where the final product is assembled – after many transport activities – as close as possible to the final market (secondary production). It is foreseen that value added logistics will increasingly become a major feature of a modern post–Fordist industrial nation. Consequently, in particular *central nodes* of a transport system tend to become places of strategic importance. As a result, the *quality* of the organization of transport as a material and immaterial process chain through links and nodes is becoming the new competitive feature of modes in a transport system.

For many shippers and passengers *travel costs* and *travel time* are the most important decision criteria for the choice of transport modality from any origin A to any origin B. It is important to note that travel costs depend – apart from distance – mainly on volume as a result of scale advantages in the transport sector. This means that large nodes which attract sufficiently high volumes tend to be more competitive as a result of economies of scale. Besides, travel time depends on distance, speed and frequency. The latter implies once again that flows between large centres are offering more competitive advantages. In conclusion, there is a 'natural' tendency to seek transport routes and modalities which ensure large volumes, a phenomenon which is clearly illustrated in the hub-and-spokes model.

The above tendencies clarify also the role of two main actors in the transport market, namely *carriers or operators* who offer transport capacities and facilities (trucks, vans, cars, trains and so on), and *shippers or integrators* (forwarders) who are responsible for a least cost organization of transport. Clearly, in the case of private passenger transport these roles combine in one and the same actor, namely the car driver.

The above distinction in roles is once again important in the case of multimodality, as in this case there may be a *double competition*, namely *between different transport modes* on the same routes (or parts thereof) and between different *operators* who have to provide competitive services on this route. As a result, the transport system's operation – especially in an international context – becomes a complicated activity in which many actors play a role. From the above observation it is also clear that multimodal international hubs are becoming major action centres in the global transport and logistic system, in particular if such hubs are able to attract new value added activities (mainly based on logistics, complementary services, assembly and collection/distribution in a component industry). A simple representation of this new force field of transport systems can be found in Figure 2.1.

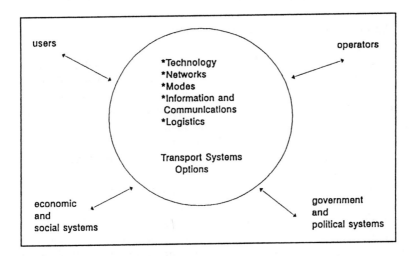

Source: Pesquera and Ibeas 1990

Figure 2.1 Transport system and its environment

In this context also the idea of a *mainport* deserves special attention. A mainport aims to fulfil many transport functions, although traditionally emphasis has mainly been on physical movement. In the past decade it has increasingly been recognized that purely physical transport is not an extremely beneficial activity, but generates sometimes even a marginal economic profitability. Several mainports have in the meantime tried to attract additional activities as a spinoff of their mainport function, for example, services and logistics centres, consultancy companies, and assembly firms. This seems to be the only way of coping with the negative environmental externalities which are necessarily connected with massive transport flows. By generating a higher value added in the same area, more resources will become available in order to finance environmental investments. Consequently, traditional mainports which do not adopt a new environmentally friendly strategy tend to become modern 'pollution havens'. Concentration of transport activities in one mainport should thus necessarily be accompanied by value added logistics and/or services and by intensive pollution abatement (or prevention) investments.

Furthermore, a multimodal and multifunctional mainport has also many more possibilities for *rapid transshipment*. For instance, a deep sea harbour like Rotterdam has an enormous unused potential in terms of connecting short sea links. Such a more environment-benign strategy for waterway transport is of course a major advantage of an international mainport.

2.2 Impediments in European Transport

The structure of production, distribution and transport is going through a rapid transition phase. Integrated logistics inside firms is increasingly linked to external distributional and market logistics, a tendency which leads inter alia to *logistic platforms* in an international network in order to fulfil the needs of just-in-time (JIT) delivery and material requirements planning (MRP). Multimodal transport will play a critical role in this new development, as is also witnessed in recent policy documents of the European Commission.

The trend towards globalization (or at least internationalization) and the need for more competition at all levels in the new European setting have provoked a profound concern over the functioning of networks in Europe. Traditionally, the interest in networks was instigated by supply side motives, but it is clear that new competitive behaviour of firms in Europe requires more focus on those actors who coordinate, manage and operate flows in this network. Consequently, much more attention is needed for *demand driven* activities in the transport sector. Unfortunately, a profound interest in a *European* orientation of users and organizers of transport in cross-border networks has until recently not been very significant, as transport policy and planning were seldom performed on this scale. National frontiers have always provided a clear physical and institutional barrier between countries, even though creative behaviour of network actors has induced growing transport demand in Europe. Intra-European transport infrastructure networks have not followed this rising trend in international mobility and show nowadays various bottlenecks in terms of *missing links* and *missing networks* (see Nijkamp et al. 1994). The emerging Internal Market between the fifteen members of the European Community has set the focus of European politicians and industry (in a more pronounced way) on issues of socioeconomic harmonization in order to remove distortions to free competition between industries in its member states. As a result, increasing consideration is now given to transportation and new actors creating a new economic potential. The Maastricht Treaty reinforces the critical function of transportation (infrastructure) for economic cohesion in Europe.

Clearly, economic development and infrastructure development generally, reinforce one another. Therefore, the European economy will remain critically dependent on *well functioning core networks as catalysts for future development*, so that networks become a vehicle for indigenous development. There is, however, a growing awareness that the current European infrastructure network is becoming outdated, without being sufficiently upgraded or replaced by modern facilities which would position the European economies at a competitive edge. *Missing networks* emerge because transportation systems are developed in a segmented way, each country seeking for its own solution for each transport mode without keeping an eye on the synergetic effects of a coordinated design and use of advanced infrastructures by various actors. Another reason for missing networks is the focus on hardware and the neglect of software and organizational aspects as well as financial and ecological implications. Cabotage, protection of national carriers, segmented European railway companies, and lack of multimodal transport strategies are but a few examples of the existence of low performing European networks. A European orientation towards the needs and behaviour of key actors for the integration of transport modes is necessary to cope with the current problems of missing and competing networks. It seems therefore necessary that the idea of Trans European Networks is now strongly supported in Europe. But it is equally important that the strategic position of public and private actors (suppliers and users) is better understood and taken care of in network policy. Creative use of multimodal networks may turn competition into complementarity and offer a contribution to sustainable transport.

2.3 Interoperability in European Networks

The above considerations have clearly demonstrated that a new element to be considered in the current European transport policy scene is the changing role of actors in this field, in both the public domain (for example, infrastructure owners or transport authorities) and the private domain (for example, freight forwarders or logistics suppliers). A major issue is whether and how transport regulatory policy can be used to create conditions for fair competition, based on a creative division of tasks between public authorities and private actors with the aim to generate added value on using intermodal networks in Europe.

This issue is once again important in light of changes in decision processes of freight forwarders, new acquisitions and mergers in the freight industry, and company diversification into non-core business.

The notion of *interoperability* of networks, as advocated in the Maastricht Treaty, generates a series of important issues which deserve thorough attention from the side of policy makers and the research community:

- the operation of transnational networks, seen from the viewpoint of European cohesion and East-European (re)integration;
- the close connection between the development of transport networks and (tele)communication networks (including new logistical systems) and their potential implications for the European space (for example, polarization tendencies towards larger metropolitan areas);
- the new roles of public and private decision makers, where a creative division of tasks has to be found between public authorities (urban/regional, national, European) and private actors (transport operators and logistics suppliers), in order to generate value added networks;
- the interconnectivity of high speed long distance networks and new regional-local infrastructures in central nodes of the European network;
- the role of physical barriers (and organizational impediments) which reduce the benefits of economic integration in Europe (including the connections with Eastern Europe);
- the emerging conflict between environmental sustainability, infrastructure expansion and competing networks (notably competing transport modes);
- the impact of new transportation, logistic and (tele)communication technologies on infrastructure life cycles in the European space;
- the lack of standardization of transport systems technologies in Europe, which hampers the full benefits of an interoperable European network;
- the completely different financing regimes for European transport modes, which prevent fair competition;
- the lack of strategic insight into the linkage between European networks and global networks developed in other regions outside Europe;
- the behaviour of 'network actors' who aim to fulfil the needs of a global (or European) economy.

Only recently, awareness is growing that interconnected networks (supported inter alia by modern telecommunications and information technology) may offer a high added value. Despite its potential, *interoperability* between different modes with a view on *cohesion* of European transport systems in order to use the transport capacity as efficiently as possible appears to be very difficult to achieve in practice, mainly as a result of a missing solid underpinning methodology. It is clear that the goal to maximize value added from the use and operation of a multimodal international network will, in general, best be reached if the impediments to free access of networks are at a minimum. Only reasons of socioeconomic distributive impacts or sustainability requirements may (temporarily) restrict free entry, but economic efficiency through competition is normally best served through actors with a free choice of different modes. This means that integration benefits will be higher as third parties are able to reap the advantages of an interconnected infrastructure network. In a deregulated transportation network the network performance is customer driven, so that ultimately the user (or customer) value – in terms of benefits or cost-effectiveness for various actors and users – is determining the overall economic performance of a network. Since transportation in a network is a very complex undertaking which covers a long chain from production – via storage, collection, transport, warehousing and distribution – to final use, the role of integrators in generating value added – in particular, via cost savings on the transport chain or via a spatial reshuffling of certain activities in the chain – is of decisive importance. As mentioned above, there is a variety of integrating activities which are performed by different players – operators, consolidators, forwarders, shippers or carriers – and which are fulfilling complementary roles in a competitive market.

It should be added that the performance of an interoperable network is – apart from demand factors, capacity limits and network design – strongly influenced by two complementary driving forces:

- *institutional organization and management* of a network (usually called *orgware*); such control functions of a network serve to increase the efficiency of infrastructure services, to enhance the access and equity conditions and to ensure sustainable operation and development in an environmentally conscious society;
- *network configuration* in terms of structure, cohesiveness, synergy, accessibility and flexibility for the operator or customer; a network configuration aims to offer services which are tuned to customer (or user) wishes and which are in agreement with the product specifications of the goods to be shipped or the user wishes of network customers. In this respect it is noteworthy that there is not a single network configuration, but a wide array of ramifications (for example, multihub systems, hierarchical structures, point-to-point connections) which may serve interconnectivity, interoperability and intermodality. It goes without saying that especially the volume or critical mass on a certain

corridor is of critical importance for the type of network configuration
that may emerge.

In light of the previous observations it should thus be noticed that the
evaluation of network performance will normally take place within a
constrained domain that is shaped by a force field comprising environmental
sustainability, institutional decision and managerial structures, spatial
interconnectivity at various (local, regional, national or international) levels,
and degree of standardization of various transport technologies. On top of
this, new management and control functions of operators (including logistics
and informatics) have to be envisaged, such as fleet management, integrated
logistic services, telematics opportunities (for example, tracking and tracing)
and so on, which will increasingly cover multiple transport modalities.
Finally, it should be noted that a focused fare policy is a sine qua non in order
to increase the value added induced by infrastructure investments. Especially
in the case of competing modes or competing types of vehicles on the same
route, contestable markets may increase efficiency – by their orientation
towards differences in willingness-to-pay. As a consequence, the quality of a
network – and its value added generating capability – does not only depend on
the quality and capacity of links connecting transfer points, but also on the
quality of transfer and terminal points in a network. Therefore,
interoperability (aimed at improving the technical compatibility between
networks), interconnectivity (aiming at improving the accessibility at all
geographical levels) and intermodality (aiming at improving the customer (or
use) value of different modes) are focal points of European infrastructure
network policy, as these concepts are crucial handles for enhancing the
socioeconomic benefits of European networks. A methodological framework
for transport systems evaluation which may offer concrete indications for
assessment is however missing thus far. A first sketch will be offered in
Section 3.

3. AN EVALUATION FRAMEWORK FOR EUROPEAN NETWORKS

In view of a proactive European infrastructure policy that aims at maximizing
the performance, and thus benefits, of interconnected networks for European
countries, it is necessary to develop an appropriate analytical framework for
assessment and evaluation, based also on a set of meaningful and practical
indicators. It seems reasonable to measure the added value and synergy of a
(European) network configuration by means of a benefit criterion which we
will indicate here by the general term *network performance*. Here we will

assume that this performance is determined by (i) *quantitative use indicators* related to actual demand (function, fulfilment or use) in relation to capacity and (ii) *qualitative structure* characteristics which depict the cohesiveness (or synergy) of a network in terms of modes, regions, interconnectivity etc.

We will first focus on *quantitative* demand features. If we take for granted that the final objective of a cohesive European infrastructure network policy is the maximization of its performance P, for example its contribution to GNP (or GEP, Gross European Product), we may assume the following relationship between the *network performance* (for example, growth in GNP as a result of transport operations) and the use D of transport services on a network (measured in values or volumes) in the country or in the network concerned (see Figure 2.2). The slope and shape of this curve is codetermined by managerial abilities, sustainability constraints, capacity limits and network interoperability.

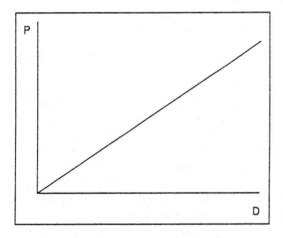

Figure 2.2 The performance-use curve

It is also clear that a high inflow of many users will encounter access and use limitations caused by a limited capacity C and hence will create congestion phenomena and other external costs (for example, environmental decay). This may then mean that we have to relate the network performance to the use-capacity ratio D/C. This is conceptually depicted in Figure 2.3.

The average D/C ratio is essentially a measure for demand intensity and its value reflects a potential growth possibility of the network use. It may also be interpreted as some sort of average productivity of a network, if the demand would materialize as actual use. Figure 2.3 depicts clearly diseconomies of scale beyond a threshold value of D/C, caused by congestion.

Underutilization of a network creates of course also a low contribution to P. Clearly, an operationalization of this curve would require an assessment of relevant empirical indicators.

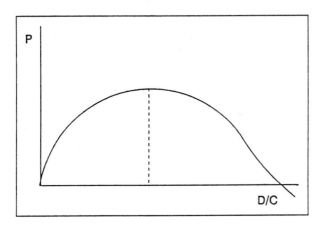

Figure 2.3   Relationship between demand intensity and network performance

Next, we will focus on *qualitative structure* features representing different perspectives on the *cohesiveness* of a network. This cohesiveness is made up of different characteristics which – according to the discussion on transport policy that emerged after the Maastricht Treaty – can be summarized under three headings: *intermodality*, *interconnectivity*, and *interoperability*. The measurement of these concepts is clearly a difficult research task and deserves due attention. It is clear that, ceteris paribus in the given use of a network, its performance will be higher the higher the scores on these three characteristics. It would be important to construct one aggregate cohesiveness score.

If it were possible to derive a single compound *cohesiveness indicator* H from these three background factors, we might assume the relationship between network performance P and cohesiveness H shown in Figure 2.4.

Here we have assumed declining marginal network performance for increasing cohesiveness. Combination of Figures 2.3 and 2.4 would yield the overall result shown in Figure 2.5.

The economic rationale of Figures 2.2 to 2.5 might in principle be used to make a *comparative* analysis of different countries, different modes or even entire networks. Furthermore, the economic significance of network improvement as a result of European strategies might also be traced in this way.

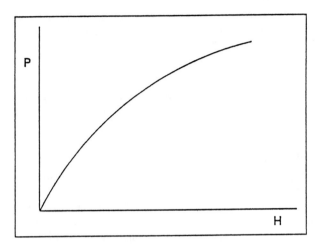

Figure 2.4 Network performance as a function of cohesiveness

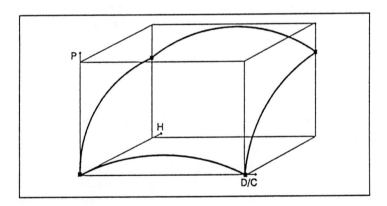

Figure 2.5 Network performance as a result of demand intensity and cohesiveness

Unfortunately, there is a serious lack of data on P, D/C and H and, therefore, we have to resort to measurable proxy indicators which mirror only part of the characteristic features of European networks and which may be used as a partial basis for assessment and evaluation of the performance of European networks. Such indicators may relate to whole networks, to separate modes or even to links or nodes. It seems useful to describe the indicators here on the basis of the well-known *Pentagon* model which has been used in earlier studies (see Nijkamp at al. 1994) to identify weak and strong elements in networks and to propose remedial policy strategies. By using this approach, the strategic factors responsible for a substandard functioning of networks and for a lower service delivery compared to its maximum potential can be identified. The components of the pentagon prism are:

- *hardware* which refers to the tangible material aspects of transport infrastructure. They serve to physically facilitate transport services or flows generated by consumers or firms;
- *software* which refers both to computer software used to control sophisticated hardware and related services like information systems, computerized booking and reservation systems, communication facilities, route guidance systems and so on;
- *orgware* which comprises all regulatory, administrative, legal, management and coordination activities and structures regarding both the demand and the supply side in both the private and public institutional domain;
- *finware* which refers not only to the socioeconomic (cost-benefit) aspects of new investments, but also to the way of financing and maintaining new infrastructures, to fare structures, or to state contracts for guaranteed finances for public transport deficits;
- *ecoware* which refers to environmental and ecological concerns (including safety and energy questions).

Now, for each of these five components we will successively describe the type of indicators which might be used to analyse the cohesiveness of networks in Europe. This will illustratively be done in a concise tabular form, which includes the three above mentioned major cohesiveness characteristics of infrastructure networks (see Table 2.1). An important step will be to translate the characteristics of Table 2.1 into measurable indicators. This will of course depend on the modes considered, the actors at hand, the regions under investigation, the policies pursued etc. Thus an important task is to design an *assessment/evaluation methodology* for transport network policy making (see Nijkamp and Blaas 1994). This would have to be based on the practical and measurable *performance indicators* for both private and public actors. It should be added that data on such indicators have to be collected over a time span which would allow for change. Thus some sort of an *observatory* based on a systematic monitoring of information is needed.

Based on the information incorporated in Figures 2.2 to 2.5 and in Table 2.1, we may give an overall characterization of the quality of European networks by combining H and D/C in one figure (see Figure 2.6).

Table 2.1 *Cohesiveness characteristics in relation to five critical success factors*

Pentagon factors

Cohesiveness features	Hardware	Software	Orgware	Ecoware	Finware
I. Intermodality	compatibility of technologies; uniform standards for rolling stock; intermodal competition and complementarity	compatibility of information systems; logistic platforms; informatics services; telematics	management of mainports; design of transfer points	sustainable transport behaviour	cost effectiveness; user charges
II. Interconnectivity	accessibility of terminals or transfer points; access to network modes; standardized technology	tracking and tracing; EDI; telematics	localization of transfer points or terminals; development of hub and spokes systems; Trans European connections	savings in energy use	efficiency; line haulage
III. Interoperability	advanced transshipment equipment	sophisticated logistics; surveillance and guidance systems; training and education	coordination of transport operations; efficient control; hazardous goods control; local distribution	efficient enforcement of environmental regulations; safety regulations	competitive strategies

31

In a simplified way we might use a trichotomic-quattrotomic classification to typify the expected performance of networks (see Figure 2.7).

It is clear that Table 2.1 and Figures 2.6 and 2.7 can not only be used to *map* the features of the structure of European networks, but also to *monitor* its evolution, either as a policy forecasting tool or as a long run scenario tool (what-if). Clearly, the demand side of transport systems is much more flexible than the supply side which is much more inert. This means that for a monitoring study time series have to be available, which cover the P, D/C and H indicators from Figures 2.2 to 2.5.

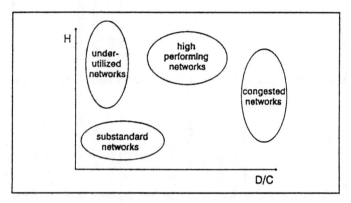

Figure 2.6 A characterization of networks

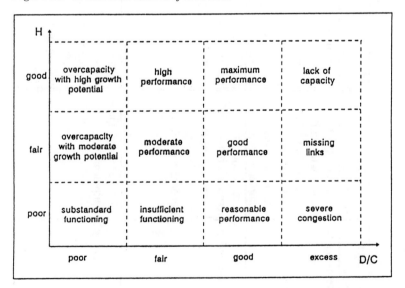

Figure 2.7 Typology of networks

After the design of a monitoring and forecasting/scenario approach, the *appraisal* of European infrastructure developments is in order. The main task here is the identification and use of *evaluation indicators* and *identification of critical success factors* for improving the performance of European transport systems.

Particular attention would have to be given to evaluating the most efficient and environmentally acceptable package of modes in an international network linking all regions and countries in Europe, while taking into account the potential for various actors of using combined transport, telecommunications and intermodal interchange.

4. THE EUROPEAN DIMENSION

Transportation fulfils a key role in modern societies, not only for road users, but also to many other actors: public authorities, network operators, industry and society at large. In the same vein, transport is assuming a central role in the new European force field. The context and nature of European trade and transport is entering a new era. In recent years, Europe has offered a scene with dramatic changes: integration of the EU market, desintegration of various nation states, and more openness between all countries and regions in Europe. To maximize the competitiveness of such a network, and thus to maximize its socioeconomic potential and performance, the quality of its infrastructure is of critical importance, in particular since transport has become an integral part of modern production processes, amongst others due to an intensified division of tasks between firms (in different countries) and a logistic integration of business processes. At the same time, large metropolitan areas appear to become poles of competition in an international context, so that the quality of a metropolitan network also plays a pivotal role.

The variety of approaches towards the assessment of European transport networks shows convincingly that – despite the glamour embodied in the three appealing missionary statements for European transport policy, viz. interconnectivity, intermodality and interoperability – it has to be recognized that there is still a long way to go. Although the needs and potentials of a coherent transportation system for both passengers and freight are widely acknowledged, the current practice offers at best examples of project oriented modal solutions and hardly any successful implementation of an integrated blend of synergetic transport solutions. There is thus a need for a systems based evaluation approach that regards the European space as a comprehensive window of transportation opportunities which may generate a substantial value added in a competitive global economy.

REFERENCES

Banister, D., R. Capello and P. Nijkamp (eds.) (1995), *European Transport and Communications Networks: Policy Evaluation and Change*, Chichester/New York: John Wiley.

Bayliss, B. (1992), *Transport Policy and Planning*, Washington, DC: The World Bank.

EC (1994), *Road Freight Transport in the Single European Market*, Report of the Committee of Inquiry, Brussels, July.

Nijkamp, P. and E. Blaas (1994), *Impact Assessment and Evaluation in Transportation Planning*, Boston/Dordrecht: Kluwer.

Nijkamp, P., J. Vleugel, R. Maggi and I. Masser (1994), *Missing Transport Networks in Europe*, Aldershot, UK: Avebury.

OECD (1992), *Advanced Logistics and Road Freight Transport*, Paris.

Pesquera, M.A. and A. Ibeas (1990), 'Transport intermodal chain in European Community ports', paper for European Transport Planning Colloquium, Brussels, March.

World Bank (1994), *World Development Report 1994*, Washington, DC.

3. Synergy in Networks: Concepts

Cristina Capineri and
Dirk-Jan F. Kamann

1. INTRODUCTION: THE GLOBAL CONTEXT

The European industrial organization and its transport system are facing events with long lasting effects. These events stem from the institutional context, from market requirements and technological innovations and are influenced by global trends. Examples are the introduction of the single market, recent 'geopolitical disorder' (that is, the changes in Eastern Europe), the increase of deregulation and privatization, new mobility patterns, new production and activities distribution (that is, JIT) and the transnational networks which have emerged in many fields (enterprises, research, technology, and so on).

These global trends require a network model of development which is based on complementarity rather than on hierarchical relationships and this acts on the pattern of exchanges and mobility. This model represents post-Fordism and also implies a more flexible industrial organization to replace Fordist mass production and mass consumption oriented models. The effects of these changes on the analysis and evaluation of networks of firms, of transport networks and communication networks are that instead of individual actors, network segments (or projects), *constellations* of networks and the *synergies* that can be created, must be taken into account.

This contribution discusses components and environments in which synergy can develop, both for physical and non-physical networks. Although suggestions about the actual measurement are made, it does not contain an empirical analysis but focuses on conceptual aspects.

2. THE MEANING OF SYNERGY

To enable a proper discussion about synergy in networks we need to clarify the terms involved. Although the term synergy has been referred to in literature (for example, Haken 1983) it has not been discussed extensively in a context relevant for both physical networks – infrastructure – and non-physical networks – socioeconomic interactor networks.

2.1   Definitions

We define a *network* as a collection of nodes (actors, cities) connected by facilities (links, arcs, ties, relationships, waves) through which entities (such as goods, cars, passengers, services, power) pass (Kamann 1993a). In *physical* networks, facilities can be roads, rails, pipes. Facilities in *non-physical* networks are relationships, paths, ties, flows of goods, services, information, capital, waves and so on (Kamann 1989; Capineri 1993b). Examples of the first type of network are railway networks and electricity networks, while   examples of the second type are networks of inter-actors, social interaction, airline routes and satellite telecommunications.

The word *synergy* literally means syn+ergos = work together for joint benefits or, better, 'cooperation of various factors or organs with a common goal or performance'. Usually, it is known under the rule '1+1 = 3', that is, the total exceeds the sum of the individuals; in other words synergy results from complementary activities and from the carry over of management capabilities. It refers to the synergetic network surplus that arises out of the combination and redistribution of resources and skills over actors enabling increased specialization of each of the actors while increasing the need for interaction because of the required coordination (Kamann and Strijker 1991:148). The non-Paretian equations introduced here resemble the *agglomeration effects* described by, for example Hoover (1975:78) and relate to 'economies of scope'.

Applied to *infrastructural* networks, Nijkamp and Reggiani (1995) describe it 'as a situation of positive user externalities through (spatial) interactions between various operators (actors and users) of a network as a result of an efficient interconnectivity of the network concerned (in terms of connectivity between nodes, accessibility of centres, or intermodality) which generates value added from scale advantages – and hence increasing marginal benefits (or decreasing marginal costs) for all users involved. This means that synergy is a users' externality caused by a favourable supply – based on architecture or design of a network'.[1] Thus a fundamental aspect of synergy is externality[2] which is based on the concept that 'the rate of growth in the demand for interrelated technologies is dependent on the number of the subscribers or clients already using that technology'.

Researchers focusing on networks of firms stress the point that both the nodes – actors – *and* the nature of the relations – links – between those nodes continuously adapt to the dynamic developments in the interrelationships and the configuration of the network. It affects both the *internal profile and the external behaviour* of each node or actor.

In this context, we distinguish the *club* type network from the *web* type network (Kamann 1993a). In the club type nodes or actors share a common goal, activity or service and therefore have parallel interests and transaction chains. Examples are subscribers in telecom networks or members of a tennis club. For club type networks, *positive* externalities are induced by the number of actors involved - subscribers, members. *Negative* externalities – congestion – are induced when all actors *actively* use the network linkages at the same time, for example, when every subscriber dials a number or all members show up to play tennis. In web type networks, actors' activities and interests are rather complementary and/or supplementary than parallel; they are linked in a serial way. In a web type network, agglomeration effects enable specialization of actors and these are induced by the volume of entities involved rather than the number of actors. In fact, the number of actors is an outcome rather than a cause of the process. The optimal network size in terms of nodes/actors involved in a web type network is a balance between the minimum required size to obtain sufficient specialization effects – or agglomeration effects – and the maximum size to allow effective and efficient coordination scope inside the network.

The traditional infrastructural view seems to relate to the club type network that comes closer to the 'classical' systems view of synergetics (Haken 1983). Researchers who refer to the web type nature of networks tend to be more critical of the systems view, pointing at, for example, the discretional and collusive behaviour of actors and the lack of atomistic actors in general. However, all authors agree that synergy requires a high level of interaction (spatial and 'intellectual') which can be achieved through improving the performance and the management of the network by acting on factors which generate any form of cohesion. This basic principle strongly affects the development of networks as regards both structural aspects (links and nodes) and economic and management aspects (such as adoption costs and competition) (Capello and Nijkamp 1993).

2.2 Synergy and Networks

Networks are a recurring theme in the description, analysis and representation of events involving interaction between actors. These are performed by a variety of disciplines, from economics to social sciences and from geography to engineering. On the one hand, networks display a well defined geometrical structure which can be expressed by variable patterns of nodes and facilities; on the other hand, they can be seen as a conceptual support defined by agreements, relationships among the elements, converging and diverging flow patterns.

Networks can be perceived as a relational model where each element contributes to maintaining the network.[3] This general principle guarantees the system permanence and its development does not follow an arithmetic but rather a geometric order, ruled by its own laws.[4] Laws of self-regulation are strongly determined by 'revolutionary' innovative factors such as telematics, globalized production, JIT logistics and so on, which have deeply affected the transport system and the territorial organization.

Traditional network development theories describe the development of networks by a sequence of different stages each referring to a topological structure of the network: from non-graph structures to more complex structures with circuits and with pockets of high density and pockets of low density of interaction. Once the network has achieved a considerable level of complexity (such as length, territorial distribution, connectivity degree) it undergoes a process of rationalization of the structure and then of specialization of the services offered. This phase is characterized by structural restructuring, by technical adjustments and by an increase of specialization of supply (multifunctional or differentiated supply).[5]

Thus if a network achieves a simpler topological structure, it must interact with other networks in order to cover larger spaces while meeting a demand which is more and more differentiated. At the same time, the network has to remain sustainable and effectively operational. The result is a juxtaposition of different network segments for differentiated activities or services operating at different levels, each representing a spatial level to be covered[6] and creating a sort of hypernetwork. This implies 'communication' among the levels and complementarity (between modes and actors) rather than competition seems to become one of the leading concepts of the development. This process implies also an increase of specialization: 'since in a network tasks and activities are distributed over actors according to their competence, every actor can specialize'. Both in physical and non-physical networks, numerous actors take part in the network coordination mechanism at different levels in both geographical and economic space. Here, barriers (physical, institutional, border type, technical, financial, cultural, and so on) influence the network development and the positions of nodes/actors and the nature of facilities. They affect synergy as they directly affect the efficiency and the agglomeration potential of the network (Rietveld 1992; Ratti and Reichman 1993; Kamann 1993b).

In conclusion, a new developmental phase can be envisaged which improves network cohesion through a process of interconnection among different networks or network *segments*. The idea is not new: in any transport cycle, a journey is allowed to be broken up into different parts where each part may correspond to a change of mode. Similarly, the flow of goods through a product chain can be broken up into the separate value chains of the actors involved in the value system (Porter 1985). The new aspect is the increasing degree of improving the *interconnection* process which amplifies the network effect and the fact that a network becomes an environment in which the performance and *behaviour* are crucial. In the past century, physical networks were designed to connect the highest number of places to be 'socially' efficient. In this phase efficiency is not measured by the extension but by both the quality of the service offered and accessibility, especially in relation to a process of distance-time contraction. In the context of regional dynamics, increased cohesion plays some important roles: it develops complementarity in non-hierarchical relationships, it adds values to endogenous resources, it is adaptable to the context, it contributes to the diffusion of urban effects and social relationships, it produces peripheral development (Capineri 1993a).

In other words, synergy is expressed by the rise in performance of a network by means of efficient and effective interaction among different spatial levels by adapting and specializing actors. In this sense we can say that synergy *only* is an implicit concept in the network model, when actors redistribute activities and resources over the network partners in an ongoing process, even if the hierarchical organization of nodes and links still persists and in certain cases even is increasing. Synergy will be absent in a network consisting of nodes that are *unwilling*, unable or unaware of the need to adjust their internal transformation process in the light of the interaction process (Håkansson 1992).[7]

3. THE PARADIGMATIC ADJUSTMENT

In this section we will deal with the changes in the real world and the paradigmatic shifts that resulted from these.

3.1 The Local/Global Perspective

In the information era the global dimension is ever present in everyday life and also in the local dimension which maintains its vitality. Contemporary culture aims at building sciences of universal validity whose first goal is to simplify the understanding of human behaviour neglecting the variety of the local worlds and the same 'local–global' relationship in which everyday life takes place. In this sense the transport and communication revolution has introduced the technological premises for a radical change of the static aspect of the traditional perspective. The scant attention paid to transport and communication theoretical matters – especially in social sciences – is also due to a lack of interest in scientific theories for a 'localist' perspective. The local still exists and has not disappeared as was expected and the 'long waves' (that is a trend towards uniformity of the world and the self-producing space) and the global village of McLuhan as the final stage of the modernization process cannot be proved either at the political, sociological or subjective level. The local level is the basis for the socialization process and can be expressed through the 'historical memory', 'the sense of place', time continuity or, at the institutional level, through any social group that can be recognized even at a political level. The global level is where the uniformity process takes place as a result of both the contraction of space and the process of information diffusion which does not imply geographical proximity. It is first of all the case of scientific knowledge and the related technology whose trend towards uniformity overcomes any other trend. This can be explained by the way in which technology spreads: price reduction for the use and adoption of intelligent systems, public investments in high cost infrastructure and equipment that are considered fundamental.

The relation between local and global can be described as dialectical and can be defined by cooperation and exchange, competition and antagonism. Although understanding this relationship does not solve the problem, it certainly helps to understand the process. An isolated 'local world' separated from the rest of the world would be meaningless: similarly the global world needs to be aware of the fundamental role of the local. In terms of networks: global events are of great importance to their development, but the local level is part of the contemporary space theory and synergy interpretation.[8]

3.2 Shift from Actors towards Relations and the Role of Cognitive Elements

The phenomena described in the previous section implied a changed set of technological, environmental and behavioural parameters. These changes can be seen as threats for nodes/actors who are unable to adapt and as opportunities for those actors who can. To enable proper analysis of the changing behaviour of actors in the real world, we find a paradigm change towards emphasizing the importance of *relationships* between actors and the internal and *mutual adjustment process* of nodes/actors. The individual performance of an actor is related to an important extent to the position of the actor in the network, the nature and the quality of the configuration of network relations the actor is part of. At the same time, the actor's behaviour and strategy becomes more and more conditioned by the cognitive set prevailing in the network.

In networks, tasks/activities and resources are distributed over actors according to their competence, enabling each actor to specialize. Hence, the individual performance of actors in terms of effectiveness and efficiency can improve; they can abandon activities that deviate from their main – core – activities which unnecessarily absorb energy and efforts. Because of this, more net energy is available for a smaller range of activities. In addition to this, routines and mental maps can focus on the core activities leading to a more homogeneous set of routines, only focusing on these core values and skills.

However, this positive effect is to some extent absorbed by two negative effects: the need to coordinate activities and the increased dependency on other actors in the network.

(i) *Internal coordination*: here, either hierarchy or internal prices are the common coordination mechanisms inside organizations. This may vary from a single site single technology single mode single product organization (with low costs of coordination) to a multiple site, multitechnology, multimode, multinational multiproduct organization (with higher costs of organizing coordination). The latter involves coordination and communication among individuals from various departments, divisions, business units inside the organizations. More complex organizations also face dangers of incompatible techniques, standards, recipes and practices but also incongruous mental maps and embedded goals between departments, sites, divisions and so on. This may well result in internal communication errors and coordination failures, distrust, or lack of loyal behaviour.[9]

(ii) *External coordination* costs fall into two categories: external through market forces and external network coordination. External 'market' costs are comparable with transaction costs in case the actor decides to buy: information, coordination, monitoring changes and positions of actors vis-à-vis the 'Five Forces' (Porter 1985). Here, the organization is very likely to face dangers of incongruence of a technical nature like standards but also in terms of interests, loyalty and mental maps between their departments and those of other actors (the contract partners). This may result in more or less serious cases of communication error, distrust, lack of loyal behaviour or even betrayal. External 'network' costs are costs related to coordinating, communication and monitoring network developments, both at the micro level – the individual actors – and the meso level – the network as an aggregate unit. Here, we come to questions whether a particular network has a shared network goal, or a network culture – with common, shared mental maps, codes, norms, methods, recipes typical for that entire network and its actors. Most likely, participating actors are not homogeneous. Even when the differences between the actors inside a network are significantly smaller than the differences between actors of different networks, we have to realize that factors like size, market share, technologies applied, organizational culture, territorial determinants and financial clout are not identical for each actor and therefore, individual actors will differ not only in behaviour, strategy and strength, but also in routines and cognitive sets.

Coordination in a network tends to focus on: (i) smoothing out changes in product specifications, properties of products and processes used, of new technologies and adoption of standards; (ii) increasing the competitiveness of the network segment; (iii) an efficient and effective use of resources in the optimal configuration of actors and relations. Coordination is in some cases an instrument of centralized network control. This is not a single actor in all cases. Sometimes, various actors are involved. Then, the role of coordinator is performed by different actors, depending on their specific function in the total process (see, for example, Johannisson 1987). Coordination in a network tends to focus on rigid 'chains' of relationships between actors. When deviation from the 'standard' easily upsets the chain – and since the chain is part of the network segment, it will upset the network segment – effective coordination makes the entire segment more efficient. When deviation from standard practice does not have repercussions for the segment, much more flexibility is allowed for. Methods to enforce appropriate behaviour of actors vary, ranging from rewards (subsidies, premiums, guaranteed price funds) to punishments (levies up to exclusion). Coordination of other actors goes through contracts and contacts. The interlocking system is an important element here. Contacts draw on normal social cohesion and group loyalty. Contracts are in practice a last resort to fall back on to force actors to behave well (see in this context Nooteboom 1996).

Actors have the choice between independent 'stand alone' strategies where they perform all activities themselves usually at higher costs resulting in lower performance and strategies of cooperation which result in the transfer of activities and/or resources to other actors increasing a large range of types of dependencies but also improving their performance (Kamann and Nijkamp 1991). 'Connection exists within networks because activities, potential or realized, bring different firms into juxtaposition. A desired activity (necessary to realize a valued outcome) will require, by definition, resources from all linked firms' (Easton and Araujo 1992). It leads to structural and multiple dependencies. Elsewhere (Kamann and Nijkamp 1991; Kamann and Strijker 1992) we described the various types of dependencies that may occur. We concluded that each actor tries to minimize dependency and maximize performance. Each actor tries to balance dependency, internal and external coordination costs with performance, perceived profitable prospects, and surplus in its relations. In other words: each actor wants to get more out of the new situation than he had in the 'old' – pre-network – situation. The sum of the energy involved for an actor equals the sum of all the net balances of energy given in all relationships this actor has, minus the revenue (or net balance of energy) received in each relation.

Dependency however goes further than just this 'technical' dependency. Being linked to other nodes/actors – being part of a network – also has a cognitive dimension. It means that when an actor does something, he has to take into account the existence, interests, potential hazards to the group, possible criticism and so on which implies a broader mental scope.

Symmetry between actors is related to dependencies and combined with the position of individual actors on their scale of 'trust <> opportunistic behaviour'.

Above, we already referred to cognitive elements: shared recipes, the 'modus operandi', recipes applied, the social paradigm of a network influencing the technological paradigm and through this the technological trajectory. Actors inside networks become conditioned by past experiences and successfully applied routines. This implies that the nature of challenges and threats from the past to which the network has been exposed moulds the way the network participants perceive present threats and formulate their strategies to deal with them. This conditioning nature may be spatially differentiated because of spatial differences in the task environment of the networks. This also explains why networks in the same industrial sector show different strategic responses to the same threat that they face (Kamann and Strijker 1994; Camagni and Rabellotti 1994).

4. HOW TO APPROACH SYNERGY IN NETWORKS

4.1 Three Steps towards a Synthesis

The first step in this section focuses on synergy in physical and territorial networks (4.2), the second step on non-physical inter-actor networks in economic space (4.3). The third step in Section 4.4 will incorporate the territorial dimension into inter-actor networks whereafter section 4.5 will combine the elements of all steps into a synthesis: a general conceptual approach of synergy.

4.2 Physical and Territorial Network Structures

It emerged above that synergy in network evolution means higher degrees of cohesiveness, that is, a combination of some cohesion factors taking part in a process which can be called an inter-networking process.[10] This process can be described with reference to the following aspects: interconnectivity, intermodality and interoperability. Each of them reflects one aspect of synergy. The main features can be summarized as follows:

- network oriented synergy (interconnectivity). This refers to horizontal cohesion between different networks and accessibility at different scales;
- vehicle oriented synergy (intermodality). This implies that the transport cycle consists of a sequential use of different means of transport;
- an institution oriented synergy (interoperability) which aims at operational and technical integration and coordination which enables the functioning of interconnectivity and intermodality at different spatial levels by the users and the actors.

The inter-networking process requires adjustments at structural, functional, operational, and institutional levels (Capineri 1993b) as it has been summarized in the 'Pentagon Model' which distinguishes five areas of interventions: hardware, software, orgware, finware and ecoware (Maggi et al. 1992).

In order to develop synergy, networks must combine cohesiveness (expressed by indices of interconnectivity, intermodality and interoperability) with network utilization/performance which has been described as the relationship between demand and capacity. By representing these two measures on separate axes, we can identify four possible situations where synergy is more or less likely to develop and each situation corresponds to a particular feature of the network and territorial contexts (Conti 1993). The anti-synergy factors must also be taken into consideration (bottlenecks, congestion, barriers).

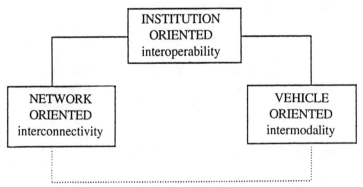

Figure 3.1   Three-sided synergy in networks

Each section of Figure 3.2 refers to territorial situations which are to develop synergy. The four following situations can be distinguished: (1)

complete and stable, (2) complete but unstable, (3) incomplete, (4) hierarchically based.

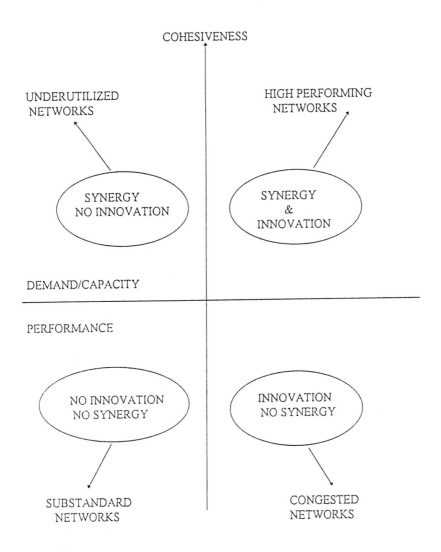

Figure 3.2 Trends in network evolution and effects on network performance

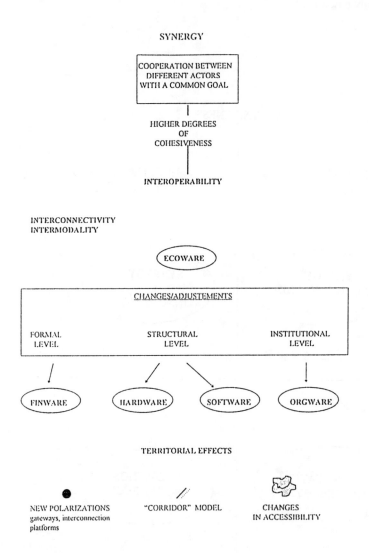

Figure 3.3 A representation of synergy and its effects on networks and territorial structures

(1) *Complete and stable situations* refer to territorial situations which are functionally open towards the outside environment due to high and varied specialization; several networks both visible and invisible are interconnected.

They include:

- gateways and global towns which need a multidimensional environment and interconnection to support the concentration of advanced service activities;
- technopoles and technology oriented areas as their activity refers to an international audience (Sophia Antipolis, Cambridge Science Park, North Carolina and so on); moreover they develop strong cooperation/complementarity relationships among the firms and the external environment.;
- industrial areas undergoing technological and organizational change which require innovations, information and production services, skilled labour and interconnection opportunities;

(2) *Complete but unstable situations* refer to structures which are linked more to the global than to the local level where it is difficult to forecast their reaction to the environment shifts. We may identify:

- tourist resorts (most of the Spanish Mediterranean coast, for example);
- multimodal platforms (for example, near ports for goods handling);
- new science parks.

(3) *Incomplete situations* refer to areas or nodes characterized by few traditional functions with limited external relationship; interconnection is limited to a few networks (road/rail, rail/air). Examples of this kind are:

- medium size towns;
- traditional industrial districts with strong internal relationships;
- growth poles with a highly specialized production structure.

(4) *Hierarchically based situations* consist of several situations which show low endogenous potentialities and are dependent on – and not complementary to – higher rank connections; for example:

- small towns;
- peripheral areas.

In this section we have defined possible directions of synergy development in networks. From these situations new structures and new forms of organization can be identified. We refer to the emergence of new polarizations (gateways, hubs, multimodal platforms, and so on); to a redefinition of well established models of regional structures, where the 'corridor model' (hierarchical organization of links, privileged paths) redefines or substitutes the centre-periphery model; to changes in accessibility and rank.

4.3 Non-physical Inter-actor Synergies in Economic Space

We described how synergy arises out of the linking complementarity and similarity of actors, redistributing resources and activities over the participating actors. In this process of redistribution and mutual adaptation, the potential for optimizing the organization of production is explored as fully as possible, increasing its efficiency and effectiveness. This optimization can be utilized in fields like R&D, production, marketing, distribution, lobbying and so forth. The *process* of optimization is subject to normal learning curve behaviour. Actors have to familiarize themselves with each other, mutual trust has to be developed and potential (internal) sources of resistance among stakeholders have to be eliminated or accommodated. The process of internal and external adaptation is an ongoing process, since individual actors will try to innovate their products and processes to strengthen their competitive position.

Whether synergy is equally distributed over all actors involved depends on the power distribution in the network. Furthermore, coalitions and cliques of countervailing or conspiring actors manage to increase their share by increasing their joint power. In some cases, this shift in synergetic surplus from one clique of actors towards another clique as a result of countervailing power *can* be measured (Kamann and Strijker 1991). However, many compromises between actors or shifts in the power balance between them are translated into changed supply arrangements that do not necessarily affect the prices or direct revenues and therefore are difficult to trace.[11] We may take a more formalized approach to describe the net balance of the energy involved for a particular actor which equals the sum of all the net balances of energy *given* in all relations this actor has, minus the revenue (or net balance of energy) *received* in each relation.[12]

In a network with n actors P_i stands for the total increase in Performance of actor i, C_i stands for the total increase in coordination Costs of actor i. S_n represents the total Synergy of the n-actors network.

For

$$S_n = \sum_{i=1}^{n} (P_i - C_i) > 0$$

we have a case of positive synergy and a potential *win-win* situation. Whether it really is a win-win situation or a win-lose situation depends on the distribution of power over the actors involved. A $S > 0$ situation implies a win-win when for *each* of the n actors holds, that $P_i > C_i$.

For a case where

$$S_n = \sum_{i=1}^{n} (P_i - C_i) = 0$$

we see a zero sum game: if someone wins, there has to be someone else losing at the same time.

We assumed in the above, that C_i in fact stands for $C_i = C_{h,i} + C_{m,i} + C_{nw,i}$ where $C_{h,i}$ stands for Costs, actor i has to make to coordinate *internal* activities/actors, $C_{m,i}$ stands for costs involved in coordinating *market* relations with actors (including monitoring, analysing, interpreting, and so on); and finally $C_{nw,i}$ stands for costs involved in coordinating (n-1) network relations with actors.[13]

Synergy for the network would then occur, when

$$\sum_{i=1}^{n} (P_i - (C_{h,i} + C_{m,i} + C_{nw,i})) > 0$$

In this formula, we can also trace the effect of substitution between internal/external relations and between market/network relationship.

The formulae above refer to the *actual* performances of actors. These actual performances include in fact two factors that can be seen as a network cost: (i) costs of compromising (Porter 1985) and (ii) costs of rigidity or its opposite, premium of rapid adjustment (Kamann and Strijker 1992). Especially when the goals and interests of actors deviate significantly, the final solution may not be the best for either or all participants. Deleting (= excluding) one or more specific actors may well reduce the costs of compromising and because of that increase the total values of S_n to a higher value for S_{n-m}, where m is the number of excluded actors or relationships where compromises had to be found. Costs of rigidity are relevant in fast changing competitive environments where a rapid change in any activity by an actor may be of strategic importance. This *cost* is difficult to measure. However, in many cases it can be derived from its opposite, the *premium* of rapid action, for instance, with subsidies given to networks for certain new products or technologies. The most effective network will be able to get more subsidies (cf. Kamann and Strijker 1992).

Networks based on and assuming complementarity of activities in order to enable specialization are of the web type. Does this mean that the club type networks with completely similar actors or activities cannot do this, or is it limited to only certain aspects? Similar actors can exchange products in production to reach scale effects; joint production, distribution and so on: 'pooling things'. For club type networks we refer to *horizontal synergy*. Ansoff (1965) refers in this context to (i) *turnover synergy* – derived from joint distribution channels, marketing; (ii) *operational synergy* – lowering operational costs by sharing scale effects, joint procurement; (iii) *investment synergy* – lowering individual investment needs by joint use of plants, machines and R&D; (iv) *management synergy* – because of less mistakes, faster and more effective decisions through shared experiences and routines.

Porter (1985) gives with his concepts of *value chain* and *value system* a down to earth methodology to actually effectuate synergy this way. Porter's value chain/system not only applies to horizontal synergy between club type actors, but also to horizontal and vertical synergy between web type actors. He divides all activities of a unit (node, actor) into five *primary activities* and four *support activities*. The primary activities are (i) inbound logistics; (ii) operations/processing; (iii) outbound logistics/distribution; (iv) sales and marketing; (v) after sales/service. The support activities are (i) infrastructure; (ii) human resource management; (iii) technology policy and (iv) procurement. Apart from infrastructure – for example, a Chamber of Commerce number, telephone line, bank account, general overhead and a physical site – that is more or less general to all primary activities, the other support activities are differentiated between the primary activity they support. The value chains of the individual actors link up into the value *system*.

Horizontal and vertical synergy can then be reached by an improved organization and distribution of the participating actors' value chains through joint operations and/or through learning. Joint operations refer to pooled activities and resources or externalized activities from one value chain into another value chain. *Learning* refers to copying – even after adjustment to specific needs – the technology, processes, software, or knowhow used by other actors in corresponding activities. Since these can be seen as resources, learning refers to the transfer of tangible and intangible resources.

4.4   The Intersection between Economic and Geographic Space: The 'Milieu'

Network studies that include both spatial dimensions use the term *milieu*. Maillat (1993:4), describes milieu as 'a spatial set which has a territorial dimension but which presents a unity and coherence that are reflected by identifiable and specific behaviour patterns and by a technical culture, understood as the elaboration, transmission and accumulation of practices, knowledge and knowhow, standards and values connected with an economic activity'. The 'réseaux d'innovations' consist of the *réseaux territoriaux* and the *réseaux industriels*. The first follows the logic of the (localized) actors involved, the second follows the logic of the (segmented) production: industry and technology. In the context of synergy we could add an extra element in that *proximity* and *spatial specificity* are sources for potential competitive advantage in value system terms. They can also be a disadvantage where actors have to spend much of their energy in overcoming the shortcomings of the 'réseaux territoriaux', giving them a handicap in their 'reseaux industriels'. Therefore, it is important to find the *proper balance* between a network that is too territorially focused and a network that has no 'embeddedness' at all.

The *physical elements* refer to the nature of the infrastructure, the role of barriers or bottlenecks and how they affect the milieu. This implies that any *changes* in these elements also change the possibilities of actors inside the milieu both in positive *and* negative directions. Improved infrastructure reducing travel time is likely to decrease the perceived (hard) distance with other actors. This increases contacts and changes the functional span of the milieu encompassing more actors. The same applies to the removal or reduction of barriers and bottlenecks. However, removing bottlenecks/barriers may also have negative effects on the 'indigenous' milieu and the networks inside, opened up to external competitors to enter more easily. Many milieux adapt to situations with bottlenecks, finding solutions to overcome them. Removing bottlenecks, effectively changing the parameters of competition may upset or remove the viability of the niche in which these actors were operating in. Changes in the physical elements *may* be important improvements in the innovation stimulating determinants. However, they can never guarantee that indeed the milieu will become (more) innovative as a result of these changes.

4.5 The Synthesis on Synergy

Although Section 4.2 focuses on physical and territorial networks, these networks are implemented, operated, designed and controlled by organizations, transport companies, public authorities and so on. Many of these actors transcend the territorial local scale. Therefore, Sections 4.3 and 4.4 also apply the analysis of physical networks. The terms interconnectivity, intermodality and interoperability from Section 4.2 in their turn can be related to the terminology used in Sections 4.3 and 4.4. Interconnectivity relates to the horizontal synergy in club type networks and to interaction between different spatial levels, both geographic and economic.

It refers to the need to avoid chasms between two densely connected groups of actors (nodes) or networks, the so called structural holes (Burt 1992). Interoperability relates to value system adjustments or interweaving of activity cycles between nodes/actors and interoperability to (i) the adjustments of nodes/actors in terms of common standards, recipes and 'mental maps'; (ii) the 'milieu' elements described in Section 4.4.

5. CONCLUDING REMARKS

Synergy originates from a number of sources. Depending on the nature of the network we study – club type or web type – we found different mechanisms that can create synergy. In real life, we will find that networks have both club type aspects and web type dimensions. Interconnectivity for club type aspects can be combined with intermodality and interoperability that is more related to web type aspects. However, club type aspects will have different optima vis-à-vis number of nodes/actors included and amount of entities passing through the facilities from web type aspects. Nodes/actors who are more focused on synergy arising out of the club type aspects will therefore show different strategies than actors who are more focused on the web type aspects. This may lead to friction inside the total network as to the perception of the 'best' network strategy. Uncertainty about the nature of networks and the potential of synergy may reinforce this phenomenon. Coalitions between similarly oriented actors may force the network into a strategy that is suboptimal. A good insight and analysis of *all* potential synergy creation could prevent or at least reduce the risk of such a development.

REFERENCES

Ansoff, H.L. (1965), 'The firm of the future', *Harvard Business Review* **38/6**, p. 85.

Axelsson, B. and G. Easton (eds.) (1992), *Industrial Networks,* London: Routledge.

Bood, R.P. and D.J.F. Kamann (1994), 'The ABC of outsourcing' (Het ABC van uitbesteden), *Maandblad voor Accountancy en Bedrijfseconomie* **68** (12), pp. 686–96.

Burt, R.S. (1992), *Structural Holes*, Cambridge, MA: Harvard University Press.

Camagni, R. and R. Rabellotti (1994), 'Footwear production systems in Italy; a dynamic comparative analysis', paper presented at the GREMI Meeting, Grenoble, 11th June.

Capello, R. and P. Nijkamp (1992), 'The role of network externalities on corporate and regional performance', paper presented at the Nectar Workshop Cluster 2, Leiden, Netherlands, 21 November.

Capello, R. and P. Nijkamp (1993), 'Measuring network externalities', paper presented at the Nectar Cluster 2 Workshop, Certosa di Pontignano, Siena, 4–5 June.

Capineri, C. (1993a), 'Italian Geography and Networks', *Flux,* Groupe Reseaux, Paris, **11**, pp. 5–17.

Capineri, C. (1993b), 'Interconnectivity: its role in network structural and functional development', paper presented at Nectar Workshop, Certosa di Pontignano, Siena, 4–5 June.

Conti, S. (1993), 'Tecnologia e nuova territorità', *Riv. Geogr. Ital.* **100**, pp. 671–702.

Easton, G. and L. Araujo (1992), 'Non-economic exchange in industrial networks', in Axelsson and Easton (eds), pp. 62–87.

Håkansson, H. (1992), 'Evolution processes in industrial networks', in Axelsson and Easton (eds), pp. 129–143.

Haken, H. (1983), *Synergetics: An Introduction,* 3rd edn Berlin: Springer Verlag.

Hoover, E.M. (1975), *Regional Economics,* New York: Alfred Knopf.

Johannisson, B. (ed.) (1987), 'Organizing: the network metaphor', *International Studies of Management and Organization,* **XVII**, 1.

Kamann, D.J.F. (1989), 'Actoren binnen netwerken (Actors inside networks)', in Boekema, F.W.M. and D.J.F. Kamann, *Sociaal-economische netwerken,* Groningen: Wolters-Noordhof, pp. 29–84.

Kamann, D.J.F. (1993a), 'Strategy and networks', in Beije, P., J. Groenewegen, and O. Nuys (eds), *Networking in Dutch Industries,* Apeldoorn/Leuven: SISWO/Garant, pp. 117–64.

Kamann, D.J.F. (1993b), 'Bottlenecks, barriers and networks of actors', in Ratti and Reichman (eds), pp. 65–102.

Kamann, D.J.F. and P. Nijkamp (1991), 'Technogenesis: origins and diffusion in a turbulent environment', *Technological Forecasting and Social Change* **39** (1–2), pp. 45–66.

Kamann, D.J.F. and D. Strijker (1991), 'The network approach: concepts and applications', in Camagni, R. (ed.), *Innovation Networks,* London: Belhaven Press, pp. 145–173.

Kamann, D.J.F. and D. Strijker (1992), 'Mechanisms of coordination in the Dutch horticultural complex', *European Review of Agricultural Economics* **19**, pp. 393–416.

Kamann, D.J.F. and D. Strijker (1994), 'Pork production in the EC: some observations on endogenous institutions', in Biemans, W.G. and P. Gauri (eds), *Meeting the Challenges of New Frontiers,* selected proceedings IMP, Groningen: University of Groningen, pp. 779–91.

Maggi, R., I. Masser and P. Nijkamp (1992), 'Missing networks in European transport and communications', *Transport Review* **12** (4), pp. 311–21.

Maillat, D. (1993), 'Territorial development, milieu and regional policy', Working Paper, Université de Neuchâtel (IRER) nr. 9306.

Muscarà, C. (1996), 'La geografia dei trasporti e delle comunicazioni tra teoria dello spazio geografico e dialettica locale-globale', in Capineri, C. and M. Tinacci Mossello, *Geografia delle comunicazioni: reti e strutture territoriali,* Milano: Giappicchelli.\

Nijkamp, P. and R. Reggiani (1995), 'Multilayer synergy and networks', paper: Communication au Rencontre européenne NECTAR/GDR 'Reseaux'/INRFTS Lille, 28 January.

Nooteboom, B. (1996), 'Trust, opportunism and governance: a process and control model', *Organizational Studies* **17**, pp. 985–1010.

Porter, M.E. (1985) *Competitive Advantage,* New York: Free Press.

Ratti, R. and S. Reichman (eds) (1993), *Theory and Practice of Transborder Cooperation,* Basel: Helbing and Lichtenhahn.

Rietveld P. (1992), 'International transportation and communication networks in Europe: the role of barrier effects', paper presented at the Nectar Workshop Cluster 2, Leiden, Netherlands, 21 November.

NOTES

1. For the authors synergy is a particular case of the more generic phenomenon of synergetics, which refers to morphological changes in complex dynamic systems; synergetics focuses its attention on those situations where systems change their macroscopic behaviour qualitatively where new qualities of a system emerge. Synergetics can be considered as a strategy to cope with complex systems.

2. In economic theory an externality is said to exist when a person external to a transaction is directly affected (positively or negatively) by the events of the transaction (Capello and Nijkamp 1992).

3. The main difference between infrastructural – physical – networks and socioeconomic inter-actor networks is here that relationships in physical networks – the links – are slower to establish and slower to change. The *sunk costs* involved in abandoning a link are significant. Links – relationships – in non-physical inter-actor networks can be established faster and switching costs may be lower, tempting actors to show opportunistic behaviour in some cases. Both cases can be treated as transaction cost type decisions.

4. The network permanence is achieved by more or less radical adjustments in the time span and it shows that the network 'works', that is, it is able to supply the service (transport or other) and expresses the adaptation of the network to the system (self-regulation). It can be measured by efficiency and impact indices.

5. This is demonstrated by the trend to cut off network branches, especially the unprofitable ones ('rami secchi' in Italy) and by the differentiated supply of, for instance, public transport services (local, regional, intercity, high speed rail services). In non-physical networks, these phenomena are found as reducing the number of suppliers to only certified suppliers and relocation of production while eliminating uncompetitive production sites and suppliers and customer accounts.

6. For example, local, interurban, regional, interregional, international for transportation in geographical space, segmented markets in economic space.

7. The GREMI research group make in this context a distinction between a 'network' and an 'innovative network'. The first can be viewed as a loosely coupled set of nodes/actors, the second as a set of interwoven activity cycles of dynamically adjusting actors.

8. The notion that spatial patterns are wholly a consequence of spatial variables has been challenged by researchers who argue that events at the local level are determined by economic and political events at the national and global level ('top-down' approach). But the features of the 'locality' and the influence of other circumstances are of such crucial significance for the analysis that they cannot be omitted in the theoretical framework.

9. Many complex organizations try to reduce the organizational costs of coordination by reducing overheads, decentralizing decision power and outsourcing activities. The overall result of this often does not meet expectations and very rarely is even accurately measured in financial terms (Bood and Kamann 1994).

10. The concept of cohesion is broader than connectivity which generally refers to structural aspects of networks.

11. Bood and Kamann (1994) proposed a methodology to actually measure this by using Activity Based Costing.

12. To be accurate, the *shadow* revenues and costs for alternative situations should be compared with *current* rather than with *historical* situations. The question is rather 'what would have been the cost/performance if we would have continued in the old way' rather than 'what did it cost us in the past'. Even when performance at t=2 did not improve compared to t=1, the shadow performance at t=2 may well have been much less.

13. Whether an actor is classified as market actor or network actor depends on the nature of the relationship. This implies that two actors may have

relationships that are typically network, but at the same time, may have relationships that may be classified as market (transactional) relationships.

4. The Concept of Network Synergies in Economic Theory: Policy Implications

Roberta Capello and Piet Rietveld

1. INTRODUCTION

In recent years much attention has been devoted to the concept of *networks* which has assumed an important role when the idea of an '*Information Economy*' came into being. By this term the literature refers to an economy where there is a large share of all economic activities associated with the production, distribution and consumption of information. The rapid rise of the service sector – not only for domestic but also for international activities – mirrors the fact that the Western world is increasingly marked by a wide variety of communication and interaction patterns ranging from a local up to a global scale. This tendency is, moreover, reinforced by the emergence of the information and telecommunications sectors, also denoted as the New Information Technology (NIT) sector or the Information and Communication Technology (ICT) sector and by advanced transport systems (see also Giaoutzi and Nijkamp 1988).

The wide technological changes and innovation taking place in telecommunications and transport systems have been regarded as the driving forces pushing society into the so called 'Information Economy'. In this kind of economy, communication and transport networks define the competitive advantages for firms and comparative advantages of regions; in fact, it is widely recognized that those local, regional and national economic systems which will not have advanced transport and telecommunications systems in the coming years risk losing much of their competitiveness (Gillespie and Williams 1988).

There is ample evidence of the fact that transport and telecommunications networks may be seen as the 'carriers' in both a literal and symbolic sense of the spatial configuration of the economy (Banister et al. 1995; Capello and Gillespie 1993). For this reason many studies have focused attention on telecommunications and transport networks, analyzing the diffusion mechanisms associated with these networks, and organizational, spatial and industrial impacts that these networks have on firms and local systems.

In the last years the concept of 'network' was not limited to the configuration of physical networks; currently the concept of network is widely used to explain 'corporate growth', as well as specific organizational forms for urban development. The concepts of firm networks and city networks are advocated to explain the way in which, respectively, firms and urban systems grow in these years (Camagni and Gambarotto 1988; Chesnais 1988; Camagni and De Blasio 1993; Johansson et al. 1994).

Thus, the literature emphasizes the importance of both material and non-material 'networks' to explain competitiveness of economic actors and comparative advantages of local economic systems. The more obvious interpretative aspect of the success of the network concept is the fact that within a network an economic actor exploits *synergies* and thus obtains advantages. However, although the word synergy is widely used in network theory, its definition is still fuzzy. Moreover, policy implications which emerge in the presence of synergies deserve careful analysis.

This chapter attempts to provide a first insight into the concept of synergy, an analysis which encompasses both the definition of this concept, and the policy implications associated with it. For what concerns the definition of the concept of synergy, Section 2 presents some ideas on the role this concept has played in traditional microeconomic theory. Section 3 relates the concept of synergy to that of material networks, and finally Section 4 presents some policy implications which emerge when synergies are present.

2.   SYNERGIES IN TRADITIONAL ECONOMIC THEORY

As mentioned before, the word synergy has received much attention in the development of studies on networks and network behaviour. However, an analysis of traditional microeconomic concepts shows that in reality the idea of synergy is also important for other phenomena, where the network concept is more implicit.

Synergies may be associated to both material and non-material networks. As a starting point, we describe the notion of synergy as a situation where two consumers (or producers) benefit from joining their consumption (or production) activity, compared with the situation that both consume (or produce) independently. In other words, synergy breaks the value additivity principle of utility (that is, $1+1 > 2$).

In this section we will look for examples from the economic literature where the notion of synergy seems to be relevant. This will lead to more specific descriptions of the notion of synergy and the reasons for the existence of synergy. Table 4.1 contains some examples taken from theories which present different levels of analysis; a micro, a meso and a macro level are underlined, for both material and non-material networks. In particular, this section deals with the synergy concept in traditional microeconomic theory, and is related to *non-material networks*. In this section, then, by network we refer to situations of market transactions where the relationship among economic actors is stable, and has a long term duration. Section 3 will instead take into consideration the concept of network synergies stemming from *material networks*. In that case, telecommunications and transport networks will be considered.

Table 4.1   Typology of network synergy based theories

Networks Approaches	NON-MATERIAL NETWORKS	MATERIAL NETWORKS
MICRO	Oligopoly cartels theory Public goods theory	Network externality theory
MESO	Cooperation agreements theory Industrial districts theory	Filière economies in transport and telecommunications network theory
MACRO	Urban agglomeration theory Milieu innovateur theory City network theory	Regional symbiosis effects theory

2.1 The Micro Approach

The first approach which can be used for the definition of synergy is a *micro approach*. The reference here is to traditional microeconomic theories. Take as an example the microeconomic theory of public goods. These goods are characterized by features such as non-excludability, non-rivalry, and indivisibility. As a consequence, markets will not lead to appropriate levels of supply of these goods. Consumers would benefit from cooperative behaviour. However, a tendency exists that some individual users will break the agreement because of free rider considerations; this holds true especially when the number of consumers is large. Thus, cooperation often does not solve the problem of the lack of supply of public goods. A third way of supplying public goods would be public provision, although also this alternative does not necessarily lead to appropriate levels of supply (Frey 1978). The non-rivalry and indivisibility features appear to be crucial factors explaining why cooperation of users, or public sector involvement in the supply are important for public goods.

Public goods theory is not the only microeconomic theory where the synergy concept plays a crucial role. Another quite similar example is present in the theory of oligopoly market structures, where a cartel is decided among firms operating in the market. A cartel represents a market structure where an agreement is signed among firms to behave as monopolists, thus fixing quantity and price at a monopolistic level. The advantage in the cooperation for each firm is the low degree of competition in the market. However, the tendency towards a more individual behaviour is present; a firm fixing a lower price of the good in the market immediately obtains market shares at the expense of others. Thus, as in the case of public goods, also here *synergy effects* take place when cooperation exists. When the cooperative behaviour is not present, advantages from synergies are no longer there. It is clear, of course, that the advantages discussed here only relate to the producers, not to the consumers.

A first definition of what is meant by synergy may be given after these examples: synergy means a situation where two (or more) economic actors cooperate to produce or consume a good obtaining advantages from a cooperative behaviour.[1] The essential elements that lead to benefits from cooperation in these examples are non-rivalry and indivisibility in the first example, and market power in the second.

The examples given, however, underline that even though cooperation is good for all actors involved, there are forces at work with the effect that cooperation does not actually take place. The reason is that individual actors will find it profitable not to join (or to cheat by secretly offering a discount). Thus, although the aggregate benefits of cooperation are higher compared with the situation of non-cooperation, individual actors will find that a free rider approach is more advantageous. This threatens the opportunities of cooperation and the exploitation of synergies. It undoubtedly has policy implications, because it implies that the synergy opportunities cannot be exploited by markets, and often not by voluntary cooperation; thus government may play a key role here.

2.2 The Meso Approach

If we move to the *meso approach*, other examples can be given of theories where the concept of synergy is present. During the eighties much attention was paid to new ways firms grew. The traditional dichotomy between 'make' or 'buy' (à la Williamson 1975) is no longer sufficient to explain firms' behaviour and corporate strategies of growth. A new way of growing experimented with by firms is *cooperation agreements among firms belonging to different sectors of the economy*. The increasing turbulence and volatility of markets, the increasing technological upgrading of products (among others in the telecommunications sector, where informatics is increasingly playing an important role) require different skills and technological knowledge. The complementary skills necessary to face the new markets are obtained by firms with cooperative agreements, which characterized what has been labelled the 'make together' (Camagni and Rabellotti 1992); the 'make together' implies a cooperative behaviour among firms, where synergies are achieved by complementary inputs to produce a common output.

The choice of the 'make together' instead of a 'make' or 'buy' choice has different reasons, which have been emphasized by many authors,[2] and which are linked to specific advantages for the firm:

- the achievement of economies of scale, towards the merging of R&D, production and marketing functions;
- the control of the market of complementary assets in order to be able to reduce the risk of failure in front of strong market volatility;
- to control the dynamics of the market of complementary assets, which for a single firm would imply very high R&D expenditure. Cooperation agreements in R&D allow the division of expenses among different firms and the decrease of risks.

The role of policies in stimulating cooperation agreements is rather limited, and related to the role of facilitating the process of cooperation among firms, by assuring communications and transport infrastructures among firms located in different areas.

This example underlines another aspect of a synergic behaviour. *Synergies are present when a cooperative behaviour is put in place in order to exploit complementarity in the production of a particular good.*

A second example may be found in the theory of 'industrial districts'. Going back to the work of Marshall, his theory justified the presence of a group of firms in a specific area by the existence of what he called the 'industrial atmosphere', a sort of collective agent which was influencing the locational choice of firms by assuring the presence of external economies to the local firms. The concept of industrial atmosphere has been developed further and has been associated to industrial economies, that is, those economies (external to the sector, but internal to the area) which stem from proximity and industrial specialization effects. A vast literature on 'industrial districts' has explained this phenomenon through the cooperative behaviour of local firms, due to advantages that each firm achieves by being linked to the network. External economies have been recently reinterpreted as '*collective effects*', underlining the important aspect of collective behaviour.[3] Recently it has been underlined that these collective effects are the result of two different positive effects, external economies and cooperation. The difference between the two is that external economies are obtained only by being located in a local district. They are a kind of public good available to every agent in the area. Cooperation is instead something which is obtained by actors only if they pay for it. It becomes a sort of club good available to a specific group of people who paid for it (Rabellotti 1994). The synergy concept refers more to external effects, that is, to spontaneous behaviour stemming from the advantages obtained by individuals. For this reason, at the basis of the theory on local districts there is the common idea that the efficiency of the whole district is greater than the sum of the efficiency of individual firms.

2.3 The Macro Approach

Let us move to the third level of analysis, the *macro, or territorial, level*. This is an area of study where the concept of synergy is not only at the basis of important theories, but also has been studied and mentioned clearly.

  In urban theory, the concept of synergy is at the basis of the explanation of agglomerations. The very basic existence of a city is explained by agglomeration economies: people live in cities because they can exploit a series of advantages by exploiting external economies. These advantages may be classified under different labels (Camagni 1992 and 1994):

- *indivisibilities*, namely in the provision of public goods (scale economies in public services), in the dimension of the urban market for outputs, in the dimension and diversification of the urban market for inputs, in the dimension and diversification of the labour market, in the presence of managerial capabilities and specialized functions;
- *synergies*, namely information exchange and face to face contacts, transfer of tacit information, imitation in business decisions and behaviour, supplier-customer relationships due to diversification of activities.

In urban theory, therefore, the concept of synergy is associated with collective behaviour between economic agents or individuals, where the advantages of the collective behaviour are generally obtained by individuals or economic agents by locating their activity in an area and thus exploiting external economies. Policy implications in this case are rather important. Local governments may apply rules in order to keep the 'size of the city' under control, in order to avoid agglomeration diseconomies when cities become too big. Control of the accessibility to a city through the imposition of limits on new entrants who want to join the city is an important way not to exceed the optimal size of the city (Camagni 1992; Richardson 1973).

This example underlines that synergy effects are associated with collective behaviours which guarantee collective advantages to be greater than individual advantages, irrespective of which kind of individual behaviour (cooperative or non-cooperative) is put in place. This means that collective advantages which are obtained do not depend on cooperative behaviour, but stem from external factors.

The same mechanism of synergies may be at the basis of the 'milieu innovateur' theory. This theory, which has been studied extensively and carried out by the GREMI group,[4] is a sort of industrial district theory, where the emphasis is put on two particular aspects:

- the role of the local environment (milieu) as a generator of innovative behaviour. The 'spatial' aspect is given much more emphasis than in the case of the 'industrial district' theory;
- the role of innovation and dynamic externalities as the main driving forces for the economic development of these areas. The 'dynamic' aspect is another important issue which distinguishes this theory from the more traditional 'industrial district' theory.

The two elements that theoretically define this role and justify the advantages stemming from the local environments are (Camagni 1993):

- the collective learning processes that enhance the local creativity, the capability of product innovation and of 'technological creation';
- the processes of reduction of the elements of dynamic uncertainty that are intrinsic in technological development and innovative processes.

Thus, in this literature, as in the case of the industrial district theory, synergy refers to spontaneous collective behaviour stemming from the advantages obtained by individuals.

Another example of synergy in non-material networks is related to the theory of city networks. It has recently been argued (Camagni 1993 and

1994) that the well known paradigm of city hierarchy, based on the works of Christaller and on the subsequent central place theory, should be complemented by a new paradigm, the 'city network' paradigm, taking care of other kinds of linkages and relationships that cities entertain among themselves beyond the gravity type relationship with the surrounding market areas. The new paradigm which seems to emerge implies a strong specialization of each city and the development of many non-hierarchical relationships among specialized centres, providing externalities from complementarity/vertical integration or from cooperation among centres.

While the organizational logic underlying the central place model is a 'territorial logic', emphasizing a gravity type control over market areas, in the network model another logic prevails, referring to long distance competition and cooperation regardless of the distance barrier (Camagni 1994). While transport costs and economies of scale were the principal forces shaping the spatial organization of functions and centres, in the new logic other kinds of economies come to the fore: economies of vertical and horizontal integration, and network externalities similar to those emerging from 'club goods' (Capello 1994).

In the examples discussed above, already three meanings of synergy have emerged which explain economic mechanisms associated with it, namely:

- synergy means that when two or more actors *cooperate*, there is a positive result for both of them;
- synergy means that when cooperative behaviour is implemented in order to exploit *complementarity* in the production of a particular good, advantages are obtained by economic actors taking place in the group;
- synergy means that when individuals or firms 'voluntarily and non-voluntarily' are part of a group, *externalities* may be present and exploited by these individuals or groups in conducting their economic activity.

After this general discussion about synergy, we now proceed in our analysis with a more specific treatment of synergy in the context of networks.

3. SYNERGIES IN NETWORK THEORY

As mentioned before, there is a vast literature on networks, in which the concept of synergy may be applied. Also in this case there are different levels of study, micro, meso and macro. Examples treated in this section are summarized in Table 4.1 in the column dealing with 'non-material networks'.

3.1 The Micro Approach

A theory related to material networks where the concept of synergy is widely present is the theory of network externalities. This theory underlines the diffusion mechanisms associated particularly with telecommunications networks. The user value of these networks, in fact, greatly depends on the number of already existing subscribers (Rohlfs1974), and the higher the number of subscribers, the greater the possibility of having a new subscriber joining the network. The advantage of entering the network is not entirely paid for by already existing subscribers, since they have more possibility to communicate (at the same marginal price) when a new subscriber joins the network. At the same time, the new subscribers may value the service by more than the amount that they are required to pay for it, that is, there might be consumer surplus that is not quantified.[5]

The actual economic value of telecommunications networks and services is only partially represented by the benefits that individual consumers derive from telecommunications because (Saunder and al. 1983):

1. subscribers may value the service by more than the amount that they are required to pay for it, that is, there might be *consumer surplus* that is not quantified;
2. new telephone subscribers not only incur benefits for themselves, but also increase the benefits of being connected to the system for those who have already joined, that is, there are *subscriber network externalities*;
3. the willingness to pay a given price to make a telephone call reflects only a minimum estimate of the benefits incurred by the caller and does not reflect the benefits received by the recipient of the call or those whom the caller or recipient of the call then contact, that is, there are *call-related externalities*.

The mere existence of a telecommunications network depends on the number of already existing subscribers, and gives rise to another interpretation of the word 'synergy': synergy means that when a particular number of actors is using a network, the benefits that these users get increase when there will be an additional user.

Positive network externalities do not only relate to telecommunications networks; they may also be relevant for transport networks. Take as an example users of public transport for a trip between A and B. The frequency of the service provided will depend among other things on the number of users. An increase in the number of users leads to an increase in the frequency of the service. This is beneficial for the average user, because a higher frequency means that the average waiting time is shorter, or that the actual time of departure is nearer to the desired time of departure. Thus, the average public transport user benefits from an increase in demand.

In reality, the situation may be more complex because of indivisibilities in public transport. When demand increases slightly, the public transport company will usually not respond by increasing the frequency, but by letting the degree of capacity utilization increase. This leads to a decrease of convenience of travelling (this is actually an example of a negative externality). Only when the capacity utilization becomes higher than a certain critical level, the company will increase the frequency of the service. Thus, with a small increase in the number of public transport users, the existing users may experience a loss, and with a larger increase, a benefit.

Examples of this nature can also be found in other respects. When total demand for public transport trips between A and C increases, public transport suppliers may find that the market is large enough to justify direct (more convenient) trips between A and C, instead of indirect trips via B. Thus, when there are more public transport users, one may expect higher frequencies and a larger number of directly connected destinations.

This reasoning does not only hold true for links, but also for the nodes in a network. Owners of terminal facilities with increasing numbers of passengers will be inclined to invest in better terminal facilities, leading to a higher level of convenience for users. In addition, with an increasing number of users of a terminal, the level of services of the underlying network may be expected to increase, leading to a higher level of connectivity for the link concerned.

According to the above definition, synergy (a positive externality) is the opposite case of congestion (a negative externality). Congestion in the transport network means that when a network user enters, the average costs of using the network increase. For example, the speed on a highway decreases with an increasing number of car users. This implies higher time costs of travelling. An important consequence of congestion is that when another user enters the network, the travel time of all existing road users increases. This leads to an increase in social costs which is however not taken into account in the decision of the new entrant. The gap between private costs and social costs that occurs in congested networks has major policy implications, such as the introduction of congestion pricing or other travel demand reducing strategies (Verhoef et al. 1993). With synergy, as the mirror image of congestion, one may expect opposite policy directions.

It must be added that synergy and congestion may also occur at the same time. For example, in a telephone network with limited and fixed capacity, the entry of a new subscriber means a positive externality (more contact opportunities for existing users) and at the same time a negative externality (a higher probability of unsuccessful attempts to establish telephone contact). This is an interesting case for further study.

3.2 The Meso Approach

At the meso level, an example of a theory where the synergy concept is relevant is the theory on 'filière economies' among transport and telecommunications sectors, or among different transport modes. Filière economies relate to a vertically integrated sector, where the increase of forward production market shares generate increases in market shares of backward production markets. In the telecommunications sector, the increase in the services (such as the one of the cellular radio) has provided economic advantages not only to the service providers but to all the related backward production markets, such as manufacturing firms for the production of cellular radio equipment and switching equipment.

This holds true also for the transport sector among suppliers of services in a certain chain. For example, when rail fares decrease, the demand for rail transport will increase, and also the demand for bus transport will increase, because the bus will be used by rail passengers to get to the railway station.

Filière economies also exist between related sectors. An example of this is the relationship between the transport and the telecommunications sectors. Many studies have been made to decide whether there is a complementarity or a substitution effect among transport and telecommunications services. However, a relationship exists, which means that when the demand for transport services increases, this influences also the demand for telecommunications services, and vice versa.

An interesting example is the video conference, which at the time of its launch was expected to decrease the demand for air travel, being a substitute for face to face meetings. The reality has shown that this was not very much the case, and that video conferencing (still not well developed) plays a rather neutral effect on the amount of air travel.

A more ad hoc example is the case of the development of new logistic systems in firms, based on advanced telecommunications services and computer networks. The increase of the demand for these telecommunications services stimulates the need to transport larger qualities of goods. Policy implications emerge in this case by ensuring telecommunications and transport plans are developed by taking into account the common needs that the development of new technologies in the two fields generate.

3.3 The Macro Approach

At the macro level, synergies exist and can be identified when a region or a local system obtains productivity advantages by being connected to the network. The achievement of greater economic performance by exploiting benefits derived from joining a network is what has been called an *economic symbiosis* effect, an improvement in economic performance based on non-paid-for synergies among firms (Capello 1994). The 'economic symbiosis' may be better defined on the basis of a set of firms strongly interrelated via a physical network. This set of firms and its interdependent sectors have a relatively high productivity because of the achievement of strong advantages in comparison with the non-networked firms. The definition of direct advantages is related to the fact that the advantages a firm gets via a network directly affect (positively) the productivity of a firm.

The existence and exploitation of network externalities are not confined to the firm level. The 'economic symbiosis' concept can in fact be translated into a spatial setting. This can be done, first, by the simple extension that the set of networked industries is spatially clustered, and secondly, by focusing on spillover effects not for the economy as a whole, but in the immediately surrounding hinterland. In other words, a *'spatial symbiosis'* effect takes place when a set of 'networked firms' are present in a specific region. This leads to a non-zero sum of the positive effects on the firms' performance generated by the non-paid-for advantages of being networked. A set of spillover effects is in this way generated in the local (regional) economy, which can be measured in terms of better regional performance. This phenomenon can give rise to cumulative effects à la Myrdal (1959) and can guarantee a local sustainable development (see also Krugman 1991).

Both 'economic symbiosis' and 'spatial symbiosis' take place when a group of firms interacts; also in this case one can claim that synergy describes a situation where a number of firms (or regions) is using a particular network and the advantages of using the network increase with the number of firms (or regions) linked to the network.

From all these examples, three important meanings of synergy have emerged, which in general are associated to the existence of a (paid or unpaid) advantage for an individual (or a firm or a local economic system) by collaborating with others. This collaboration may be expressed as:

- a *cooperation* (voluntary or not) in an economic activity,
- a *complementarity* in an economic activity,
- an *externality* in the existence of and participation in a network which creates advantages in the pursuit of an economic activity.

Having these three characteristics in mind, some policy implications in the presence of synergy may be formulated, which are the subject matter of the next section.

4. POLICY IMPLICATIONS IN THE PRESENCE OF SYNERGIES IN ECONOMIC ACTIVITY

One main conclusion of the first part of the analysis is that network synergies take place in different situations and may be defined with the use of some economic concepts. These concepts have been identified as cooperation, complementarity and externality. In the presence of one of the three a network behaviour generates synergies, and thus advantages for economic actors.

Network synergies mean advantages, which take different forms according to the different situations in which they are exploited. It seems thus rather important to underline the policy implications which may be put in place in order to protect these 'natural' economic advantages stemming from network behaviour.

In most examples mentioned above markets are not sufficient to guarantee the exploitation of network synergies, for a number of different reasons, among which free rider behaviour is one of the most important. Thus, in most cases government intervention is useful for four reasons:

- to increase *positive effects* stemming from network synergies;
- to take care of *distributive effects* among actors of the advantages generated by network synergies;
- to mitigate *negative effects* when network disadvantages take place;
- to correct for monopolistic tendencies if synergies would lead to high market power of conglomerates.

One has to take into consideration that a government intervention may also have negative effects on network synergies, by preventing private groups of actor from exploiting network advantages to protect public interests or by manipulating the situation in favour of public interests. Moreover, there might be also the case that a government intervention in favour of network synergies (such as the construction of a public road) is in conflict with a different public goal (the control on environmental pollution); in this case, it may happen that the government itself does not favour the achievement of network synergies in order to protect the conflicting public interest.

In this section some policy implications are presented associated with the existence of network synergy stemming from the examples mentioned above.

Table 4.2 contains some examples of policy implications concerning the three levels of analysis mentioned above, micro, meso and macro, and the three strategic economic features existing in the presence of network synergies.

Table 4.2   Policy implications in the presence of network synergies

	Cooperation	Complementarity	Externality
Micro	Incentives to avoid free rider behaviour	Control on tariffs of related services	Taxes and incentives to limit congestion
Meso	Control on interconnectivity Control on technical standards Incentives to cooperation agreements in firms belonging to the same industrial districts	Common planning of telecommunications and transport networks	Incentives for filière sectors
Macro	Control on compatibility among telecommunications and transport networks between regions and countries	Incentives for specialized urban networks	Control on urban size Incentives for the exploita-tation of local external effects Incentives for the widespread development of transport and telecommuni-cations networks

4.1   Cooperation

In most cases mentioned above, at the basis of network synergies is the concept of *cooperation*, which is put under constraints by free rider behaviour.

A *micro level* analysis of policy interventions may be linked to the theories of both public goods and oligopoly cartels. In both these examples, there is wide possibility for policy interventions in order to protect network synergies among free rider behaviour. In public goods theory, consumers may be protected by taxes or penalties in the presence of unfair behaviour.

In the case of oligopoly cartels, penalties and taxes on free rider behaviour may be implemented by firms themselves, that is, those belonging to the cartel. Public policies in this case may take the form of legal rules imposed in some sectors in order to work as cartels, by imposing minimum prices. These kinds of legal impositions have the possibility of being implemented at the national level, while at the international level there is the need for a supranational body governing cross-national legal rules. However, if one takes the interests of the consumers as a starting point, it is not easy to defend government intervention in favour of cartels. The opposite would rather be the case.

A *meso level* analysis in the case of cooperation has some policy implications which are related to the example of cooperation agreements among firms. As said before, also in this case space for policy interventions is rather limited, since it is very much related to strategic decisions within firms. However, public intervention can support this process by ensuring interconnectivity and common technical standards on communications networks. In this way, electronic communications among firms are facilitated, for example by imposing EDI standards. These technologies do not play a role in the decision to start cooperation, but once this decision is made, common technological standards in communications technologies facilitate and support cooperative activities.

More space exists in terms of policy measures when we speak about cooperation among firms belonging to an industrial district. Here, policies may regard the promotion of cooperation among firms belonging to the same sector, through local Chambers of Commerce. Other local actors, such as banks and credit authorities, may offer incentives to local cooperation by ensuring more easy and attractive conditions for mortgages or credits when they deal with local consortia of firms.

Finally, at a *macro level* cooperation giving rise to network synergies may be supported by policies governing compatibility among telecommunications network standards and advanced transport networks (such as high speed trains) among countries and regions. Advantages stemming from being linked to an advanced transport and telecommunications network depend on the possibility of having access to the network, and the advantages for users increase with the increase in the number of users. National policies of transport and telecommunications network development should take interconnectivity and common network standards into account. These technical aspects guarantee the physical connection among telecommunications and transport networks among countries. The larger the geographical dispersion of the network, the greater the advantages users receive in using the network.

4.2   Complementarity

Let us move to the *complementarity* issue. In this case, there are possibilities for policies related to network synergies. A first insight into policy implications when complementarity is taken into account is at a *micro level*. In this level of analysis, complementarity concerns the use of complementary services and modes of communication and transport. In many cases complementarity relationships take place entirely within the domain of free markets and there is not much scope for a positive contribution of governments. However, government involvement may be relevant in cases such as:

*   complementarity between actors with different market powers leading to exploitation of some actors by an actor with large market power (for example, large shipping company versus many small carrier companies). In cases like this government intervention can be directed towards increasing the power of the weak market partners, or decreasing the power of the strong partner;
*   complementarity between actors operating in the public domain. An example is the complementarity between services of buses of two companies in two interconnnected areas, or between the services of a bus company and a railway company. In this case the government may become active in order to ensure that these companies arrive at an appropriate coordination of schedules;
*   complementarity between actors where one is operating on the free market, and the other in the public domain. Given the chain character of many transport activities, such complementarities easily arise. An example is the transition from a car to public transport. Here, the public sector can contribute to a smooth change by providing the necessary facilities such as park and ride locations;
*   complementarity between actors in the private market where a transport chain cannot develop without public sector involvement in the determination of a node. An example is the development of city distribution centres near large cities.The inflow of goods takes place by large trucks. In the city distribution centres grouping takes place after which the goods are transported to destinations in the city by means of smaller trucks. This system can in principle lead to a considerable reduction in the traffic intensity in large cities due to freight transport.

However, such city distribution centres do not easily develop spontaneously with competitive market conditions. Government intervention may be needed both in terms of restrictive measures for trucks entering city centres, and in terms of facilities to make the city distribution centre successful.

At the *meso level*, policy implications emerge in the attempt to exploit all advantages associated with network synergies among complementary modes in order to put in place new corporate organizations, such as new logistic chains. In this field there is the need for a coordinated initiative between policy makers in these sectors. It is in fact becoming more and more evident that the strategic importance of the future organization of society at large depends on the simultaneous use of both physical and virtual means of transport.

Transport and telecommunications sectors have often been regarded as two distinct and separate fields, growing at different growth rates, according to different technological advances, and facing a different growth in demand. The technological revolution in the telecommunications sector at the beginning of the eighties had a particular influence on the corporate organization, by allowing new forms of external contacts with suppliers and customers (for example, via the use of Electronic Data Interchange). At the same time, these new external linkages could only be introduced with a different transport structure. A recent study on this aspect (Capello and Gillespie 1993) has concluded that the most likely future scenario of the industrial organization is the 'network firm' scenario, built on the assumption that the inadequacies of Fordist mass production are overcome, but that the oppositional outcomes suggested by the 'flexible specialization' school are more verbally advocated than firmly based on empirical evidence. The 'network firm' scenario will be attracted to intermediate forms of 'quasi-organization' that are assuming an ever more important role as an alternative to full vertically integrated or vertically disintegrated production systems. The 'make together' organization – à la Williamson (1975) – among firms seems to be one dominant organizational structure which will emerge in the future.

If this is true, the 'make together' form of organization implies a high volume of information transmitted between firms, in the form of horizontal intercorporate information flows. At the same time, high volumes of intermediate products need to be transported between cooperative firms. This new industrial organization has a peculiarity in respect to previous organizations; it needs at the same time both advanced transport and telecommunications systems, and these systems have to be integrated in terms of organization, planning, technological aspects and spatial development.

The just-in-time system and the new logistics systems are evident examples of the new organizational structure taking place. However, in order to have an efficient just-in-time system, or an efficient logistic chain, advanced telecommunications and transport systems need to be integrated; both networks have to be developed with the same geographical patterns, with the same technological advances and with the same carrying capacity. It is difficult to envisage an efficient logistic organization in a region, when advanced transport systems are put in place but where telecommunications networks are still very old. The strength of these industrial organizations is related to the implementation of technological and geographical integration of strategic factors in both the transportation and communications systems (Banister et al. 1995).

Traditionally, the way of thinking of policy makers in these two fields has been dictated by problems of individual sectors. At present an integrated policy strategy has to be advocated for the sake of efficiency of these two sectors in the future, and for the possibility of exploiting synergies from these complementarity modes.

At a *macro level* a good policy example of how to protect and even increase network synergies when complementarity exists stems from the city-network theory. As mentioned above, this theory emphasizes the new organizational paradigm of cities which develops in parallel with the traditional 'gravity type' territorial model. The characteristic of this new organizational paradigm is the specialization of cities in particular activities and the cooperation with complementary cities in a network organization. Experts in this field have emphasized that there are many intervention policies which may assure network synergies due to complementarity among cities (Camagni and Gibelli 1993). In particular, these kinds of policies may be reflected, for example, in public financial support from local governments for joint innovation projects between cities, where each urban system participates with its specificities and its specialized knowhow, and obtains advantages both from the division of labour and from economies of scale stemming from the dimension not of the single project, but of the sum of all centres.

4.3   Externalities

Much space for policy intervention exists when network synergies hide an *externality* mechanism. In this case, policies may be divided into three categories: (a) those policies aiming at avoiding negative externality mechanisms, (b) those aiming at keeping distributive effects of externalities under control, and (c) those aimed at increasing positive externality effects.

At the *micro level*, examples of policy implications in front of network synergies stemming from externality mechanisms can be found among policies to avoid negative effects of externalities. All traditional economic tools to control negative externalities may be implemented. The internalization of a negative externality through taxes is one possible policy, where the 'polluter pays' principle is used; the economic actor which creates the damage to the others pays for its negative behaviour. In our examples on congestion in telecommunications networks, when the telephone company is a profit maximizing monopolist, the externality is already accounted for in the tariff. In the case of the public monopoly, however, cross-subsidization may take place, leading to the above optimal levels of congestion. In the case of transport networks, congestion on the road may be controlled by increasing the price of petrol. This is only a second-best policy, however, since such a price increase does not differentiate between congested and uncongested roads; neither does it differentiate between different points in time. The first-best solution to congestion on roads is obviously congestion pricing, but given the social and political obstacles, one may not expect that congestion pricing will soon be implemented on a large scale (Emmerink et al. 1994a).

Another well known way of internalizing negative externalities is the 'pollutee pays' principle; this principle states that economic actors who are potentially damaged by a negative externality pay for not being affected by the external costs.

In addition to correction of negative externalities, the government may also correct undersupply as a consequence of positive externalities. As is well documented in the literature, the introduction of videotex systems, and other similar telecommunications systems such as the Minitél system in France, is characterized by positive externalities in the adoption process. Given the high fixed costs involved, this leads to a problem of a critical mass of users. Subsidies may be needed to get the system off the ground. Indeed, government subsidies can be defended here, although one should not forget that once the system becomes successful, the owner can easily make monopolistic profits since the barriers to entry by other firms are very high. Thus, at a later stage, governments may wish to influence price setting behaviour to protect consumer interests.

Another area where there is the possibility of positive externalities concerns the introduction of motorist information systems in cars. Drivers who have installed such equipment in their cars experience benefits since they are in a better position to avoid heavily congested roads in their route choice. In addition to this effect on one's own welfare position, there is also an effect on the welfare position of other road users. The reason is that informed road users stay away from heavily congested roads, and this improves the travel times of the other road users. Here, again, it can be shown that a subsidy to car users buying the equipment has a positive effect on overall welfare (Emmerink et al. 1994b).

At a *meso level* there are network externality effects which may be assimilated into 'filière economies'. As mentioned above, filière economies are those economies stemming from sectors which are vertically integrated, so that the increase in forward markets generates advantages also to backward markets. In this case policy implications concern the possibility of increasing these advantages by stimulating forward markets. Public financial expenditures for high speed trains have certainly not only the positive consequence of producing a very useful service, but on the supply side that of introducing a chain of positive effects to all backward related markets. The same can be said for the telecommunications sector. The launch of a new advanced service, such as the Minitél in France, has the immediate consequence of providing a useful service to economic actors, but also of stimulating the switching equipment market and the market of terminal equipments. Many other examples may be quoted here, where policy implications associated to filière economies play a role. One could be the role of government in giving extra support to introduce a new service. In the example of the Minitél above, the subsidy given to users of this new service has the effect of stimulating the adoption of this service, and thus its market and its related backward markets.

Once we move to the *macro level* of analysis, externalities in networks are related to theories of spatial symbiosis and of local districts, as well as of city dimension and city size. The theory of local districts emphasizes the role of external economies associated with a certain location. Policy implications here may concern incentives for the exploitation of network synergies; in particular, the creation of local actors who facilitate cooperation among local firms and exploitation of local knowhow would be extremely useful for local firms to exploit local synergies. We are thinking here of local Chambers of Commerce and of local bodies whose role, among others, would be to reinforce local specificities and local economic strengths. This could be done by increasing managerial, technical and organizational knowhow, via seminars, and by supporting firms in their marketing activity both in their own country and abroad. Moreover, the development of efficient information systems and channels within the district, sectorally oriented, may help firms in exploiting the specific advantages of their location.

At a macro level, policies to increase the exploitation of positive externalities stemming from network synergies are always related to network externality advantages. In this case there is a need for policies which guarantee the widespread development of telecommunications and transport networks, which have been recognized as the main weapons upon which the competitiveness of firms and the comparative advantages of regions will increasingly depend. In this case, policies are oriented towards the increase of network synergies due to network externalities and towards the control of distributive effects stemming from these externalities.

Policies associated with the increase of positive network externalities concern the development of telecommunications and transport networks with a wide geographical spread. For this reason, and for the reason of giving to all regions the same opportunity to exploit network externalities by being linked to a telecommunications network, in terms of economic policy, the European Union itself has interpreted telecommunications systems as a way to decrease the gap between advanced and backward regions of the Union. A large EU programme, called STAR, was launched in 1987 in order to enhance economic development in 'Objective 1' regions of the Union. The success of the programme in increasing economic growth in these regions and in giving all regions the same opportunity of exploitation of network externality depends largely upon various specific local conditions which have to be present and taken into account.

The first crucial precondition for assuring continuous adoption of these technologies (and thus greater real connectivity) is the achievement of a *critical mass* of adopters especially for interrelated services, such as electronic mail. The user value of these technologies is in fact related to the number of already existing subscribers, since the attraction for a new potential subscriber to join the network is the possibility of being linked to a great number of subscribers. The existence of a certain number of subscribers is a necessary condition to stimulate a *cumulative self-sustained mechanism*.

Another critical factor for the achievement of a great number of adoptions is the *clear identification of the way these technologies may be useful for business purposes*. Policies should be implemented in order to help firms in understanding the most competitive way of exploiting these technologies for their businesses. This process requires a strong organizational effort on the part of the subscriber, who most of the time needs organizational support from specialized telecommunications experts.

A crucial resource for the development of these technologies is *entrepreneurship*. In other words, the presence of risk aversion and of non-competitive market structures discourages adoption processes of these technologies, since no market force exists under those conditions which can stimulate firms to bear the organizational, managerial and financial costs necessary for a successful adoption. Thus, local entrepreneurship turns out to be a strategic element for successful adoptions. If this is the case, innovative policies have to take this aspect into consideration, choosing, among other factors, local areas where *entrepreneurial capabilities* are available. Thus, instead of supplying these technologies to all areas in less developed regions, as has been the case with the STAR programme in Italy, innovative policies should rather be focused on the most dynamic areas in terms of both technical and entrepreneurial capabilities (Capello 1994).

A last example of policy implications in the presence of network synergies when externality mechanisms are concerned is related to urban growth theory. As mentioned before, the existence of a city is explained by the exploitation of agglomeration economies by people and firms located in the city. However, as the neoclassic approach to urban growth underlines, there is an optimal size of the city, which defines the boundaries between agglomeration economies and diseconomies. In fact, when the urban system exceeds a certain size, all sorts of negative effects are put in place, such as congestion, noise, pollution and so on. In this field, policy implications may concern the control of a certain size of the city, by establishing high prices for urban location (Richardson 1973).

The examples of policies presented above which may be developed in the presence of network synergies do not take account of all indirect effects. The purpose of this chapter, in any case, has been to identify a list of possible policy interventions which could be introduced in the presence of synergies. Some concluding remarks are highlighted in the next section.

5.   CONCLUSIONS[6]

The aim of the present chapter is twofold. First of all, a more careful definition of what is meant by network synergy is given, on the basis of some examples of different theories, all exploiting the concept of network synergy in a different way. Secondly, a careful analysis is developed of the role for policy implications. The examples of theories given in the first part of the chapter have helped in defining the role of public policies in the presence of network synergies. Some interesting conclusions can be drawn from the analysis, namely:

- *synergy is not a simple concept*, as it appears at first glance. It is widely used in economic literature in different theories, but a more careful analysis shows that it hides different economic mechanisms. This represents already an important aspect. In fact, at first glance, network synergies are associated with cooperative behaviour. A first result which emerges from this analysis is that the concept of network synergy does not only take place when a cooperative behaviour is implemented. Other mechanisms, in fact, may be associated with the concept of network synergies, that is, complementarity in economic actions and externalities;

- moreover, *network synergies do not mean by definition non-paid-for advantages*. The advantages associated with synergies are in some cases similar to positive externalities. In this case the non-paid-for mechanism is present. In other cases, instead, when cooperative behaviour is implemented, advantages stemming from network synergies are all paid, that is, the marginal advantages are equal to marginal costs associated with these advantages;
- *synergies do not always hide an advantage for people or economic agent in the network*. As mentioned several times, when networks are exploited by too many people, the synergy mechanism turns into a congestion mechanism, where negative externalities are generated instead of positive external effects. Moreover, when an individual or an economic agent enters a network, the advantages he gets depend on the capacity of this agent to impose himself in the network and to become one of the leaders. A weak position in comparison with the partners may lead the individual or the economic agent to be exploited by the network;
- in some cases government policies are not useful since market mechanisms guarantee the existence and development of these kinds of advantages. However, and this is the case in most of our examples, governments may play a role in:

  - increasing positive effects stemming from network synergies;
  - controlling distributive effects of network synergies;
  - abolishing negative effects, when negative network externalities are put in place;
  - correcting monopolistic tendencies.

In some cases, public policies may be implemented to protect some groups of people (or agents in a market) by the negative effects caused by the exploitation of network synergies by another group of people. It is the case of the oligopoly market: policies may be envisaged to protect cartels from free rider behaviour, thus maximizing network synergies for everybody. However, when the same analysis is done on the side of the consumers, it may very well be the case that some policies have to be implemented to 'limit' network synergies and thus protect users from a monopolistic behaviour.

Different kinds of policies may be useful, according to the mechanisms hidden under the label 'network synergy', that is, cooperation, complementarity and externalities mechanisms. All policies presented are formulated on the three above mentioned objectives, that is, with special attention to network synergies. Some reflections on all *indirect* effects of policy implications presented above may perhaps need further attention.

REFERENCES

Allen, D. (1988), 'New telecommunications services: network externalities and critical mass', *Telecommunications Policy*, September, pp. 257–71.

Allen, D. (1990), 'Competition, co-operation and critical mass in the evolution of networks', paper presented at the 8th Conference of the International Telecommunications Society, on 'Telecommunications and the Challenge of Innovation and Global Competition', held in Venice, 18–21 March.

Amiel, M. and J. Rochét (1987), 'Concurrence entre réseaux de télécommunications: les conséquences des externalités négatives', *Annales des Télécommunications* 42 (11–12), pp. 642–49.

Antonelli, C. (1990), 'Induced adoption and externalities in the regional diffusion of Information Technology', *Regional Studies* 24 (1) pp. 31–40.

Antonelli, C. (1991), *The International Diffusion of Advanced Telecommunications: Opportunities for Developing Countries*, OECD.

Antonelli, C. (ed.) (1992), *The Economics of Information Networks*, Amsterdam: Elsevier.

Aydalot, Ph. (ed.) (1986), *Milieux Innovateurs en Europe*, Paris: GREMI.

Aydalot, Ph. and D. Keeble (eds) (1988), *High Technology Industry and Innovative Environment*, London: Routledge.

Bagnasco, A. (1977), *Le Tre Italie*, Bologna: Il Mulino.

Banister, D., R. Capello and P. Nijkamp (eds) (1995), *European Transport and Communications Networks: Policy Evolution and Change*, London: John Wiley and Sons.

Becattini, G. (ed.) (1987), *Mercato e Forze Locali: Il Distretto Industriale*, Bologna: Il Mulino.

Bental, B. and M. Spiegel (1990), 'Consumption externalities in telecommunication services', in de Fontenay, M. and D. Sibley (eds), *Telecommunications Demand Modelling*, Amsterdam: Elsevier Science, pp. 415–32.

Cabral, L. and A. Leite (1992), 'Network consumption externalities: the case of the Portuguese telex service', in Antonelli, C. (ed.), *The Economics of Information Networks*, Amsterdam: Elsevier, pp. 129–40.

Camagni, R. (1989), 'Cambiamento tecnologico, "milieu locale" e reti di imprese: verso una teoria dinamica dello spazio economico', *Economia e Politica Industriale* 64, pp. 209–36.

Camagni, R. (ed.) (1991), *Innovation Networks: Spatial Perspectives*, London: Belhaven-Pinter.

Camagni, R. (1992), *Economia Urbana*, Rome: La Nuova Italia Scientifica.

Camagni, R. (1993), 'From city hierarchy to city networks: reflections about an emerging paradigm', in Lakshmanan, T.R. and P. Nijkamp (eds), *Structure and*

Change in the Space Economy: Festschrift in Honor of Martin Beckmann, Berlin: Springer Verlag, pp. 66–87.

Camagni, R. (1994), 'City networks: an analysis of the Lombardy region in terms of communication flows', in Cuadrado-Roura, J., P. Nijkamp, and P. Salva (eds), *Moving Frontiers: Economic Restructuring, Regional Development and Emerging Networks*, Aldershot: Avebury, pp. 127–48.

Camagni, R. and G. De Blasio (eds) (1993), *Le Reti di Città*, Milan: Franco Angeli.

Camagni, R. and F. Gambarotto (1988), 'Gli accordi di cooperazione come nuove frome di sviluppo esterno delle imprese', in *Economia e Politica Industriale* **58**, pp. 93–128.

Camagni, R. and M.C. Gibelli (1993), 'Reti di città e politiche urbane', in Camagni, R. and G. De Blasio (eds), *Le Reti di Città*, Milan: Franco Angeli, pp. 219–65.

Camagni, R. and R. Rabellotti (1992), 'Technology and organisation in the Italian textile-clothing industry', *Entrepreneurship and Regional Development* **4**, pp. 271–85.

Capello, R. (1994), *Spatial Economic Analysis of Telecommunications Network Externalities*, Aldershot: Avebury.

Capello, R. and A. Gillespie (1993), 'Transport, communication and spatial organisation: future trends and conceptual frameworks', in Nijkamp, P. (ed.), *Europe on the Move*, Aldershot: Avebury, pp. 43-66.

Chesnais, F. (1988), 'Technical cooperation agreements among firms', *STI Review*, OECD, **4**.

Colombo, M. (1989), 'Accordi di cooperazione, complessità relazionale ed organizzazione degli oligopoli internazionali', *Economia e Politica Industriale* **64**, pp. 241–66.

David, P. (1985), 'Clio and the economics of qwerty', *AEA Papers and Proceedings* **75** (2), pp. 332–7.

David, P. (1992), 'Information network economics: externalities, innovation and evolution', in Antonelli, C. (ed.) (1992), *The Economics of Information Networks*, pp. 103–106.

Emmerink, R.H.M., P. Nijkamp, P. Rietveld and K. Axhausen (1994a), 'The economics of motorist information system revisited', *Transport Review* **14** (4), pp. 363–88.

Emmerink, R.H.M., P. Nijkamp, P. Rietveld and K. Axhausen (1994b), 'How feasible is congestion pricing?', Amsterdam: Tinbergen Institute Discussion Paper.

Frey, B.S. (1978), *Modern Political Economy*, Oxford: Oxford University Press.

Garofoli, G. (1992), 'I sistemi produttivi locali: una rassegna della letteratura Italiana', in Garofoli, G. (ed.), *Economia del Territorio*, Etas Libri.

Giaoutzi, M. and P. Nijkamp (eds) (1988), *Informatics and Regional Development*, Aldershot: Avebury.

Gillespie, A. and H. Williams (1988), 'Telecommunications and the reconstruction of regional comparative advantage', *Environment and Planning A* **20**, pp. 1311–21.

Hayashi, K. (1992), 'From network externalities to interconnection: the changing nature of networks and economy', in Antonelli, C. (ed.) (1992), *The Economics of Information Networks*, Amsterdam: North-Holland, pp. 195–216.

Johansson, B., C. Karlsson and L. Westin (eds) (1994), *Patterns of a Network Economy*, Berlin: Springer Verlag.

Katz, M. and C. Shapiro (1985), 'Network externalities, competition and compatibility', *The American Economic Review* **75** (3), pp. 424–40.

Krugman, P. (1991), *Geography and Trade*, Cambridge, MA: MIT Press.

Maillat, D., M. Quévit and L. Senn (1993), *Réseaux d'Innovation et Milieux Innovateurs: un Pari pour le Développement Régional*, Neuchâtel: EDES.

Markus, M. (1992), 'Critical mass contingencies for telecommunication consumers', in Antonelli, C. (ed.) (1992), *The Economics of Information Networks*, Amsterdam: Elsevier, pp. 431–50.

Myrdal, G. (1959), *Teoria Economica e Paesi Sottosviluppati*, Milan: Feltrinelli.

Nijkamp, P. and A. Reggiani (1995), 'Multi-layer synergy and networks', paper presented at the International NECTAR Conference, Group 2, held in Lille, 28 January.

Rabellotti, R. (1994), *External Economies and Cooperation in Industrial Districts: A Comparison of Italy and Mexico*, University of Sussex, Brighton, unpublished PhD thesis.

Richardson, H. (1973), *The Economics of Urban Size*, Saxon House.

Rohlfs, J. (1974), 'A theory of interdependent demand for a communication service', *Bell Journal of Economics and Management Science* **5**, pp. 16–37.

Saunder, R., J. Warford and B. Wellenius (1983), *Telecommunications and Economic Development*, London: The Johns Hopkins University Press.

Teece, D. (1989), 'Concorrenza e cooperazione nelle strategie di sviluppo tecnologico', *Economia e Politica Industriale* **64**, pp. 3–16.

Verhoef, E.T., P. Nijkamp and P. Rietveld (1993), 'Second-best regulation of road transport externalities', *Journal of Transport Economics and Policy* **29**, pp. 147–67.

Williamson, O. (1975), *Markets and Hierarchies: Analysis and Antitrust Implications*, New York: Free Press.

NOTES

1. For a paper dealing with the modelling of the network synergy see Nijkamp and Reggiani 1995.

2. See among others Camagni 1989; Colombo 1989; Teece 1989.

3. A vast literature on local districts exists, dealing with the concept of external economies. For a review, see, among others, Bagnasco 1977; Becattini 1987; Garofoli 1992; Rabellotti 1994.

4. For the basic ideas of the 'milieu innovatuer' theory developed by the GREMI group, see, among others, Aydalot 1986; Aydalot and Keeble 1988; Camagni 1991; Maillat et al. 1993.

5. See, among others, Allen 1988 and 1990; Amiel and Rochét 1987; Antonelli 1990, 1991 and 1992; Bental and Spiegel 1990; Cabral and Leite 1989; Capello 1994; David 1985 and 1992; Hayashi 1992; Katz and Shapiro 1985; Markus 1989.

6. Though the contribution is the result of a joint research effort of the two authors, R. Capello has written Sections 2, 3 and 4, while Sections 1 and 5 have been jointly written.

5. Managing Openness in Transport and Regional Development: An Active Space Approach

Marina van Geenhuizen and Remigio Ratti

1. INTRODUCTION

In the past several years the geopolitical and socioeconomic positions of many European regions has undergone major changes. Four basic forces are reshaping the regional 'landscape' of Europe. First, the unification of Europe means a geopolitical and territorial shift of historical importance in terms of increased openness of regions. One can observe gains from trade, benefits from integration and deregulation, but also emerging impediments, for example, as a result of new nationalistic motives (Ratti 1993; Mlinar 1992). A second megatrend is the shift to a new local-global network economy, in which new competitive forces are responsible for win-lose situations in the business world (see Geenhuizen and Nijkamp 1995a; Nijkamp 1994). A third megatrend is the fast progress in information technology (Perriard 1994) with a variety of impacts on patterns of consumption, production organization and location, as well as communication and transport.

The above trends clearly lead to increased competition between European regions and cities (see Cheshire and Gordon 1995). In the concomitant force field, communication and transport are vital ingredients for a continued competitive position of regions and cities. At the same time, however, the policy framework of sustainable environmental development may set limits to an increase of transport in particular regions or advance substitution of one transport mode by another. Policies for an environmentally sustainable growth are the fourth force reshaping the 'landscape' of European regions.

Freight transport is currently facing radical changes in the relationship between the actors involved, such as manufacturers, suppliers and logistics service companies. This is the result of the use of new internal logistics systems and external distribution and market logistics (see NEA/Cranfield

1994) which may, in turn, lead to logistics platforms being established to enable the growth of international networks of delivery systems linked with material requirements planning. Consequently, new use of networks and nodes will emerge in new spatial configurations (Priemus et al. 1995a, 1995b; Ratti 1995).

Most of the above indicated changes are mutually dependent and have strong implications for the spatial organization of production systems and regional economic development. The first issue to be discussed is therefore the perspective on space (regions, cities) used in transport studies and regional economic analysis.

Space can be considered from various perspectives in view of communication and transport, namely:

- as source and destination (localization approach);
- in terms of distance and population concentration (gravity models approach);
- as bridge/contact zone, attraction zone and nodal points (network approach);
- as carrier, medium, or milieu (functional space approach);
- as territory (system and evolutionary/ecological approaches).

The first two approaches use a passive perspective, in which space is conceived of as physical support to transport and communication. However, the latter three approaches enable space to be viewed as an active factor in transport and communication. This perspective will be emphasized in this chapter.

This chapter begins with a discussion of two case studies of regional development in relation to openness connected with transport (Section 2 and Section 3). This is followed by the introduction of a new approach to regional economic development (the active space approach). Particular attention is paid to factors of change in active space development (Section 4). In a complementary theoretical section, the active space approach will be elaborated, leading to a framework for the identification of various trajectories of regional economic development (Section 5). Furthermore, various empirical insights that can be achieved by the active space approach will be discussed based upon the previous two case studies (Section 6). The conclusion will briefly indicate the advantages of the approach (Section 7).

The chapter is based on recent reflections of regional science (particularly a network approach) and institutional economics (Grabher 1993; Ratti 1993; Williamson 1985). It is not the end product of thorough exploration and testing but merely a starting point for such activity.

2. INNOVATION IN DUTCH FREIGHT TRAFFIC: THE REGION OF ROTTERDAM

The Netherlands is located in the delta of the river Rhine which connects the seaport of Rotterdam with major economic centres in Europe. The natural openness of the Netherlands cannot be equalled by other European regions. This has caused a strong focus of the Dutch economy on transport and logistics. For example, in the newly emerging transport and distribution patterns of large manufacturers in Europe, the Netherlands turns out to be an attractive location for European Distribution Centres (Buck Consultants Int. 1993; NEA/Cranfield 1994; Priemus et al. 1995b).

The Dutch seaports, particularly Rotterdam, have an important role in transport and logistics in the Netherlands. Transport by sea has a share in inward bound flows of 70 percent (tonnage). For outward bound transport this share is 22 percent. Rotterdam clearly has a leading position within the range of ports from Le Havre to Hamburg. Of all throughput in these ports 43 percent is handled in Rotterdam (1994). Antwerp is in second position (16 percent), with Hamburg as third (10 percent). The leading position of Rotterdam is, however, under pressure regarding specific types of good (MVW 1995). Rotterdam is the leader in bulk (with Antwerp as the second largest port) but there has been a small decrease in its share (from 45 percent in 1986 to 43 percent in 1994). Rotterdam is also the leader in the container segment. Here, despite an absolute growth, a significant decrease has become evident in the share of Rotterdam, that is, from 42 percent (1986) to 37 percent (1994). The runner-up ports are Antwerp and Hamburg.

The latter development needs particular attention in view of the increased containerization in freight transport. The main points of concern in this respect are the price/quality level of port services in Rotterdam (particularly compared with Antwerp) and road congestion in the connecting inland system (MVW 1995). With regard to the latter point, this section will discuss responsiveness to innovation in the Dutch road freight sector and potential implications of this responsiveness for regional economic development.

Road transport in the Netherlands has undergone strong growth in the past decade. In international freight, it has grown faster than any other mode (except for pipeline): witness an increase by 36 percent for unloaded goods, and an increase by 55 percent for loaded goods and 26 percent for transshipment (in the years 1986–1992) (Table 5.1). With shares of 16 percent (unloaded), 20 percent (loaded) and 6 percent (transshipment) road transport is nevertheless still rather modest. What is more important is that alternative modes for road transport have lost importance in absolute and relative terms, particularly the railways. Between 1986 and 1992 rail has decreased by 24 percent and 33 percent for unloaded and loaded goods respectively (Table 5.1).

Table 5.1   International freight transport in the Netherlands (million tonnes)
(1986 = 100)

	1986		1992		Change (% share)
	Abs.	%share	Index	%share	
UNLOADED					
Sea	249.4	71.8	112	69.7	− 2.1
Inl. Waterways	43.4	12.5	95	10.2	− 2.3
Rail	4.9	1.4	76	0.9	− 0.5
Road	47.1	13.6	136	15.9	+ 2.3
Remaining (a)	2.6	0.3	500	3.2	+ 2.9
All Modes	347.3	100	116	100	−
LOADED					
Sea	71.7	26.7	104	21.7	− 5.0
Inl. Waterways	110.3	40.8	103	33.0	− 7.8
Rail	7.2	2.7	67	1.8	− 0.9
Road	44.4	16.4	155	20.0	+ 3.6
Remaining (a)	36.5	13.5	220	23.5	+10.0
All Modes	270.1	100	127	100	−
TRANSHIPMENT (b)					
Sea	89.5	88.3	101	87.2	− 1.1
Inl. Waterways	6.0	5.9	103	5.9	0
Rail	0.8	0.8	83	0.7	− 0.1
Road	5.0	5.0	126	6.1	+1.1
Remaining (a)	0.1	0.1	183	0.1	0
All Modes	101.4	100	102	100	−

a.   Largely pipeline (except for transhipment)
b.   Partial overlap with unloading

Source: Netherlands Central Bureau of Statistics (various years)

When we focus in on the region of Rotterdam and the modal split of hinterland transport, it can be stated that inland waterways have a more important role than in the previously discussed national pattern (47 percent of tonnage) (1991) (B&W Rotterdam 1993). Road transport is in second position (24 percent), whereas rail transport performs a modest role (4 percent) (1991). The two patterns clearly compare in that road use has increased in transport via Rotterdam, that is, from 43.5 million tonnes (1986) to 56.1 million tonnes (1991), meaning a growth by 29 percent.

Ever increasing road use now starts to hamper the accessibility of the Randstad (Rimcity), particularly the region of Rotterdam. It is estimated that direct economic costs amount to 1.2 milliard DFL (540 million ECU) per year nationally (Venemans 1994). What is necessary is both a smaller growth of road transport and a move towards other modes. Here lies an interesting field, that is, how to substitute road transport by inland shipping and rail when the trend seems to be the reverse? One strategy is to advance the use of multimodal transport, particularly including inland shipping and rail on major tracks. The recent decision of the Dutch government (1995) to construct a major railway link (Betuwelijn), connecting Rotterdam with Germany, needs to be understood within this framework.

In policies for reducing road congestion, a main point of concern is the problem awareness and responsiveness among the principal actors, that is, large forwarders and transport/logistics companies. Various explorative studies of such companies in the Netherlands indicate a low responsiveness to change and innovation. Instead of radical shifts, there has been a small and stepwise application of new logistic concepts (such as value added logistics) among large manufacturing companies (Buck Consultants Int. 1993). In addition, strategic adjustment of transport/logistics companies seems to be rather reactive (Riet et al. 1993). This is exemplified by a small application of complex forms of information technology such as fleet management and electronic data interchange (Weijers 1994). Information technology has been adopted in single tasks and separate activities, not in an integrated way.

It needs to be emphasized that the above indicated strategic response is not uniform. There is a large differentiation within manufacturing (Buck Consultants Int. 1993; NEA/Cranfield 1994) and within transport/logistics (Riet et al. 1993; Wang and Ruijgrok 1994). For example, general cargo road transport is very diverse, based upon different submarkets regarding distance, product nature, logistic concept (time and accuracy), and so on. The size of road haulage companies seems to be a further differentiating factor in responsiveness to innovation. This observation is important because the Dutch road haulage sector is composed of a small number of large and medium sized companies and a large number of small companies.

An appropriate scale is often absent among Dutch road haulage companies (80 percent employ less than ten people) leading to particular impediments in organizational structure (Riet et al. 1993; Weijers 1994). One can observe a dominance of truck drivers in the workforce (80 percent) with generally low levels of education. In addition, there is often a decision structure based on intuition, ad hoc action, and small time horizons (90 percent of all firms).

Only a few Dutch road haulage companies (the large ones) make use of strategic planning and qualify as early adopters of innovations.

The above indicated low responsiveness among the majority of Dutch road haulage firms, together with a low problem awareness of congestion and reduced accessibility (Groot 1994) imply the rise of important difficulties in the mitigation of road congestion. The active space approach – to be discussed in Section 4 and Section 5 – will clarify the role of local learning in solving and preventing this type of problems.

3. TRANSALPINE FREIGHT TRAFFIC IN THE CHIASSO REGION

This section will discuss the restructuring process in transport and logistics services in the region of the railway and highway node of Chiasso. Chiasso is located on the Swiss-Italian border on the major axis between Southern and Northern Europe, including the passage of the St Gotthard. This passage absorbs roughly 30 percent of all transalpine freight traffic (Ratti and Rudel 1993).

The development of Chiasso illustrates an interesting trajectory of regional development. With the first construction of the tunnel and the railway of the St Gotthard the Swiss–Italian border region of Chiasso/Como (up to those days a peripheral region) started to gain importance. This development was mainly rooted in the regional function as an intra- and intermodal platform, and in the existence of strong barriers in Italian export trade. The St Gotthard route is the shortest connection across the Alps between the economic centres of Southern and Northern Europe. This factor and the existence of the border as a trade barrier favoured the position of the Ticino Swiss–Italian border region which could develop various value added transport services successfully. In 1970, at the peak of its growth, the region counted for more than 2500 forwarding employees. In addition, a supporting cooperation has been established with the Swiss federal railway company. Various alliances and cooperative relationships between the more than one hundred forwarding and transport firms contributed also essentially to this niche growth.

The subsequent development of transit traffic across the Alps was characterized by a specific new demand for transport and logistics services (differentiated demand, intermodal capacities, integrated logistics for tailormade solutions) (see Table 5.2). For the border forwarding agents this implied a significant change in services (a shifting away from the exclusively physical handling of goods), tighter relationships with clients and, most important, a new supporting environment based on new strategic alliances, (hierarchical) cooperation and new institutional aspects.

Table 5.2   Main factors of change for forwarding agents in the Chiasso region

---

Production Space

- Widespread introduction of information services (goods handling and clients management).
- Innovation in transport technologies (piggy backing on rail).
- High differentiation in the organizational structure of logistics firms.
- Need for new infrastructure (decay of traditional customs warehouse).

Market Space

- Radical change in services connected with different types of customs transactions (elimination and organizational innovation).
- Increasing demand due to trends for outsourcing by industrial producers.
- Structural change of demand (just-in-time; diminishing share of mass products, shift to road freight traffic).
- Decline of old networks (as intermediate services), and high competence and financial barriers to enter new logistics markets.
- New logistic demands (flexibility, reliability).

Supporting Space

- Diverging interests and loss of identity.
- Important reduction of support by national institutional agencies.
- Important (new) privileged relations with specific clients or operators.

Important investments in highway infrastructure in France and Austria, and a restricting transport policy (limit of 28 tonnes for heavy trucks) aiming at a sustained dominant position of the Swiss railway company in transalpine freight traffic, have caused a rapid change in the Ticino transport economy (Ratti and Rudel 1993). This development was reinforced by a tremendous restructuring process in production and distribution systems, requiring flexible, reliable and punctual transport services. The demand for these services could easily be satisfied by road transport, with railway transport only in a complementary role. In fact, the region was facing great difficulties in adjusting to these new market conditions (Ratti 1995). As a consequence, the region adopted a corridor function while experiencing a throat cutting market competition. A few forwarding firms in Chiasso were able to adjust adequately, others have relocated in the Northern Lombardian area, and the remaining firms have contracted or closed down.

The above characteristics can be formalized by the framework of the three functional spaces of economic activity as follows (see Table 5.2) (Ratti 1991, 1995):

- the production space, including location, physical networks, technological and social division of labour;
- the market space, including basic market conditions, market(ing) networks and information (a)symmetries;
- the supporting space, including governance structures and alliances, social networks and learning infrastructure.

The number of employees in the forwarding houses of Chiasso has dropped today to roughly half of the number of 25 years ago. With the decline of the traditional transport firms and forwarders in the border area, new logistic services emerged in the area of Milan (Creti 1994; Ratti 1995), where a close contact with the transport market and the production system became more and more important, for example, in view of supplying tailormade solutions (see Table 5.2). Whether the developments in the Milan region – where the expanding market creates new opportunities – may apply to a certain extent to the Ticino border region depends on the regional capacity to take advantage of emerging conditions following from a new railway infrastructure and environmental restrictions to road transport. First results would indicate that the Ticino border region has great difficulties in recovering and that new infrastructure favours increasingly the Milan region.

4. THE ACTIVE SPACE APPROACH: INTRODUCTION

The active space approach is a new approach to regional development which connects changes in openness of regions (related with transport) with the capacity of regions to manage the consequences of these changes in openness (see Figure 5.1). Starting from a systems approach, regions are considered as territorial organizations (Morin 1977; Rallet 1988; Thireau 1993). Openness of a territorial system refers to potential interaction between various components of the system (internal openness) and between the system and external systems. This interaction includes forms such as competition, cooperation, and complementarity. An increase in openness causes new momentum in the region at hand.

From a dynamic point of view, territorial systems are subject to an evolutionary development with active space and passive space as extremes.

Actors in active space (such as firms and institutes) are capable of managing – in terms of coherent behaviour and routines – dynamic internal and external relationships in order to achieve the best economic output of resources in a (socially and environmentally) sustainable way.

The concept of active space has a normative connotation as it emphasizes the best output of resources. This gives rise to the question of which interests (actors) are involved. A large openness may be considered beneficial in economic terms when it advances economic efficiency in regional economies (through changes in transaction costs). In a social (cultural) framework, however, a large openness may be considered favourable as long as external influences enrich the local culture and no threats emerge in terms of loss of cultural cohesion and social stability (see Mlinar 1992).

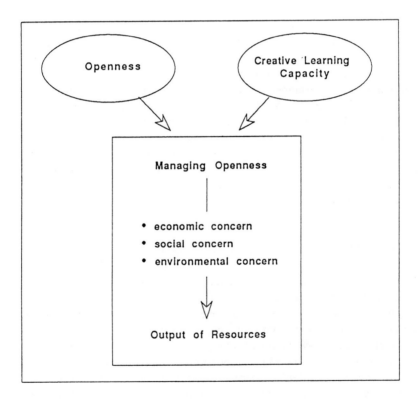

Figure 5.1   The force field in active space development

The key force in active space development is creative learning. It represents the capacity of a local system to respond to internal and external changes in terms of objectives, norms, and particularly system oriented strategic rules. It rests on a variety of local assets such as human capital (skills, experiences, and so on), transactional relationships between manufacturers, local suppliers and customers, informal contact networks, and synergy effects between various local actors such as universities, higher education institutes, firms and Chambers of Commerce.

It is self-evident that cities and regions offer different opportunities in terms of local learning. Stocks of knowledge, production and exchange of new knowledge vary considerably between network nodes (cities, firms) and their links. It is particularly the quality of the network in the sense of incorporating enforceable social habits and routines, which underlies local technical and organizational learning (cf. Camagni 1991, Storper 1993). It needs to be mentioned, however, that tight local networks may also preclude open learning. A high degree of (personal) cohesion may lead to a low alertness and low receptivity for new opportunities and innovative ideas (Grabher 1993).

The influence of openness (closedness) and learning capacity can be used in a two-way classification of regional development (see Figure 5.2). The conditions in Box 1 indicate obstacles to a development toward active space. Such conditions can be observed in peripheral areas outside major transport flows and in areas with an increasingly isolated position based upon new regionalism or specific network dynamics that cause tight local ties with a decreasing sensitivity for innovation. Box 2 represents a rather exceptional development by combining closedness and strong local learning. Regions aiming at economic self-sufficiency while using production methods under strict ecological rules get near to this type of development. Conditions in Box 3 may be observed in specific border regions with a corridor function based upon an increasing openness in international transport. There is, however, no capacity to manage a selective use aimed at gaining benefits from this openness. This type of region will suffer permanently from negative externalities of heavy transport flows without improvement through an adequate strategic response.

Finally, conditions in Box 4 advance a development toward active space. Accordingly, openness is managed in a selective way leading to the best results in economic, environmental and social terms. Such conditions can be observed, for example, in mainport regions which are able to establish new logistic services while moving toward environmentally sustainable approaches, such as integrated product chain management and reversed logistics. In addition, a strong anchoring of the main transport/logistics actors in the local economy and community is accompanied by well developed learning mechanisms, evident in a strong focus on transport/logistics in local education (research) programmes and a broad support for environmental and social concern among local actors.

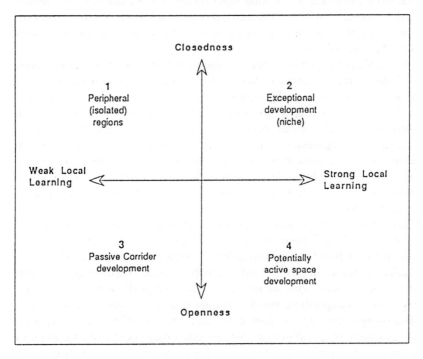

Figure 5.2 A two-way classification of regional development

Regional systems, managing their dynamic relationships, face four classes of features which influence their development (see Nijkamp 1990):

1. Location, in terms of national and European core-periphery systems, nodal points and network links (barriers), competing (complementary) regions, and so on.
2. A (limited) carrying capacity, in terms of economic resources and land (including human capital), ecological resources, and social absorption capacity.
3. A configuration of networks, in terms of capacity, coverage and connectivity of physical and socioeconomic networks (Håkansson 1988; Kamann 1993). The institutional framework is also important here (see Nijkamp et al. 1990; Suarez-Villa et al. 1992).

4. Multifunctionality, in terms of particular functional mixes in the region. Multifunctionality is associated with costs of transaction and benefits for innovation.

In a dynamic approach, a further distinction can be made between the capacity of regional actors to advance openness (remove barriers) and their capacity to use new openness in a selective way. The former capacity includes changes in the institutional environment (deregulation) and governance structures (transaction costs), the adoption of new technology (organization) and the establishment of new infrastructure (Grübler and Nakicenovic 1991).

Removing barriers in infrastructure (faster and cheaper transport, less capacity constraints, increased reliability) may imply a further openness and integration of regions. In addition, the capacity to remove sociocultural barriers (caused by a long term separation) may be important in order to gain economic benefits from vanished political borders, such as in cross-border corporate networking (Geenhuizen et al. 1994; Ratti 1993).

The capacity to manage openness in a selective way rests on various basic conditions associated with local learning. This will be illustrated in the remaining part of this section with the establishment of policies reflecting environmental concern (see Haughton and Hunter 1994). The key conditions to achieve an environmentally sustainable regional growth and the concomitant problem areas can be summarized as follows:

1. A sufficient availability of knowledge. Sustainable development is a highly complex matter, including complicated source – emission – immission chains in environmental pollution and socioeconomic mechanisms. Ways to policies for sustainable growth are, however, still hampered by a shortage of knowledge, including systems of sustainability indicators and databases.
2. A certain level of political consensus and acceptance of sustainability aims. This is associated with the development of enforceable habits and routines. However, within one society sustainability issues may be evaluated differently among different actors. There is no unambiguous profile of sustainable regional growth and sustainable transport, and so on.
3. Availability of appropriate policy and planning tools. The complexity of sustainable growth (e.g. multidisciplinarity and multiactor situation) causes a need for an integrated approach. Such an approach and the concomitant planning tools are not (yet) well developed.

The above indicates that local learning processes are vital in developing policies for a selective management of openness. The next section will now elaborate the active space approach, particularly the perspective of regional development trajectories.

5. THE ACTIVE SPACE APPROACH: A THEORETICAL PERSPECTIVE

In general, an increase in regional openness implies growing economic benefits from specialization and integration (complementary resources), as well as newly available resources for investment in environmental and social aspects. It is assumed here that after exceeding a certain level of openness, regional systems have a preference for social and environmental aims (instead of only economic aims).

The logic behind the relationship between a change in openness and a move towards or from active space is given in Figure 5.3. In fact, by using this type of figure it is possible to establish a typology of regional development trajectories according to different curves and positions in the various boxes. In order to explain the reasoning Figure 5.3 shows a simplified case leaving, for example, the behaviour of other regions (in terms of competition) and complex shapes of the curves aside.

The starting point is a difference in openness ($t_0 \ldots t_1$). The consequence of a change in regional openness can first be evaluated in terms of transaction costs. A higher degree of openness means generally a lower level of transaction costs (Box 1). Secondly, a decrease (or increase) of transaction costs determines – following the theory on new industrial economics – a benefit (or loss) in external exchange through comparative advantage and specialization, and hence a different level of integration (Box 2). Box 2 (the integration box) represents the capacity of regional companies to use markets, hierarchies and alliances in such a way that low transaction costs and a strong integration are combined.

Third, the amount of transaction costs and the degree of integration of regional companies have an impact on the regional development curve (Box 3). It needs to be emphasized that the case represented in Figure 5.3 is a positive one, whereas in many other cases the curve is different, for example, more steep or even inverse, the latter indicating a decline of the regional economy. Finally, Box 4 represents the result, namely the point in the trajectory in terms of active space development. In the specific case displayed in Figure 5.3, an increase in regional openness leads – given the above assumptions – to an increase of social and environmental concern and hence, to a move to active space (A_0 to A_1).

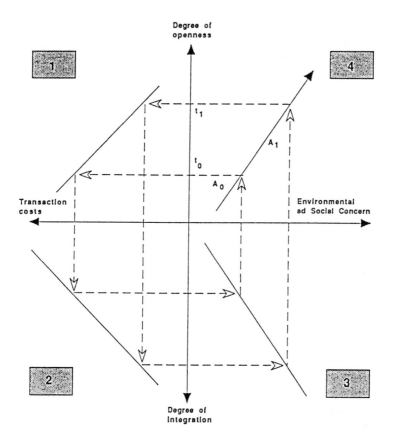

Figure 5.3   The logic of the active space development (simplified case)

In the next section we will turn back to the two case studies and discuss various changes (turns) in regional economic development by using the active space approach.

6.   THE ACTIVE SPACE APPROACH: EMPIRICAL CONCLUSIONS

With regard to the region of Rotterdam, two extreme scenarios of future development can be identified by using an active space approach. In the first scenario, road transport continues to increase rapidly leading to further reduced accessibility and increased transaction costs with various negative implications for integration. In a second scenario, there is a better use of the learning capacity in the region. This implies the advancing of strategic response, based upon a broad consensus and support among the main regional actors. In addition, supportive economic institutes have a strong receptiveness to changes in the market and technology, in such a way that they advance quality control and produce early warning signals.

In fact there are signs that the second scenario is a realistic one, given recent efforts to improve the openness of the region. For example, two managing organizations have been established for improving the regional learning capacity (1995/1996). These aim at (1) the coordination of research on transport and (2) the dissemination of results of this research to transport companies, and improvement of education in the field of transport.

The establishment of new interfaces between knowledge (technology) institutes and transport companies is a very important issue in present day Dutch national policy (cf. CROW 1994). Research projects that are now being carried out are concerned, for example, with faster services (container processing) in the port of Rotterdam and the use of multimodal transport in inland connections, and with finding new potentials for value added activities connected with the seaport. The regional support for such research projects is now much larger than previously, due to the use of public–private partnerships (joint financing by the national government and regional transport companies). This joint financing implies also a shift from technology driven to demand driven research which may improve the use of research results, based upon a larger commitment by the companies involved.

The past development of the Chiasso region will now be explained by using the following three periods: the 1950s (A_0), around 1970 (A_1), and the 1980s (A_2) (Figure 5.4). During the 1950s (t_0) the international trade of Italy faced a high level of transaction costs with, as previously explained, the development of value added niche services (Box 2). The concomitant growth reached its maximum in 1960–1979 (t_1), evident in an improved regional development (Box 3) and concomitantly, a move toward active space (A_0 to A_1).

However, it appears that in the case of a trend to a fully free market (1990, t_2) and lowest transaction costs, the benefits from strategic alliances can break down or be substantially modified by new external conditions (Box 2). This is the situation in which border regions are pushed into a corridor role. In the theoretical illustration here, the consequence is a much weaker integration (equilibrium in Box 2) and even a modified regional growth curve (Box 3). Furthermore, environmental and social concern in the region are given much less attention causing a move away from active space (A_2).

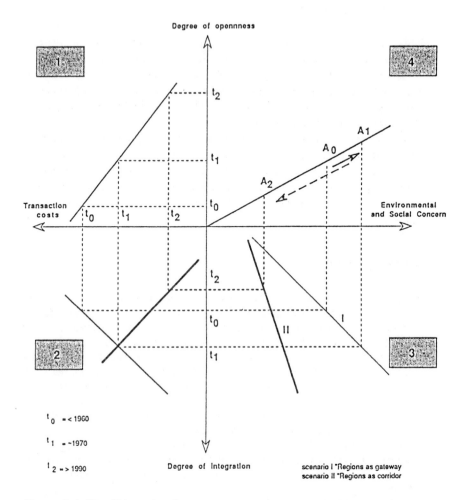

Figure 5.4   The Chiasso border region: a development trajectory in terms of active space

What is remarkable in the above trajectory is the apparent weakness of local learning mechanisms, particularly the lack of early warning signals and a (pro)active response of companies. An early strategic response might have prevented the dramatic turn in development and perhaps led to a better complementary relationship with the region of Milano.

7. CONCLUSION

This chapter has introduced the active space approach in the analysis of regional development. As a dynamic approach, it integrates the role of transport in openness of regions with the capacity of regional actors to manage this openness in a sustainable way. Such an approach is particularly useful given the many vanished political borders in Europe today and a tremendous increase of transport.

The advantage of the approach rests upon the opportunity to identify various development trajectories (scenarios) of regions with transport as the basic factor of change and to clarify the role of local learning mechanisms in preventing or advancing turns in regional development trajectories. Now steps need to be undertaken to arrive at a further operationalization of the approach.

REFERENCES

Buck Consultants Int. (1993), *Netwerken en ruimtelijke patronen van bedrijvigheid: een sectorale benadering* (Corporate Networks and Spatial Patterns: A Sectoral Approach), Nijmegen: Buck Consultants International.

B&W Gemeente Rotterdam (1993), *Havenplan 2010*, Rotterdam.

Camagni, R. (1991), 'Local "milieu", uncertainty and innovation networks: towards a new dynamic theory of economic space', in Camagni, R. (ed.), *Innovation Networks: Spatial Perspectives*, London: Belhaven Press, pp. 121–44.

Cheshire, P. and I. Gordon (1995), *Territorial Competition in an Integrating Europe: Local Impact and Public Policy*, Aldershot: Avebury.

Creti, A. (1994), La logistica industriale-distributiva. La globalizzazione di un milieu: Osservatorio permanente sull'evoluzione dei sistemi produttivi in Lombardia, Milano: *Universita Commerciale L. Bocconi Queaderno 4*, pp. 1–55.

CROW (1994), *Naar nieuwe onderzoeksprogrammering voor verkeer, vervoer en infrastructuur* (Towards a New Research Programme for Traffic, Transport and Infrastructure), Ede: Stichting CROW.

Geenhuizen. M. van, and P. Nijkamp (1995a), *Sustainable Cities: Challenges of an Integrated Planning Approach*, RM-1995-18, Amsterdam: Free University.

Geenhuizen, M. van and P. Nijkamp (1995b), *European Regional Science: In Search for New Combinations*, Amsterdam: Tinbergen Institute.

Geenhuizen, M. van, B. van der Knaap and P. Nijkamp (1994), *Transborder European Networking: Shifts in Corporate Strategy?*, Amsterdam: Tinbergen Institute.

Grabher, G. (1993), *The Embedded Firm. On the Socio-economics of Industrial Networks*, London: Routledge.

Groot, P.J. (1994), *Economische perspectieven voor ondergronds (gecombineerd) vercoer op lange termijn (Long Term Economic Perspectives for Subterranean (Combined) Transport*, Amsterdam: Economisch Instituut voor de Bouwnijverheid.

Grübler, A. and N. Nakicenovic (1991), *Evolution of Transport Systems: Past and Future*, Laxenburg: International Institute for Applied Systems Analysis.

Håkansson, H. (1988), *Industrial Technological Development: A Network Approach*, London: Croom Helm.

Haughton, G. and C. Hunter (1994), *Sustainable Cities*, London: Jessica Kingsley.

Kamann, D.J. (1993), 'Bottlenecks, barriers and networks of actors', in Ratti, R. and S. Reichman (eds), *Theory and Practice of Transborder Cooperation*, Basel: Helbing and Lichtenhahn, pp. 65–101.

Mlinar, Z. (1992), *Globalisation and Territorial Identities*, Aldershot: Avebury.

Morin, E. (1977), *La méthode, la nature de la nature*, Paris: Seuil, Tome I.

MVW (Ministerie van Verkeer en Waterstaat) (1995), (*Paper on Progress in Seaport Policy*), The Hague.

NEA (NL) and Cranfield School of Management (1994), *Future Logistics Structures*, Tilburg/Cranfield.

Netherlands Central Bureau of Statistics. Statistiek van de aan-, af- en doorvoer (various years) (Statistics of loaded and unloaded transport, and transhipment), Voorburg/Heerlen.

Nijkamp, P. (ed.) (1990), *Sustainability of Urban Systems: A Cross-National Evolutionary Analysis of Urban Innovation*, Aldershot: Avebury.

Nijkamp, P. (1994), 'Borders and barriers: bottlenecks or potentials', in Nijkamp, P. (ed.), *New Borders and Old Barriers in Spatial Development*, Aldershot: Avebury, pp. 1–11.

Nijkamp, P., P. Rietveld and I. Salomon (1990), 'Barriers in spatial interactions and communications. a conceptual exploration', *The Annals of the Regional Science* **24**, pp. 237–52.

Nijkamp, P., A. Perrels and L. Schippers (1995), 'The strategic role of new infrastructure networks in Europe', in D. Batten, J. Casti and R. Thord. (eds.), 1995, *Networks in Action: Communication, Economics and Human Knowledge*, Berlin: Springer, pp. 229–50.

Perriard, M. (1994), *Information et dynamique spatialisee de l'economie*, Fribourg (CH): Editions Universitaires, pp. 117–260.

Priemus, H., J.W. Konings and E. Kreutzberger (1995a), *Goederentransport knooppunten: typologie en dynamiek (Nodes in freight transport: typology and dynamics)*, Delft: Delftse Universitaire Pers.

Priemus, H., Konings, J.W. and E. Kreutzberger, (1995b), *Goederentransport knooppunten en modaliteit: Een inventarisatie (Nodes in Freight Transport and Modes: An Inventory Analysis)*, Delft: Delftse Universitaire Pers.

Py, B. (1992), 'Comportement des micro-espaces face à une recession économique: une approche théorique', *Revue d'économie régionale et urbaine*, **5**.

Rallet, A. (1988), 'La région et l'analyse économique contemporaine', *Revue d'économie régionale et urbaine*.

Ratti, R. (1982), *Les relations commerciales européennes à travers les Alpes: l'espace de marché du St. Gothard*, Zurich: DISP, ETH-Zurich **68**.

Ratti, R. (1991), *Innovation technologique et developpement regional*, Bellinzona: IRE-Meta Editions.

Ratti, R. (1993), 'Strategies to overcome barriers: from theory to practice', in Ratti, R. and S. Reichman (eds.), *Theory and Practice of Transborder Cooperation*, Basel: Helbing and Lichtenhahn, pp. 241–67.

Ratti, R. (1995), 'Dissolution of borders and european logistic networks', in Banister, D., R. Capello and P. Nijkamp (eds), *European Transport and Communication Networks*, Sussex: John Wiley & Sons, pp. 69–86.

Ratti, R. and R. Rudel (1993), 'Tableau de l'évolution des transports dans l'arc alpin', *Revue de Géographie Alpine* **4**.

Riet, J. van, M. van den Heuvel, C.J. van den, Ruijgrok and A.J.M. Vermunt (1993), *De vervoerder van de toekomst (A Future Perspective on Freight Transport Firms)*, Delft: INRO-TNO.

Storper, M. (1993), 'Regional worlds' of production: learning and innovation in the technology districts of France, Italy and the USA', *Regional Studies* **27**, pp. 433–55.

Suarez-Villa, L., M. Giaoutzi and A. Strategea (1992), 'Territorial and border barriers in information and communication networks: a conceptual exploration', in *Tijdschrift voor Econ. en Soc. Geografie* **83**, pp. 83–119.

Thireau, V. (1993), 'Vers un renouvellement du rôle d'espace dans la dynamique des territoires', *Revue d'économie régionale et urbaine*.

Venemans, M.J. (ed.), (1994), *Goederenvervoer over korte afstand (Short Distance Freight Transport)*, Alphen aan den Rijn/Zaventum: Samson.

Wang, W.H.J.B. and C.J. Ruijgrok (1994), 'De organisatie van voorraden en vervoerstromen' (The organisation of inventory and transport), in Venemans, M.J. (ed.), *Goederenvervoer over korte afstand (Short Distance Freight Transport)*, Alphen aan den Rijn/Zaventem: Samson, pp. 14–24.

Weijers, S. (1994), 'Information technology and organization in freight road haulage: questions on flexibility and bureaucracy', paper for the Zesde Sociaal–wetenschappelijke Studiedagen 1994, Amsterdam, 7–8 April.

Williamson, O.E. (1985), *Economic Institutions of Capitalism*, New York: Free Press.

6. Traffic Congestion and Behavioural Reactions: Policy Implications Exemplified for the Dutch Case

Eliahu Stern, Piet H.L. Bovy and Mart Tacken

1. INTRODUCTION

Most larger conurbations suffer from traffic congestion. It manifests itself predominantly as recurrent queue occurrences in suburban network parts and during rush hours. More and more congestion is spreading out in space and time, and in non-recurring forms also, often caused by unpredictable incidents. The increasing levels of traffic congestion and the inability to find appropriate solutions have triggered a new scientific interest in the economic, behavioural and environmental impacts of congestion. The present chapter is an effort to analyse behavioural impacts. Various actors on the demand and supply sides of the transportation system have a variety of potential responses at their disposal to counteract negative impacts of congestion. All actors develop policies to prevent or minimize congestion impacts covering the whole range from short to long term types of reaction. We can distinguish at least three classes of relevant actors. The first comprises public bodies responsible for spatial planning, temporal organization, infrastructure provision, traffic operation, and so on. Secondly, there are the organizations of the private economy, the firms which indirectly suffer from traffic congestion and can react to this, for example, through adapting their work schedules. Finally, the travelling individuals and hauliers can be distinguished as the direct victims. The individual consumers can respond in a variety of ways by their lifestyle, time-space activity, travel and driving choices respectively.

Several interesting empirical studies have been performed in the last five years to obtain an insight into the real response behaviour with respect to changes in congestion conditions, however, they are often disconnected from any comprehensive conceptual framework. This chapter therefore aims at presenting a theoretical framework for the study of behavioural responses to changing congestion. We confine the contribution to individual travellers and their behavioural responses in the space and time domains. Accordingly, theoretical expectations regarding behavioural responses are discussed and supported by empirical findings.

2. NATURE AND EXTENT OF CONGESTION

Most people know what is meant by traffic congestion but will fail in giving a precise scientific definition. A common element in the definitions of congestion is the concentration of people in time and space. The difficulty is much more with defining when congestion occurs rather than what the actual level of congestion is. Thus, we will not try to define congestion but rather describe this peculiar traffic status by some of its observable symptoms. Congestion is characterized by high densities (number of vehicles per kilometre), lack of freedom of movement for drivers, low speeds, queues of slowly moving bunches of vehicles, stop-and-go traffic, and so on. Various levels of congestion may be distinguished. A speed of less than 70 km/h on freeways is often considered as a first sign of congestion. Queue building is the next stage. As queues grow, blocking back occurs where entry and exit points and crossings get blocked. Finally, a complete gridlock, a standstill in an extended network of links and nodes can occur.

Recurrent congestion is caused by a structural lack of capacity (or an equivalent excess in demand), whereas non-recurring congestion stems from an incidental lack of capacity because of road works, accidents, weather conditions or incidental excess demand. It is important to note that even in cases of recurrent congestion, the travel characteristics can change from day to day; it is uncertain where queue building starts, when it starts, when it ends, how large waiting time loss will be, and so on. So, apart from the existence and travel time losses of queues, the unreliability of queue location, queue duration and queue moments are major aspects of congestion having a great impact on traveller behaviour.

Congestion has two faces: on the one hand, it is an attribute of the network so we can say how many queues have occurred in the network during the morning peak, how long they were and how long they lasted, how many kilometres of road were over-saturated and how many links were blocked.

On the other hand, congestion is also an attribute of a trip. This is what interests us most because these attributes influence the traveller's behaviour. Such trip-related characteristics are, for example whether a trip gets stuck in congestion (percentage of trips with congestion), amount of time or distance travelled under congested conditions, and share of delay time in total trip time. Unfortunately, empirical data on trip-related congestion variables are very rare. With respect to the extent of congestions, some statistics of the Dutch Randstad area may serve as an illustration (Ministry of Transport 1994). On an average working day in 1993 about 40 queues of minimum length of two kilometres built up mainly at the fringes of the four big cities. As indicated previously, congestion is highly variable, so the number, location and times of queues change from day to day. Bridges and tunnels across major waterways are well known queue locations. Also, discontinuities in the freeway network (entries, exits, weaving sections, lane number alterations) are favourite queuing places. The typical location of recurrent queues around the larger cities for a large part stems from changes in the spatial orientation of travel demand in the last 20 years such as reversed commuting and crisscross travel demand between suburbs.

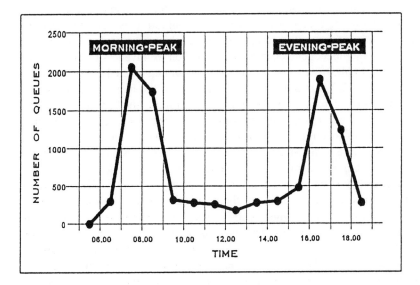

Figure 6.1   Hourly distribution of queues in the Dutch Randstad network, 1993

Concerning the timing of congestion, 80 percent of the queues in the Randstad occur during peak periods (see Figure 6.1, totalled over the year), of which 45 percent are in the morning peak (from 7.00 to 9.00 a.m.) and 35 percent in the afternoon peak (from 4.00 to 6.00 p.m.). From the average of 40 daily queues about ten queues take place during off peak times. These are mainly queues caused by incidents.

3. CONGESTION AND TRAVEL CONDITIONS

The occurrence of congestion leads to a number of changes in objective travel conditions at the level of the individual trip maker. The main changes are:

- changing travel time on network segments,
- increasing waiting time at bottlenecks (waiting in queues),
- increase in total trip duration,
- decreasing reliability of trip timing (i.e. arrival time reliability),
- decreasing reliability of trip duration (i.e. travel time reliability), and
- deteriorating driving conditions (i.e. stop-and-go, speed changes, and so on).

These congestion-related travel conditions have consequent effects on both the individual traveller and the local-national economy. Empirical evidence on who suffers where and how much from congestion is very rare. In the Netherlands a few studies have been done which give only a fragmented picture of the direct consequences of congestion to travellers (McKinsey and Company 1994). If we look which travellers get into traffic jams on freeways (see Figure 6.2a) it is not surprising to find that the majority is formed by commuters (57 percent). Another significant group is the business travellers. Travellers for other personal purposes are a minority (13 percent). From a comparison of locations, it is clear that the higher the congestion level, the lower the share of non-must travellers. These travellers have, for example, more opportunities to travel at other times.

The distribution of waiting time losses in queues among traveller categories appears somewhat different from the occurrence figures above (see Figure 6.2b). On average, commuters who get stuck in traffic jams suffer less than travellers for other purposes. This has, among other things, to do with their travel distances. At traffic jam locations, the median trip length of commuters is less than 20 kilometres, whereas all other trip purposes show median trip lengths of 30 kilometres or more. If we add a monetary value of the travel time losses, it appears that the business traveller suffers most from traffic congestion (see Figure 6.2c). The value-of-time for the purposes of commuting, business, goods and others currently amounts in the Netherlands to 12, 40, 63 and 9 Dutch guilders respectively.

From a dedicated congestion survey among commuters in congested areas (Korver et al. 1994) we can learn that about half of the car commuters regularly suffer from traffic congestion. These commuters on average have a travel time loss of about 15 minutes per commuting trip. The longer the commuting distance, the higher the congestion time loss. Congestion time losses cause trip duration to be about one-third longer than without congestion (average trip duration is about 36 minutes). There is a clear variability in congestion time losses among trips of an individual commuter: only about 20 percent of delayed commuters suffer each day from travel time losses of at least 15 minutes. In most cases, congestion occurrence as well as congestion delays are highly variable from day to day. This reliability aspect of congestion is valued highly by respondents. This is even more true for business travellers who appear to value travel time reliability even more than delay times (Korver 1992).

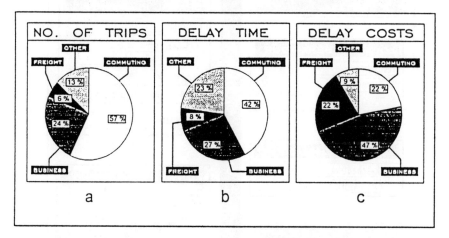

Figure 6.2 Composition of traffic in queues

4. THEORETICAL FRAMEWORK OF CONGESTION RESPONSE BEHAVIOUR

4.1 General Introduction

Since congestion is argued here to be a stochastic process, reactions to congestion are assumed to be dynamic. Based on this we assume that the frequency of decision making with regard to each of the possible reactions to traffic congestion is related to the type of behavioural response.

Figure 6.3 presents a concise overview of the possible reactions of both individual travellers (i.e. consumers) and authorities (i.e. providers). A hierarchical order is assumed to exist between the frequency of behavioural reactions and the type of behaviour. For the individual traveller, the least practised responses are changes in lifestyle and location, and the most frequently practised responses are changes in driving and travel behaviour.

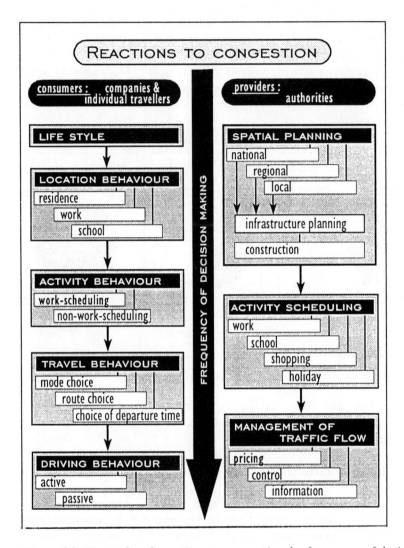

Figure 6.3 Hierarchy of reactions to congestion by frequency of decision making

Evidence for this statement has been found in a Dutch study conducted among 400 employees of two offices in Amsterdam. Tacken and De Boer (1990) asked office workers who experience traffic jams several times a week to value behavioural alternatives with potential to avoid congestion. The respondents could rank five alternatives from one to five. Table 6.1 shows that workers' first behavioural reaction to congestion is choosing different working hours, whereas moving house is the least favoured option.

Table 6.1   Average rank of alternative behavioural reactions to congestion

alternative	averaged rank
change working hours	1.9
other route	2.6
mode choice	2.9
other work	3.2
move house	3.8

Source: Tacken and De Boer 1989

Some other evidence relating to these rankings was found in a recent study conducted among executives and employees of 15 firms in the Netherlands (Korver et al. 1994). Executives were asked about the responses of the firm to increased interurban road traffic congestion. The employees were asked about their likely responses to a further increase of congestion on their home to work trips. From a catalogue of potential responses the most likely reactions of the firms are changing work schedules and stimulating shorter home-work distances, whereas the least likely responses are locational change of the firm and encouraging employees to work more at home. It should, however, be mentioned that responses differ greatly between types of firms. Industrial firms see much less potential for adaptation to congestion than the service sector industries. The responses of individual trip makers in order of likeliness were the following: (1) earlier departure from home, (2) changing working times, (3) changing route to/from work, (4) working more often at home, (5) using public transport more often, (6) changing job, (7) working fewer days a week and (8) changing home location. Thus, the least attractive to workers is changing their home, whereas employers and the government see it as a realistic option.

On the provider's side, we may expect that the most practised behaviour would be the management of traffic flow where the least practised one may be the reorganization of space on national and regional scales.

4.2   Reactions of Providers

As previously mentioned, this chapter deals primarily with the individual traveller and therefore, this section only briefly describes the reactions of authorities, or various level governments (i.e. providers), to congestion. The individual reaction is always embedded in and conditioned by legal regulations and decision space. The hierarchical order of authorities' behavioural reactions, as presented in Figure 6.3, includes three basic reaction categories: reactions related to management of traffic flows, reactions related to activity scheduling, and reactions related to spatial planning. The order by frequency of decision making can also be looked upon as an order of perceived difficulty of implementation. In these types of reactions, the basic dimensions of space and time are respectively stressed on the module of spatial planning and the module of activity scheduling. The third module of traffic flow management will be much more a mixture of both dimensions and these measures are more directly focused on the reactions of individual users.

There is some agreement in the literature regarding the hierarchical order of the solutions. The short term responses include transport management actions and promotion of variable working hour programmes. The long term solutions include land use development and technological changes. It is argued that the task over a longer term will be more difficult because it may exact a price that is now unacceptable. The cost may not be simply in monetary terms, but may also require changes in lifestyle and the way we do business. As implemented in the Netherlands, for example, the short term solutions developed by the state included demand management techniques like ride sharing, pool subsidies, motorist information, transit improvements and others. The long term reactions were concerned with land use development strategies such as the encouragement of households and firms to relocate in areas called 'areas of economic opportunity', and the initiation of a strategic planning grant programme for cities and towns to enable them to use a more systematic approach to development that allows people to live closer to their work.

At first glance, adapting departure times seems to be a short term reaction and the easiest way to respond to congestion. This is true for the incidental individual decision, but decisions on time schedules must fit into a larger decision structure. The easiest and most personal decision concerns the departure time for commuting trips. The personal planned work schedule is conditioned by arrangements in the work situation mostly imposed by the employer: fixed or flexible working hours, range of working hours, compressed work week, weekend. The national government and the labour unions negotiate about legal working time regulations: the amount of working hours, the maximum hours per time period, the flexibility in working hours. These are related to opening hours of shops and public facilities, the schedules of schools, and so on. A whole system of coherent measures is built up as a context for time decisions.

In several ways, the flexibility of work has been encouraged (Ministry of Transport 1995). Flexitime, spread of working hours, compressed work weeks and teleworking are examples of this policy. Twenty-two percent of the workers participated in an experiment for a compressed working week of four working days of nine hours. Eighteen percent completed this experiment. Evaluation showed that the productivity of the participants increased and that the accessibility of the Ministry improved during the experiment. The effects on mobility were very interesting; participants were commuting 10 percent less and travelling during peak hours decreased by 11 percent within this group.

Another experiment concerned teleworking of employees of the Ministry of Transport. Evaluation showed that the productivity increased during the experiment. The total car kilometres during peak hour decreased by 25 percent. This experiment resulted in a continuation of the telework project for this ministry. The introduction of telework gained broader support from the labour unions and the organizations of employers. Both organizations benefit from flexibility of work. The experiments show that time policy combined with other measures offers opportunities to respond to congestion.

4.3   Reactions of Consumers

Dynamic decision making implies that both choice and knowledge should play a major role in explaining the decision order of the five reaction categories of travellers to traffic congestion as illustrated in Figure 6.3. Choice depends first on the alternatives subjectively considered by the individual traveller as being feasible. These alternatives are constantly changing with the updating of knowledge. Knowledge, in our case, may be described as learning from day-to-day, firsthand, experience (that is, exposure to congestion), complemented by exogenous information from the various media outlets, word-of-mouth and others. Knowledge is directly connected to two types of expectations that may affect individual reactions to traffic congestion:

1.   expectations about the performance of the feasible alternatives, and
2.   expectations about future solutions to the congestion problem.

The first expectation is assumed to affect short term reactions, mainly those related to daily activity and travel-driving behaviour, whereas the second type of expectation is assumed to affect long term personal reactions such as change in location and/or in lifestyle.

It is assumed that the more frequently practised reactions are stimulated more by congestion consequences. The less practised responses depend on other considerations, mainly personal constraints and the anticipated long run consequences of the individual's response. Since the frequently practised reactions are more associated with congestion consequences, we propose a personal stimulus-response model (Figure 6.4) as an expectancy framework for the study of congestion and personal behavioural reactions.

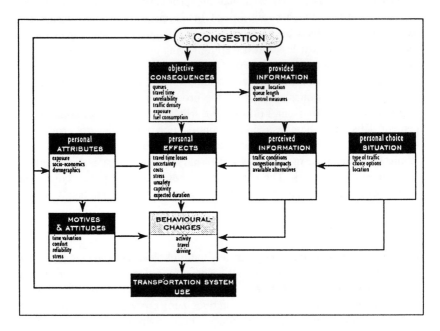

*Figure 6.4 A personal stimulus-response model in a congested transport
environment*

Behavioural responses to congestion result directly from the perceived personal effects of congestion, the personal choice situation, and the congestion-related motives and attitudes developed by the traveller on the basis of his/her personal attributes and experience – often an outcome of previous choices. The latter are demonstrated in Figure 6.4 by the loop connecting the 'transport system use' box and the 'exposure' attribute. The perceived personal effects are subject to the amount of perceived information and the objective consequences of congestion (the stimuli). The latter also determine the contents of the provided (objective) information. The consequent perceived information includes not only traffic conditions but also perceptions of individual congestion impacts and subjective estimates of available alternatives. Finally, the model can be viewed as a closed subsystem showing the interface between congestion and transport system use through the mediation of personal behaviour. The following sections examine a selection of specific behavioural responses to congestion along with supporting empirical evidence.

5. IMPACTS OF TRAFFIC CONGESTION ON ACTIVITY BEHAVIOUR

Activity behaviour refers to work and non-work personal scheduling. Changes in work scheduling due to congestion include both daily working times and working days, and chaining of daily activities. The same may be applied to non-work out-of-home activities where people change their schedules. The main motive for work rescheduling will be decreasing reliability and travel time duration.

'Before' and 'after' studies undertaken by Tacken and De Boer (1989 and 1991) focused on the way employees use flexible working hours to avoid peak hour traffic. The 'after' study was done after an improvement in the urban beltway around Amsterdam resulting in a decrease in congestion levels on the former bottlenecks.

The 'before' study (1989) gives information on the role of flexitime as a possibility to respond to congestion. Over the long term the scheduling of *planned, normal* working hours shows minor differences between weekdays. The most important factors for this scheduling are: congested roads (4 percent), personal attitudes (28 percent), time schedules of public transport (27 percent), workload (27 percent). Time schedules are less fixed than expected on the basis of the planned times. The findings stress the importance of flexitime as one of the conditions for behavioural reactions to congestion; people use the flexibility to respond to expected congestion. They adjust their planned time schedule to the experienced congestion. Workers adapt their travel behaviour within the margins they have and the next part shows that they want more flexibility.

About 60 percent of the sample had the option of a major change in work schedule. Twenty-five percent were prepared to start more than one hour earlier and 40 percent were willing to start much later.

This leads to the hypothesis that this finding is strongly related to the actual situation of flexitime. Many workers have already used the margins of the existing regulation in the company by an early start. Advancing the present departure time would cause too much trouble at home or the arrival at work would be too early, outside the allowed working hours. To enable workers to use their maximum margins in departure times, the existing regulations for working hours must be extended by a start between 6.30 and 9.30 and finish between 15.30 and 18.30. This hypothesis about the early start leads to the expectation that departure times will return to the peak after a congestion relief.

Tacken and De Boer (1991) repeated the 1989 study one year later with the same sample of office workers with flexitime. Meanwhile, the urban beltway around Amsterdam was completed with the opening of the Zeeburger Tunnel crossing the North Sea Canal. Congestion at existing bottlenecks was reduced or disappeared. Relevant in the context of this chapter is the way people changed their planned, 'normal' departure times. The results given in Table 6.2 show the reaction of employees who changed their activity patterns due to former congestion levels in the new situation of 1990 where congestion levels have decreased. A clear 'back to normal' reaction is observed with workers returning to more convenient departure times, usually 'back to the peak'.

Table 6.2   Changes in starting times of work between 1989 and 1990 during all interview days

start work 1990

start work 1989	before 7.00	7.00– 7.30	7.30– 8.00	8.00– 8.30	8.30– 9.00	after 9.00	total # trips
before 7.00	22	1	5	0	0	0	**38**
7.00–7.30	21	110	43	20	8	4	**206**
7.30–8.00	5	46	149	58	7	5	**270**
8.00–8.30	0	22	57	179	40	8	**306**
8.30–9.00	0	3	8	46	127	11	**195**
after 9.00	1	0	3	14	10	51	**79**
total trips	**49**	**182**	**265**	**317**	**192**	**79**	**1094**

Source: Tacken and De Boer 1989

Research shows that strict lateness regulations influence the choice process. An interesting remark for future time policy is: the impact for peak spreading may not be greatest where individuals have the freedom to adjust their work schedules according to their preferences but where regulations enforce non-standard working hours for a significant proportion of workers. Next to flexitime this introduces a second way to handle time policy in reduction of congestion. In many European countries the discussion has started between employers and labour unions about flexibility of working hours; flexitime, compressed working weeks, reduced working hours, Saturdays as working days.

6. IMPACTS OF TRAFFIC CONGESTION ON TRAVEL BEHAVIOUR

Travel behaviour includes three types of reaction to recurrent congestion in the following decreasing order of adoption frequency: change in departure time, change of route and change of transport mode. In the case of non-recurrent congestion we should expect to find 'change of route' to be the most frequently practised response. The major congestion-related motives affecting changes in travel behaviour are loss of time, decreasing reliability, and feelings of captivity stemming simply from 'queue occurrence'. As indicated in Figure 6.5, travel behaviour is also likely to change due to information provided to the traveller. The types of effect of some of these factors supported by empirical evidence is presented below.

6.1 Loss of Time

Time loss is by far the most important influencing variable. Only slight increases in travel time give rise to changing routes by travellers. A recent literature survey (Jansen et al. 1990) indicated, however, the lack of studies that show the specific separate effects of congestion as such. Only a single later study (Jansen et al. 1991) showed the route choice impact of time loss due to congestion. The stated preference survey among 300 commuters, users of congested motorways, revealed that on average, the commuters were prepared to drive an extra 12.5 kilometres to save ten minutes time loss in a queue. This means that on average they accept a few minutes extra travel time in a queue before taking alternative routes that are longer in distance.

About 25 percent of drivers are willing to accept longer trip times as well as longer trip distance to reduce the time lost in queues. As time lost in queues gives extra disutility to commuters, already with low travel time losses in queues they switch to alternative routes even if this takes more time. Another 25 percent show a reverse sensitivity; they are only willing to make a detour with extra kilometres of driving if the travel time loss in the queue is quite significant. There are, however, studies (for example, Vanderschuren and Tacken 1989) showing that departure time is the most decisive factor in reaction to congestion.

As adapting departure times is one of the travellers' opportunities to respond to changes in congestion conditions, we may assume that travellers try to minimize travel disutility also with respect to the timing of their trips. Travellers will trade off the various disutilities by advancing departure time. The disutility of early arrival schedule delay will be compensated by lower congestion delay and parking costs. Accordingly, Figure 6.5 presents hypothetical disutility curves for a number of time dependent trip variables. For a recent overview of the theory see Polak et al. 1992.

From a number of studies (see HCG 1990 and Polak et al. 1992) it appears that the disutility of one minute extra congestion delay equals more or less the disutility of two to three minutes schedule delay. On average, larger congestion delays more often cause advancing departure times than delaying departure times. Moreover, travellers are more sensitive to late arrival than to early arrival by a factor three to four. One of the few empirical studies into congestion sensitivity of departure times was the Amsterdam Orbital Opening Before-and-After Study (Bovy et al. 1991). A sudden decrease in congestion levels due to the opening of a new tunnel caused about one-third of the channel crossing car drivers to adapt their trip times during the morning peak. Most of these changes involved departure time shifts towards the centre of the peak, also called the return-to-the-peak phenomenon. The peak appears to be clearly the most preferred travelling period for commuters.

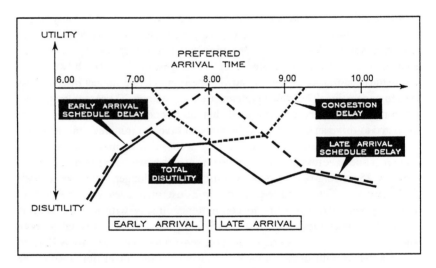

Figure 6.5 Disutility components of morning commuter departure time choice

6.2   Unreliability

Unreliability, measured by travel time variability, was shown in a number of studies (for example, Bates et al. 1987; Foster 1982) to have a separate impact on travel behaviour. It affects all the discussed behavioural choices – departure time, route and mode choice. In the experimental study conducted by Bates et al. (1987), it was expected that for a given level of variability, the highest utility will be assigned to the most preferred combination of departure/arrival times. The results show that the highest utilities, for a given level of variability, are found for the traveller's current departure time and a mean arrival time about 15 to 20 minutes later. As the departure time is earlier, utility falls extremely fast, while for later departures, it only begins to fall when the mean arrival time is 40 minutes later than the current departure time. For all situations there is a drop in utility as variability increases, particularly as we move to high variability.

Unreliability is equivalent in the case of congestion to uncertainty. A study conducted among the executives of fourteen firms in the Netherlands showed, for example, that uncertainty due to congestion is most relevant to business travellers. The costs involved with uncertainty are much higher than those related to delays (Korver 1992). Since executives usually have more freedom of choice than their employees, their reactions to congestion will first be a change in departure time, second they would adapt their trip schedules (order of visits), and third, they would change their route choice.

6.3 Queue Occurrence

The occurrence of a queue expresses a number of congestion consequences that are difficult to measure like driving conditions or feelings of captivity. Often drivers say they like to keep moving even if it takes more time (see, for example, Jansen and Den Adel 1986). The quantitative effect of such consequent 'declarations' to captivity has, however, hardly been investigated (Bovy and Stern 1990). Only a few studies (for example, Wachs 1967; and to a certain extent also Jansen et al. 1991) dealt explicitly with this choice factor. From the few studies it can be learned that there are large individual differences with respect to congestion sensitivity.

7. POLICY IMPLICATIONS OF CONGESTION ISSUES

The behavioural reactions of road users towards congestion as described earlier give clues to effective policy measures to reduce congestion problems. Figure 6.3 shows an overview of the types of policy interventions that authorities can exert in order to improve congestion conditions. When looking at the various policy instruments, we are now aware of the dangerous ambiguity of the classical countermeasure to congestion, that is, building more roads. Only in very specific situations with severe bottlenecks will the addition of extra road capacity at the bottlenecks (for example, second bridge or tunnel) result in a significant and longstanding reduction in congestion. In many cases of infrastructural enlargement however, the improvement of traffic conditions gives rise to actuating latent demand.

As a result of travel time improvements, the demand for road capacity at the improved location increases strongly, where this new demand follows from mode, destination and route changes of travellers. In addition, adaptation of departure and arrival time decisions leads to the well known 'return-to-the-peak' phenomenon, so that peak hour congestion levels after improvement often equal those prior to infrastructural improvements. These processes have been analysed intensively in a before and after study of the recently completed orbital freeway around Amsterdam (see Bovy et al. 1991).

Policy makers are now convinced that other strategies for congestion relief are needed which tackle the problem much more at the roots. The term congestion management as an umbrella label for these strategies expresses a different approach to the problem. According to a recent OECD report on this topic (OECD 1994), the collection of congestion management policy measures may be grouped into two basic strategy classifications; demand side and supply side. Whereas the latter group focuses on the increase of capacity of existing infrastructure and better utilization of given capacities in order to improve traffic flows for all modes, the demand side measures intend to reduce car dependency and car demand on the system by increasing vehicle occupancy, increasing public transport share, reducing the need for travelling at peak periods and/or to specified locations. Table 6.3 gives a classification of congestion management measures that are being successfully applied in European countries.

Despite the positive experiences with current congestion relief measures it is clear that their contribution to the total mobility problem is limited. If we look at the expected long term growth in the demand for road space in most of the European countries, this category of measures compensates for the demand growth of a few years only. For the future, new classes of policy instruments are needed to distribute scarce road space among competing consumers. New technologies such as telematics may help to develop, for example, various forms of rationing. Tradable permits of using spatiotemporal slots in the infrastructure supply could solve a lot of equity and financial problems related to the future scarcity of transport facilities. These new types of congestion management measures constitute challenging research subjects for the near future.

Table 6.3 *Congestion management measures used in European countries*

Strategy Class	Types of Measure	Measures
DEMAND SIDE	LAND-USE ZONING	•Land-Use & Zoning Policy •Site Amenities & Design
	COMMUNICATIONS SUBSTITUTES	•Telecommuting •Teleconferencing •Tele-Shopping
	TRAVELLER INFORMATION SERVICES	•Pre-Trip Travel Information •Regional Rideshare Matching
	ECONOMIC MEASURES	•Congestion Pricing •Parking Pricing •Transportation Allowances •Transit & Rideshare Financial Incentives •Public Transport Pass Programmes •Innovative Financing
	ADMINISTRATIVE MEASURES	•Transportation Partnerships •Trip Reduction Ordinances and Regulation •Auto Restricted Zones •Parking Management
SUPPLY SIDE	ROAD TRAFFIC OPERATION	•Entrance Ramp Controls •Traveller Information Systems •Traffic Signal Improvements •Motorway Traffic Management •Incident Management •Traffic Control at Construction Sites
	PREFERENTIAL TREATMENT	•Bus Lanes •Car Pool Lanes •Bicycle & Pedestrian Facilities •Traffic Signal Preemption
	PUBLIC TRANSPORT OPERATIONS	•Express Bus Services •Park & Ride Facilities •Service Improvements •Public Transport Image •High Capacity Public Transport Vehicles
	FREIGHT MOVEMENTS	•Urban •Intercity Source

Source: OECD 1994

8. CONCLUSIONS

This chapter has dealt with various aspects of behavioural responses to congestion. First we have presented a framework for the various types of behavioural options people have to adapt to changing congestion conditions, including changes in lifestyle, in location behaviour, in activity behaviour, in travel behaviour and in driving behaviour.

With respect to travelling options it appears clearly from the many empirical studies that trip timing is the mostly preferred and used option to counteract congestion changes. Route choice is second best. Mode choice switches are only seldom considered as a solution. An important consequence is the so called return-to-the-peak phenomenon. After removing bottlenecks, the peak in travel demand at the bottleneck location is often not removed or shaved but remains more or less the same because of temporal shifts of drivers towards the middle of the peak period. This does not, however, mean that the capacity improvement was useless.

With respect to factors relevant in congestion behaviour, researchers appeared to be very myopic in the past. Often only extra travel time was considered as a trigger of behavioural changes. It is however clear that reliability of both travel durations and arrival times are at least as important if not even more important. Reliability becomes more and more an issue because of changing lifestyles of people towards so called just-in-time living with fully booked diaries. Also, the mere occurrence of a queue regardless of duration is a factor causing behavioural response in many cases such as in route choice.

With regard to the choice process it is clear that thresholds, that is, transaction costs, exist in adaptations of regular behaviour. People try to maintain their current behaviour as long as possible. Uncertainty about travel conditions leads to stability in travel habits. Information can play an important role here since better knowledge appears to lead to more conscious decisions where travellers are willing to switch more often according to dynamically changing conditions.

Another threshold is created by the position of individual decision making in the whole hierarchical structure of decision making. The individual often has to act within the small margins allowed by official rules for working hours, working weeks, opening hours, or allowed by the spatial planning on several levels.

Despite the enormous impact of traffic congestion upon individuals and society, not very much is known about its characteristics, especially at the level of individual trip making. We need more precise operational definitions of the various dimensions of congestion and more and better measurements of congestion variables at the level of trips.

This lack of knowledge makes it difficult for policy makers to make effective decisions. Learning from experiments and past experience one thing may be clear, people often have to pass higher thresholds than expected. From the theoretical framework we can learn about the diversity of policy measures reducing or handling congestion. Part of these must focus on the locations of activities: tele-activities, concentration of residential areas and work locations, whereas others have to focus on time behaviour of people: flexitime, compressed working weeks, work scheduling, departure times. Often a mixture of measures creates the best conditions for individual behavioural reactions. Transport coordination and the provision of information support decision making.

REFERENCES

Bates, J., M. Dix and T. May (1987), 'Travel time variability and its effects on time of day choice for the journey to work', *Proceedings PTRC*, Seminar C, pp. 293–311.

Bovy, P.H.L. and E. Stern (1990), *Route Choice: Wayfinding in Transport Networks*, Dordrecht: Kluwer Academic Publishers.

Bovy, P.H.L. et al. (1991), *Effects of Opening the M10 Amsterdam Orbital Motorway*, Rijkswaterstaat, Rotterdam: Transport and Traffic Research Division.

Foster, N. (1982), *A Study of Travel Time, Variability of the Journey to Work*, University of Leeds: unpublished MSc thesis.

Hall, W.R. (1993), 'Non-recurrent congestion: how big is the problem?' *Transportation Research C 1* (1), pp. 89–103.

HCG (1990), *Stated Preference Investigation: Changes in Departure Time Choice Due to Congestion*, The Hague (in Dutch).

Jansen, G.R.M. and D.N. Den Adel (1986), *Car Drivers' Route Choice: An Investigation into Qualitative Choice Factors*, ISO Report no. 59, Delft University of Technology (in Dutch).

Jansen, G.R.M. et al. (1990), Variable Message Signs on the Amsterdam Ring Road – *A Literature Study into Route Choice Behaviour and the Appropriate Design*, Delft: INRO TNO (in Dutch).

Jansen, G.R.M. et al. (1991), *Route Choice Behaviour on Congested Motorway Networks: A Stated Preference Experiment*, Delft: INRO TNO (in Dutch).

Korver, W. (1992), *Congestion Delays in Personal Business Travel: Behavioral Changes of Companies*, Delft: INRO TNO (in Dutch).

Korver, W. et al. (1994), *Behavioral Changes of Companies as a result of Congestion – Part III: Commuter Traffic*, Delft: INRO TNO (in Dutch).

McKinsey & Company (1994), *Better Utilization Besides Building*, The Hague: Dutch Ministry of Transport (in Dutch).

Meyer, M.D. (1990), 'Dealing with congestion from a regional perspective: the case of Massachusetts', *Transportation* **16**, pp. 197–220.

Ministry of Transport (1994), *Queues: How Do We Cope?*, The Hague: Dutch Ministry of Transport (in Dutch).

Ministry of Transport (1995), *All People Travelling at the Same Time or Spread of Traffic in Time*, The Hague (in Dutch).

Murphey, T. (1990), 'Suburban congestion: recommendations for transportation and land use responses', *Transportation* 16, pp. 221–40.

OECD (1994), *Congestion Control and Demand Management*, Paris.

Polak, J. et al. (1992) *An Assessment of Some Recent Studies of Travellers' Choice of Time of Travel*, Oxford University, Transport Studies Unit, TSU Ret. 698.

Tacken, M. and E. De Boer (1989), *Flexitime and the Spread of Traffic Peak Hour: An Analysis of Conditions and Behaviour*, OSPA, Delft University of Technology (in Dutch).

Tacken, M. and E. De Boer (1991), *Change in Spread of Travel and Working Times Due to Opening of the Amsterdam Orbital Motorway*, OSPA, Delft University of Technology (in Dutch).

Vanderschuren, M. and M. Tacken (1989), 'Choice of working hours in avoiding congestion', in Meurs, H. (ed.), *Transport Policy between Urban Fringe and City*, Colloquium Vervoersplanologisch Speurwerk, The Hague (in Dutch).

Wachs, M. (1967), 'Relationships between drivers' attitudes toward alternative routes and driver and route characteristics', *Highway Research Record* 197, pp. 70–87.

7. Models and Tools to Design Strategies for Freight Transport: An Example for the Netherlands

Odette van de Riet and
Patricia Twaalfhoven

1. INTRODUCTION

The FORWARD (Freight Options for Road, Water, And Rail for the Dutch) project was a broad policy analysis focused on ways of coping with the projected massive growth in road freight transport in the Netherlands. The primary purpose of this multidisciplinary study was to examine possible ways to mitigate the negative impacts of increasing freight transport on the Netherlands' highways, while also attempting to retain its economic benefits.

Begun in December 1992, the project was carried out by the European American Center for Policy Analysis (EAC) of the California-based RAND Corporation, for the Netherlands Ministry of Transport, Public Works and Water Management (hereinafter, the Ministry). The project team was composed of researchers from the EAC, RAND, and the School of Systems Engineering, Policy Analysis and Management of Delft University of Technology. With the support and active participation of staff members of the Ministry, a set of policy analysis tools were designed and built to assess the impacts of various policy alternatives and identify the most promising policy options.

Section 2 defines the FORWARD project in terms of its goals, scope, and approach. Section 3 gives an overview of the project and describes the models and tools that were used to identify promising *tactics* (single actions taken to affect the freight transport system) and to design promising combinations of tactics (called *strategies*). Section 4 describes the major conclusions and observations. A glance at the future, including the use of the project's results by the Ministry, is given in the last section. A complete description of the research carried out on the FORWARD project is contained in a main report

(Hillestad et al. 1996) and two supporting volumes (Carrillo et al. 1996 and Bolten et al. 1996).

2. BACKGROUND

2.1 The Research Problem

In 1990, the Netherlands Minister of Transport, Public Works and Water Management and the Minister of Housing, Physical Planning, and Environment issued a policy statement on transport called the *Second Transport Structure Plan* (SVV) (Second Chamber of the States-General 1990). This document describes the current and projected problems associated with transport in the Netherlands and proposes adopting a number of specific steps to deal with them. With respect to freight, there are specific policy recommendations designed to maintain the Dutch market share, improve freight hauling efficiency, and develop additional infrastructure.

Although the *Second Transport Structure Plan* was fairly comprehensive in its policy recommendations, there has been continued debate about the importance and effect of specific policy options. The debate focuses not only on the predictions of effects, but, depending on the interest group involved, also on which effects are most important. It has also been argued that there may be more attractive alternatives to a number of the Plan's options. The continuing public debate about the alternatives to deal with freight transport in the Netherlands and the importance of this transport to the Dutch economy motivated the Ministry of Transport, Public Works and Water Management to commission a broad study of freight policy options and their impacts and costs.

The problem originally posed to the FORWARD project team was to find the best ways to shift freight off the highways and onto other modes. However, this was soon realized to be too narrow and more of a solution statement than a problem statement. Asking the client why freight should be shifted off the highway revealed a desire to reduce the negative effects of road freight transport. But there are other ways of dealing with the negative effects of road freight transport besides shifting it off the highways, such as making better use of the existing infrastructure and truck fleet, or by directly mitigating the negative effects, for example, with cleaner diesel engines.

It was also realized that there were likely to be many policy actions for coping with the negative impacts of road freight transport, and that preferences among these actions would depend on the relative importance placed on their effects. People concerned about environmental effects are likely to evaluate the policy options differently from people concerned about the economic effects. A major component of the problem is how to provide some rationale for choosing among a large number of policy options and making tradeoffs among many measures of effectiveness.

The goal of the research was eventually defined as: find the best strategies to mitigate the negative impacts of the growth of freight transport while retaining the economic benefits.

This was done for alternative economic scenarios for the year 2015. The study was to look at as many policy options as possible and to evaluate each policy option's effects on a broad range of performance measures, including noise, safety, congestion, emissions, costs, added value to the economy, and employment.

2.2 The Policy Analysis Approach

The research was performed using a structured approach developed at RAND to evaluate public policy options (each of which is called a *tactic* and combinations of which are called *strategies*) specifically for situations involving complex systems with multiple measures of performance and involving competing interest groups with different and frequently conflicting goals. The approach is simply called *policy analysis* (Miser and Quade 1985). It has been applied successfully to such different problems as national water policy, drug policy, educational policy, and national defence planning and budgeting.

Policy analysis is an *iterative* process. When the first batch of strategies is presented to the policy makers, they may ask whether it is possible to design a strategy that emphasizes, for example, modal shift a bit more. Or new tactics may be suggested, which may help to shore up weaknesses in the strategies initially presented. The analysis and planning team must then design new strategies and return for further direction.

Properly applied, this approach helps policy makers do their jobs better. At various stages the policy makers are asked to participate and advise. They are shown the effects of a number of different strategies. They are then asked for their preferences, or to suggest areas in which they would most like improvement or could best tolerate degradation. The end result is not only a set of promising strategies, but a deeper understanding of the rationale for why certain strategies and tactics perform as they do, and a set of results that has involved the policy makers and stakeholders in their development. This is the approach that we used in the FORWARD project.

2.3   Some Unique Features of the FORWARD Project

There have been many other studies of policy options for transport in the Netherlands and Europe, including the Ministry's own SVV (Second Chamber of the States-General 1990). The natural question is how the FORWARD project differs from the others, and what unique insights it provides for making informed policy decisions. The differences are in both approach and outcomes.

Generally, transport projects, even policy projects, have been narrowly defined to look at one or two specific policy actions and to focus on a particular impact category, such as the economic impacts, environmental impacts, or safety impacts. Thus, one finds studies of the 'cost of time' for transporters, of the environmental impact of a dedicated rail line for freight, and on the effect of road pricing on traffic intensity.

The FORWARD study took a *broad perspective* in terms of the policy actions investigated and the impacts of those actions. The attempt was to consider as many tactics as possible and to compare their impacts on the measures of interest to the broad spectrum of stakeholders. The project was *integrative*, in that it attempted to bring together multiple tactics to provide robust strategies that would mitigate the negative impacts of freight transport on all of the measures. FORWARD was also integrative in the sense of utilizing existing Dutch research (for example, research by DAF on cleaner diesel engines and *Trendbreuk* results (Werkgroep '2duizend 1993) on certain efficiency options) and existing Dutch models (Blok et al. 1992). The computer programme that was used to estimate the impacts of the various tactics (which is called PACE-FORWARD) was largely based on traffic conversion and impact models developed by other groups in the Netherlands. The freight demand data were obtained from NEA, and were based on research they had done with respect to origin and destinations of freight as affected by the Central Planning Bureau scenarios of economic growth (NEA 1991a/b; NEA 1992a/b). In its breadth, FORWARD was also *multimodal*, in that it considered the interactions among modes (for example, how shifting freight from highway to rail decreases road emissions but increases rail emissions), the elasticities of demand for the various modes (that is, how demands might be affected by changes in costs), and actual intermodal freight transport. The project treated each tactic as a separate research project, and, in some cases, went into considerable depth to understand how to represent and quantify a tactic. In other cases, cursory examination was enough to eliminate an option. Thus, the project *used depth where necessary*.

FORWARD did not attempt to find a single solution, but rather it *produced alternative promising strategies and conclusions*, together with their evaluation and rationale. The research and the final results are developed *through iterations with the stakeholders and policy makers*, thus providing important inputs and more assurance that the conclusions and recommendations are understood and accepted.

The project *developed* PACE-FORWARD, which is expected to have a usefulness beyond this research effort. Given appropriate support and data, this model and its architecture provide the Ministry with the capability to reevaluate the policy actions investigated in this project as more information on tactics becomes available or changes in scenario projections of demand occur. It can be used to investigate changes in the relative emphasis applied to the various impact measures, and it can be used to evaluate new tactics and strategies once they are fully defined and implemented in the model and data structure.

Finally, the FORWARD project *demonstrated a policy analysis methodology* that can be applied to other policy areas such as civil aviation, passenger transport, infrastructure priorities, etc., in the Netherlands and elsewhere. Indeed, the methodology provides an approach that can be used to address high level, cross-cutting issues when there are large numbers of policy options and when there are competing objectives and measures.

3. OVERVIEW OF THE FORWARD PROJECT AND ITS RESULTS

3.1 Tactics and Performance Measures

One of the key elements in the FORWARD project was to develop a detailed picture of transport and traffic in the current situation, and for several future situations. The Netherlands Central Planning Bureau (CPB) has outlined three scenarios for the development of the Dutch economy to the year 2015: the Balanced Growth scenario (BG), the European Renaissance scenario (ER), and the Global Shift scenario (GS) (Central Planning Bureau 1992). Based on the freight demand data developed by the Dutch research institute NEA, we developed freight demand scenarios for the year 1990 ('current situation') and for the three CPB scenarios for the year 2015.

The performance measures that were considered in the FORWARD study are divided into six categories: emissions, noise, safety, congestion, costs, and national economy. The emissions category consists of six types of emissions: CO_2, NO_x, CO, C_xH_y, SO_2, and aerosols. The effect on the noise nuisance is measured by the average distance from the highways to the 55 dB(A) contour. To measure safety, the impacts on the number of accidents, injuries, fatalities, and truck accidents related to the transport of hazardous goods are estimated. Total congestion severity (number of incidents * average length of tailback * average duration of incident) is taken as a measure of congestion on the Netherlands' highways. The net incremental cost of a tactic (that is, its net additional cost over all stakeholders) is taken as a measure for the cost. The cost of a tactic is split into four parts: delay costs, investment costs, operating cost and maintenance costs. For the macroeconomic impacts, the changes in employment and value added for the transport and production sectors are estimated.

The tactics evaluated fall into three main categories:

1. *Direct Mitigation Tactics*. These tactics are addressed specifically to reducing one or more of the negative impacts at their source. Most of them are technical improvements to trucks to reduce the emissions and noise of trucks, or to increase safety on the highways. Examples are the use of soot filters, cleaner engines, low-noise tyres, electric vans, and the reduction of the power/weight ratio of trucks. Tactics that change the road infrastructure in order to reduce congestion, such as using a separate lane for trucks, are also included in this category.

2. *Transport Efficiency Tactics*. These tactics seek to use the truck fleet and transport infrastructure more efficiently. Examples of efficiency tactics include the use of City Distribution Centres and larger trucks.

3. *Mode Shift Tactics*. These tactics are specifically designed to stimulate the shift of freight off the roads and onto other modes of transport. They include various ways to make rail and waterway transport of freight more attractive by making these modes faster and more reliable (for example, using a regional dispatching system at ports, and having the railroads give priority to freight transport over passenger transport). They also include ways to improve transshipment capabilities (for example, building multimodal centres), and ways to provide regulatory or price incentives for modal shift (for example, introducing tolls on roads and making rail transport free). Besides shifting freight to rail and waterways, we considered possibilities for transport of freight by alternative modes, such as moving pavements for containers, short sea transport, and pipelines.

3.2 PACE-FORWARD

To assess the impacts of the tactics, a microcomputer-based spreadsheet model called Policy-Analytic Computational Environment for FORWARD (PACE-FORWARD) was developed. The user can directly interact with the program to gain insights into the effects of the various tactics on emissions, noise, safety, congestion, costs, and the national economy. PACE-FORWARD is integrative in that it uses data, factors, and relationships from existing Dutch transport models and databases. PACE-FORWARD is designed for use by policy analysts knowledgeable about the freight transport policy area; its use requires little training for an analyst already familiar with spreadsheets. It was used to assess the impacts of the various tactics and strategies on a range of performance measures, as depicted in Figure 7.1.

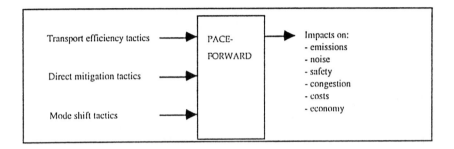

Figure 7.1   Use of PACE-FORWARD in the FORWARD project

Performance measures ->	CO2 Emissions	Congestion	Noise	Injuries	Employment	Net societal cost	...
Tactics							
Build City Distribution Centers	...	...	...	...	...	...	...
Use cleaner diesel engines	...	...	...	...	...	...	...
......	...	...	...	...	...	...	...
......	...	...	...	...	...	...	...

Figure 7.2   Sample scorecard

We had planned to use existing analytic tools to estimate the effects. A substudy was performed to identify the characteristics of existing Dutch freight transport system models and some other models for which documentation was readily available. This substudy concluded that no existing model or combination of models could satisfy our requirements. As a result, PACE-FORWARD was developed. It uses equations and data from existing models, as well as new equations and data that were developed as part of the FORWARD project to fill the remaining gaps (Carrillo 1995).

The model allows the user to choose one of the modelled tactics and one of the scenarios: the current situation (1990) or one of the future scenarios of the CPB (for the year 2015). It then calculates the impacts related to air pollution, noise pollution, safety, congestion, costs, and the national economy. The user chooses the impacts to be displayed and how they are displayed. The results can be given as absolute numbers or in percentage changes from a base case. Alternative formats for displaying the results include maps, graphs, and scorecards. A scorecard is a matrix in which the columns represent impacts and the rows represent tactics. A row shows all the impacts of one tactic, while a column shows the impacts of all the tactics on one specific performance measure (see Figure 7.2).

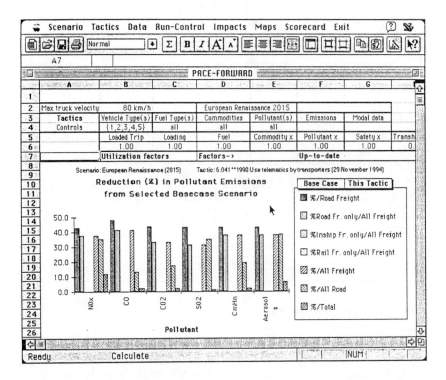

Figure 7.3 User interface and sample display from PACE-FORWARD

To run the model for a single tactic takes about five minutes on a Macintosh Powerbook 180c. So, PACE-FORWARD provides the user with a way to quickly estimate the performance of tactics as part of the process of formulating a policy. The way policy makers use this information, and the final choice and selection of preferred policy options is, of course, up to them.

The reductions for each type of pollutant are shown in several ways:

■ percentage reduction in emissions caused by road freight transportation

▣ percentage reduction in emissions caused by road freight transportation relative to the emissions caused by all freight transportation

▤ percentage reduction in emissions caused by waterway freight transportation relative to the emissions caused by all freight transportation

☐ percentage reduction in emissions caused by rail freight transportation relative to the emissions caused by all freight transportation

▨ percentage reduction in emissions caused by all freight transportation

▧ percentage reduction in emissions caused by all road traffic (passengers and freight)

▨ percentage reduction in emissions caused by all human activities

Figure 7.3 shows the user interface of PACE-FORWARD and gives an example of a graphical display of the results generated by the model. The tactic and scenario being examined are displayed on the screen, as is the date of the run. The vehicle types, fuel, and commodity types related to this tactic are indicated as well. Input data defining the tactic in terms of its effect on the number of loaded trips, truck utilization factor ('Loading'), fuel use, emissions, and so on, are given in terms of indices. The user can make changes to these factors to modify the tactic or implement it selectively. In this way, the policy maker may choose, for example, to use speed limiters only on heavy trucks.

Figure 7.3 displays upper bounds on the effects from implementing a tactic in which road transporters use telematics to identify loads to be transported and, therefore, increase their truck utilization factors. The figure shows upper bounds on the estimated reduction of the six types of emissions, compared to the 2015 European Renaissance situation without the tactic implemented.

We made optimistic assumptions about the effects of tactics, so that we would not screen out any tactic that might be promising. In this case, we assumed that trucks would increase their average utilization factors to those identified as upper bounds in the Dutch Trendbreuk study (Werkgroep '2duizend 1993). Increased utilization factors lead to fewer truck trips, and, thus, fewer trucks on the road. As a result, the model estimates that emissions from road freight would be reduced significantly (see Figure 7.3), injuries and fatalities from truck accidents would be reduced to below their 1990 levels, and noise and congestion would also be reduced. The tactic would result in some extra delay costs for the goods being transported, because they will have to wait somewhat longer to be picked up. There will also be small investment costs. But these costs will be more than offset by the cost savings from having fewer truck trips (and, therefore, fewer vehicle kilometres driven).

3.3 Strategy Design

A strategy is a combination of promising tactics designed to achieve a certain goal, where promising means that the tactic is beneficial relative to the costs. In trying to use the output from PACE-FORWARD to develop strategies, we had to deal with a number of complexities:

- For each tactic the values of a large number of impact measures were estimated, and the large number of tactics provide many different ways of achieving certain goals.
- Since there were goals associated with each of the negative impacts (on the environment, congestion, noise, and safety) as well as with the impacts on the economy, strategy design had to consider the relative importance of the various impacts and the tradeoffs among them. Depending on the importance weighting, the best tactics to include in a strategy would differ. Indeed, it was necessary to develop different promising strategies to account for different sets of weights on the impact measures.
- A third complexity related to the constraints placed on the tactics to be combined into a strategy. For example, which tactics focus on mode shift? Which tactics should be pursued by the Netherlands and which are better implemented within the European Union? Which tactics can achieve goals in the near term and which are longer term improvements?
- It is not possible to simply add tactics together. Related tactics interact in non-linear ways. And some tactics cannot be implemented together. An extreme example of this interference is that there is a tactic to require freight movement at night to reduce congestion and one to disallow freight movement at night to reduce noise. Other tactics might be alternatives for other tactics; that is, one tactic might do the same thing as another (but in a less cost-effective way). So, they would not be implemented together.

We developed an approach to deal with these complexities. The approach is based on a Cost-Effectiveness Model (CEM), which uses the output of PACE-FORWARD (scorecards, which contain the estimated impacts for each of the tactics) for a particular scenario and a given set of weights on the impacts to rank the tactics based on their cost-effectiveness. The outcome of this approach is not only a set of strategies, but also strategy design tables that can be used by policy makers to design their own strategies based on their own goals, constraints, and specific wishes.

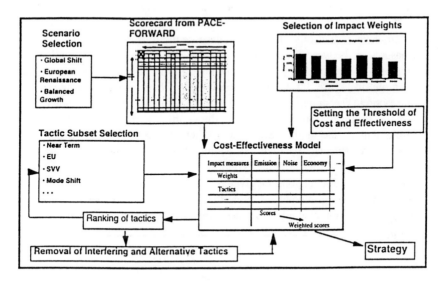

Figure 7.4 Use of models in the FORWARD project

We used the CEM to develop a broad range of strategies. We thought that the ranked components of the strategies would depend on the scenario for 2015 because of different demands on the freight system. But, with only a few minor exceptions, the ranked lists did not change as a function of the scenario. The ranked lists of tactics produced by the CEM does depend on the importance weighting of the tactic impacts, on the subset of tactics considered, and on various nonlinearities in the combination of tactics (some tactics interfere with other tactics and many do not provide strictly additive effects). Thus, there is a strategy for focusing on NO_x emissions, a strategy to focus on mode shift, and so on. Figure 7.4 shows how PACE-FORWARD and the CEM were used to identify promising tactics and strategies. In all, we designed 12 illustrative strategies. To determine the effects of a strategy, we used the CEM to produce graphs of the cumulative effectiveness and the cumulative costs of a given set of tactics that are part of a strategy.

One of the illustrative strategies is a 'uniform strategy', which focuses equally on all impact measures without making a selection among them. Figure 7.5 presents results from running the CEM for this strategy. The horizontal axis shows the number of promising tactics from the ranked list (after removal of the alternative and interfering tactics) that are included in the strategy. In the example shown here, the strategy includes 17 separate tactics. The – □ – graph is an upper bound estimate of the cumulative percentage reductions in truck-related emissions, noise, safety, and congestion. The —■— graph shows the estimate of the impact measure with the lowest cumulative reductions. The cumulative reductions of the other impact measures are between the minimum and the maximum graph. The reduction increases as the number of tactics included in the strategy is increased. For example, in Figure 7.5, the reduction increases from about 45 percent with one tactic in the strategy to about 65 percent with all 17 tactics included. The —•— graph is an estimate of the cumulative annualized cost of implementing the tactics. Some tactics actually save money, so the cost curve starts out negative. The remaining graph, the —◊— graph, gives an indication for the effects on the economy; it shows the percentage increase in value added. All reductions are given relative to a ER base case in which none of the tactics is implemented. Note that there is a net cost savings for the strategy. Also note that all impact measures are improved dramatically.

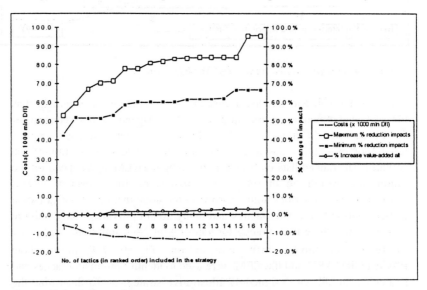

Figure 7.5 Costs and impacts of a uniform strategy

4. CONCLUSIONS AND OBSERVATIONS

It is possible to reach some general conclusions about an overall approach to mitigating the negative effects of road freight transport based on the strategies generated by the FORWARD project. And these conclusions, which are scenario independent, are unlikely to change as the result of more detailed analysis or consideration of different tactics. We were able to identify common tactics among all the various strategies. We were able to determine which strategies or types of tactics are relatively robust among a range of importance weights on impacts. And, we were able to identify which types of strategies and tactics offer the greatest improvement in benefits at the lowest possible cost. The major conclusions from the FORWARD project are:

The most important tactics focus on transport efficiency improvements.
Transport efficiency tactics are disproportionately represented at the top of all lists of cost-effective tactics for a very broad range of weights. They improve many impact measures (for example, reducing the amount of truck movements affects all impact measures), and by their nature they tend to save money because of their efficiencies. In other words, if you can reduce the number of kilometres travelled, many negative impacts are reduced, and you also save money (because of a reduction in the investment and operational costs, including labour cost). In fact, four of the first seven tactics in the list of cost-effective tactics in a strategy that takes into account the full range of impacts are transport efficiency tactics, and all lead to a reduction in the overall cost of freight transport. Two of the best tactics in this set are *use telematics in road transport* and *equalize rules of transport on own and professional account.*

There are other reasons why transport efficiency tactics tend to be important in most strategies. Most of the top-ranked transport efficiency tactics can make dramatic improvements. And, since many of the transport efficiency tactics do not rely on future technological developments, they can be implemented in the near term. (Of course, the political feasibility of certain regulatory changes may imply a longer term change for some.) Finally, these tactics call for the involvement of many stakeholders, so the burden of implementation does not fall on a single agency or group.

Certain direct mitigation tactics are cost-effective and are complementary to transport efficiency improvements.
Certain direct mitigation tactics are cost-effective and either produce net reductions in the overall cost of freight transport, or only small increases. Two examples of such tactics are *use quieter tyres* and *use electric vans in urban areas.* These tactics, although sometimes showing dramatic improvements for the measures on which they focus, generally rank lower in cost-effectiveness than the transport efficiency tactics because they focus on only a few impacts and they have net positive costs. The importance of these tactics is that they can 'fill in' for gaps in improvement by focusing on particular impacts not provided by the transport efficiency tactics.

However, because these tactics focus on particular negative impacts, whether they are promising or not depends to a great extent on the importance weighting of the impact measures. For example, someone who cares only about NO_x emissions would favour the cleaner engine tactic, while someone who cares only about CO_2 emissions would not. Furthermore, although direct mitigation tactics tend to cost more than the transport efficiency tactics, the costs might be manageable by targeting the largest contributors to an impact. For example, they could be selectively implemented to target urban vehicles, international (or national) trucking, and even selectively implemented in certain regions for haulers of specific commodities. In addition, most of these tactics would be implemented in the mid to long term, since they generally require some technical change. This would make the cost impacts easier to bear, but would also mean that their benefits would only be realized gradually.

Mode shift tactics are either not cost-effective or make little difference.
Our analysis has shown that mode shift tactics tend to be inferior in both absolute effectiveness and cost-effectiveness to the combination of transport efficiency and direct mitigation tactics. A reason for this is that waterway and rail improvements are relatively expensive, and they do not realize very much mode shift for a number of reasons. First, there is only limited opportunity for mode shift. The average distance travelled by national freight is less than 50 kilometres, so it is unlikely that rail or waterway transport, which usually also require pre- and after-road transport and transshipment, will be attractive to forwarders for national goods movement. Second, the quantity of longer haul, international trucking is much smaller than the quantity of national trucking, whether measured in terms of tonnes or tonne-kilometres. Thus, the quantity of road haulage that can be affected by mode shift tactics tends to be smaller than that affected by other tactics.

Mode shift tactics that attempt to focus on the international movement of goods between specific regions affect an even smaller quantity of transported goods, because these goods are already shipped mostly by water.

We note that we have not considered the port competition effects of the various tactics. The consideration of port competition is not likely to change the set of promising tactics, but some tactics having to do with port improvements or improvements in the movement of freight from the port would probably become higher ranked.

A qualification, however, is that improving service characteristics of rail and waterway transport could make mode shift more attractive to freight forwarders and thus be more promising.

The economic effects of most of the promising tactics are small.
The macroeconomic module of PACE-FORWARD shows the effects of the freight tactics on national value added and employment in the production and transport sector. Almost all of the promising tactics show only small macroeconomic effects because they involve low costs or even cost savings. There is likely to be little effect on market share from implementation of any of these promising tactics, since they either save money or would have to be implemented internationally.

5. A GLANCE AT THE FUTURE

5.1 Broadening the Context

The FORWARD project made major strides toward enabling a broad range of freight policy options for the Netherlands to be compared on quantitative and consistent grounds. A set of policy analysis tools has been designed and built to assess the impacts of various policy options and to identify the most promising ones. The architecture of the models and tools developed, as well as the general approach can be applied in other (broader) contexts.

For example, the context could be broadened to include passenger transport. The FORWARD study focused on freight, but there are substantial interfaces with passenger transport in the use of infrastructure and in terms of impacts. It would be desirable to study these interfaces by filling the architecture of PACE-FORWARD with expanded modules and databases that include passenger transport and developing an integrated set of tactics for freight and passenger transport.

The context could also be broadened to a European level. We focused on freight transport in the Netherlands and did not consider the international movement of freight beyond the Dutch borders, except in terms of destination and distance travelled. Many tactics cannot be implemented by the Dutch alone, so a broader EU-based study of freight (and passenger) transport would be useful. A policy analysis model could be built to evaluate an EU transport policy by modifying PACE-FORWARD to include data and models on European networks, European demand and supply data, European safety data, etc.

5.2 Use of the Project's Results by the Ministry

The policy analysis approach used in the project is clear and straightforward. That made it easy for the project members to communicate the results to the policy makers in the Ministry. It also made it easy for the policy makers to communicate the results to stakeholders outside the Ministry.

The results of the FORWARD study have already been used in a number of ways. First, they are used at the early stages of freight transport policy making, since the results provide a good overview of the effects of different (combinations of) tactics. For instance, the Dutch government is currently trying to reach agreement with freight transport organizations concerning ways to mitigate the effects of (freight) transport on the environment. The conclusions of the FORWARD study are being directly used in this project. The results of the study also play a role in helping the Netherlands look at international (EU) issues.

Secondly, the results of the FORWARD study are used to give direction to the Ministry's research efforts in the field of freight transport. They are being used to suggest tactics that should be examined more carefully (ways to implement promising tactics, for example), and tactics that should not be investigated further.

PACE-FORWARD itself has been found to be a useful (additional) product of the study. The model is easy to use and runs very fast, so it is possible to take a quick look at tactics and strategies that were not examined in the project, and assess their contribution to policy goals. For example, the model has been used by the Ministry during its recent discussions with Parliament about a new (freight) railway line from Rotterdam to Germany (the Betuweline).

The model has been turned over to the Ministry, which has decided to support its maintenance. This will guarantee that it will be kept updated, and will be available when needed. The Ministry is also looking into the possibility of applying the same general methodology to other segments of the transport system, such as passenger transport and maritime transport.

REFERENCES

Blok, P.M.J. et al. (1992), *Verkennend onderzoek: verbeteringen efficiency in het goederenvervoer: trends & maatregelen*, Rotterdam: Nederlands Economisch Instituut, YD/T1840, 27 July.

Bolten, J.G. et al. (1996), *FORWARD – Freight Options for Road, Water, and Rail for the Dutch: Tactic Definitions*, DRU–138–EAC/VW, RAND, Santa Monica, USA.

Carrillo, M.J. et al. (1996), *PACE-FORWARD: Policy Analytic and Computational Environment for Dutch Freight Transport*, MR–732–EAC/VW, RAND, Santa Monica, USA.

Central Planning Bureau (CPB) (1992), *The Netherlands in Triplo, A Scenario Study of the Dutch Economy 1990–2015*, Summary, The Hague.

Hillestad, R.J. et al. (1996), *FORWARD – Freight Options for Road, Water, and Rail for the Dutch: Final Report,* MR–736–EAC/VW, RAND, Santa Monica, USA.

Miser, H.J. and E.S. Quade (eds) (1985), *Handbook of Systems Analysis: Overview of Uses, Procedures, Applications, and Practice,* United Kingdom: John Wiley & Sons.

NEA (1991a), *TEM II, Deelrapport 6: Constructie database,* Rijswijk, August.

NEA (1991b), *TEM II, Hoofdrapport,* Rijswijk, August.

NEA (1992a), *Hoofdlijnen TEM,* Rijswijk, July.

NEA (1992b), *TEM II, Het goederenvervoer in drievoud tot 2015,* Rijswijk, November.

Second Chamber of the States-General (1990), *Second Transport Structure Plan (SVV) Part D: Government Decision,* The Hague: SDU Uitgeverij.

Werkgroep '2duizend (1993), *Goed op Weg: Naar een Trendbreuk in Het Goederenvervoer,* Amersfoort, November.

8. Risk Behaviour, Network Adoption and Use under Uncertainty and Externalities

Heli Koski

---

1. INTRODUCTION

Access to new sources of information by means of advanced communications technology (ACT) can profit both individual firms and the regions in which they are located. The use of advanced communications networks may also facilitate intrafirm coordination and interfirm cooperation both within countries and across national borders. Information and communications technology will play a key role in the creation and success of the Single European Market as well as in intensifying global competition of firms. This means that the competitiveness of European countries in the international marketplace is closely related to their ability to utilize new communications technology and advanced communications networks.

Despite the fact that non-negligible benefits are expected to be obtained from the utilization of ACT, the use of advanced communications systems – in particular as a strategic means to cope with a competitive environment – is still in the early phases. This chapter considers two potentially decisive factors which may hinder the diffusion process of advanced communications systems. We propose that an inertia in the spread of new network technologies refers to two interrelated characteristics of the ACT market: (i) the presence of network externalities and (ii) the presence of several sources of uncertainty.

The concept of network externality means that the value of a network technology or network use varies with the number of users and that this interdependence of the users' utilities or profits is not fully or partially intermediated by the market mechanism. Network externalities stress the importance of compatibility of technologies. Rapid continuous technological progress in network industries gives rise to uncertain timing and prominence of future improvements in network technologies and also to uncertainty in the compatibility of future technologies with existing ones. In addition, several other sources of uncertainty may complicate the ACT adoption decision of a potential network user, for instance, uncertain productivity effects of a new technology and uncertain quality and price of information in a network. Consequently, potential network subscribers cannot know for sure what the network size will be in the future if they now decide to join a network. We suppose that – as communications technologies involve substantial interdependence among the utilities or profits of the network users – uncertainty regarding the network size may play a decisive role in ACT adoption decisions along with economic factors.

In this chapter we present a neoclassical model regarding a firm's decision making in the network. We consider the firm's adoption and use decision of a network or a new network technology when information or a network is used as an input in the firm's production. We extend traditional microeconomic analysis of the actors' decision making under uncertainty (see, for example, Gravelle and Rees 1992 and Laffont 1989) to the case of network externalities. Our aim is, on the one hand, to present a formal model which shows how the combination of uncertainty and network externalities affect a firm's decision making, and, on the other hand, to examine how a decision maker's attitudes towards risk affect his behaviour in the networks.

Section 2 discusses potential forms of network externalities and a distinction between network externalities and network effects. Network use and information transmitted via a network are assumed to appear as inputs in the production function of a firm. Furthermore, we assume that the existence of network externality may affect both the production function and the costs of a firm, that is, there exist both technical and pecuniary network externalities. In Section 3 we show how network externalities influence a firm's cost minimization problem and the level of network use it chooses under certainty.

Section 4 considers the network adoption decision of economic actors under the presence of uncertainty and positive network externality. In addition to the indigenous quality and price of a network technology, the expected number of network users also influences the adoption decision regarding a new network technology. This highlights the significance of private critical mass (PCM) in the adoption behaviour of potential network users. Under uncertainty, private critical mass is the smallest expected user size at which a potential user is indifferent to joining the network. We point out the importance of the adopter's risk attitudes in the determination of the PCM point. Moreover, we show how changes in expectations of the number of network users and an increase in the risk related to network use affect the risk averse actor's adoption behaviour.

Section 5 examines the short run cost minimization problem of a firm under the presence of pecuniary and technical externalities and uncertainty. The traditional neoclassical microeconomic framework is applied to the examination of the effects of network externalities and uncertainty on the firm's behaviour in the networks. We point out that the presence of technical and pecuniary network externalities necessarily implies both technological uncertainty and market uncertainty, when either of these two sources of uncertainty exist initially. Then, we explore how economic actors with different risk attitudes choose their (optimal) level of network use. Finally, we examine how a change in the number of network users affects the level of network use chosen by a network subscriber. Section 6 highlights the main conclusions of the formal analysis and discusses some implications of these results for practical network policies.

2. NETWORK EXTERNALITIES AND NETWORK EFFECTS

A communications network is, unlike most other input factors, a resource whose value seems likely to increase with the number of other firms (especially business related) joining the network. The presence of network externality, that is, interdependence among the utilities or profits of the network users, implies that the use value, and consequently the adoption decision regarding a new technology, critically depend on the size of a network. There is considerable theoretical research on network externalities (see, for example, Antonelli 1992; Capello 1994; Capello and Nijkamp 1993; Farrell and Saloner 1985; Katz and Shapiro 1986; Oren and Smith 1981; Rohlfs 1974). The presence of network externality implies that a certain critical mass of users has to be obtained before a potential subscriber is willing to join a network. This means that a profitable network size is never reached – even if that size were an economically feasible welfare maximizing network size from a society point of view – unless the critical network size is obtained by other means. Previous literature has stressed the role of pricing policy in the early stages of networks as a means to correct market failure and reach a critical mass point (see, for example, Heal 1990).

Recent economic literature has increasingly paid attention to network externalities and their effects on network markets (see, for example, Economides 1994; Church and Gandal 1993). Discussions have also raised some doubts concerning the presence of market failures on network markets. Liebowitz and Margolis (1994) criticize the broad use of the expression 'network externality' due to the deficient empirical evidence on the presence of this market failure on the network market.

They distinguish *a network effect* from network externality, and determine the former to be *the circumstance under which the net value of an action is affected by the number of agents taking equivalent actions* and the latter to consist of – besides a network effect – a market failure. They claim that most of the examples presented in earlier literature have been closer to the illustrations of network effects than of network externalities. However, the literature does not provide any contradictory evidence; there are no empirical studies concluding that the network market exhibits only network effects which then lead to an optimal size or to a market clearing solution.

The controversial use of the definitions of network externality and network effect is not, however, just a question of the use of exact terminology. It is very important in particular for the success of practical network policies to be able to distinguish network externalities from network effects. Empirical evidence on the presence and order of magnitude of network externalities – as well as information on which markets and in what forms network externalities exist – is of great importance in determining whether, where and what sort of market intervention is needed to correct potential market failures.

Interdependence among network users may originate either from direct communication connections between the network subscribers or indirectly, from the influence of the demand for network technologies for the amount of services supplied in the network. In the former case, an increase in the number of network users does not necessarily profit a user, since the contributiuon of an additional user to the value of network use depends on *who* a new network user is. In the latter case, the network users care merely for *the network size* regardless of the character of a new network subscriber; a higher number of network users is associated with an increase in the number of services available in a network. Interdependence among network users via direct network connections refers to *direct network externalities*, whereas the effect of additional users on the supply of network services represents *indirect network externalities*.

In the entrepreneurial context, the presence of network externality due to direct user interdependence is related to a firm's business relationships creating a demand for interfirm communication. Direct business related communication needs may emerge, for instance, among separate business units of a multinational firm, among the rivals which cooperate in R&D or in the buyer-supplier relationship. An advanced communications technology can offer a more efficient means to transfer data and information between business units. Also, it is possible that a firm profits from some firms, for example, rivals with which a firm is not willing to cooperate, staying outside the network. On the other hand, fear that rivals may achieve a competitive advantage by using the network may push a firm to join the network.

Direct positive (negative) network externality means that a user's benefits from access to a network increase (decrease) with the number of possible connections or with additional users joining the network. Whether an additional user profits the existing users or reduces their gains may also depend on the network size and on its capacity to transmit information and data flows. Positive externality is likely to be dominant as long as the capacity of a network is sufficient to handle information loads without delays. Negative network externality arises when the number of network users exceeds the capacity of a network. Consequently, the network becomes congested and data and information transfers may be delayed.

Indirect externalities arise from the complementarity of technologies: when the number of users of a technology increases, the market for complementary goods or services responds to the demand growth by increasing the variety of complements supplied. This implies that when the networks of technologies are close incompatible substitutes, a user prefers a larger network even if any direct externalities are not related to the networks. A great number of products fall under this category of network technologies exhibiting indirect network externalities. Examples include video recording systems (recorders and cassettes), personal computers (hardware and software) and the networks of automatic teller machines (terminal equipment and ATM cards).

Besides the division of network externalities into direct and indirect, the literature also presents (see, for example, Antonelli 1992; Capello 1994) the classification of direct network externalities by their nature. Direct network externalities are divided into four main categories, viz. *consumption externality, adoption externality, technical externality* and *pecuniary externality*. Consumption externality describes direct interdependence among consumers. It means that network adoption and use decisions of other economic actors enter into the utility function of consumers. Adoption externality relates to the diffusion process of network technologies and refers to the intertemporal interdependence among the user generations. Technical externality and pecuniary externality – also called *production network externalities*[1] – emerge as a result of interfirm dependence in network use.

This chapter considers network adoption and use decisions of firms which use a communications network and information as inputs in their production process. A crucial difference with most other input factors is that the value of network use depends not only on the utilization of this resource in a producing firm, but also on other firms' investment decisions and their resource utilization. We will concentrate on the effects of production network externalities on a firm's network adoption and use decisions. Therefore, we will briefly discuss the potential forms of the appearance of production network externalities on the network market before going into the theoretical exploration.

Pecuniary network externality means that the profit of a producer depends on the actions of other producers through input costs. Positive (negative) pecuniary externality indicates that a firm's profit increases (decreases) with the new firm joining a network. Positive pecuniary externality may appear, for instance, as a result of a decline in transaction and communications costs, when a larger share of the firm's external communications is handled via the advanced communications channels. The effect of positive pecuniary externality on a firm's profit through a decline in the input costs is also dependent on the reactions of a firm's competitive environment and on the degree of competition in the product market. Monopolists certainly benefit from the cost reduction, but in a competitive market – due to the rivals' identical adoption behaviour – a firm's adoption of a new technology may possibly result in no change in the firm's profit. In reality, it seems quite credible that even if the rivals would make identical network adoption decisions, the behaviour of other actors may still have non-zero effects on a firm's profit. The number of communication partners as well as the share of communications partners joining the network may differ among the firms resulting in divergencies in the order of magnitude of pecuniary externality.

Technological externality affects the productivity of input factors. For instance, a higher share of a firm's business partners using compatible advanced communications technology, may profit the firm by increasing its labour productivity. This increment in efficiency can, for example, refer to a better quality of information achievable via the use of the advanced communications network and/or to the time savings which the employees may be able to obtain by the more efficient means of communication.

Advanced communications technology may involve both pecuniary externality and technical externality. It is plausible that these external effects are positive, that is, they decrease a firm's input costs and/or enhance efficiency in production. It is possible that rough competition on the product market drives a change in a firm's profit to zero, but then consumers will profit from the firms' use of new network technologies. This suggests that the overall welfare effects of the use of ACT are likely to be positive and the diffusion and exploitation of advanced communications technology should thus be encouraged by society. In the next sections we explore how network externalities and uncertainty affect a firm's network adoption decision.

3. NETWORK EXTERNALITIES AND NETWORK USE UNDER CERTAINTY

Consider first how network use and network externality appear in a network user's short run cost minimization problem under certainty. Assume that a firm has already joined a network. We denote the production function of a firm by $y = f(x(N))$, where y = output, $x = (K, K^I, L, I, n)$ is a vector of inputs, K = non-information capital, K^I = information capital, L = labour, I = information, n = network use and N = network size or the number of a firm's business partners in the network. We assume here that all inputs are non-decreasing in N, i.e. $\partial x/\partial N \geq 0$, in the short run.

Now, positive (negative) technical network externality implies an increase (decrease) in the marginal productivity of a given input vector, x, when the network size increases (decreases), i.e. $\partial f_x/\partial N > 0$ ($\partial f_x/\partial N < 0$), where $f_x = \partial f/\partial x$. Here, $\partial f_x/\partial N > 0$ ($\partial f_x/\partial N < 0$) means that adding up the partial derivates of the marginal products of input factors with respect to N results in a positive (negative) outcome. Consequently, in the case of positive (negative) technical network externality, at least one of the partial derivates has to be strictly positive (negative).

The cost equation of a firm is $c = r_k K + r_{ik} K^I + wL + p_I(n)I + p_n n$, where r_k, r_{ik} = cost of non-information and information capital, w = wages, $p_I(n)$ = cost of information and p_n = unit price of network use. Let us assume that the firms can transmit and receive information both through the ACT network and by means of traditional communication channels (for example, the telephone). Moreover, we assume that an increase in N implies that information needed for production is obtained at a lower unit (or average) cost – i.e. $\partial p_I(n)/\partial N < 0$ – in the case of positive pecuniary externality. The presence of negative pecuniary externality, instead, implies an increase in the unit cost of information. We assume that the unit cost of information is twice differentiable and that the second derivate is decreasing in N, i.e. $\partial^2 p_I(n)/\partial N^2 > 0$.

We apply the neoclassical economic framework and assume that firms buy all input factors besides information from competitive markets and sell their own production also on the competitive market. Then, both the output prices (p) and the input prices (r, w and p_n) are exogenous to a single firm. Cost of information depends on the level of network use chosen by a firm and on the number of the firm's business partners in the advanced communications network. A profit maximizing firm chooses the level of its network use such that the marginal value of network use equals the cost of network use. Mathematically this can be formulated as follows:

$$p\frac{\partial f}{\partial n} = \frac{\partial p_I}{\partial n} I + p_n \tag{8.1}$$

Consider next how positive and negative network externalities affect a firm's network use under certainty. Partial differentiation of the first order condition with respect to N gives:

$$\frac{\partial(\partial\pi/\partial n)}{\partial N} = p\frac{\partial(\partial f/\partial n)}{\partial N} - \frac{\partial(\partial p_I/\partial n)}{\partial N} I - \frac{\partial p_I}{\partial n}\frac{\partial I}{\partial N} \tag{8.2}$$

where π denotes a firm's profit. In the case of positive (negative) technical network externality, an increase in N implies an increase (decrease) in the marginal product of network use. This means that the first term on the RHS of Equation (8.2) is positive (negative). Moreover, a positive (negative) pecuniary externality indicates that an increase in N leads to a further decrease (increase) in $\partial p_I / \partial n$. Then, the second term on the RHS is negative (positive). When a network exhibits positive externality, the price of information is non-increasing in n and the amount of information a firm used is non-decreasing in N and thus, the last term of Equation (8.2) is positive or zero. Consequently, the RHS of Equation (8.2) is positive (negative) in the case of positive (negative) technical and pecuniary externalities. In other words, the higher the number of a firm's business partners in the ACT network, the higher the level of network use chosen by an individual firm in the network.

Network externalities differ from the usual production externalities (for example pollution) considered in the literature in the sense that a firm usually has more freedom of choice regarding the exploitation of positive network externalities than suffering negative production externalities. For instance, using a common textbook example, a laundry cannot avoid smoke from a steel mill, whereas any firm is able to choose whether it joins a communications network. A firm cannot, however, choose the size of a network which would maximize its own profits. Also, the use of some advanced communications network may be a precondition for staying in the market, when a firm's business partners and rivals use a new technology for their transactions.

This section has highlighted the importance of the number of network users in a firm's behaviour in the networks. Typically, new network technologies involve several sources of uncertainties. Then, especially uncertainty related to the future network size can play a prominent role in a firm's ACT adoption decision. The next section points out that besides the current network size, also the expected number of network users can have clear implications for the adopter's behaviour.

4. NETWORK ADOPTION DECISION UNDER UNCERTAINTY

A new communications technology may embrace various uncertain properties. For instance, the quality and price of information in a network as well as the effects of a new technology on labour productivity in a firm can be uncertain. In addition, rapid continuous technological progress – which is characteristic to the network industries – gives rise to uncertain timing and prominence of future improvements in network technologies. Also the degree of compatibility of future network technologies with existing ones can be uncertain. It seems quite credible that in – and due to – this multitude of uncertainties, a potential network user cannot know for sure what the number of network users of a current technology in the future will be.

Let us keep the assumption of competitive firms in the production market. To simplify the analysis, we assume that a firm has a single owner who maximizes his expected utility over the firm's profits and makes the network adoption decision. The other firms' behaviour in a network may affect the utility of a network user in at least two ways. First, the business partners of a network user may create direct positive network externality. Second, the total number of network users – irrespective of their essence – can be the source of indirect network externality. For simplicity, we do not distinguish these two user groups, but use a single definition of network externality which incorporates both direct and indirect external effects.

A firm's profit can be expressed as a function of prices and the number of network users. We define the maximum profit of a firm which has adopted a network technology by π^1 (p, A, N(T)), and correspondingly, the maximum profit of a non-user by $\pi^0(p)$. A price vector of inputs and output is here denoted by p. A describes a lump sum access fee charged to a network subscriber or the price of a new technology and N is the number of network users. We suppose that the demand for a new network technology or the network size is determined by the indigenous quality of a network technology, T.[2] We assume that the higher technological expectations relate to a larger network size, i.e. $\partial N/\partial T > 0$. In addition, we assume that the utility function of a firm $U[\pi^1(\cdot)]$, is a continuous and (twice) differentiable function of profits such that $U''<0$ ($U''=0$), when a firm is risk averse (risk neutral).

We assume that the market for communications technology exhibits positive network externalities. This means that a firm's profits increase with the number of network users – i.e. $\partial \pi^1/\partial N > 0$ – when the firm is the user of a communications technology. This presumption embodies further an implicit assumption regarding the capacity of a network: it is assumed that the network incorporates sufficient technological capabilities for transmitting information without delays or for excluding the possibility of crowding. Moreover, we assume that the variation in a network size does not cause any changes in the utility of a non-user $(\partial U(\pi^0)/\partial N) = 0$.

We assume that a decision maker knows his utility if he does not join a network, that is, $E[U(\pi^0)] = U(\pi^0)$. The market for network technologies is assumed to supply only one type of communications technology (current standard). Then, a firm joins a network or adopts a new technology if its expected utility of network use exceeds the utility of non-adoption. We assume that uncertainty in the network market may involve both the current indigenous quality of a new technology and the future evolution of network technology.[3] This indicates that the development of a network (or the future market share of a new technology) depends critically on the current value of a technology and also on the expected future value of this technology.

Technological uncertainty is closely related to network externalities, since the quality of a new communications technology largely determines the demand for it and non-neglible benefits are created either directly or indirectly by the other network users. Next, we will explore how this uncertainty appears in a firm's adoption decison regarding a new network technology and how it affects the determinaton of the private critical mass point. The expected utility related to network use can be approximated by taking a second order Taylor series expansion around point $(p, A, N, (\overline{T}))$:

$$E[U(\pi^1(p, A, N))] = \overline{U}^1 + \overline{U}_N^1 E(N(T) - N(\overline{T})) + \frac{1}{2}\overline{U}_{NN}^1 \sigma_N^2 \qquad (8.3)$$

where $N(T)$ denotes a network size at the expected value or quality of a network technology,

$$\overline{U}^1 = U[\pi^1(p, A, N(\overline{T}))], \overline{U}_N^1 = (\partial U(\pi^1)/\partial N) \cdot (\partial N/\partial T), \overline{U}_{NN}^1$$
$$= \partial[(\partial U(\pi^1)/\partial N) \cdot (\partial N/\partial T)]/\partial T \text{ and } \sigma_N^2 = E(N(T) - N(\overline{T}))^2$$

Since $E(N(T) - N(T)) = 0$, the second term on the RHS of Equation (8.3) vanishes. Consequently, a decision maker is indifferent to joining a network at price A if

$$U[\pi^0(p)] = E[U(\pi^1(p, A, N(\overline{T}))] = \overline{U}^1 + \frac{1}{2}\overline{U}_{NN}^1 \sigma_N^2 \qquad (8.4)$$

Equation (8.4) corresponds with Heal's (1990) definition of private critical mass under certainty. Because of an uncertain value of a new network technology, the network size is also unknown. Private critical mass, PCM, under certainty is then the smallest *expected* number of users such that the user of a technology and a non-user are equally well off.

Now, we explore how a decision maker's attitudes towards risk affects his adoption decision of a network technology, when the market for the new technology exhibits uncertainty. We consider two divergent attitudes towards risk, viz. risk neutrality and risk aversion. The risk neutrality of an economic actor implies that $\bar{U}^1_{NN}=0$. In this case, Equation (8.4) reduces to the following condition:

$$U[\pi^0 (p)] = \bar{U}^1_N \qquad\qquad (8.5)$$

where $\bar{U}^1_n$ denotes the utility of a risk neutral actor at the expected user size. Equation (8.5) suggests that in the case of a risk neutral actor, the PCM condition is satisfied, when the utility of a network user at the expected user size is equal to his utility in the case of non-adoption. Correspondingly, if a potential adopter of a technology is risk averse, then $\bar{U}^1_{NN}< 0$. It follows that the PCM for a risk averse actor is defined as the smallest expected number of network users satisfying the following equation:

$$U[\pi^0 (p)] = \bar{U}^1_a + \frac{1}{2}\bar{U}^1_{NN} \sigma^2_N \qquad\qquad (8.6)$$

where subscript a symbolizes risk averse investment behaviour and $U\beta^1_a$ is the utility of a risk averse decision maker at the expected number of network users. In order to be able to focus on the effects of different risk attitudes on PCM, we assume that the firms are otherwise identical – also in their expectations – but differ with respect to their attitudes towards risk. It follows that $\bar{U}^1n$ equals $\bar{U}^1a$, when the decision makers have equal technological expectations and consequently, the actors also share equal expectations regarding a network size. Then, Equation (8.6) suggests that the expected utility of risk averse firm is always lower than the expected utility of a risk neutral firm at a given expected user size, since the second term on the RHS of Equation (8.6) is negative. It follows that Equations (8.5) and (8.6) are satisfied simultaneously only if

$$\bar{U}^1_a = U [\pi^1 (p, A, N(\bar{T})_a)] > U[\pi^1 (p, A, N(\bar{T})_n)].$$

This implies that the PCM conditions of risk netural and risk averse firms can hold coincidentally only when $N(\bar{T})_a > N(\bar{T})_n$. That is – $\partial N/\partial T > 0$ – a threshold (expected) network size required before a firm joins a network under uncertainty is always larger in the case of a risk averse firm compared with the PCM point of a risk neutral firm (see Figure 8.1).

Equation (8.6) stresses the importance of three factors in the determination of PCM in the case of a risk averse economic actor and, consequently, in his decision making regarding the adoption of a new network technology. The expected value of a network technology depends critically on the following components: (i) the expected number of network users or the network size at the expected quality of technology ($N(\overline{T})$), (ii) the variance of network size with technological expectations (σ^2_N) and (iii) a decision maker's order of magnitude of a risk aversion ($\overline{U}^1_{NN}$). Next, we briefly examine how changes in these parameters affect the adoption behaviour of an economic actor.

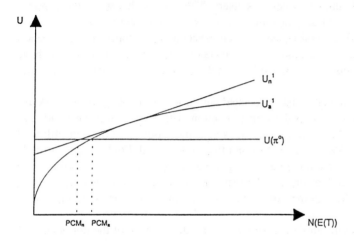

Figure 8.1   *The private critical mass (PCM) of network use under uncertainty*

Consider first how a change in the probability distribution of a network size influences the critical mass point in the case of a risk averse firm. We assume here – in order to make a clear point regarding actors' risk behaviour – that the firms are identical apart from their order of magnitude of risk aversion. In other words, the value of network use is the same for all firms, when there is no uncertainty regarding a new technology. We use Equations (8.3) and (8.4) for solving the Arrow-Pratt measure of relative risk aversion, which describes the smallest level of risk aversion at which a firm attaches equally high values to network use as to the non-adoption of a network technology. Then, a threshold level of risk aversion at the critical mass point can be written as follows:

$$p = -\frac{\overline{U}^1_{NN}}{\overline{U}^1_N} = \frac{2(\overline{U}^1 - U^0)}{\overline{U}^1_N \sigma^2_N}$$

(8.7)

Assume that technological expectations change, resulting in a shift in the mean of the distribution of a network size. An increase (decrease) in the expected number of network users implies – due to the definition of positive network externality – an increase (decrease) in $\overline{U}^1$. Then – as $\partial U^0/\partial N = 0$ by definition – the numerator of Equation (8.7) is obviously increasing with N. Since the variance term is always positive and $\overline{U}^1_N$ decreases with the network size, the threshold level of risk aversion increases (decreases) with the expected number of network users. This means that when the expected network size increases, the more risk averse firms are indifferent to joining a network. And as a consequence, when the economic actors differ with respect to their order of magnitude of risk aversion, the number of firms which are willing to adopt a new network technology increases with the expected user size.

Assume now that a risk associated with a new technology or network use increases. Concavity of the utility function with respect to the network size implies that the mean preserving spread decreases the expected utility of network use. Thus, the PCM conditions remain valid only if the threshold level of risk aversion decreases suggesting further that – as a consequence of the mean preserving spread – the firms in the critical mass point are less risk averse and the number of technology adopters on the network market decreases.

Next, we shall relax the assumption of independence of the non-adopters' utility on the network size. We assume that a non-user of a network technology is worse off when the number of network users increases, that is, $\partial U(\pi^0)/\partial N < 0$. This negative network effect may emerge, for instance, due to an increased competitiveness of a firm's rivals as they adopt a new technology. The network users may achieve competitive advantage if the utilization of a new technology increases their efficiency, decreases their production costs and/or improve their market position. For instance, a large plant which uses the communications network for the delivery of raw materials and intermediate products may favour subcontractors which use a compatible communications technology with it.

Under the presence of negative network effects and positive network externality, it is easy to show that irrespective of the decision maker's risk preferences, private critical mass is always smaller than without the existence of negative network effects. In this case, we can define the PCM point as follows: $E[U^1(p, A, N)] = E[U^0(p, N)] < U^0(p)$ at any positive network size due to the definition of negative network effects and thus, the PCM point is always located to the left of the PCM point which was defined in Equations (8.5) and (8.6). We conclude the discussion of the adoption behaviour of economic actors under uncertainty and proceed to the next section where we explore the network users' behaviour after the adoption of a new network technology.

5. NETWORK USE UNDER UNCERTAINTY

Let us assume that a firm has already made a decision regarding its network use and has adopted a new network technology. Section 3 considered how network externality affects the cost minimization problem of a network user under certainty. This section extends the analysis to conditions of uncertainty and explores the consequences of uncertainty, risk behaviour and network externalities on the chosen level of network use. We assume as above that the network market may exhibit two types of external effects, viz. pecuniary and technical network externalities. Furthermore, we assume that the market for a new network technology embodies both *market uncertainty* and *technological uncertainty*. In fact, as we show below, the presence of technical and pecuniary network externalities necessarily implies both technological uncertainty and market uncertainty, if either of these sources of uncertainty exists initially. The actors' investment behaviour on the network market is assumed to be based on either risk averse or risk neutral attitudes towards risk.

Market uncertainty means uncertainty regarding input and/or output prices, whereas technological uncertainty implies that a firm is not able to fully control its output by its own production choices, but the firm's production is also affected by some random factors beyond its control. Market uncertainty may appear, for instance, as a result of an uncertain price of information in a network. Technological uncertainty can be related to the unknown productivity effects of a new technology: a firm may be uncertain whether the network use substitutes other input factors – and if it does, to what extent – and whether (and how much) a cooperation with its business partners via the network increases its productivity. Both market and technological uncertainty result in uncertainty about the size of a network. The third reason for an uncertain number of network users can be *asymmetric information* regarding the quality of a new network technology. Even a decision maker with perfect technological information cannot know the network size for sure, when this information is unequally spread among the potential users.

We assume that a firm has to make its production decision before it knows for certain what the state of the world at the production period will be. It is worth noting that in the presence of pecuniary network externality, technological uncertainty further results in market uncertainty via an uncertain network size. As the price of information in the network depends on the network size, uncertainty about the number of network users leads to an uncertain price of information, $P_I(n(N))_s$, where s denotes the state of the world. Correspondingly, the simultaneous presence of technological network externality with market uncertainty gives rise to technological uncertainty – again via uncertainty on network size. Technological externality implies uncertain productivity of input factors and, consequently, a stochastic production function. We assume that the technological uncertainty a firm faces is multiplicative, i.e. a firm's marginal product is state dependent. Thus, the production function of a firm can be written as follows: $y_s = f_s$ $(x/N))$ e_s, where $Ee_s = 1$ and $e_s > 0$. And the expected utility of a firm's profit is: $E(U(\pi)) = E(U(p\ f_s(x(N))\ e_s - wL - r_kK - r_{ik}K^I - p_I(n(N))_sI - p_nn))$.

We consider first how market and technological uncertainty affects the level of a firm's network use. Now, the level of network use is chosen to maximize the firm's expected utility of profit as follows:

$$\frac{\partial EU(\pi)}{\partial n} = EU'(\pi)(p\ \frac{\partial f_s}{\partial n}e_s - \frac{\partial p_{I_s}}{\partial n}I - p_n) = 0 \tag{8.8}$$

We can rearrange the terms and write Equation (8.8) in the following form:

$$pE\frac{\partial f_s}{\partial n} = \frac{cov(U'(\pi),\ p\frac{\partial f_s}{\partial n}e_s) - cov(U'(\pi),\ \frac{\partial p_{I_s}}{\partial n}I)}{EU'(\pi)} + E\frac{\partial p_{I_s}}{\partial n}\bar{I} + p \tag{8.9}$$

where $\bar{I} = E(I)$. When a firm is risk neutral, its marginal utility from an increase in profit does not vary with the profit level; $U'(\pi)$ is constant. It follows that both covariance terms are equal to zero and consequently, the first term on the RHS of Equation (8.9) vanishes. A risk neutral firm's use decision rule regarding the level of network use under uncertainty seems to be quite similar to the one under certainty (see Equation (8.1)). The only difference is that a risk neutral decision maker uses the *expected* marginal product of network use and the expected price of information in his decision making under the presence of uncertainty, whereas the certain values of the coresponding variables are used under certainty.

Next, we explore how a risk averse firm chooses its level of network use under uncertainty. The assumption of multiplicative technical uncertainty implies positive correlation between marginal product and total product.

Then, the marginal product of network use and profit are also positively correlated and

$$\text{cov}(U'(\pi), p \frac{\partial f_s}{\partial n} e_s) > 0.$$

Since a decrease in the cost of information increases profit, π and $\frac{\partial p_{I_s}}{\partial n} I$ are negatively correlated and $\text{cov}(U'(\pi_s), \frac{\partial p_{I_s}}{\partial n} I) > 0.$

It now follows that the first term on the RHS of Equation (8.9) is positive in the case of a risk averse firm and it chooses a smaller level of network use under uncertainty than a risk neutral firm.[4]

Consider next how uncertainty regarding the network size, due to any source of uncertainty mentioned above,[5] affects a firm's network use and production decisions. The effect of a change in the network on the level of a firm's network use can be written as follows:

$$\frac{\partial(\frac{\partial EU(\pi)}{\partial n})}{\partial N} = EU''(\pi)(p\frac{\partial f_s}{\partial x}\frac{\partial x}{\partial N} e_s - \frac{\partial p_{I_s}}{\partial n}\frac{\partial n}{\partial N} I - p_n\frac{\partial n}{\partial N})(p\frac{\partial f_s}{\partial n} e_s - \frac{\partial p_{I_s}}{\partial n} I - p_n)$$

$$+ EU'(\pi)(p\frac{\partial(\frac{\partial f_s}{\partial n})}{\partial N} e_s - \frac{\partial(\frac{\partial p_{I_s}}{\partial n})}{\partial N} I) - \frac{\partial p_{I_s}}{\partial n}\frac{\partial I}{\partial N}) \qquad (8.10)$$

We can see from Equation (8.10), by comparing it with (8.2), that the effect of network externality on a risk neutral firm's network use level under uncertainty does not differ that much from the certainty case (since $EU''(\pi)$) = 0 in Equation (8.10)). A change in the expected network size implies changes in the expected values of the variables which were certain in Equation (8.2). The conclusions are similar to those presented in Section (8.2); an increase in the expected number of network users increases (decreases) a risk neutral firm's network use under positive (negative) pecuniary and technical network externalities.

In the case of a risk averse firm, the interpretation of Equation (8.10) is a bit more complicatd. A risk averse firm increases its network use level under positive network externalities, since since $EU'(\pi) < 0$, only if the following condition holds:

$$(p\frac{\partial f_s}{\partial x}\frac{\partial x}{\partial N} e_s - \frac{\partial p_{I_s}}{\partial n}\frac{\partial n}{\partial N} I - p_n\frac{\partial n}{\partial N} I - p_n\frac{\partial n}{\partial N})(p\frac{\partial p_{I_s}}{\partial n} I - p_n) < 0 \qquad (8.11)$$

Since the combination of the first three terms on the LHS of Equation (8.11) is just $\partial\pi/\partial N$, the contents of the first brackets are obviously positive due to the definition of positive externality. This means that the outcome from the second brackets has to be negative. We can deduce from Equation (8.11), after some calculations,[6] that a risk averse firm increases its network use when the (expected) network size increases only if the following condition holds:

$$\frac{\partial f_s}{\partial x} \frac{\partial x}{\partial N} > \frac{\partial f_s}{\partial n} \frac{\partial n}{\partial N} \qquad (8.12)$$

Equation (8.12) suggests that as the network size grows or as the expectations of a risk averse firm regarding the network size increase, the firm increases its network use only if an increase in N results in a larger increment in the marginal product of 'all inputs' than in the marginal product of network use. In other words, the input vector x has to include at least one input – in addition to network use – of which marginal product increases with N.

The mathematical exercise of this section indicates that risk averse investment behaviour can both hinder a firm's adoption of new network technologies and lower the level of network use in the firm after the adoption of a network technology, when the network market involves network externalities and uncertain components. Consequently, the diffusion of new communications technologies and systems may be deferred and positive network externalities underutilized in the networks.

6. DISCUSSION

It seems quite credible that new communications technologies involve several sources of uncertainty as well as substantial network externalities. Our analysis suggests that under the presence of production network externalities – that is, pecuniary and technical network externalities – uncertainty regarding a new network technology can have prominent effects on network adoption and use decisions of a firm. The order of magnitude of these effects depends on the actors' attitudes towards risk: the higher the risk aversion of economic actors or the greater uncertainty related to a new technology, the higher the PCM point is and the later the adoption of a new technology takes place and the lower the level of network use. Risk averse investment behaviour can cause the emergence of three types of inefficiencies in the network market: (i) the diffusion of a new network technology can be inefficienctly slow or (ii) a superior technical standard is not adopted and (iii) positive network externalities related to the use of a network are underutilized.

When the critical mass of network users is not yet reached, the diffusion of a new network technology can be inefficiently slow and consequently, a society may forego the benefits of a superior technology as well as positive externalities related to its use. Risk averse investment behaviour of economic actors can have even more serious consequences from a societal point of view; risk aversion is likely to strengthen 'excess inertia'[7] in the early phases of network development and consequently, it is possible that a new superior technical standard is not adopted even if the benefits of its adoption exceed the costs of the adoption (at and after passing the PCM point). In addition, uncertainties related to a new network technology can hinder the exploitation of production network externalities after the adoption of the technology.

Next, we briefly discuss some assumptions about our analytical exploration and their implications for the results. Our theoretical framework was based on the simplified assumption of the single manager/owner of a firm. This situation is, however, not very common in the real world. On the contrary, ownership is increasingly separated from control (Ihamoutila 1994). The separation may create informational asymmetries and thus, possibly some agency problems between the managers and the owners of a firm. Managers are usually more risk averse than the owners of a firm, when the ownership is separated from the control of the firm.[8] It follows that a firm is likely to adopt a new network technology later and then choose a lower level of network use, when managers make decisions regarding a firm's network investments instead of the owners of the firm. This means that the managers can be too risk averse not only from the shareholders' or owners' point of view, but also from a societal point of view.

We can also question the feasibility of an assumption that the level of network use is chosen by the profit maximizing interests of an owner. First, the owners of the firms are certainly not the users of a firm's network technology, when the ownership is separated from the control. In addition, the employees of a firm may be unwilling to put any effort into learning to use a new communications technology and their manager may necessarily not – due to his risk aversion and the presence of uncertainties – encourage the use of advanced communications networks. Second, when the manager of a firm owns the company, he is rarely the only user of a communications network, but the employees of a firm will probably also use the communications technology. This situation may give rise to some agency problems between the manager and the employees.

The points made above stress that intrafirm conditions and relationships can play an important role in the adoption and use of new communications technologies in the firms. These include the owner-manager relationship, the manager's control over the employees and the employees' attitudes towards learning and using the new means of communication. These complexities which may arise in practical decision making in the firms do not reduce the importance of network externalities and uncertainties in the diffusion of the advanced comunications systems. However, the authorities who decide on the practical network policy should keep in mind that the underutilization of advanced communications networks may also be related to some internal problems of the firms. Then, these intrafirm factors can affect both the appropriateness of certain policy means and the efficiency of the policy instruments applied by public authorities.

The critical role communications networks and technologies already play – and will certainly increasingly play in the future – in international trade and competition highlights the importance of network policies European countries now practise and will practise in the future. The utilization of advanced communications systems is still in its early phase in many industries and regions in Europe and community policies facilitating the use of ACT are still needed. A crucial question which should be paid particular attention in network policy decisions is how the chosen policy instruments affect the diffusion of new communications technologies as well as their utilization by economic actors.

This chapter suggests two policy means which might accelerate the diffusion and utilization of advanced communications networks: (i) the reduction of uncertainty regarding the new communications technologies and (ii) the encouragement and support of ACT investments in firms. For instance, commitment to the compatibility of communications technologies by regulation and legislation (for example, technical standards) and the distribution of information regarding the new technologies can reduce uncertainty in the network market and consequently facilitate the diffusion of network technologies. Also, a policy means which supports risk taking in entrepreneurial network investments – for example, favourable tax treatment for firms' network related investments – could accelerate the utilization of advanced communications networks.

Before adoption and use of advanced systems is supported by public funds, it is of great importance to ensure that there is an actual need for government intervention. The successful implementation of practical network policies requires answers to a multitude of questions. This section has raised some relevant, but still unsolved questions regarding the spread and utilization of advanced communications technologies. First, it would be important to explore what is the role and significance of uncertainties and risk averse investment behaviour in the diffusion of new communications technologies. Second, the order of magnitude of positive network externalities which a society forgoes without government intervention should be evaluated. And third, the sectors and regions of European economies where advanced communications technology is still underutilized should be identified. After these stages of research have been done, it will be time to consider the allocation of funds for supporting the adoption and use of advanced communications systems.

ACKNOWLEDGEMENT

The author is grateful to Peter Nijkamp, Rune Stenbacka, Rauli Svento and an anonymous referee for their helpful comments.

REFERENCES

Antonelli, C. (ed.) (1992), *The Economic Theory of Information Networks*, Amsterdam: Elsevier Science Publishers.

Capello, R. (1994), *Spatial Economic Analysis of Telecommunications Network Externalities*, Aldershot: Avebury.

Capello, R. and P. Nijkamp (1993), 'Measuring network externalities: their role on corporate and regional performance', paper presented at the 33rd European Congress, held in Moscow, Russian Federation, 24–27 August 1993.

Church, J. and N. Gandal (1993), 'Complementary network externalities and technological adoption', *International Journal of Industrial Organization* **11**, pp. 239–60.

Economides, N. (1994), 'The economics of networks', Discussion Paper no. EC–94–24, NYU: Stern School of Business.

Farrell, J. and G. Saloner (1985), 'Standardisation, compatibility and innovation', *Rand Journal of Economics* **16**, pp. 70–83.

Gravelle, H. and R. Rees (1992), *Microeconomics*, London: Longman.

Heal, G. (1990), 'Price and market share dynamics in network industries', *First Boston Working Paper Series*.

Ihamoutila, M. (1994), 'Corporate ownership, capital structure and investment', A:97, Helsinki School of Economics and Business Administration.

Katz, M. and C. Shapiro (1985), 'Network externalities, competition and compatibility', *American Economic Review* **75**, pp. 424–40.

Laffont, J-J. (1989), *The Economics of Uncertainty and Information*, Massachusetts: MIT Press.

Liebowitz, S.J. and S.E. Margolis (1994), 'Network externality: an uncommon tragedy', *Journal of Economic Perspectives* **8**, pp. 133–50.

Nijkamp, P. and A. Reggiani (1994), 'Multi-layer synergy and networks', paper given at NECTAR Meeting, 19–20 August, Stockholm.

Oren, S. and S. Smith (1981), 'Critical mass and tariff structure in electronic communications markets', *Bell Journal of Economics and Management Science* **12**, pp. 467–86.

Rohlfs, J. (1974), 'A theory of interdependent demand for a communication service', *Bell Journal of Economics and Management Science* **5**, pp. 16–37.

NOTES

1. Capello (1994) considers extensively production network externalities. Moreover, her empirical results support the existence of positive externalities – at least under certain spatial and corporate conditions – in the use of advanced telecommunications technology.

2. This indigenous quality of a network technology can be assumed to include implicitly also the firm-specific adoption or learning costs regarding a new technology such that T represents the net value of a new technology to a user.

3. We might as well assume that uncertainty arises from some other source (for example, uncertainty regarding prices). The implications of any form of uncertainty for a firm's network adoption decision were similar to the ones which will be presented below.

4. It should be noted that this unambiguous interpretation is achieved due to the assumption of multiplicative technical uncertainty. When this assumption is relaxed, it is unknown whether the relationship between marginal and total product is positive or negative. Consequently, the sign of the first covariance term in Equation (8.9) is also unknown. This means that whether a risk averse firm chooses a smaller, the same or a greater level of network use than a risk neutral firm depends on the sign and magnitude of the first covariance term.

5. For simplicity, we use straightforward uncertain network size, irrespective of whether it is caused by market uncertainty, technological uncertainty or asymmetric information, throughout the analysis. This simplification does not affect the essence of the results, but helps to demonstrate the point clearly.

6. Equation (8.11) implies that $p_n > p(\partial f_s / \partial n) \, e_s - (\partial p_I / \partial n)I$ and $p_n < p(\partial f_s / \partial x)(\partial x / \partial N)(\partial n / \partial N)^{-1} \, e_s - (\partial p_I / \partial N)I$. Thus, $p((\partial f_s / \partial n) - (\partial f_s / \partial x)(\partial x / \partial N)(\partial n / \partial N)^{-1}) \, e_s < 0$.

7. See Farrell and Saloner (1985) for a more detailed discussion on excess inertia.

8. The managers 'invest' their human capital in a firm and when the firm is the only source of income, they cannot diversify their human capital. The owners of a firm, however, are able to diversify their wealth to a large number of assets.

9. Measurement and Measures of Network Accessibility: Economic Perspectives

Dino Martellato, Peter Nijkamp and Aura Reggiani

1. THE ACCESSIBILITY ISSUE

Transportation and communication infrastructure serve to improve the competitive advantage of regions and cities by enhancing the relative accessibility of these areas.

For the assessment of the impact of transport policies on the economic performance of different regions or urban areas it seems appropriate to use practical concepts and measurable indices of accessibility in space. There is indeed a quite long tradition in the available literature which attributes to infrastructure the ability to influence land use in a region or an urban area as well as the level of standard economic performance indicators like unemployment rates and growth rates (Wegener 1983). For example, Rietveld and Nijkamp (1993) have recently investigated the relationship between transport and regional development by focusing on the response of the private sector to transport infrastructure improvement. In particular, they address the relationship between transport infrastructure and relocation of investment and employment which bears on the relationship between infrastructure, accessibility and productivity.

In the present chapter we will focus on the concept of accessibility. There are many definitions of accessibility and many ways to measure it. The basic concept of accessibility of a location site contains nevertheless different, but complementary aspects. Any specific location offers socioeconomic possibilities to agents that have chosen it. They can reach other locations and thus interact with other agents; however, in doing so they must make some effort in relation to the distance, the price of the service, the time required, and the shadow price they attach to their time.

Table 9.1 Measures and formulations of accessibility: a selective review

Accessibility Measures	Potential of Opportunity	Physical Measure	Utility	Inverse Function of Competition	Joint Accessibility	Dynamic Accessibility
Formulations	$Acc_i=\sum_j D_j e^{-\beta c_{ij}}$	$Acc_i=\sum_j d_{ij}$ or $Acc_i=\sum_j W_j d_{ij}$	$Acc_i=\ln \sum_j D_j e^{-\beta c_{ij}}$	$Acc_i=\frac{1}{A_i}$	$Acc_i=\sum_j Acc_j D_j e^{-\beta c_{ij}}$ where $Acc_j=\sum_k D_k e^{-\gamma c_{jk}}$	$Acc_i(t)=\frac{1}{A_i^*(t)}$
Authors	Hansen, 1959 Ingram, 1971 Wilson, 1971 Domanski, 1979 Weibull, 1980 Bröcker, 1989 Bruinsma & Rietveld, 1993 a,b Rietveld & Nijkamp, 1993 Forslund & Johansson, 1993 Suarez, 1995	Wachs & Kumagai, 1973 Vickerman, 1974 Mattson & Weibull, 1981 Moretti, 1989 Cattan, 1992	Neuberger, 1971 Wilson, 1976 Williams, 1977 Leonardi, 1978 Williams & Senior,1978 Ben-Akiva & Lerman, 1979 Leonardi & Tadei,1984 Bröcker, 1989 Forslund & Johansson, 1993	Wilson, 1982 Fotheringham, 1983 Reggiani, 1985a Matthes, 1994	Domanski, 1979 Fotheringham, 1986 Reggiani, 1985b Nijkamp & Reggiani, 1992	Nijkamp & Reggiani, 1988

Surveys: Vickerman, 1974; Domanski, 1979; Pirie, 1979; Weibull, 1980; Bruinsma & Rietveld, 1993a; Vickerman, 1995

Notes: 1: D_j is a measure of opportunities/activities in j   2: W_j is a weight related to location j

3:   $A_i=\dfrac{1}{\sum_j D_j e^{-\beta c_{ij}}}$ is the calibration factor in a spatial interaction model

4:   $A_i^*(t)=\dfrac{1}{\sum_j B_j^* D_j e^{-\beta c_{ij}}}$ where $=B_j G_j$, B_j is the usual (dynamic) calibration factor and G_j a dynamic accessibility factor

162

Velocity, density and congestion in transport networks are related concepts. All these elements should be considered in the definition of accessibility, since they enter as arguments in the utility function of agents. They will not change their current location when the perceived utility – that is, the net benefit – is at its maximum, but they may change the mode, the route and the timing of their movement.

Section 2 is devoted entirely to an assessment of various measures and formulations of accessibility. In this review it will be shown that the concept of accessibility may receive various and different interpretations. In Section 3 new definitions are provided leading to a new analysis of accessibility effects. Accessibility will be related to actual, rather than potential, flows and costs. In particular, due attention will be paid to traffic composition and route choice. Some concluding observations are provided in Section 4.

2. MEASURES AND FORMULATIONS OF ACCESSIBILITY: A REVIEW

2.1 Introduction

The accessibility concept, and hence the related measures, have a long tradition in regional science and transport economics. The concept came to the fore in the 1950s after the rigorous legitimation of gravity theory offered by Isard at the First Regional Science Meeting in 1954 (for a historical review on gravity theory/spatial interaction models see Nijkamp and Reggiani 1992). One of the first foundation stones for the use of accessibility 'theory' can be found in the work of Hansen, who defined accessibility as *potential of opportunities for interaction* (1959, p. 73). The quantification as well as the formulation of a theoretical structure of this concept has assumed various forms in the course of history.

This part of the chapter briefly reviews the main concepts and related measures/formulations of the accessibility concept. It is worth noting that in the following subsections we do not intend to offer an exhaustive list of all scientific contributions related to accessibility indices/notions, but essentially an illustration of the various research directions which have been carried out so far in this context. This is also illustrated in Table 9.1. These different interpretations will now successively be discussed in a succinct way.

2.2 Accessibility as Potential of Opportunity

Accessibility as a measure of the nearness to opportunities is still the most popular concept starting from Hansen's definition, as the long list of authors in Table 9.1 witnesses. 'By accessibility I mean the possibilities of using the opportunities that the economic, social, cultural and political facilities and institutions provide' (see Domanski 1979, p. 1190). This quotation shows how the concept of accessibility is usually related to the concepts of nearness, proximity, ease of spatial interaction, potential of opportunities for interaction or potentiality of contacts with activities or supplies (Weibull 1980, p. 54). In other words, accessibility is considered a property of configurations of opportunities for spatial interaction (see Weibull 1980, p. 53). These opportunities may concern employment places, medical care centres, production places, shops, parks, and so on, each particular type of opportunity having relevant attributes such as distance, mode of transport, travel time/cost, supply capacity, price, quality, congestion, queuing time, and so on. It is clear that the concept of potential of opportunities includes a certain measurement of the opportunities at destination j, discounted (in relative or absolute value) by the spatial distance (travel/time/cost) of j from some reference point (origin) i. Consequently, the *total accessibility* of all opportunities implies discounting the total number of opportunities at all nodes (destinations) by the sum of distances from the reference node. In formal terms:

$$Acc_i = \sum_j D_j\, f(c_{ij})$$

$$(9.1)$$

where Acc_i defines accessibility in some reference point (origin i), D_j is a measure of opportunities in j, c_{ij} is the cost of travelling from origin i to destination j, and $f(c_{ij})$ is the impedance function from place i to destination j. After some proposals concerning the analytical form of $f(c_{ij})$, in terms of a function of distance d_{ij}, as given, for example, by Hansen (1959):

$$f(c_{ij}) = d_{ij}^{-\alpha}$$

$$(9.2)$$

or by Ingram (1971):

$$f(c_{ij}) = \exp(-d_{ij}^2/\delta)$$

$$(9.3)$$

the exponential decay function conceived by Wilson (1971) – which also substituted the travel cost c_{ij} to the related distance d_{ij} – has been widely adopted:

$$f(c_{ij}) = \exp(-\beta\, c_{ij})$$

$$(9.4)$$

However, apart from the different formulations of the travel impedance function – which should be tested in an empirical setting – Equation (9.1) involves two main related limitations: one concerning the aggregated approach (considering that all individuals in the same zone have the same level of accessibility), and the other one regarding the use of zone centroids, by neglecting intra-zonal improvements to the transport system (see, for example, Bröcker 1989 and Pirie 1979). It should also be noted that in the related Equation (9.2), a *high value* of Acc_i will roughly mean – for location i – a *good transport infrastructure.*

Despite all limitations involved, Equation (9.1) is still widely used in empirical applications. It is interesting to refer here to recent contributions by Bröcker (1989) who applied a modification of the potential formula to German regions; by Bruinsma and Rietveld (1993a, 1993b) for the accessibility analysis of European cities; by Forslund and Johansson (1993) for the measurement of international freight accessibility as well as municipality's accessibility in Sweden; by Reggiani (1985b) for the analysis of zoning systems in Lombardia (Italy) and by Suarez (1995) in measuring accessibility for peripheral European regions. In this context, an interesting result is also given by Domanski (1979), who relates the increase of accessibility to spatial concentration. In particular, this author uses *accessibility as a measure* to represent *spatial equity,* essentially by applying the potential formula (9.1) to a hypothetical spatial system. Finally, in Rietveld and Nijkamp (1993) a survey of recent scientific contributions to the exploration of the relationship 'infrastructure/accessibility' is given by means of formulation (9.1), which emphasizes the existence of a positive relationship between accessibility and total employment.

2.3 Accessibility as Physical Measure

A second line of research concerning accessibility indicators is related to the definition of accessibility as a direct function of the distance d_{ij} (from origin i to destination j). In other words, the *physical separation* of two places is treated as a measure of the accessibility of one place to another as follows:

$$Acc_i = \sum_j d_{ij} \tag{9.5}$$

Obviously, the above index may also be weighted by means of variables related to activities in j:

$$Acc_i = \sum_j W_j d_{ij} \tag{9.6}$$

where W_j expresses the weight related to location j.

It is then clear from (9.5) and (9.6) that accessibility, here defined as a direct function of average distance (or time/cost), will show a *low value* corresponding to a *high* efficiency of the *network infrastructure* (in contrast to the previous approach outlined in Section 2.2). In some studies of accessibility to certain opportunities (for example, employment) the number of these opportunities (for example, jobs) within a predetermined travel time is used as a quantitative indicator (see, for example, Mattson and Weibull 1981 and Wachs and Kumagai 1973).

The accessibility measure, as defined in (9.5), is often used in graph theory in connection with other topological measures such as the number of network vertices or the number of connected links (see, for example, Vickerman 1974 and Cattan 1992). Applications of the physical accessibility are mainly found in geography and network analysis (see, among others, Moretti 1989, who applied (9.5) for the analysis of the rail network in Lombardia, and Cattan 1992, who used (9.5) for investigating the centrality of European cities).

2.4   Accessibility as Utility

A further interesting approach, in the framework of the accessibility issue, relates accessibility to the notion of consumer surplus in microeconomic theory (see, for example, Ben-Akiva and Lerman 1979, Leonardi 1978, and Williams and Senior 1978). In particular, discrete choice theory is employed here to model the behaviour and the (net) benefits of different users of a transportation network. By considering, for example, a logit model, the welfare or benefit associated with network opportunities j, which are given to an agent i, can be derived as follows:

$$u_{ij} = v_{ij} - \beta c_{ij} \tag{9.7}$$

where u_{ij} represents the net gain consisting of a component v_{ij} (referring to the value of making the trip ij) minus communication costs c_{ij}, while ß is a cost-sensitivity parameter. In this situation the maximum net gain is a natural indicator of locational advantage L_i (see Bröcker 1989):

$$L_i = E \left[\max_i (u_{ij}) \right] \tag{9.8}$$

where E denotes the expectation operator.

Expression (9.8) can then be interpreted as a measure of *spatial surplus* in the context of the location of public facilities (see Leonardi and Tadei 1984) as well as an *accessibility measure* or the preference value of a given accessibility pattern (see Ben-Akiva and Lerman 1979 and Forslund and Johansson 1993).

It is well known from the theory of stochastic choice that a standard result of (9.8) is the following (see also Small 1992):

$$L_i \stackrel{\sim}{=} Acc_i = \ln \sum_j \exp(u_{ij})$$

(9.9)

or, in relation to formulation (9.1) (see Williams 1977 and Wilson 1976):

$$Acc_i = \ln \sum_j D_j \exp(-\beta c_{ij})$$

(9.10)

where now $D_j = \exp(v_{ij})$ by reflecting a measure of utility in j rather than opportunities in j. Consequently, the expected maximal net gain is formally a monotone increasing function of the potential formula (9.1) (see also Bröcker 1989).

The above interpretation is certainly interesting, offering an 'economic' background for the potential approach advocated in Section 2.2. However, despite its 'methodological significance', the utility concept of accessibility – as expressed in (9.9) and (9.10) – is rarely used in empirical applications.

2.5   Accessibility as Inverse Function of Competition

A further approach, conceptually close to those discussed in Sections 2.2 and 2.4, relates accessibility to the *inverse* balancing factor A_i (usually interpreted as a *competition factor*; see Wilson 1982) in a *singly-constrained spatial interaction model*.[1] Thus, from the well known theory of spatial interaction models, we conjecture:

$$Acc_i = \frac{1}{A_i} = \sum_j D_j \exp(-\beta c_{ij})$$

(9.11)

where D_j is a measure of attractiveness of j.

Consequently, even though expression (9.11) is formally equivalent to equation (9.1) (including (9.4)), the value of Acc_i emerges from the calibration process determining A_i and is not given a priori. In this framework, Acc_i in (9.11) can also be interpreted as a measure of the *benefit* of facility size, as underlined in the previous section. It is interesting to note that Neuberger (1971), Williams and Senior (1978) and Wilson (1976) were the first authors who interpreted the inverse balancing factor as an indicator of *economic benefit*.

It is also interesting to mention here the work by Matthes (1994), who applies a logarithmic form of the spatial interaction models by estimating the accessibility factors (9.11) in the case of mobile communication traffic in the previous Federal Republic of Germany.

2.6   Accessibility Conceived of as Joint Accessibility

A concept often advocated in the literature is the sequential decision making process. This 'mental' structure constitutes the basis of the well-known nested logit model, whose counterpart is a spatial interaction model embedding a double accessibility function (see, for example, Domanski 1979 and Fotheringham 1983).

In particular, in the case of a two-stage decision process towards two levels of destinations j and k, the joint accessibility results as follows (see, for example, Reggiani 1985b):

$$Acc_i = \sum_j Acc_j \, D_j \, exp \, (-\beta \, c_{ij}) \tag{9.12}$$

where

$$Acc_j = \sum_k D_k \, exp \, (-\gamma \, c_{jk}) \tag{9.13}$$

embeds the accessibility of a destination j to further destinations k with a cost-sensitivity parameter γ.

It is then evident that formulation (9.12) can also emerge as an inverse balancing factor of a *doubly-constrained spatial* interaction model, by regarding the usual balancing factor B_j as a measure of Acc_j as defined in (9.13) (see, for details, Nijkamp and Reggiani 1992). In this context it is worth referring also to Anas (1983) who demonstrates the equivalence of doubly constrained spatial interaction models and logit models of joint origin-destination choice.

Applications of (9.12) embedding (9.13) can be found in Fotheringham (1986) in a discussion on competing destination models incorporating a hierarchical destination choice, as well as in Reggiani (1985a,b) where the empirical results emerging from the joint accessibility (9.12) are compared with those emerging from the usual potential formula (9.1), in order to design homogeneous zoning systems.

2.7 Dynamic Accessibility

Investigations concerning the 'dynamics' of accessibility, in addition to the 'static' accessibility previously illustrated, are still rare, owing to the theoretical/computational difficulties inherent both in the dynamic aspects of the related methodological tools and in the dynamic setting of the empirical experiments.

An attempt in this direction is given by Nijkamp and Reggiani (1988) who obtain, by means of a dynamic entropy approach as an optimal solution, the dynamic form of a spatial interaction model, and hence the related dynamic accessibility factors which result analogous to those emerging in a static framework. In this way a theoretical foundation is shown which allows the use of the dynamic accessibility.

In particular, the dynamic accessibility factor reads as follows:

$$Acc_i(t) = \frac{1}{A_i^*(t)} \tag{9.14}$$

where $A_i^*(t)$ is the (dynamic) calibration factor:

$$A_i^* = \frac{1}{\displaystyle\sum_j B_j^* D_j \exp(-\beta c_{ij})} = A_i G_i^{-1} \tag{9.15}$$

and

$$B_j^* = B_j G_j \tag{9.16}$$

In (9.15) and (9.16), A_i, B_j are the usual calibration factors for a *doubly constrained spatial* interaction model, even though *here all variables are time dependent*, and G_j *is a dynamic accessibility factor* (see Appendix 9A in Nijkamp and Reggiani 1988).

It is then clear that the above approach, despite its theoretical significance, ends up with a sort of 'dynamic version' of the potential formula illustrated in Section 2.2, with all intrinsic limitations.

2.8 Concluding Remarks

The overview illustrated in the previous section underlines the crucial role of accessibility in spatial interaction and location theory. However, some remarks are still in order here.

First, it is evident that, despite the various theoretical frameworks, the accessibility function always emerges, in its analytical form, as a potential of opportunities (see Table 9.1). However, this result is not surprising, given the strict link between accessibility and spatial interaction models, as well as the 'universal' role of spatial interaction models in most spatial models (even dynamic) adopted so far (see Nijkamp and Reggiani 1992). It should be noted that an intrinsic limit of this approach, in its empirical setting, lies both in the degree of aggregation and in the lack of theoretical elements concerning the (efficient) use of infrastructure.

A second remark concerns the majority of static measures (see again Table 9.1) which hamper the evaluation of changes in transport supply, and consequently in patterns of transport demand and potentially in sectoral structure (Vickerman 1994).

In this framework new indicators, trying to overcome the above limits, have recently been proposed, for example, by taking into account the *connectivity structure* or the *joint use of modes* (see Vickerman 1995).

Starting from the above considerations, in the next section a new approach will be proposed, taking into account the 'economic' aspect of accessibility as well as the impact of the related network. This approach will be a new stage in a research direction aimed at generating new insights into the complex measurement of the accessibility concept.

3.   THE ECONOMICS OF NETWORK ACCESSIBILITY

3.1   Accessibility in Networks

In the previous sections we have shown how the concept of spatial accessibility is at the very core of cost-based theories of location and spatial interaction models. The definitions of accessibility and their interpretations are numerous. The available definitions, however, appear to be slight variations of the potential accessibility which is basically the sum of masses weighted by some inverse function of geographical distance. A standard formula for potential accessibility indeed is the following (see Section 2):

$$Acc_i = \sum_j [D_j/f(C_{ij})]$$

(9.17)

where D_j is the mass location j and $f(C_{ij})$ is an impedance function which is directly related to cost C_{ij}. The mass acts as a proxy of the possibilities of contacts open to agents located in j, while the impedance function is related to the effort of reaching j from the reference point i.

The main weakness of potential accessibility is the likely impact of a change in the masses, that is, in the intensity of use of the infrastructure, on the accessibility. In the context of this definition, any increase of the masses in the connected nodes yields a proportional increase of accessibility, as if unused transport capacity would always be available. It is evident, however, that a larger use of existing infrastructure may imply congestion, that is, lower velocity, higher time and more costs.

Other unsatisfactory aspects of potential accessibility defined in (9.17) are the impossibility of taking into account the composition of traffic flows as well as the existence of differences in the number of alternative routes connecting the different pairs of cities in the network. It is safe to assume that the higher the number of routes and, more in general, the number of modes connecting a pair of cities, the lower the risk of a bottleneck in the link and the higher the accessibility of the two cities.

Accessibility seems indeed to be influenced by many more factors than the masses and costs suggested in (9.17). These different factors can bring about various effects which in Table 9.2 are listed and classified.

Table 9.2   Factors influencing accessibility in a given time horizon

	short run	long run discrete changes	long run smooth changes
monetary price	*		
economic activity level	*		
distance		*	
infrastructure capacity		*	
total price			*
location decision			*

Table 9.2 deserves some comments. A change of a toll, i.e. a change of the monetary price, can influence drivers' decisions, even in the short run. Any change in the general economic activity also has an instantaneous effect on accessibility via its effects on congestion. Any investment decision concerning infrastructure furthermore has an impact, discrete in nature, on the capacity of transport infrastructure which unfolds with a time lag. Finally any change in the total price and in any other factor is able to influence the location decisions of agents. When more and more individuals perceive the change and reset to it there is a further impact on transport flows.

Many of these elements influence the level of congestion and consequently the time spent on the journey as well as the time delay (that is, the cost). It is then clear that impedance is affected by everything that is able to influence congestion and time.

Since time is the reciprocal of velocity and velocity depends on infrastructure and thus on capacity and density, it is worthwhile considering a definition of accessibility in which accessibility depends on demand and costs (or demand and velocity), as will be suggested in the following section.

Besides, the concept of accessibility in a network seems to have received insufficient attention. The existence of different routes or combinations of links, the composition of traffic flows, and the unsteady level of congestion are factors to which attention must also be paid to reach a satisfactory index of network accessibility.

Starting from the above observations, we will examine the concept of network accessibility by adopting an economic perspective which takes into account the capacity of infrastructure and the intensity of use.

3.2   Network Accessibility and Costs: A First Example

Given a specific transport mode, actual accessibility seems to be a concept more related to actual costs of a trip (or shipment), along a specific route, rather than to a weighted sum of all possibilities open to agents. *Actual cost* is the sum of monetary cost and the value of travel time including the time lost for congestion and the rescheduling time. In the following, we will only refer to road transportation, because congestion phenomena have in this case the highest importance. This section draws mainly on Martellato and Nijkamp (1995, Section 9.6).

It should be noted that a route between two distinct locations can be direct or indirect and usually implies the use of a combination of different links as well as the crossing of some urban areas or districts and a choice between different alternatives. We need then a definition suitable for measuring the *ease of access to or via a network formed by links and nodes*. Such a definition will appear to be rather different from the definitions of potential accessibility found in the literature.

With regard to the various factors having an impact on accessibility, we are then arguing that distance, transport infrastructure, time price and locations can be assumed as given, at least in the short run.

Changes in relative prices of transport modes – when realized by rational agents – and changes in the general activity level execute their impact on accessibility through demand, even in the short run. Taking these two elements as given, the time required for a trip (or a shipment) and the schedule delay are seen as being dependent on the degree of congestion related to the various elements like route characteristics, route assignments, traffic composition and the time schedule chosen by agents.

Travel costs are obtained by adding a non-monetary component to the monetary component (the toll and the car operation cost). The former is the time spent on travelling and the scheduling delay (properly priced). The time spent on travelling is obtained by adding the extra time caused by congestion to the normal time. The scheduling delay can be due to the time before or after the planned trip.

We will assume a non-linear relationship between travel cost and travel time, and an elastic flow with respect to costs, on any specific route. Changes in the road density, reassignment, rescheduling and car-pooling are examples of phenomena sensitive to costs, and the number of cars at a certain point and in a certain moment.

A general impedance function relating travel costs to density, for a specific group g and for a given route, may be defined by adding to the specific monetary component p_{rg}, the component related to the travel time and the schedule delay. It is safe to assume that, after a certain density threshold, the costs that any group of travellers incurs for waiting at a bottleneck and for the change in departure or arrival time are an increasing function of density, given the characteristics of the route, its peculiarities, the time schedule, and the mix of user groups.

The number of vehicles entering a particular route r without congestion will be less than or equal to the threshold value S_r^*. D_{rh} is a measure of the actual flow level on route r. There are two cost 'regimes', one without and one with congestion. In the latter case we have externalities among road users, which can be represented by an implicit function Ω relating travel costs per kilometre (C_{rg}) to the flow level. We have then the following possibilities:

$$C_{rg} = p_{rg} \qquad \text{when} \sum_{h=1,G} D_{rh} < S_r^*$$

$$(9.18)$$

$$C_{rg} = p_{rg} + \left(\sum_{h=1,G} \Omega_{rgh}(D_{rh}) \right) \quad \text{when} \sum_{h=1,G} D_{rh} > S_r^*$$

where G is the total number of groups of drivers and $\Omega' > 0$. We believe it is correct to introduce cross-congestion effects which means that we assume that each group has an effect on the remaining groups. The value of the implicit function $\Omega_{rgh}(D_{rh})$ for a group 'g' different from group 'h' is the cross–congestion cost (that is, the impact of a group 'h' density on drivers of group 'g'), while for g=h, the same function gives the internal congestion effect (that is, the impact of group 'g' density on the drivers of the same group). The presence of a private cost and a cost inflicted on others implies that C_{rg} is the marginal cost of a vehicle conditional to the mix of groups.

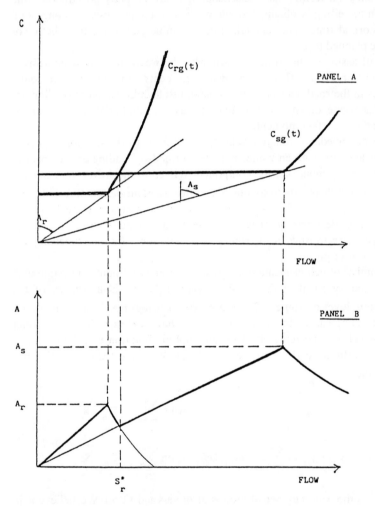

Figure 9.1 Cost and accessibility in relation to traffic flow

Figure 9.1 (panel A) above gives an example of two routes, r and s, respectively. Notice that the steepness of the upward tail reflects the physical characteristics of the route, the characteristics of the group concerned (g) and the mix of groups which are found on the route. Other elements, like weather conditions, may of course have an impact on the steepness. In the picture, the mix is assumed as given.

It should be clear that, from the point of view of group (g) and given a specific mix, the concerned routes (r) and (s) have different cost levels and different degrees of accessibility, at least if we adopt definition (9.18). Accessibility is no longer seen as a function of masses and it is deemed to change with the level and the composition of the flow as well as the capacity of the network.

We can now address the problem of measuring actual accessibility for the same group in the connection between a pair of nodes. In doing this, we observe that the rising cost which accompanies the flow increase above the capacity limit is essentially the consequence of the increase in the use of the resource time. In other words, above a critical number of vehicles, any increase in the flow is accompanied by an increase in travel time, that is, a reduction of the velocity.

It is surprising that the similarity between the (rising) supply price of an industry and the (rising) travel cost on a road has, to our knowledge, hardly been recognized before. A road, the cars and the drivers deliver transport services incurring some costs (some of which are imputed costs) much in the same way an industry does.

The angle with the vertical axis spanned by any point in the envelope curve (heavily shaded in Figure 9.1, panel A) indicates how strongly increasing is the cost at which the actual user flow is routed. Above a certain threshold, the cost increases with the use, something which resembles the increasing supply price at which a firm or a sector sells its output.

The bold curve in Figure 9.1 (panel A) corresponds to the optimal choice and entails a yes-no assignment pattern: everybody on route (r) until S* and every S-S* on route (s), if demand falls above that threshold. This is essentially an application of Wardrop's second principle. If this flow pattern is actually realized, then the profile of actual accessibility can be easily drawn. The angles are reported in Figure 9.1 (panel B) which depicts the level of actual accessibility, under the stated assumption of a social optimum.

Each angle is the demand level divided by the cost defined above (9.18) and gives the index of actual accessibility for the road link concerned (or crossing) and for the group concerned, given the mix:

$$\text{Acc}_{rg}(t) = D_{rg}(t) \ / \ C_{rg}(t) \tag{9.19}$$

One interesting feature of this definition of accessibility is that with (9.19) we credit to any increase of the traffic flow (which is one of many factors affecting it) two separate effects on accessibility. There is a direct and positive effect on the accessibility and an indirect one which may be positive or negative depending on its specific effect on congestion and travel cost. Another interesting feature of a measure of accessibility based on the ratio between the flow and the cost is seen in the possibility of discriminating between an increase in the traffic flow and an increase in its capacity. The first (see Figure 9.1) has an impact which may be positive or negative, the second has an effect which is positive as it reduces the cost.

By adopting the suitable use shares as weights, we may aggregate over groups in order to obtain the following accessibility index by route:

$$Acc_r(t) = \sum_{h=1,G} \frac{D_{rh}(t)}{C_{rh}(t)} \frac{D_{rh}(t)}{\sum_{g=1,G} D_{rg}(t)} \qquad (9.20)$$

or, alternatively, the accessibility index by user group:

$$Acc_g(t) = \sum_{r=1,R} \frac{D_{rh}(t)}{C_{rh}(t)} \frac{D_{rh}(t)}{\sum_{r=1,R} D_{rg}(t)} \qquad (9.21)$$

Note that the first term appearing in both equations is decreasing with a use above the limit S_r^*. Initially, the cost is simply the monetary price and in this instance the index is easy to measure. Above the capacity limit, it implies extra travel time and some schedule delay, which is much more tricky to measure.

By aggregating over groups and routes, one is left with an index of overall accessibility, conditional to the mix:

$$Acc(t) = \sum_{h=1,G;r=1,R} \left(\frac{D_{rh}(t)}{C_{rh}(t)} \frac{D_{rh}(t)}{\sum_{g=1,G;r=1,R} D_{rg}(t)} \right) \qquad (9.22)$$

All the stated indices of accessibility are conditional on the mix of groups of users and on the number R of available routes, i.e. on time. The main conclusion we may draw at this stage is that actual accessibility cannot be measured with a time invariant index, as is the case with other traditional indices. It is obvious that the ease of access, that is, cost and accessibility, changes over time.

4. CONCLUDING REMARKS

In the previous section we have tried to reformulate and expand the concept of accessibility on the basis of considerations emerging from an overview of available definitions. In particular, we have abandoned the concept of potential and constant accessibility in favour of actual and variable accessibility. In the new proposed concept of accessibility we have replaced the 'masses' and thus potential flows by actual flows. This has brought us to define accessibility as a function of choices made by individuals, that is, a function of actual flows and costs (Section 3.2). Actual accessibility turns out to be conditional on the mix of routes and groups and change in time. The attention paid to traffic composition, capacity and intermodality in a network requires the use of complex definitions of accessibility. They are all related to the performance of a transport network.

An important strategic question is whether transport policy is capable of expanding capacity and/or regulating the level and composition of demand. The proposed new concept of accessibility aims at highlighting this often vaguely defined relationship between transport policy measures and accessibility.

A first policy conclusion perhaps is the following. Any demand and infrastructure policy, or any combination of the two, should be judged from their combined effects on a suitably defined total or actual accessibility concept and not from their isolated effects.

Another conclusion to be drawn is that an expansion of origin or destination masses leading to an increase in traffic demand may not necessarily have a positive effect on accessibility; analogously, a capacity expansion may have a positive effect on accessibility, which is smaller than expected, next to an increase in the traffic demand. The above new concept of accessibility may facilitate the evaluation of accessibility effects in various transport policies, provided it is put in an empirical research context with operational results.

ACKNOWLEDGEMENT

The third author would like to thank the Italian CNR Project PFT2 – Contract n° 96.00098.PF74.

REFERENCES

Anas, A. (1983), 'Discrete choice theory, information theory and the multinomial logit and the gravity models', *Transportation Research B* **17** (1), pp. 13–23.
Ben-Akiva, M. and S.R. Lerman (1979), 'Disaggregate travel and mobility choice models and measures of accessibility', in Hensher, D.A. and D.R. Stopher (eds), *Behavioural Travel Modelling*, London: Croom Helm.
Bröcker, J. (1989), 'How to eliminate certain defects of the potential formula', *Environment and Planning A* **21**, pp. 817–30.

Bruinsma, F. and P. Rietveld (1993a), 'Accessibility of cities in European infrastructure networks: a comparison of approaches', *Research Memorandum 1993–18*, Department of Regional Economics, Amsterdam: Free University.

Bruinsma, F. and P. Rietveld (1993b), 'Urban agglomerations in European infrastructure networks', *Urban Studies* **30** (6), pp. 919–34.

Cattan, N. (1992), 'Air and rail accessibilities and attractivities of European metropolis', paper presented at the 6th World Conference on Transport Research, Lyon.

Domanski, R. (1979), 'Accessibility, efficiency and spatial organization', *Environment and Planning* **11**, pp. 1189–206.

Forslund, U. and B. Johansson (1993), 'Assessing road investments: accessibility changes, cost benefit and production effects', ISRN KTH/RO/AR 93/2-SE, Stockholm: Royal Institute of Technology.

Fotheringham, A.S. (1983), 'A new set of spatial-interaction models: the theory of competing destinations', *Environment and Planning A* **15**, pp. 15–36.

Fotheringham, A.S. (1986), 'Modelling hierarchical destination choice', *Environment and Planning A* **18**, pp. 401–18.

Hansen, W.G. (1959), 'How accessibility shapes land-use', *Journal of the American Institute of Planners* **25**, pp. 73–76.

Ingram, D.R. (1971), 'The concept of accessibility: a search for an operational form', *Regional Studies* **5**, pp. 101–107.

Inman, R.P. (1978), 'Congestion function for highway travel', *Journal of Urban Economics*, pp. 21–34.

Leonardi, G. (1978), 'Optimum facility location by accessibility maximizing', *Environment and Planning A* **10**, pp. 1287–1305.

Leonardi, G. and R. Tadei (1984), 'Random utility demand models and service location', *Regional Science and Urban Economics,* **14**, pp. 399–431.

Martellato, D. and P. Nijkamp (1995), 'Old and new concepts of accessibility', Tinbergen Institute, Amsterdam (unpublished manuscript)

Matthes, N. (1994), 'Allocation of mobile communication flows. From micro-economic demand theory to a gravity model', *The Annals of Regional Science* **28** (4), pp. 395–409.

Mattson, L.-G. and J.W. Weibull (1981), 'Competition and accessibility on a regional labour market', *Regional Science and Urban Economics* **11**, pp. 471–97.

Moretti, A. (1989), 'Le misure dell'accessibilità e le sue utilizzazioni territoriali', in Moretti, A. and A. Reggiani (eds), *Sperimentazioni e Analisi Comparate Riferite alla Misura di Accessibilità*, Milan: CLUP, pp. 25–2.

Neuburger, H. (1971), 'User benefit in the evaluation of transport and land use plans', *Journal of Transport Economics and Policy* **5**, pp. 52–75.

Nijkamp, P. and A. Reggiani (1988), 'Entropy, spatial interaction models and discrete choice analysis: static and dynamic analogies', *European Journal of Operational Research* **36**, pp. 186–96.

Nijkamp, P. and A. Reggiani (1992), *Interaction, Evolution and Chaos in Space*, Berlin: Springer Verlag.

Pirie, G.H. (1979), 'Measuring accessibility: a review and proposal', *Environment and Planning A* **11**, pp. 299–312.

Reggiani, A. (1985a), 'L'accessibilità nei modelli di interazione spaziale', in Moretti, A. and A. Reggiani (eds.), *Sperimentazioni e Analisi Comparate Riferite alla Misura di Accessibilità*, Milan: CLUP, pp. 5–24.

Reggiani, A. (1985b), 'Il sistema della mobilità in Lombardia: sperimentazioni di modelli di interazione spaziale con riferimento alla misura di accessibilità', in Reggiani, A. (ed.), *Territorio e Trasporti*, Milan: Franco Angeli, pp. 214–27.

Rietveld, P. and P. Nijkamp (1993), 'Transport and regional development', in Polak, J. and A. Heertje (eds), *European Transport Economics*, Oxford: Blackwell, pp. 130–51.

Small, K.A. (1992), *Urban Transportation Economics*, Reading: Harwood Academic Publishers.

Suarez, C.G. (1995), 'Measuring accessibility of peripheral European regions', paper presented at the ISINE/COST Conference, Lausanne.

Vickerman, R.W. (1974), 'Accessibility, attraction and potential: a review of some concepts and their use in determining mobility', *Environment and Planning A* **6**, pp. 675–91.

Vickerman, R.W. (1994), 'Regional science and new transport infrastructure', in Cuadrado Roura, J., P. Nijkamp, and P. Salva (eds), *Moving Frontiers*, Aldershot: Avebury, pp. 151–66.

Vickerman, R.W. (1995), 'Accessibility and peripheral regions', in Cocossis, H. and P. Nijkamp (eds), *Overcoming Isolation,* Berlin: Springer, pp. 29–40.

Wachs, M. and T.G. Kumagai (1973), 'Physical accessibility as a social indicator', *Socio-Economic Planning Science* **7**, pp. 327–456.

Wegener, M. (1983), 'A simulation study of movement in the Dortmund housing market', *Journal of Economics and Social Geography* **74** (4), pp. 267–81.

Weibull, J.W. (1980), 'On the numerical measurement of accessibility', *Environment and Planning A* **12**, pp. 53–67.

Williams, H.C.W. (1977), 'The generation of consistent travel-demand models and user-benefit measures', in Bonsall, P.W., P.J. Hills and M.W. Dalvi (eds), *Urban Transportation and Planning*, Tunbridge Wells: Abacus Press, pp. 161–76.

Williams, H.C.W. and M.L. Senior (1978), 'Accessibility, spatial interaction and the spatial benefit analysis of land use - transportation plans', in Karlqvist, A., L. Lundqvist, F. Snickars and J.W. Weibull (eds), *Spatial Interaction and Planning Models*, Amsterdam: North-Holland, pp. 253–87.

Wilson, A.G. (1971), 'A family of spatial interaction models and associated developments', *Environment and Planning A,* **3**, pp. 1–32.

Wilson, A.G. (1976), 'Retailers' profit and consumers' welfare in spatial interaction models', in Hasser, I. (ed.), *Theory and Practice in Regional Science*, London: Pion, pp. 42–59.

Wilson, A.G. (1982), 'Transport location and spatial systems', School of Geography, University of Leeds, Leeds LS2 9JT.

NOTE

1. A double constrained spatial interaction model has the meaning of joint accessibility (see further).

PART TWO

Network Policies: Efficiency and Sustainability

10. The Public–Private Nexus in Financing Infrastructure Investment

Peter Nijkamp and Sytze A. Rienstra

1. INTRODUCTION

The influence of public policy on society and the regional and national economy has drastically increased since 1945. As a result, government expenditures have risen significantly (absolutely and relatively), while also many more regulatory measures have been introduced. Social security systems were, for example, widely expanded, while the government assumed inter alia responsibility for the financing and operation of transport infrastructure (Nijkamp and Rienstra 1993).

In the 1980s however, the societal and institutional environment in which economic agents were used to act changed dramatically (Fokkema and Nijkamp 1994). This holds for the public as well as the private sector: the devolution movement has induced increased competition between companies and countries. As a result, a growing need for restructuring and renewal has come to the fore, and hence the Schumpeterian paradigm of 'creative destruction' has gained popularity. Even large companies like IBM and Philips appear to face problems when lags in renewal cause structural inefficiencies. The same may hold for countries: the economic development of most Western European countries for example lags behind that of the US and the Pacific, which may be due to a more regulatory and conservative institutional environment in Europe.

The response of successful companies to this challenge has been diverse:

* an increasing emphasis on scaling up by fusions and take-overs (for example, in the financial sector);
* an aggressive market penetration (for example, consumer electronics);
* 'back to basics' strategies with repulsion of other activities (for example, car industry, microelectronics);
* emphasis on quality and flexibility (just-in-time principles, temporary contracts for employees);

183

- developing national and international strategic alliances, in order to secure the competitive position (car industry, chemical sector).

These trends are not only found in the private, but also in the public sector. As a result, much more cooperation between countries seems to occur (EU, NAFTA, ASEAN), several activities are repulsed (transport, telecommunication), while unnecessary regulations are abolished (labour market, capital market). It may be clear that good management in the public and private sectors may be of increasing importance for the economic development and welfare of countries, regions and their citizens.

Also in the transport sector – which is traditionally very much a regulated sector – many changes are now occurring. Traditionally, natural public monopolies were thought to be the best market organizations. Now it is widely acknowledged that incentives should be introduced to make this sector more efficient (see also Button and Pitfield 1991).

In the 1980s, investments in infrastructure in many EU countries decreased largely because of public budget problems and increasing attention to environmental impacts of transport (Bruinsma 1994). During the past few years, attention to transport infrastructure has again increased, which may be a result of increasing congestion, while attention to Trans European Networks has emerged because of the integration of the European market (Nijkamp et al. 1994).

As a result it may be interesting to analyse how far the above discussed developments may influence the management of transport infrastructure and whether it is possible to increase the influence of private parties in this sector. We will restrict ourselves to road and rail infrastructure, although the arguments may also hold for other kinds of infrastructure (harbours, airports, telecommunications, and so on).

The chapter is set out as follows. First, in Section 2 the strategic importance is discussed by assessing the economic impacts of transport infrastructure and identifying trends in the use of governmental policy instruments. In Section 3 the traditional arguments for government influence are discussed. Next, Section 4 focuses on problems relating to private financing and operation of infrastructure by analysing transport infrastructure from the viewpoint of a 'normal' economic good. In Section 5 we investigate how private infrastructure provision may in practice be analysed. Finally, some conclusions are drawn in Section 6.

2. THE STRATEGIC IMPORTANCE OF TRANSPORT INFRASTRUCTURE

2.1 Introduction

Increasing attention has been paid to transport infrastructure as a vehicle for stimulating economic growth and improving the competitiveness of countries or regions. It is questionable whether such presuppositions are valid, however, as there may be contrasting developments. For example, interregional trade theory claims that the construction of infrastructure has a clear positive impact at several spatial scale levels (Bruinsma 1994). Several costs for economic firms are reduced, because travel times are lower and become more reliable (which makes, for example, just-in-time delivery possible). Therefore, production factors may be used more efficiently, which improves the competitiveness of companies. In this way the construction of infrastructure may have a positive impact on a national or regional economy. On the other hand, it is quite possible that the improved accessibility will increase the competition from other regions or countries, which may then hamper the expected economic growth.

The final result is unclear and therefore empirical research should offer more insight into such impacts. To analyse this question, we will first present a concise overview of some case studies at the national, regional and urban level.

2.2 Empirical Research

At the national level several studies have been carried out on the impacts of public investments in general and of those in transport infrastructure in particular (see, for example, Aschauer 1993; Bruinsma and Rietveld 1993; Seitz 1993). It appears that investments in several kinds of infrastructure – especially roads – contribute largely to economic growth. This occurs by means of increasing sales of private companies; the impact on employment may be smaller however, since the productivity of labour also increases.

An important question in this respect is whether these impacts are temporary or permanent. First, construction of infrastructure may only stimulate economic growth because of the multiplier effects of the construction activities themselves. When the project is finished, the impacts fade away. Second, better infrastructure and accessibility improve productivity, which will stimulate economic growth. As observed by Bruinsma (1994), some studies make a distinction between these impacts, but others do not.

Transport infrastructure may not only be important for national, but also for regional economic development. In empirical research, positive economic impacts are often found, especially on employment, the level of investments and regional economic growth (see for an overview Bruinsma and Rietveld 1993). Other studies, however, do not find significant impacts (see, for example, Rienstra et al. 1997).

An important analytical distinction to be made is between generative and distributive impacts. In the first case there is clearly additional economic growth resulting from the construction of infrastructure, in the second case there is only a shift of economic activities, while at a macro level there is no impact at all. It often appears to be difficult to disentangle these impacts, because all may occur at the same time.

2.3 The Increasing Importance of Infrastructure

It may be clear that – especially at the national level – generative impacts occur, which emphasize the importance of transport infrastructure of a high quality. This importance is reinforced by some general trends at the European and global levels.

First, because of integration of, for example, the European markets and the liberalization of global capital markets, attention to the competitive position of distinct countries has increased. At the same time the possibilities for governments to influence this position have decreased, since the traditional policy instruments – adaptations of the exchange rate, monetary and budgetary policies – cannot be used because of EMU conditions and the liberalization of capital markets. Therefore, the construction of infrastructure (not only transport, but also, for example, telecommunications) is one of the few policy fields left to influence the competitive position of a country. As a result, many countries compete with each other to a greater extent, by improving the business climate via tax cuts, subsidies and offering (semi)public facilities.

Second, there appears to be increasing competition from 'low wage countries'. Next to the competition of Pacific countries, the competition from Eastern European and North African countries has dramatically increased. Therefore, labour intensive production may be repulsed to these countries. The only way for high wage Western European countries to curb this trend is to offer products and services with a high quality and productivity. This increases the need for R&D and a high education level, but also for high quality infrastructure.

As a result there is increasing emphasis not only on the quantity of infrastructure, but also on its quality. Examples are the 'digital highway', the introduction of mobile telephone networks, the construction of an HST network, and so on.

2.4 Success Factors Influencing Infrastructure

The quality of infrastructure may be analysed by using the so called Pentagon model, which contains the five critical success factors which contribute to the efficiency of an infrastructure network (see also Nijkamp et al. 1994).

Hardware aims at the physical features of the infrastructure (terminals, roads, railways, harbours). Software focuses on the control of it, for example by introducing telematics systems to provide information to users. There is a danger that most attention will be paid to the hardware and software, while other strategic factors may be largely forgotten. The model emphasizes, however, that a variety of other factors are also of major importance for improving economic structure, welfare and well-being of countries and people.

As a result also the orgware – the organization and management – is of major importance for the efficiency of a country or region. However, the construction and use of infrastructure causes many – especially negative – externalities, like noise, stench and visual annoyance or local and global air pollution. Government and society have to make a tradeoff therefore, in which these negative externalities are weighed against the positive economic impacts (ecoware). It may be clear, however, that a private delivery of physical transport infrastructure may cause more problems than that of, for example, telecommunications.

Finally, the way new infrastructure is financed (finware) is also an important success factor, which may be entirely public, entirely private or by both sectors (joint venture). In the next sections we will analyse some strategic policy factors which influence the orgware and finware of transport infrastructure, especially when new infrastructure projects are introduced. Particular attention will be paid to possibilities for improving overall efficiency by increasing private sector involvement in the operation and financing of infrastructure.

3. GOVERNMENT INTERVENTION

3.1 Introduction

It is clear that there is – and should be – a large difference in the financial and socioeconomic targets and democratic responsibilities of the private and public sectors. As a result there are several reasons for the government to intervene in the economy and to assume responsibility for the provision of several goods. It may be clear that pure collective goods (like defence) are normally an exclusive governmental responsibility. When the use of a good is competitive however (as is the case with infrastructure), this good may in principle be provided by the private sector as well.

The question of how far goods should be provided by the private sector may be analysed by using the transaction costs approach. Transaction costs include those of, for example, negotiating, making contracts, control and requiring information. Within the Coase theorem of a world without transaction costs, there is no efficiency difference between provision by the public or the private sector, because negotiations continue until there is a Pareto optimal allocation of goods (Coase 1988).

In reality however, there are of course many kinds of transaction costs. A good should now be provided by that sector, which can offer it against the lowest transaction costs. For normal goods, provision by the private sector will be optimal. For some goods however, this may not be the case, which may justify public intervention. In this respect it should be acknowledged that intervention also causes costs, leading to so called government failures, which should be weighed against the resulting benefits.

In order to analyse how and to what extent government intervention is desired (in order to correct a biased market allocation), we will first present a concise overview of arguments to intervene, while next the concept of government failures will be elaborated.

3.2 Validity of Traditional Intervention Arguments

There are several standard reasons for governments to intervene in the market. In light of the above mentioned trends in society, it is questionable, however, whether these arguments are still valid (Fokkema and Nijkamp 1994; Nijkamp and Rienstra 1995).

First, there is the *infant industry* and *infant region* argument. Here it is argued that in an initial stage of industrial or regional development, the economic basis of a sector or region is too weak to be competitive and to survive, and therefore economic actors should be protected temporarily. In practice however, it appears that these measures are very hard to abolish, and that they may lead to inefficiency and a Pareto suboptimal allocation. Therefore, there is at present a greater trend to establish an attractive general business climate, while – at least in Europe – protection is also decreased by European legislation. Another argument is that in recent decades the accessibility of peripheral regions has increased substantially by constructing new infrastructure (Rienstra et al. 1997), which reduces the validity of the infant region argument.

Second, *market failures* may occur because a market system does not always result in a Pareto optimal allocation. The aim of government intervention is then to remedy this suboptimal allocation and in this way to move towards the theoretically optimal situation of perfect competition. There are several causes of such market failures:

- *imperfect competition*; infrastructure is an example of this situation, because it is in most cases not efficient to operate two links on the same corridor. Also the special network character of infrastructure causes imperfect competition: one given link may contribute to the profitability of other links, and therefore an unprofitable link may be profitable when the impact on the total network is taken into account. Often however, there is competition with other modes (while for highways also a high quality underlying road network is available), which reduces the importance of this argument;
- *imperfect information*; this seems (besides telematics systems) to be of lesser importance in the case of infrastructure;
- *absence of markets*; governments intervene in transport to eliminate negative externalities or to generate positive externalities as discussed above. In environmental and transport policy however, there is a trend to cope with negative externalities in a more market based way, for example, by increasing fuel costs and introducing tolls or road-pricing systems. Such measures might also be carried out by private instead of public companies however, since there is in principle a direct user charge for the operator of the infrastructure.

Finally, there is the *ethics and justice argument*; an obvious example is the provision of non-profitable public transport, because the government wants to provide a minimum mobility level for everyone at reasonable fares. In this respect, there is again a clear trend towards a market based provision, by using franchising contracts in order to link social policies to efficiency incentives (see Section 5.2).

It may be concluded that there are still reasons for governments to intervene in the transport sector, especially for environmental reasons and in order to integrate markets by constructing infrastructure. However, the necessity for governments to intervene has been reduced because of the above discussed factors. As mentioned above, there is at the same time a growing awareness of government failures, which will be reviewed next.

3.3 Government Failures

When the government intervenes in the market, the market mechanism will be (partly) replaced by a budget mechanism which has its own rules. These may lead to a suboptimal (that is, too high) level of intervention, because of two important reasons (Frey 1983):

- civil servants have their own goals and utility functions;
- decision making is influenced by lobby and pressure groups.

These two arguments will now briefly be discussed. Civil servants may have a utility function, which differs from the societal function; this may lead to a suboptimal allocation of funds. An example is the budget maximization theory, which takes for granted that the utility function of civil servants correlates positively with the public budget they have at their disposal. Since the civil servant has a monopoly position in the provision of information to parliament, he will supply information with the intention that the intervention level is higher than in the societal optimal situation. See for a graphical presentation Figure 10.1, in which a simple situation is presented with linear curves and without fixed costs. In this figure the level of intervention corresponds with the budget of the civil servant.

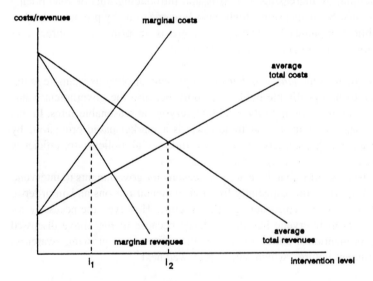

Figure 10.1 The intervention level under a budget maximizing civil servant

If Parliament would have full information, it would choose the intervention level at which the marginal costs would equal the marginal revenues, which corresponds with an intervention level of i_1, which is optimal. A civil servant may however, provide only information about the total costs, and as a result, Parliament may decide to intervene at (somewhat left of) the point where the average total costs equal the average total revenues, which corresponds with intervention level i_2. This is optimal for the civil servant since it maximizes his budget, but it is suboptimal from a societal point of view.

Also pressure groups may increase the level of intervention. Groups in society differ in power and strength: labour unions and employer organizations for example are well organized, while consumers and tax payers do not have powerful pressure groups. By negotiating, the most powerful groups may gain advantages at the expense of the less powerful ones. For each intervention measure the costs per individual (consumer, tax payer) may be so low and unclear that it is not rational to resist the measure (like minimum prices, protection measures, and so on).

Disadvantages of intervention in general are that the market allocation is disturbed, while a non-transparent and complicated legislation may be introduced, which may affect the possible allocation gains of public intervention. As a result of these factors the management of infrastructure by the public sector leads almost per definition to efficiency losses. For transport infrastructure this may have three major impacts:

- the *price* asked for using the infrastructure may be *too low*, for example, to satisfy car users (who are a powerful pressure group) and to maximize subsidies (budgets);
- *inefficiencies* in construction and maintenance of the infrastructure may emerge, because of lack of market incentives;
- *construction of (unprofitable) infrastructure* may take place, in order to satisfy pressure groups and to maximize budgets.

It is clear that a tradeoff has to be made between the costs of government intervention and the benefits because of the improved allocation, or in Coasean terms, between the transaction costs of market and public allocative regimes.

When government decides to intervene, this should be done in the most efficient way. It may be clear that in many cases market based intervention, in which the private sector takes care of the provision, may lead to lower transaction costs than in the case of public provision. In this context, it should be acknowledged that equity considerations are also important.

In order to analyse the extent to which private provision of infrastructure is possible, we will in the next section discuss infrastructure from a viewpoint of a private investor.

4.   INFRASTRUCTURE AS A PRIVATE GOOD

4.1   Introduction

In the development and construction of infrastructure, four stages may be distinguished which are important for investors. The first is the R&D stage, in which the idea and the technical features of a project are developed. This stage is followed by the financing stage in which financiers become interested, while the profitability of the project should also be analysed. The next stages are those of construction and exploitation.

The R&D stage is mainly a technical one, in which infrastructure is developed, investigated and tested. It is also important, however, that economic factors like market potential will be considered. A political decision has to be made about the introduction as well. The outcome of this stage is supposed to be a given fact in the remaining part of this section. Most attention will be paid to the financing stage, because this is the stage at which economic possibilities have to be analysed.

4.2   The Financing Stage

Four issues may be important in the financing stage, which may to a large extent influence the possibilities of a market provision; in principle these may hold for all investments. These are the characteristics of investments in infrastructure, the risks involved, the expected costs and the expected revenues of the project.

Characteristics of investments in infrastructure
Most investment costs of a project are normally made when infrastructure is constructed; the other costs (for example, rolling stock) form a smaller part of the total costs. According to Emanuel (1991) about 80 percent of the costs of a newly realized project consist of construction costs. For society, the infrastructure costs are even more important because the external costs of the construction and the operation are mainly discussed during the decision procedures about the construction and site of the infrastructure.

Investments in infrastructure may differ from competing investments such as immoveables and capital goods in several ways (Nijkamp and Rienstra 1995). Especially high investment costs and the long construction and planning periods may make an investment very unattractive for a private investor, because in the beginning of a project a lot of capital is needed while the payback period is very long. As a result the interest costs are very high at the beginning of a project, while the cashflow and the return on investments are low. In most cases there are no revenues at all before the operation starts. When it starts, the profits tend to increase over time, because more repayments are made, which reduce the interest costs. The problem is that these high profits and revenues often start decades after the initial investment, which make the uncertainty and the risks of infrastructure projects very high.

In practice, however, it is possible that there is no profit at all (Nijkamp and Rienstra 1995). The construction costs of infrastructure are (up to a certain level of demand/transport) fixed costs; the other costs are partly fixed and partly variable. From this it follows that compared to competing investments fixed costs in infrastructure are very high for an investor, while variable and marginal costs are relatively low. When the price in this case is set according to the marginal costs, it is often not possible to make a satisfactory return on investments.

Another important factor is the planning procedure. Often first a political decision is taken in which private financing is already assumed, and next a private investor has to be found. This gives private investors a competitive advantage in negotiations with public agencies.

Risks of investments in infrastructure

Risks are included in all kinds of investments, but for investments in infrastructure these are particularly high. This is the result of the long payback period, which makes it difficult to make good estimations.

The political risks are the most important difference compared to alternative investments, however (see also Section 4.4). In practice, governments always wish to influence the planning of infrastructure, because of the important positive and negative external effects and the national importance of high quality infrastructure (see Section 2). There is always also a danger of changes in laws or new regulations or even nationalization, since a change in transport policy may influence the charges which can be asked as well as the competition by other modes.

In conclusion, the risks of infrastructure investments are very high compared with alternative investment opportunities; this in turn makes these investments unattractive for private investors, therefore a high risk compensation is needed. In theory, this compensation should be given on the basis of high profit expectations, as can also be shown from recent tunnel projects in the Netherlands. Another possibility, however, is that the government guarantees (part of) the revenues in one way or another, or makes the investment attractive in a different way (for example, by tax exemptions).

The expected investment costs

Expected costs and revenues are of course important for the calculation of the return on investments. It appears, however, to be very difficult to estimate the costs of construction of major infrastructure projects. These projects are often much more expensive than estimated; well known examples are the Channel Tunnel, High Speed Train sections and the Betuwe freight railway line in the Netherlands. This problem arises especially when the project is a completely new transport mode or when new technologies are used. Then many costs are not known at the outset of the project and the estimates appear to be too low in almost all cases (Rienstra et al. 1996).

Also important as causes of rising costs are relatively expensive solutions, chosen to cope with resistance in society, for example, to avoid external effects (this may lead for example, to (half) subterranean infrastructure and noise shields). It is however very important that the cost estimates are made on a reliable basis. Otherwise it will be impossible to assess the economic viability of the project. And if no return on investment can be calculated, private investors might withdraw.

The expected revenues

To calculate the possible revenues of a project several issues are noteworthy, which are important mainly for the transport mode(s) which use(s) the infrastructure at hand. First, an assessment of the market in which the mode will operate is important. Therefore, the (sub)market(s) aimed at should be analysed. These submarkets can be distinguished according to the residential zones of clients, their destinations, the reasons for travelling, and so on. When, for instance, a project serves a mass transport mode, the price must be low, while the comfort, speed and service may be of lesser importance. When the project aims at the higher level business market, the speed, reliability, service and comfort are very important, while the price may be set somewhat higher. The latter is of course also dependent on the prices of competing modes.

Next, it is important to quantify the submarkets the mode is aiming at. The alternatives for the traveller must be analysed in light of the criteria which determine the choice. When this is known the mode may be constructed and exploited in the most competitive way. It is also important to consider the changes that are expected in the submarket(s) in the future. Several issues regarding future transportation use may be distinguished (Nijkamp et al. 1994):

- *demographic factors*; for example declining population density in urban areas, the age structure, migration, labour participation, decline in working hours, and so on;

- *political factors*; for example, the European integration, the opening up of new markets in Eastern Europe, the transport and environmental policy of the government and/or municipalities, and so on;
- *socioeconomic factors*; for example, economic growth, growth of and changes in trade flows, spread of production, the development of trade blocks, and so on;
- *technical factors*; for example, the emergence of new competing transport modes, improvements of existing modes and telecommunications, and so on.

When this is analysed, the number of travellers can be estimated. In this case it is important to investigate uncertainty about these estimates, especially because these have to be made for the long term. It is especially crucial to analyse to what extent demand depends on characteristics of the infrastructure (which may be influenced) and on external factors (which cannot be influenced). Next, the optimal price can be set; eventually there may be price differentiation in one way or another, to reach different submarkets.

For total revenues it may also be important to generate revenues other than those which are directly related to transportation. Catering on long distance travel and tax-free shopping at airports are well known examples of indirect revenues. But there may also be other possibilities. For example, railway stations are popular sites for several companies like bookshops, snackbars, flower shops, travel agencies and so on. Another possibility for generating revenues is a development based on the value of the locations around transport terminals, which may arise after the construction of, for example, a new railway station. The question here is of course whether it is possible for the investor to receive (part of) these revenues.

When all revenues are known, the expected revenues for the investor may be calculated for the long run.

4.3   The Construction and Exploitation Stage

When the financiers of a project (private and/or public) are identified and the procedures are completed, the construction of the project can start. It is at this stage very important that the costs are kept under control, because this often causes a lot of problems (as with, for example, the Channel Tunnel). It appears that often the costs of construction are higher than expected, or certain financial items have been neglected. It is also important that the construction contracts are clear as to who pays for excess costs; this often leads to conflicts, which can also have economic implications (for example, delays, higher costs).

Reducing annoyance to local people during the construction is essential, especially when the construction takes place in densely populated areas. When the annoyance is high, the resistance in society against the construction will be high, which may cause delays.

When the transport mode is relatively new, it will have to work hard to obtain its share of the transport market. In most cases new modes will have to find a new niche in the market first, while later they may also start to compete with existing transport modes. A good marketing strategy is very important to obtain a profitable market share. It is common practice that ticket prices have to be relatively low at the beginning, in order to attract new travellers and to give users of alternative modes an incentive to shift. Later on the charge may be raised towards the economic (or social) optimal level.

4.4 Current Trends and Lessons from Existing Projects

Since 1945 almost all infrastructure has been financed and operated by governments or by public organizations tied to the government. Especially in the case of railways, there is at present a trend to separate the financing and operation of infrastructure, as is the case in Sweden, Switzerland and the United Kingdom (Hannson and Nilsson 1991; Nash 1993). In this model, the management and financing of infrastructure is the responsibility of government, while the operation takes place on a private basis, where the operator imposes user charges. In this situation there may be several suppliers of transport services, which allows competition. This model corresponds with recent EU regulations and is proposed or under discussion in several countries (Germany, Italy, the Netherlands).

Road (and waterway) infrastructure is mostly the responsibility of the public sector, however, although there are in several countries discussions about introducing toll or road pricing systems.

It is noteworthy that in recent years several projects have been financed and exploited (partly) privately (Nijkamp and Rienstra 1993). This concerns car traffic projects, like toll roads (France, Italy) and several tunnels and bridges (for example, the Mont Blanc tunnel, Dutch tunnels, the Dartford bridge), but also rail projects like the TGV-Sud-Est and the Channel Tunnel. Public intervention in these projects is, however, still relatively high. Even the Channel Tunnel, which is said to be a private sector initiative, would not have been constructed without a significant indirect support by the governments concerned (Marcou 1993). Intercity rail traffic is in some countries profitable, and is therefore not subsidized by the government (UK, Sweden, Switzerland). Local and regional traffic are almost everywhere exploited at big losses. Regional rail traffic and public road transport are subsidized in most European countries, as is the case with local transport modes.

As discussed above, it is very important that traffic flows have a critical mass, and hence projects which reduce the importance of barriers (borders and natural barriers) are relatively often privately financed. It should be acknowledged that often the most profitable links are financed privately, but that the remainder of the network, which adds to the profits of the private investor, is financed by the public sector. One of the main reasons for this trend may be the budget problems of most European governments.

It should be added that in several cases the government appeared not always to be a reliable partner. This may be an important failure factor for future projects, since this increases perceived political risks. Examples are interventions of the government after the success of the Mont Blanc tunnel and the Cofi route. The government obliged investors to finance new infrastructure with the unexpected high profits they had made out of these projects. As a result, public investors may feel that governments add new conditions to the contract when their profits are high, but when a project is not profitable the private investor(s) may have to face the burden (for example, the Channel tunnel).

It may be concluded, however, that there is a clear trend towards governments stepping back and of an increasing influence of the private sector in the operation and financing of transport infrastructure.

5. PRIVATE PROVISION IN PRACTICE

5.1 General Conditions

As discussed above there is a clear privatization trend in society. The arguments for government intervention have become less important, while any case of public intervention is often conducted in a market based way. Therefore, privatization of infrastructure may be an interesting option.

One of the arguments against privatization is that the government may attract loans at lower interest rates than the private sector; public financing and operation is cheaper because no risk premium is needed. There are however two reasons which may make this argument less valid.

First, this argument holds for all investments, so that – when argued consistently – the government should finance or guarantee all investments. The reason that this is not the case is – as a second argument – that the private sector may provide the infrastructure in a cheaper way, which may compensate the higher interest costs. It is questionable, of course, whether this also holds for investments in transport infrastructure.

As argued in Nijkamp and Rienstra (1995), two conditions have to be met for private financing possibilities:

- the private investor should take the risks of the investment (at least to a large extent);
- user charges should be levied.

The first condition is, for example, not met when the government provides guarantees for the payback of loans. When the government guarantees loans, it runs the risks instead of the private investor, while possible additional revenues are handed over to the private investor. In this way there are also less incentives to provide the infrastructure efficiently. In conclusion, such a model is not economically feasible and is therefore in the long run unattractive for governments.

Next, levying user charges, for example, by introducing toll or road pricing, is also a necessary condition. An alternative is that government compensates the investor from the public budget, for example, by providing a revenue per passing car. In this case, however, government accepts long term obligations, while the private investor will ask a considerable risk premium. Therefore, the costs for the government will be much higher than with public financing, while the government still pays for the project out of the public budget. From this argumentation, it may be concluded that private financing is only feasible when there are considerable revenues from user charges. Private operation and management is therefore a sine qua non for private financing, while this relationship does not hold in the opposite direction.

Private financing constructions, which do not meet the above mentioned conditions, are sometimes politically very attractive, however, because funding of the investment can be postponed, while the public control over the infrastructure is not reduced.

5.2 Cooperation between the Public and Private Sectors

It may be clear that in theory transport infrastructure may be provided by the private sector. In practice however, the influence of governments tends to be high, not only because of the strategic importance and the specific characteristics of infrastructure, but also because of various environmental and equity issues involved. As a result, private financing and operation in practice faces many problems. Therefore, joint ventures may be an interesting option by combining the advantages of both regimes. In such joint undertakings the above mentioned conditions should of course be met, while market incentives should be introduced to a maximum extent in order to achieve an efficient management and to reduce the transaction costs of infrastructure provision.

In many cases private sector involvement tends to be introduced by franchising (Andersen 1995; Nash 1993). A franchise can be defined as a contract between a transport authority (the franchiser) and a private company (the franchisee), by which the latter obtains the right to operate a transport system. Under a conventional franchise contract, the franchisee pays the franchiser for using his property rights. In the case of transport infrastructure, this situation may be reversed: the transport authority may compensate the private company for an expected operational deficit. These franchise contracts may be allocated by means of tendering. There may be two different kinds of contracts: a given transport system is transferred to the company which offers to operate it at the lowest costs or the contract is transferred to the company which offers the best transport system for a given budget. The following management constructions may be introduced (Gidman et al. 1995):

- *affermage*; the government controls the formal regulations, but contracts out the operation (as is the case in some countries for rail infrastructure);
- *leasing* the infrastructure; this may however not meet the above discussed conditions;
- *build, own and operate* (BOO); in this model the private investor gets the concession and will become the legal owner of the infrastructure;
- *build, operate and transfer* (BOT); this system is similar to BOO, but at the end of a prespecified period the right to operate the infrastructure is transferred to a public authority; this is the option which is most often used in practice (for example, Dartford bridge, Channel Tunnel).

6. CONCLUSIONS

The trends towards liberalizing European and global markets, as well as the reduced efficiency of traditional policy instruments, have led to increasing attention to transport infrastructure. In this respect it is important that not only the 'hardware' and 'software' are considered as direct and clear success factors, but that also 'orgware', 'finware' and to a lesser extent 'ecoware' are taken into account. It should be acknowledged that the latter three factors are also of critical importance for the economic structure, the welfare and well-being of countries, regions and their citizens.

In orgware, current trends indicate increasing attention to market incentives, in order to improve the competitive position vis-à-vis other countries, while reasons for government intervention have become less valid. It is clear, however, that infrastructure – and the transport sector – cannot be left entirely to the competence of the private sector, because of the large number of externalities involved and because of equity reasons. Public intervention is therefore still necessary, although a tradeoff has to be made because of the high transaction costs of intervention (government failures). When government decides to intervene, market based measures may be most efficient, which may not hamper privatization.

It is clear that privatizing infrastructure – first in the operation (orgware), and second also in financing (finware) – may lead to efficiency gains, while at the same time other policy objectives (environment, tax level, government deficits) may be served.

In practice however, there are several problems which call for a solution. For example, it is important that the costs of construction and exploitation of infrastructure are well estimated. In this respect, it is also important that the calculations are consistent and do not underestimate real costs, as is often the case. The same holds for the expected use of infrastructure, since this is often information which is not available to private investors. Besides direct revenues, the generation of indirect revenues might be important, in order to reach an acceptable return on investment.

To attract investors, the risks have to be reduced to a maximum extent, taking into account the above discussed factors. These risks follow especially from the long payback period and the associated political risks. Reducing these risks may be (partly) a task of government, therefore joint ventures may also be attractive.

It may be concluded, therefore, that several modes of privatizing infrastructure may provoke various practical problems. On the other hand a more intensive involvement of the private sector may be essential for enhancing the competitive position of countries and regions, without having negative impacts on other relevant policy objectives.

REFERENCES

Andersen, B. (1995), 'Franchising alternatives for European transport', in Banister, D., R. Capello and P. Nijkamp, *European Transport and Communication Networks*, Chichester: John Wiley, pp. 221–47.

Aschauer, D.A. (1993), 'Is public expenditure productive?', *Journal of Monetary Economics* **23**, pp. 177–200.

Bruinsma, F.R. (1994), *De Invloed van Transportinfrastructuur op Ruimtelijke Patronen van Economische Activiteiten*, PhD thesis, FEWEC, Amsterdam: Free University.

Bruinsma, F.R. and P. Rietveld (1993), 'Infrastructure and metropolitan development: a European comparison', in Leeuw, A. de and H. Priemus (eds),

Bodenpolitik und Infrastruktur, Forschungen der Europäischen Fakultät für Bodenordnung, Strassburg, Frankfurt am Main: Peter Lang, pp. 35–57.

Button, K. and D. Pitfield (eds) (1991), *Transport Deregulation: An International Movement*, Basingstoke: Macmillan.

Coase, R.H. (1988), *The Firm, the Market and the Law*, Chicago/London: The University of Chicago Press.

Emanuel, J.D. (1991), 'Ultra light mass transit; today's costs and environmental breakthrough in mass transit and people movers', research paper.

Fokkema, T. and P. Nijkamp (1994), 'The changing role of governments: the end of planning history?', *International Journal of Transport Economics* **21**, no. 2, pp. 127–45.

Frey, B.S. (1983), *Democratic Economic Policy: A Theoretical Introduction*, Oxford:Basil Blackwell.

Gidman, P., I. Blore, J. Lorentzen and P. Schuttenbelt (1995), 'Public–private partnerships in urban infrastructure services', *UMP–Working Paper Series*, no. 4, UNDP/UNCHS/World Bank-UMP, Nairobi.

Hannson, L. and J.E. Nilsson (1991) 'A new Swedish railroad policy: separation of infrastructure and traffic production', *Transportation Research* **25A**, no. 4, pp. 153–59.

Marcou, G. (1993), 'Public and private sectors in the delivery of public infrastructure: the case of the Channel Tunnel from an international perspective', *Environment and Planning C* **11** (1), pp. 1–18.

Nash, C. (1993), 'Rail privatisation in Britain', *Journal of Transport Economics and Policy* **27**, (3), pp. 317–22.

Nijkamp, P. and S.A. Rienstra (1993), 'Private sector involvement in financing transport infrastructure: a historical sketch, current practice and some lessons', *FEWEC-Research Memorandum 1993–67*, Amsterdam:Free University.

Nijkamp, P. and S.A. Rienstra (1995), 'Private sector involvement in financing and operating transport infrastructure', *Annals of Regional Science* **29**, no. 2, pp. 221–35.

Nijkamp, P., J.M. Vleugel, R. Maggi and I. Masser (1994), *Missing Transport Networks in Europe*, Aldershot:Avebury.

Rienstra, S.A., P. Rietveld, M.T.A. Hilferink and F.R. Bruinsma (1997), 'Road infrastructure and corridor development', in Kim, T.J., L. Lundqvist and L.G. Mattson, *Network Infrastructure and the Urban Environment*, Berlin: Springer Verlag.

Rienstra, S.A., J.M. Vleugel and P. Nijkamp (1996), 'Options for sustainable passenger transport; an assessment of policy choices', *Transportation Planning and Technology* **19**, pp. 221–33.

Seitz, H. (1993), 'A dual economic analysis of the benefits of the public road network', *Annals of Regional Science* **27**, no. 2, pp. 223–39.

11. Partnerships and Responsibilities in Transport: European and Urban Policy Priorities

David Banister, Bernard Gérardin and José Viegas

---

1. INTRODUCTION

The expansion of the European Union (EU) to fifteen nations in January 1995 and the further links with the countries of the old East European block will result in new and extended patterns of transport demand. Three principal unresolved questions remain as to the future development of transport infrastructure investment:

- The priorities for investment in the Trans European Networks in terms of the types of projects (for example, road, rail or air), the location of those projects (for example, in the core or peripheral areas), and the timing of those investments.
- The means by which those projects selected should be funded, either by the public sector or by the private sector, or through some partnership between the two sectors. It is in this latter category that most attention needs to be placed.
- Cities have to continue to develop as vibrant and attractive places in which to live and work. A joint public-private commitment to keep traffic volumes under agreed thresholds would help achieve this objective, but this partnership needs to be established in advance and followed consistently over a period of time.

Two key problems are investigated in this chapter. One covers the means by which the transport infrastructure can be financed through new partnerships and the other concerns the appropriate allocation of responsibilities between the private and public sectors. Within the context of recent policy changes, the chapter argues that priorities and decision making must move away from national concerns towards pan-European priorities, particularly if the full benefits of the Single Internal Market are to be realized. It also explores the possibilities for public-private partnership in transport infrastructure networks. Similar partnerships in the development of interchanges and terminals have a much clearer history and the case for private sector involvement is much stronger (Banister et al. 1995). The final part focuses on the urban scale and the means by which public and private actors in the transport sector can take responsibility for meeting targets through demand management.

Two basic types of partnership are identified. Constructive or expansive partnerships concern the large scale investment priorities which involve putting together substantial financial packages with considerable risks. These take place mainly at the European level. Managerial partnerships involve many different actors, where the concern is to manage access to the existing infrastructure and services in situations where there is excessive demand. These take place mainly at the urban level. There seems to be a tremendous opportunity for action at all levels of decision making in transport with the full involvement of the public and private sectors, provided that priorities are set and followed consistently over a period of time.

2. TRANS EUROPEAN NETWORKS IN TRANSPORT

There is a long history of engagement of private companies in transport. Many of the original roads and railways in Europe were built and run by the private sector, but more recently the provision of transport infrastructure and services has been seen as a public monopoly with welfare objectives taking precedence over profits to the operator and investor. However, in the 1990s the priorities have again changed with pressure on public budgets, concern over waste and the need to encourage new forms of financing. There has been a move towards liberalization of transport markets and the privatization of transport services. Most recently, there has been a clear priority at all levels to fully involve the private sector in all forms of transport provision and operation.

The Trans European Networks (TEN) consist of 54,000 km of road, of which about 40,000 km is in use at present. This means that 14,000 km is to be completed by 2002, and a further 5,000 km needs to be upgraded at a total cost of over ECU 120 billion (CEC 1993a). The provision of a 30,000 km high speed network of railways in Europe would cost about ECU 100 billion (1988). Spread over 20 years, this amounts to about 0.3 percent of Gross Domestic Product (GDP) and 2 percent of the total investment of EU countries (Gérardin 1990). However, investment in transport infrastructure has been falling from 1.5 percent of GDP in 1975 (ECU 20.4 billion) to 0.8 percent in 1990. During this period, annual economic growth in the EU was 2.6 percent in real terms, the growth in passenger travel was 3.1 percent per annum and the growth in freight traffic was 2.3 percent per annum.

The cycle of production and consumption in the transport sector has been broken. Growth in demand (consumption) is often short term and relates closely to GDP and levels of individual affluence. The investment cycle (production) is longer term and requires a commitment over a substantial period of time.

The problems of transport infrastructure and its funding have been given a higher profile within the EU as special funds and guarantees have been allocated to new projects which promote European integration. In Europe, these issues are now a major concern with respect to the Trans European Networks (TEN) which are to be constructed across all European Union countries. The Edinburgh Council (December 1992) set up a new European Investment Fund (EIF) to help fill the missing links in the European network. The European Investment Fund (EIF) is a new financial agency set up to provide guarantees to support medium and long term investment in two crucial areas for the development of the European economy, including the Trans European Networks and small and medium enterprises. It was established in June 1994 and is now open for business. It is a new and unique partnership in which the European Investment Bank and the European Union, through the Commission, cooperate with the banks and the financial institutions of the fifteen member states. Its headquarters are in Luxembourg.

The Edinburgh Council also extended the lending facility of the European Investment Bank (EIB). It will now be easier for the financial markets to back large infrastructure projects for Trans European Networks, including transport, telecommunications and energy projects. The EIB will contribute 40 percent of the EIF capital of ECU 2 billion, with the remainder coming from the EU (30 percent) and the private and public sectors (30 percent). It is estimated that the EIF could support investment projects up to ECU 20 billion, but normally, no more than 50 percent of the investment cost of any particular project. The EIF will seek to share risks with the financial intermediary funding the operation. For infrastructure projects, the EIF's guarantees may be very long term so that progress is actually made. Allocations may also be made for shorter term funding of construction and pre-construction periods.

Overall, there is an optimistic assumption of a very high gearing ratio of 10 to 1 (Banister 1993). Even with this substantial commitment from the EU, the levels of funding actually needed for the completion of the Trans European Networks are far greater than those proposed above. In the White Paper on Growth, Competitiveness and Employment (CEC 1993b), a firm commitment has been made to develop the Trans European Networks, and it is estimated that ECU 220 billion should be invested by 2002 – about ECU 30 billion per annum. New investment is not just required within the EU, but also more widely in the European Economic Area and the Central and East European Countries. The Christophersen Group suggested that additional finance could be raised through taking advantage of the EU's top credit rating. Even then, the first project would not start until early 1996. At the Corfu Summit (June 1994), little progress was made in financing the 32 large infrastructure projects, costing ECU 68 billion. The list of priority projects was reduced to 11.

The Christophersen Group finally came up with a new priority list of 14 projects at the Essen European Council (December 1994), together with comments on the obstacles to action (see Table 11.1). It was decided to eliminate obstacles on a project by project basis and also to address the problems of establishing a common regulatory framework. The selection procedure ensured that all projects were of common interest (for example, covered cross-border sections), were large in scale, were viable economically, were attractive to the private sector, contributed to economic and social cohesion objectives, and included environmental protection. The criteria for selection could make it difficult for projects to be implemented as transfrontier, large scale, high risk projects; all conspire against investment, particularly if the private sector is to be involved.

The total of funding requirements for the projects listed in Table 11.1 is ECU 91 billion, and all projects had to begin work by the end of 1996. The Essen Council also adopted the main conclusions of the Christophersen Group concerning the Central and East European Countries. The European Council has confirmed the importance of cooperation with neighbouring countries to connect the Trans European Networks with Central and East European transport networks. Priority is given to rail and road links between

- Berlin–Warsaw–Minsk–Moscow (rail and road);

and further projects have been selected:

- Dresden–Prague (rail and road);
- Nuremberg–Prague (road);
- Fixed link across the Danube (rail and road) between Bulgaria and Romania;
- Helsinki–St Petersburg–Moscow (rail and road);
- Trieste–Ljubljana–Budapest–Lvov–Kiev (rail and road).

Table 11.1 Transport priority projects agreed at Essen

Project	Funding
High Speed Rail	
Brenner Axis	Open financial plans
Paris–Brussels–Cologne–Amsterdam–London	Private–public partnership
Madrid–Barcelona–Perpignan	Open financial plans
TGV Est: Paris–Strasbourg–Karlsruhe	Public finance
Lyon–Turin	Open financial plans
West Coast Main Line in UK	Open financial plans
Conventional Rail	
Rotterdam–Betuwe	Private–public partnership
Cork–Dublin–Belfast–Larne–Stranraer	EU grants, Cohesion motives
Combined Road and Rail	
Nordic Triangle	Open financial plans
Oresund Fixed Link	User charges with government guarantees
Road	
Ireland–UK–Belgium	Private-public partnership
Lisbon–Valladolid	EU grants, Cohesion motives
Greek Motorways	EU grants, Cohesion motives
Air	
Malpensa Airport, Milan	Private–public partnership

The EIB is being encouraged to give priority to these 14 projects and to start negotiations with member states, the promoters of the projects and the private sector. There is a particular interest in the full involvement of the private sector in all of these projects so that they can take a full share of the risks. This involvement is important, as the funding available from the EIB is limited in total and by the requirement for matching funding from other sources. These projects being promoted may be the most important for the EU, as they cover all EU countries and achieve objectives such as integration and cohesion. But for the private sector, they may be of less interest as they do not have the lowest levels of risk and uncertainty, nor do they necessarily have the highest rates of return. The whole success of the 14 projects depends on the public and private funding available from national and international sources, and it is this issue which is likely to determine the success or failure of the strategy.

Agreement has also been reached on the means to extend the EIB's lending facility set up at the Edinburgh Summit, and this will now cover both the EU and the CEEC countries as well as Scandinavia, the Mediterranean area and the Trans Alpine crossings. This greater flexibility in lending includes:

- provision of longer maturities and longer capital grace periods to match capital debt requirements to the cashflow characteristics of the projects;
- provision of refinancing facilities to the banks at the outset of a project;
- provision of financing of interest during construction, fixing of loan rates and credit lines provided that certain commitments are reached;
- involvement of the EIB at the earliest possible stage of the financial and contractual structuring of the project to agree the best financial arrangements;
- extension of the EIB's eligibility criteria.

In addition to the problems of funding, the decision process itself has become more complex as the number of actors in the process has increased. Previously, there had only been local, regional and national influence, but now there are community wide factors and a variety of new funding sources. The linking of networks across international boundaries will complicate the planning process and this in turn may reduce the attractiveness to the private sector of these investment opportunities. It is to these issues that we now turn.

3. CONSTRUCTIVE PRIVATE–PUBLIC PARTNERSHIPS

Most transport projects in the recent past have been funded by the public sector as they are large in scale, involve a high risk and have long payback periods. The private sector has only shown real interest where it has some degree of a monopoly position (for example, in road bridges across estuaries) or where the public sector has underwritten much of the risk in the project (for example, the European high speed rail system). However, public budgets have increasingly come under pressure and transport budgets in particular have been easy to cut as their immediate effects are not apparent. It takes many years for underinvestment in both capital and maintenance to manifest itself in terms of lower standards of service reliability and reductions in safety standards. It is also unrealistic to expect this situation to change, at least in the short term, so there must be a greater involvement of the private sector in partnership with the public sector. For the EU countries, the Maastricht Treaty has defined the limitations for budget deficits and there is now a consensus among member states that the stabilization of pressure on income tax and social security contributions is a key element in maintaining the competitiveness of a single market.

The problems of involving the private sector in transport infrastructure projects are well known (Banister et al. 1995; Gérardin 1990, 1993, 1995), and they are summarized in Table 11.2. In addition to the central question of risk, transport projects have themselves proved difficult to assess. Levels of demand have been difficult to predict accurately, there are often substantial cost overruns, and they have aroused considerable public opposition to their construction (for example, TGV Méditerranée). There is also the important problem of perception as transport infrastructure has been traditionally considered as a free good, particularly at the point of delivery. To compensate for the high levels of risk and uncertainty, the private sector is looking for higher levels of return, typically 12–15 percent. Very few transport projects fall into this category as most of these high return links have already been built (Gomez Ibanez and Meyer 1995).

Table 11.2 Summary of the risk elements in transport infrastructure projects as perceived by the private sector

1. Long periods between the start of the investment and financial returns to investors – negative cashflows during both the construction and initial operating phases (5–10 years).
2. Irreversibility of the investment, often involving substantial sunk costs – it is costly to withdraw from a project once it has been started.
3. Financial returns do not flow until the whole infrastructure is completed.
4. Political influences are still manifest in the production of transport goods and services – uncertainty increased through delays from political, legislative or environmental interventions.
5. Long amortization periods in transport projects when loan repayments are required over a much shorter period – the life spans of many transport projects range from 20 to over 100 years.

In addition there are the political uncertainties. For example, the level and legitimacy of toll collection may be jeopardized by inappropriate action from the politicians, as in the case of the concession for the second Tagus crossing in Lisbon in the summer of 1994 (Viegas 1994). At this level it seems that the odds are stacked against the private sector being fully involved – there is no level playing field. In many countries and cities the dominant supply is through free access to infrastructure and subsidized operations, and there is protection against innovation or improvement in competing infrastructure or services, except if these are also carried out under concession agreements.

However, there are a series of privately funded projects which have either been completed in Europe, or are waiting to be built (see Table 11.3). These examples, together with jointly funded projects, are becoming more common, with the contractual agreements presenting the two sectors as reciprocally supportive. This corresponds to a creative concept by which both parties of the contract are recognized as complementary servers to the implicit third party, the public. Both the public and the private sectors have an important role to play in the construction, renewal and maintenance of the road, rail and air infrastructure. Much of the funding will remain the responsibility of the public sector and the planning process needs to be strengthened so that the full range of partnership possibilities can be realized (see Tables 11.4 and 11.5). This is what we term constructive or expansive partnerships between the public and private sectors where complex financial packages and risk sharing determine the exact nature of the agreement.

Table 11.3 *Examples of private sector funded road projects in the European Union*

Road Infrastructure Already Open	Road Infrastructure Under Construction or as Proposals
1. Mont-Blanc, St Bernard and Frejus Tunnels in the Alps 2. Cadi Pyennean Tunnel 3. Tunnel under the Schelde at Antwerp 4. Tancarville Bridge over the Seine estuary 5. Dartford Bridge over the Thames 6. Bridge on the Dublin Ring Road 7. Normandy Bridge over the Seine estuary 8. Tunnel in Marseilles (Prado–Carènage) 9. Second Severn Bridge	1. Bridge over the Great Belt in Denmark 2. North Birmingham Relief Road 3. Puymorens Tunnel 4. Toll roads and tunnels in Lyons

In addition, there are two other roles for the private sector. One has been in the US through the exaction of special real estate taxation based on the added value of land brought about by transport investments (Sussna 1991; Cervero and Landis 1995). The other is the creation in France in 1982 of the 'versement transport', a special tax paid by employers of 10 or more staff, based on their salary volume, to promote the presence of public transport. In each of these cases it has been argued that public transport has both direct and indirect benefits to the city, and that these benefits should be capitalized.

Table 11.4 Partnership possibilities between the private and public sectors for transport infrastructure investment

Function	Public Sector Model	Partnership Possibilities			Private Sector Model
		Type 1	Type 2	Type 3	
Planning	Public	Public	Public	Public	Private
Design	Public	Public	Private	Private	Private
Construction	Public	Private	Private	Private	Private
Operation	Public	Public	Private	Private	Private
Ownership	Public	Public	Public	Private	Private
Finance	Public	Mixed	Private	Private	Private
Risk	Public	Public	Joint	Private	Private

4. PARTNERSHIPS IN EUROPEAN TRANSPORT PROJECTS

As can be seen from Table 11.5, three different types of partnership have been identified. The involvement of the private sector increases with each example, but in each case the particular package has been negotiated so that the risks and uncertainties to the private sector are balanced against the potential returns. A case by case approach has to be developed, with the experience from the previous situation being used to influence subsequent outcomes – a case experience approach. There are no clear rules which can be used in all situations and negotiation must form the core of successful implementation with responsibilities being allocated to all parties.

4.1 TGV Financing – Type 1

Considerable debate is currently taking place on the question of balance of the risk between the public and private sectors. Many of the French TGV routes have been funded through loans from commercial banks and the EIB, but always with government guarantees.

Table 11.5   Examples of the different financing packages

	Examples	Possibilities	Comment
Public Sector Model	Traditional road and rail investment projects	Part of the debt can be passed onto users through tolls (as in Norway)	Hypothecation of revenues for further road or public transport investment
Partnership – Type 1	Funding of the TGV	Balance of risk crucial (>8% IRR means project is worthwhile, <8% requires state guarantee)	Speeds up investment process as state support or guarantees reduce risk to private sector
Partnership – Type 2	Birmingham Northern Relief Road – ECU 350 million	Level of shadow toll and expected increase in traffic crucial	Risk shared as private sector is paid by number of vehicles using road
Partnership – Type 3	Channel Tunnel Rail Link – ECU 3.4 billion	Packaged projects could be auctioned to the private sector. Links with associated development	Front end risk to private sector reduced and construction can be started sooner
Private Sector Model	Channel Tunnel – ECU 17 billion, with a 55 year private sector ownership period	Feasible where profits can service all debts and provide a return on equity capital	Role of public sector limited to supporting actions (e.g. enabling legislation) and negotiations over length of operating and ownership period

The French railways (SNCF) have the responsibility to develop the railways, but they also have a high credit rating as the government guarantees the loans. This means that interest rates are lower than commercial rates (typically 1–3 percent less), and high rates of return are not essential (as they would be with equity risk capital). In the short to medium term, SNCF can also run at a loss and pay no corporation tax. This means that it is easier to obtain financing for investment and that the TGV system can make a profit sooner than if it had been entirely financed from the private sector. SNCF carries short term debts (FF 150 billion in 1995) which would have placed a private sector company into liquidation.

Recently, the government has decided to support more directly new TGV route investments where the internal rate of return of the project is less than 8 percent and when the economic rate of return is sufficient. This new rule will be applied for the funding of the TGV Mediterrannée and TGV Est new links. This new policy is justified by the positive impact of these projects on regional planning. For the TGV Méditerranée the contribution of the national government will be about FF 4 billion (600 million ECUs). In the case of TGV Est, regional communities (Lorraine, Alsace and Ile-de-France) will also cofund the project. The contribution of the state is not yet known.

4.2   The Birmingham Northern Relief Road – Type 2

This road may be the first section of privately funded road in the UK, and it will duplicate a heavily congested section of the M6 to the north of Birmingham. Construction was to start in 1996, after a second public inquiry (see Table 11.6). The competition for the right to design, build, finance and operate the new road took place in 1989 and added two years to the development process. Although Midland Expressway Limited (MEL) have strong indications from the international financing community that the project will be financed, uncertainty over the public inquiry process together with the market conditions has meant that no finance has actually been committed as yet. The promoters (Trafalgar House and Iritecna) have funded all MEL's costs so far (Carlile 1994), and it will only be in 1995 that MEL will be clear as to whether the project can be funded.

A substantial part of the risk and the pre-construction costs have been transferred to the private sector, yet there is no guarantee that the finance will be available for the new road or whether construction will actually take place. This high level of uncertainty in a situation where the other conditions for private sector involvement are promising may suggest that this form of road building has limited prospects. As noted in Table 11.2, capital cost outlays are high at the beginning of any project, whilst the revenues only accrue over a long period after opening. There are also substantial sunk costs, and it is costly and difficult to reverse a decision once it has been made. Road projects require long amortization periods (53 years for the BNRR), and this contrasts with many private sector projects where payback periods are medium term (about 15 years).

In the UK, four other schemes are currently being promoted by the Department of Transport. In each case, the private sector will design, build, finance and operate (DBFO) the road for a period of 15 to 20 years. They will be paid a shadow toll by government according to the traffic using the road. The schemes are:

- the 19 mile, £190 million M1–A1 Yorkshire link road which bypasses Leeds and connects with the M1 and M62 south of Leeds and the A1 south of Wetherby;
- the £145 million widening of the A1 between Alconbury and Peterborough to bring it up to motorway standard;
- the £35 million, 34 mile A419/A417 trunk road between Swindon and Gloucester, including a bypass of Cirencester and dualling of existing roads between Stratton and Nettleton;
- the 53 mile management of the A69 between Carlisle and Newcastle, including a new £10 million bypass of Haltwhistle.

Table 11.6 The Birmingham Northern Relief Road

1980	Plans for the Birmingham Northern Relief Road (BNRR) announced.
1987	After extensive consultations, Draft Orders were published for a 53 km motorway from the M54 at Featherstone to the M6 near Coleshill.
1988	Public Inquiry held.
1989	The Government announced a competition to design, build, finance and operate (DBFO) the BNRR as the first purpose built inland tolled motorway in Britain.
1991	Midland Expressway Limited (MEL), a joint venture between Trafalgar House and Iritecna, was announced as the winner.
1992	A Concession Agreement signed for 53 years. The revised preferred route was published in March 1992.
1993	Draft Compulsory Purchase Orders authorizing the acquisition of land published.
1994	Objections heard at a Second Public Inquiry.
1996	Construction scheduled to commence.
1998	Road to be opened.

The total cost of the new road estimated at £270 million (1990 prices).

Source: based on Banister, Andersen and Barrett 1995

All of these schemes are relatively small and will not require extensive inquiry stages, and they may prove attractive to larger construction consortia. In addition, the UK government is discussing the possibility of widening key motorways with the DBFO being undertaken by the private sector. This will extend the private sector's role from that of construction to the management and maintenance of existing motorways. Contracts will be negotiated with the private sector receiving shadow tolls based on the number of vehicles using the road.

4.3   Channel Tunnel Rail Link – Type 3

Auctioning a prepared project reduces the uncertainty on time and costs as construction can begin immediately. The private sector has to make a bid to complete the final design and to finance, construct and operate the project. Fielding and Klein (1993) propose a clearing-before-awarding approach of this kind, and they suggest that it would reduce the perceived risk and hence the expected rates of return. The costs to the public sector for inquiries, environmental impact assessment and land acquisition may be lower than they would be to the private sector. It also allows both sectors to work together at achieving what each of them are best at. Public sector involvement is concentrated in the approving and awarding phases, so there is less possibility for political intervention and an assurance that all procedures are followed in full.

The 108 km high speed rail link from the Channel Tunnel portal at Cheriton, Kent to the St Pancras terminal in central London will cost £2.7 billion (ECU 3.4 billion at 1992 prices). This makes it the second most expensive civil engineering project in the UK after the Channel Tunnel itself. When completed in 2002, it will cut some 33 minutes from the journey between central London and the portal, reducing London-Paris train times to 2 hours 27 minutes and London-Brussels times to 2 hours 7 minutes.

Although there will be some limited government guarantees as part of the capacity of the line will be used to ease congestion on the existing commuter lines in south east London, it will be funded primarily by the private sector. A limited competition has been held between four private consortia and these bids were submitted to the UK Department of Transport on 15 March 1995. These consortia have now been reduced to two, Eurorail and the London and Continental Rail Company. This decision was based on how much government cash each consortium required to build the link, the level of risk they were prepared to take, and the evaluation of other non-transport and transport benefits from the link. The winner was announced in late 1995 and the London and Continental Rail Company won the competition.

The Channel Tunnel Rail Link is also being used to support a major urban development initiative in the Thames Gateway (formerly the East Thames Corridor). This is the largest redevelopment project in Europe, and it involves a corridor of new urbanization and regeneration, some 100 km in length on both sides of the Thames from London Docklands to the Isle of Sheppey in Kent. The link will have one or two stations along this corridor, and these points will be used as the basis for further private investment in commercial and related activities. It is the intention of government to redress the historic imbalance between the prosperous west London and the impoverished east London, which for the last 50 years has been exacerbated by the development of Heathrow airport to the west of the capital.

Much of the publicity has been given to the Trans European Networks and the prestige international transport projects, but the importance of smaller scale investment opportunities should not be overlooked. The private sector has been involved in promoting projects (see Table 11.3), and the problems here are somewhat different. It is not so much the need to raise large sums of capital, but the speed of the planning process, particularly the time for public consultations, land acquisition, the free rider problems and more recently the prospects of direct action. In each case the risks and uncertainties are increased and this again reduces private sector interest, particularly if there are other investment opportunities. The need for partnership is even more important.

5. MANAGERIAL PARTNERSHIPS

The examples identified above are all related to what could be called *constructive or expansive partnership*, since they involve the actions and resources of both public and private institutions for the construction or expansion of certain infrastructures.

But other types of public partnership have been surging, again involving actions and resources of public and private institutions, but this time with the aim of ensuring proper operation of certain infrastructures or urban systems. These can be called *managerial partnerships*, because they often include some element of managing access to the infrastructure or services when facing actual or potential excessive demand.

Whereas the word 'private' in the first type of partnerships inevitably means large financial or contractor companies, in the second it will most likely engage coalitions of citizens bound together by place of residence or of work.

5.1 Need to Contain Excessive Traffic Generation

Constraints on the size and nature of development are often based on estimates of trip generation by new developments. Experience over several decades in many cities shows that developers frequently manage to persuade authorities to exceed the previously set limits. But, even when those limits are respected, the type and intensity of occupancy of each building may vary with time, and mobility has been systematically growing at levels in excess of those anticipated (both for persons and for goods). The consequence is that total traffic generated is far above what can be digested by the planned infrastructure.

The responsibility of the developers has been limited to building what they are allowed to at one particular point in time, and the occupants (residents or firms located in the area) are never engaged in any form of 'responsibility' related to their mobility levels which will change over a longer period of time. So the planning errors of estimation are externalized to the whole community, through the mechanisms of traffic congestion, environmental pollution and accidents. The problem is not only a lack of integrated land use and transport planning, but also the development of new patterns of uses made by people and firms. Travel seems to expand to fill the space and time available to users, and the scale of these changes could not have been anticipated in the original plans. Many of the elements that make up the land use structure change over the longer term (30–40 years), but travel patterns change over a much shorter period of time.

New ways must be found to change perceptions of those living and working in the cities. The space around them must not be seen solely as the means to travel more, but a balance must be sought between the desire for mobility and the necessity to preserve the environment (Owens 1995). If the traffic generation factors per unit area are growing, an attitude of ecological preservation of that space would imply limiting the growth of those factors or reducing the areas with functions which generate such a high mobility profile.

5.2 New Formulas for Joint Responsibilities

Changes in attitudes of the main agents responsible for the urban transport infrastructure have been easier to achieve with respect to air pollution by traffic, rather than by traffic congestion itself. In the US, there are associations for the management of mobility, with the possibility of using Transport Demand Management (TDM) ordinances, to allocate 'responsibility' to firms for the mobility of their employee. More recently, the lasting contractual engagement of real estate developers in the mobility generated by their developments has been achieved. These measures present particular difficulties for enforcement, and there is a growing feeling that the problems of air quality might well be solved through the extensive application of new technologies and fuels to vehicles. The quality of air in many cities is improving, and this is mostly due to the replacement of older, very polluting cars and lorries. However, the longer term effects are less clear, particularly the increasing contribution of urban traffic to carbon dioxide emissions and the particular problem of particulates from diesel engines. Particulates are thought to be related to health problems, in particular asthma attacks and other kind of breathing problems.

The US also seems to be taking the lead in at least one other respect. The Adequate Public Facilities Ordinances (APFOs) limit the rate of construction of new developments to the existence of adequate facilities to accommodate the expected traffic. But, in accordance with American tradition, when dealing with limitations on private rights, public authorities must be able to demonstrate their good faith in solving existing problems. Even if the concept is positive, this is only applicable during the construction period, and it again relates to expected traffic, so we are back to the planning criteria (Freilich and White 1994). The difficulties should not be underestimated, and each move in the right direction helps. In some recent concession agreements in the US, the commercial risk for private investors has been limited through minimum and maximum allowed rates of return. The maximum rate receives a premium if prespecified environmental targets are achieved.

These examples confirm the underlying message that it is no longer acceptable to engage the responsibility of the private sector (particularly if on a significant scale) only at the input stage, where the land use and the employment decisions are taken. The new logic for public-private partnership must be extended to the control of the output of the jointly created system.

There must be some evidence of this enlargement of the nature and the evolution of the new role that private organizations now have, and this is in direct contrast with the traditional role as the suppliers of a service that strictly conforms to a public specification. The clear movement in many countries and cities towards a deeper level of local consultation in project approval has also led to the emergence of new interest groups, particularly in those of a greater environmental and ecological activism.

One interesting example of such an organization of different private interests – but all transport stakeholders of one type or another – is found in the Surface Transportation Policy Project (STPP). The STPP was formed with the explicit aim of developing a model transport policy with stated goals in the areas of sustainability, economic efficiency and equity (Dittmar and Bender 1994), and which has been effective in transferring its main recommendations into the fundamental new American transport legislation –

the Intermodal Surface Transportation Efficiency Act (ISTEA, see Paaswell 1995). The STPP has in the meantime been transformed into a non-profit coalition of many groups, and remains active in the discussion and surveillance of transport policy. The lesson from the US is that these interest organizations have an increasing role to play in achieving the appropriate balance between the private and public sectors, and between transport and other economic, equity and environmental priorities. It is also important to keep these organizations active so that they can continue to monitor ex post the success of specific projects, so that their experience can be used in subsequent decisions as partners in policy and project design.

5.3   Towards a New Structure for Public-Private Partnerships

This engagement of private interests in policy and project design has existed for some years, the main difference being that it has in the past been achieved through implicit processes, usually in the form of public relations and lobbying. Now it is totally assumed through explicit processes of open negotiation with formal recognition by the public sector. It must be noticed that the presence of private interests is not confined to environmentalist or local citizens' groups, and it is not uncommon to find real estate developers or engineering firms involved in the fine tuning of projects to which they have not yet acquired any guarantees of a future building permit, planning approval or contract. The main advantages and disadvantages of the open policy negotiation for the public and private sectors are given in Table 11.7.

Table 11.7 Advantages and disadvantages of open policy negotiations

	Political Bodies	Private Organizations
Advantages	Smaller risk of uncontrolled evolution of systems needing remedial action	Smaller risk of political decision, implying very high adaptation costs
Disadvantages	Longer time for decisions Complaints from private groups not invited to the discussion	Investment in negotiation process Loss of corporatist purity

This open policy negotiation process may seem to challenge the very foundations of democracy, where elected bodies are responsible for the definition of policies and decision making in the domain of the public interest. But, in reality, this already occurs. The vote of elected representatives is no longer accepted as good enough for the true representation of local interests, and direct consultation and action is a growing exigency. The proposal here is that the technical committees preparing the decisions on policy or projects incorporate a representation of private parties more susceptible of a direct interest in the project, or particularly suited to making a fair analysis or representation of general interests. These outline proposals would then be subject to the formal decision process, thus keeping the democratic legitimacy untouched.

If a wider and more informed vision is presented at the stage of policy or project conception, the final decision may be slower to achieve but the ultimate decision at a higher level will be easier to reach. The key point here is not the speed or ease of decision, but the level of engagement in the perception of the problems and in respect to the final decisions that will have been built into all the actors in the process. This new consensus will avoid one of the main weaknesses in present democratic societies, namely that too many people feel distant from the decisions and they tend to think twice before respecting them. From this argument, we are coming to a process of transport demand management for our cities which is defined and carried out over a longer period of time than that normally argued. The short term 'solutions' of pricing of the infrastructure are replaced by a longer term view of the vitality and liveability of the city. Pricing may form part of that vision, but so do management, control, planning and investment.

The idea is to engage in serious negotiation and commitment at the planning stage, especially in what concerns land use and transport demand forecasts and the construction of new infrastructure, particularly where it involves joint public-private control of the resulting transport infrastructure over time. The novelty lies in the fact that administration and private interests engaged in negotiation remain bound by contract in the commitment to keep those traffic volumes under the agreed thresholds, and thus they are partners in the search for solutions needed to achieve it. Those solutions can also include improvements to the transport supply, but the focus would often be on the containment of traffic growth and the preservation of the quality of life in the area.

It is also obvious that ways must be found to pass on this commitment to the actual residents, shopkeepers, employers and employees of the actual buildings constructed. Monitoring traffic volumes is essential, and some means to ration individual mobility must be devised, either through pricing, or through physical restraint, or through a combination of both. There will be technical difficulties in the implementation of change, and issues of privacy may emerge, but the Intelligent Transport Systems being developed have the potential to cover all these problems. In summary, the transition in transport demand management from the concept of road pricing to that of public-private controlled mobility is explained in Table 11.8.

Table 11.8 Transition to public–private controlled mobility

	Traditional Concepts	New Concepts
Key Concept	Authority	Negotiation and Joint Responsibility
Traffic Control Mechanism	Direct payment for access and use of congested roadways	Each person/household is entitled to a certain amount of car mobility per month, and must only pay for the excess consumption
Technological Implementation	Easier universal application	More difficult application at the individual/family level
Political Issues	Equity Against belief in free access to all public goods	Selection of private partners in negotiation phase Invasion of privacy in application

6. CONCLUSIONS

In the introduction we stated the two problems addressed in this chapter – the first concerned the need for new forms of partnerships and the second the appropriate allocation of responsibilities. We have outlined the concepts of constructive (or expansive) partnerships and managerial partnerships and have addressed the problems of infrastructure investment and management at both the European and the city levels, drawing certain parallels, but essentially treating them as two separate issues. The main problem with infrastructure investment at the European level has been the sharing of risk and the reduction in uncertainties for the private sector. The sums of capital required to finance the Trans European Network are substantial; and the private sector or the public sector on its own is not likely to be able to fund the proposed new and upgraded links. At the urban level, the capital sums involved are less but the difficulties come mostly from the presence of the dense road network to which there is free access. It is on the management dimension that new forms of partnership are being developed, that involve all interested parties at the earliest possible stage in the development and design of projects and policies, directly or indirectly related to traffic generation. The proposal made in this chapter is based on negotiation and joint responsibility.

In infrastructure investment, the traditionally clear distinction between the public and private sectors is now becoming less transparent. One convenient means to combine the advantages of the public and private sectors is to set up separate quasi independent semi public companies to mobilize public and private capital. The concession holder is responsible for building the infrastructure and providing all the investment funding, with the opportunity to operate the facility over a period of time to allow for the capital plus a profit to be realized. The length of the concession may vary, particularly if there are restrictions on the prices which can be charged for the use of the infrastructure. It is in the interests of the concession holder to negotiate as long a period as possible so that all possible profit can be exacted. At the end of the concession period, the ownership of the infrastructure returns to the public sector or a new concession is negotiated with the same or a different consortium.

New approaches to funding transport infrastructure in Europe are required. It is unrealistic to expect substantial increases in public expenditure, even when economic conditions allow. Transport infrastructure is a budget which can easily be cut as there is a considerable time lag before the effects are noticed. Partnership between the public and private sectors allows the particular expertises of both parties to be fully utilized, and it also allows investment to continue as a long term priority rather than subject to the short term fluctuations associated with the annual national budgets. The EU has a crucial role to play, both in setting up the appropriate financing mechanisms for these large scale projects (for example, through the European Investment Fund), and in promoting these new forms of partnership.

Similarly in urban transport management, it is recognized that the modern urban planning process, in spite of all the technical and financial efforts invested in it, has failed (at least in part). It has not been able to ensure the creation and preservation of cities with a good spatial distribution of activities and an efficient flow of people and goods. There is an emerging trend towards the engagement of private parties in the discussion and creation of policies, from which a new paradigm of demand management will emerge.

This paradigm would be based on the joint public-private commitment to keep traffic volumes in a certain area under thresholds agreed at the planning stage. This is in clear contrast with the current practices of leaving it to the authorities alone to take remedial action when the development of land use patterns and the demand for mobility exceed the capacity of the system. This commitment will then imply the continuation of that partnership, with some form of commonly accepted rationing plan, and the managed evolution of land use in the area, but it will also ensure an urban environment where traffic volumes are kept at sustainable levels.

REFERENCES

Banister, D. (1993), 'Investing in transport infrastructure', in Banister, D. and J. Berechman (eds), *Transport in a Unified Europe: Policies and Challenges*, Amsterdam: North Holland, pp. 347–68.

Banister, D., B. Andersen and S. Barrett (1995), 'Private sector investment in transport infrastructure in Europe', in Banister, D., R. Capello and P. Nijkamp (eds), *European Transport and Communications Networks: Policy Evolution and Change*, London: Belhaven, pp. 191–219.

Carlile, J.L. (1994), 'Private funding of public highway projects', *Proceedings of the Institution of Civil Engineers* **105**, February, pp. 53–63.

Cervero, R. and J. Landis (1995), 'Development impacts of urban transport: A US perspective', in Banister, D. (ed.), *Transport and Urban Development*, London: Chapman and Hall, pp. 136–56.

Commission of the European Communities (1993a), *Trans European Networks – Towards a Masterplan for the Road Network and Road Traffic*, CEC Directorate General for Transport, Report of the Motorway Working Group, Brussels.

Commission of the European Communities (1993b), *Growth, Competitiveness and Employment: The Challenges and Ways Forward into the 21st Century*, EU COM (93) 700 Final, Brussels.

Department of Transport (1993), *Paying for Better Motorways: Issues for Discussion*, London: HMSO, May.

Dittmar, H. and C. Bender (1994), 'Reinventing planning under ISTEA: transportation partnerships', *Transportation News* **175**, Nov–Dec., pp. 2–5.

Fielding, G.J. and D.B. Klein (1993), 'How to franchise highways?' *Journal of Transport Economics and Policy* **27** (2), pp. 113–30.

Frielich, R.H. and S.M. White (1994), 'The interaction of land use planning and transportation management: lessons from the American experience', *Transport Policy* **1** (2), pp. 101–15.

Gérardin, B. (1990), 'Private and public investment in transport: possibilities and costs', European Conference of Ministers of Transport, Round Table 81, Paris, Economic Research Centre, pp. 5–32.

Gérardin, B. (1993), 'Financing infrastructures and transport systems in Central and Eastern Europe', submission by the European Conference of Ministers of Transport to the 2nd Pan-European Conference on Transport, CEMT/CS **93** (43), Paris, September.

Gérardin, B. (1995), *Financing Infrastructures and Transport Systems in Central and Eastern Europe*, Report to the Council of Ministers of the European Conference of Ministers of Transport, Paris.

Gomez Ibanez, T. and J. Meyer (1995), 'Private toll roads in the United States: Recent experiences and prospects', in Banister, D. (ed.), *Transport and Urban Development*, London: Chapman and Hall, pp. 248–71.

Orski, C.K. (1995), 'Employee trip reduction programs: an evaluation', *Transportation Quarterly* **47** (3), pp. 327–41.

Owens, S. (1995), 'From "predict and provide" to "predict and prevent"? Pricing and planning in transport policy', *Transport Policy* **2** (1), pp. 43–9.

Paaswell, R. (1995), 'ISTEA: Infrastructure investment and land use', in Banister, D. (ed.), *Transport and Urban Development*, London: Chapman and Hall, pp. 36–58.

Sussna, S. (1991), 'Real estate development and transportation financing', *Transportation Quarterly* **45** (3), pp. 369–75.

Viegas, J. (1994), 'Portagens e Coerência', *Expresso* 20.8.94.

12. Public Transit Subsidy: From the Economics of Welfare to the Theory of Incentives

Daniele Fabbri

1. INTRODUCTION

A subsidy is the difference between production costs of a good and revenues from sales to final users. Its aim is to restore profitability in the production of a good, in order to make it available in quantities and qualities otherwise not provided by the normal functioning of the market. Therefore subsidization is deliberately performed by an agent in order to let some activities exist and grow.

Good reasons for subsidizing public transit have been repeatedly suggested by economists. Standard arguments are: economies of scale, second-best problems, redistribution in kind, option value, imperfect information. For all these reasons it might be socially useful to sustain the production of public transit. But to what extent should we provide this support? The standard welfarist approach gave answers which will be analysed in Section 2.

Among the several limitations of the standard welfarist approach we find that what makes it an 'outdated' framework is its complete disregard of organizational concerns. In Section 3 we show how these issues have been normatively treated by the former advocates of the standard welfarist approach and how relevant they are in terms of positive explanations of public firms' behaviour.

Once we explicitly introduce organizational issues we should, find new theoretical paradigms allowing another question to be answered: how to subsidize a public transit firm in order to reach some specific goals given that it has its own rationality? The theory of incentives provides such a paradigm. In Section 4 we provide a model of regulation that fits very well into the typical situations we face. Then, in the last section, it will be quite easy to analyse past and recent experiences of performance based subsidization.

2. THE STANDARD WELFARE ANALYSIS OF PUBLIC TRANSIT SUBSIDY

In the welfare approach the optimal level of subsidy is defined through a welfare calculus of costs and benefits. Its comprehensiveness is limited only by the extent that direct and indirect effects, which pass through final users of the transport system, can be measured. The literature reports two ways of performing this welfare calculus: cost-benefit analysis and approaches based on optimal pricing of public utilities.

Cost-benefit analysis allows the definition of subsidization rules on the basis of a welfare comparison between alternative uses of subsidies. The alternative uses are given by different combinations of adjustments in tariff and quality of transit service with respect to the initial situation. Therefore cost-benefit analysis identifies the adjustments in tariff and quality of service that maximizes social welfare given a budget constraint on the total amount of subsidy. The main difficulty in these calculations is the presence of a quality index both in the demand and cost functions.

Let $D(b,q)$ and $C(D(b,q,),q)$ be respectively the demand and the short run cost function of transit, where b is the tariff and q is the quality index. For any given initial situation (b_0,q_0), it is possible to calculate the net benefit for each amount of money spent alternatively to lower the tariff or to improve the quality of service. In the first case, the net benefit per unit of subsidy will be given by:

$$\frac{dB_b}{dT_b} = \frac{\partial W/\partial b}{\partial b/\partial P} = \frac{-(b_0 - C_D)\,\varepsilon_b}{b_0 + (b_0 - C_D)\,\varepsilon_b} \tag{12.1}$$

where dB_b is the net benefit due to a tariff reduction, measured by the variation in total surplus $W=S+P$, dT_b is the required increase in subsidy, given by the variation of producer surplus, P, and ε_b represents tariff elasticity of transit demand. Equation (12.1) is quite easy to calculate since it is made of known ingredients: tariff, tariff elasticity of demand and marginal cost of service.[1]

This is not so in the case of subsidization of an improved quality of service. In this case we have:

$$\frac{dB_q}{dT_q} = \frac{\partial W/\partial q}{\partial P/\partial q} = \frac{\int_{b_0}^{\infty} D_q\,(v,q_0)\,dv + (b_0 - C_D)\,\varepsilon_q\,D/q_0 - C_q}{C_q - (b_0 - C_D)\,\varepsilon_q\,D/q_0} \tag{12.2}$$

The numerator of Equation (12.2) contains an integral term. It measures the variation of consumer surplus due to an increase in quality of service. No small experiment with price and quality will generate the information required to evaluate this integral term. The reason for this is that quality changes affect the welfare of the entire set of inframarginal consumers. The data generated by local changes in the parameters will not yield such estimates. Therefore in order to calculate equation (12.2) it is necessary to build a model that replicates the reactions of the entire set of inframarginal consumers.[2] Moreover we must rescale these effects in terms of welfare measures.[3] Once made operational, Equations (12.1) and (12.2) provide a sound basis for allocating public transit subsidies to different towns in the same region.[4]

In order to look at transit subsidization as a pricing problem we should remember that welfare economics defines subsidy as the difference between an *opportune* unit price and the unit cost for producing the quantity of service demanded at that price. Therefore welfare economists are mainly concerned with the extension of the concept of *opportune price*. This has usually been accomplished through the definition of second- and third-best solutions to first-best deficiencies. Production costs usually do not play any relevant role. With given technology and perfectly elastic supply of inputs it could be assumed that the service demanded is produced at minimum costs. Therefore the standard pricing problems contain a traditional cost function. The celebrated model developed by Glaister and Lewis (1978) moves within this framework. It identifies optimal pricing schemes of urban public transit in presence of congestion and defines the second-best subsidy that allows its social costs to be internalized.[5]

The welfarist approach has been criticized for several reasons. Even in its more comprehensive version cost-benefit calculation of transit subsidy, for instance, suffers from several internal limitations. Gwilliam (1987) provides the following list of criticisms:[6] (1) with respect to the objectives encompassed the use of the cost-benefit framework does not provide for any environmental or distributional objectives; (2) these models are not disaggregated by time of day and therefore they do not properly assess welfare effects due to peak shifting policies; (3) the high level of spatial aggregation and the lack of explicit geographical content result in an uncertain estimate of the real effect of congestion; (4) the short term nature of the model does not enable the impact of subsidy over cost structure and supply capacity to be evaluated. Criticisms 2, 3 and 4 still hold in the optimal pricing tradition. Moreover we should not diseregard external limits due to the narrow definition of the mobility system. The welfarist approach focuses only on direct and indirect effects which pass through final users, identifying mobility needs with transport demand. In this way the empirical relevance of the approach may be quite limited in scope.

In the following we will not discuss approaches coping with these last types of limitations.[7] We do believe that the standard welfarist approach has merits that largely exceed its limits. However there is one more typical external limit, concerning the organizational contents, that we consider interesting to focus on here. This is the limit that makes the approach 'out of date'. The standard welfarist approach deliberately disregards any references to the organizations governing supply of public transit services. It assumes that organization is simplified to a single decision maker that is a social welfare maximizer. It could be a regulator, as implicitly assumed in the cost-benefit analysis approach, or the transit firm, as is done in the second-best pricing problem. This drastic reduction changes the standard welfarist models to simple tools for evaluating transport policy options, but leaves important questions concerning the real implementation of those policy options completely unanswered. In this last respect, as we will show in the next section, organization counts.

3. THE ORGANIZATIONAL CONCERN

3.1 Optimal Commercial Criteria for Public Transit Firms

The organizational concern originally emerged among the advocates of the standard welfarist approach as a problem of bounded rationality. Since the public transit firms are separate bodies from the regulator subsidizing them, it might be that they are not rational enough to implement, by themself, a welfare maximization programme. Therefore it is necessary to provide them with simple commercial criteria which might approximate social welfare objectives.

In order to implement a social welfare maximizing programme, that is, a couple (x,q) of quantity, x, and quality, q, of transit service, each firm should solve the following problem:

$$\underset{x,q}{\text{Max}} \int_0^x b(v, q) \, dv - xb(x,q) + (1 + \lambda)(b(x,q)x - C(x,q)) \tag{12.3}$$

where $b(x,q)$ is the inverse demand function for transit.

From (12.3), the first order necessary conditions, defining price and quality of service, are the following:

$$\frac{(b - C_x)}{b} = -\frac{\lambda}{1 + \lambda} \frac{1}{\varepsilon_b} \tag{12.4}$$

$$\frac{\int_0^x p_q\,(v,q)\,dv - C_q}{x} = \lambda\left(\frac{C_q}{x} - p_q\right) \tag{12.5}$$

Ramsey's rule (12.4) is easy to implement. The transit firm knows all the elements composing it, or can easily discover them through marginal price and quality adjustments. On the other hand it is not so simple to implement rule (12.5) which prescribes increasing quality as long as net average benefit over the set of inframarginal consumers exceeds the value of social loss on the last quality improvement. In this case it is impossible to evaluate the integral term by means of simple marginal experiments on price and quality. Therefore a public transit firm will not be able to fix the optimal level of quality as long as it does not develop a demand simulation model. Since this is quite difficult, the regulator should provide the firm with the simple commercial rules we mentioned above.

Ridership maximization and vehicle-mile maximization, both subject to a budget constraint, have been the natural candidates examined in literature. Papers by Nash (1978), Glaister and Collings (1978) and Bös (1978) stressed the relative merits of the former in comparison to the latter. However the analysis does not yield any general conclusion. On the contrary the more general result in this stream of literature is the 'negative' conclusion[8] reached by Frankena (1983).

Frankena demonstrated that, in quite general conditions, both mileage and ridership maximization under a budget constraint may lead a non-profit monopolist to fix a tariff and to supply a quality higher than those implemented in the second-best allocation defined by (12.4) and (12.5). In particular this happens if marginal valuation of quality increases, as long as consumers' total willingness to pay reduces,[9] that is, if $b_{xq}>0$, and marginal cost does not change with the quality of service, that is, $C_{xq}=0$. In these circumstances a ridership maximizer will produce a level of quality higher than socially optimal because of the excessive weight he attaches to the high valuation of quality of marginal users. The same holds true for a mileage maximizer. By changing assumptions about demand, that is, by assuming that $b_{xq}<0$, Frankena demonstrated that ridership maximization enabled the firm to choose lower tariffs and quality levels than socially optimal, while the previous conclusion still holds with mileage maximization. Finally, if $b_{xq}=0$ ridership maximization may lead to the social best. Frankena concluded that without knowing the demand and cost functions one cannot determine whether ridership maximization would lead to levels of fares and quality below, equal to, or above those which would be second-best efficient under the budget constraint. Moreover, unless one has information about transport firms' objective function, demand and cost function, one cannot determine which subsidy formula would be the most socially efficient.[10]

3.2 Positive Analyses of Public Transport Firms

All the normative models we have examined up to now contain a conventional treatment of cost relationships. It is usually assumed that the transit firm is a public enterprise that produces sustaining costs given by a canonical, well-behaved, cost function. Therefore managers are not only expected to determine level of service and standards of quality according to some welfare calculus but are also implicitly requested to define inputs mix to minimize total cost. Many theoretical and empirical positive analyses of transport firms' behaviour are actually in conflict with this simplified picture.

The more recent literature of public finance suggests that the behaviour of public enterprise is such that cost minimization at given prices is constrained by demand level, available technology and some political conditions which may introduce a preference for some specific inputs. Therefore public enterprise should not necessarily produce output at minimum cost. In the specific analytical approach suggested by Rees (1984) public enterprise decisions are assumed to result from a negotiation process between the firm's management and the internal labour union. The interaction of managerial preferences,[11] union preferences and political control might easily lead far from standard cost minimization.[12]

Several statistical analyses, for example those by Pucher et al. (1983), Pickrell (1985) and Button (1988), showed that a relationship exists between the amount of subsidy and the cost level of transit. Transit subsidy is positively correlated with unitary costs and level of service and negatively correlated with labour productivity.[13] Another piece of evidence comes from the comparative studies of private and public companies. These studies repeatedly concluded that, also in the public transit sector, the former are commonly more efficient than the latter.[14]

These empirical findings confirm theoretical deductions about the public enterprise by suggesting that public transit firms generally have non-conventional objectives and therefore follow non-standard behavioural programmes. In general it is therefore reasonable to assume that a transit firm's objective function does not coincide with a regulator's objective function. It is in this context that organization may matter.

3.3   Why Does Organization Matter?

Organization matters as long as the agent in charge of producing and supplying the public transit services is different from the regulator who should subsidize or regulate him. This difference becomes relevant from the point of view of organization if both the following conditions hold:

1.   The agent and the regulator should have different, conflicting objective functions. In this respect it is not relevant if the agent is a public or a private firm.
2.   There should be some asymmetry of information that favours the agent in face of the regulator.

If 1 holds but 2 does not, it happens that, since the regulator knows everything about the agent, he could always put her in the conditions to deliberatly reach his own preferred outcome. In the reverse situation the agent would have the incentive to reveal all his private information to the regulator. If both 1 and 2 hold the regulator has an imperfect control of the regulated agent. Therefore organization matters as it becomes economically relevant to cope with the imperfectness of control.

In the early perfomance approach the agent could not share the regulator's objective function because of lack of rationality. However it was implicitly assumed that the agent would be willing to do so. Therefore the regulatory problem was to identify a good substitute for his objective function that the agent could easily follow. This organizational arrangement is quite unrealistic since there are good reasons to assume that the agent is not willing to follow the regulator's prescriptions. A private transit firm obviously has objectives that are conflicting with those inspiring the regulator. Otherwise a free market arrangement would be preferable. Moreover we have seen that the public enterprise has its own specific objective functions. These might be significantly different from a 'simple' social welfare function.

As far as information is concerned, it is quite realistic to assume that it will be asymmetric, with a fully informed management of the regulated firm and with an imperfectly or incompletely informed regulator. His lack of information results from lack of observation. Certain actions of the firm cannot be directly observed by the regulator. Alternatively or cumulatively, certain information about the state of the world can be observed only by the firm, not by the regulator. Therefore we are generally confident that organization should matter.

Within this context new questions arise concerning public transit subsidies. If organization matters, subsidy must be granted not only in order to let the sector produce in quantities and qualities otherwise not available but also to solve organizational problems, that is, taking into account the lack of control on the regulator side. Therefore the question becomes: How can a public transit firm be subsidized in order to reach some specific goals and given that it has its own rationality? The incentives theory provides the right theoretical background for answering this question.[15]

4. THE INCENTIVES THEORY APPROACH

Incentives theory provides a solution to the so-called principal–agent problems. These problems emerge whenever a principal wants to induce an agent to take some action which is costly to the agent, as long as it will require some effort. The principal may be unable to directly observe the action of the agent, but instead observes some output that is determined, at least in part, by the actions of the agent. The principal's problem is to design an incentive payment for the agent that induces the latter to make the best decision from the principal's viewpoint. He should do this by taking into account two sorts of constraints.

Since the agent may have another opportunity available that gives him some reservation level of utility, the principal should design an incentive payment that ensures that the agent gets at least this reservation level. Otherwise the agent would not be willing to participate. This is the so called participation constraint or individual rationality constraint.

The second constraint on the problem is that of incentive compatibility: given the incentive schedule defined by the principal, the agent will pick the best action for himself. As long as the agent attempts to maximize his own return he will exploit all his informational advantage in order to get the maximum payment and to exert the minimum effort. Since the principal cannot choose the agent's action directly but can only influence it by the incentive payment, he must set it by taking into account the utility maximizing behaviour of the agent.

In order to make these concepts clear we present in the next paragraph the theory of regulation recently developed by Laffont and Tirole (1993). In the following we provide an application of this theory that fits into our specific subsidization problem. In the last section we summarize the general rules for an incentive use of transit subsidy.

4.1 Incentives Theory of Regulation: The Laffont and Tirole Framework

Laffont and Tirole's theory of regulation is based on the following main features:

1. Regulation is defined through a contract between the regulator and the firm.
2. The regulated firm has private information about its technology at the date of contracting, and its cost-reducing effort is unobserved by the regulator. Cost function will be written as $C=C(\beta,e,...)q$, where ß is a technological parameter and e is the cost-reducing effort.[16] Let $\Psi(e)$ denote the firm's managers' disutility of effort expressed in monetary terms, such that $\Psi'>0$ (effort is costly) and $\Psi''>0$ (the cost of effort is convex). The model assumes that the regulator has incomplete information about the cost function but not about the function $\Psi(e)$. The firm knows ß, and the regulator has a distribution over ß in an interval $[\underline{\beta}, \bar{\beta}]$.
3. Realized cost C^r, the outputs and the prices are verifiable. However the regulator cannot disentangle the various components of costs.
4. The firm can refuse to produce if the regulatory contract does not guarantee it a minimum level of utility. Let U denote the firm's expected utility. We normalize the individually rational level at zero. $U\geq0$ will be called the firm's rent.
5. The regulator offers a monetary transfer, t, to the firm.
6. The firm and the regulator are risk neutral with respect to income.
7. By accounting convention, the government receives the firm's revenue from charges to consumer, pays the firm's cost and a net transfer t. Transfers are of the linear type in realized cost C^r, that is, $t=a-bC^r$, where a is a 'fixed fee' and b is the fraction of costs incurred by the firm.
8. The firm's objective function is given by the total amount of transfer less monetary disutility of effort, that is, $U=t-\Psi(e)$.
9. The regulator designs a regulatory contract in order to maximize total surplus in society, given that he faces a shadow cost of public $\lambda>0$.

Ignoring for the moment output and quality decisions, the regulator has two conflicting goals: to promote cost reduction and to extract the firm's rent.[17] In order to see why these two goals are in conflicts consider the two polar cases of cost-plus (that is, b=0) and fixed-price (that is, b=1) transfers. A fixed-price contract induces the highest amount of effort because it makes the firm residual claimant for its cost savings. Therefore the firm has the socially optimal incentive to reduce cost as it receives all the money it saved. However, a cost-plus transfer offers no incentive for cost reduction, as long as the firm does not appropriate its cost savings.

In the case of rent extraction the logic is reversed. Under a fixed-price transfer any exogenous reduction in cost is received by the firm. The firm's rent therefore is sensitive to the technological environment. On the other hand, a cost-plus contract is ideal for rent extraction because any exogenous variation in cost is received by the government and not by the firm.

When the regulator has perfect information about the techonology (there is moral hazard but no adverse selection), the optimal regulatory contract is a fixed-price transfer.[18] When the firm has private information about its technology optimal contracts are incentive contracts trading off effort inducement, which calls for fixed-fee transfers, and rent extraction, which calls for a cost-plus transfer. In general it is optimal for the regulator to offer a menu of incentive transfers, since the transfer should be tailored to the firm's information. An inefficient firm should not be regulated with the same contract as an efficient firm. The regulator discriminates among the different potential types of firm in the same way the monopolist price discriminates among consumers with different valuation for quantity or quality.

The regulatory contract emerges as the solution of a mechanism design game, that is a three step game of incomplete information, where the agent's type is private information. In step 1 the regulator designs a contract $[t(\mu),C(\mu)]$ that specifies for each announced value of the signal μ sent by the firm a net transfer to the firm $t(\mu)$, and a cost to realize $C(\mu)$. In step 2 the firm decides to accept or reject the contract. In step 3, the firm which accepts the contract plays the game specified in the contract. The revelation principle[19] shows that, to obtain the highest expected payoff, the principal can restrict attention to contracts that are accepted by the firm at step 2 and in which at step 3 the firm truthfully reveals its type. As we will show, the revelation principle allows the regulatory problem to be solved in terms of standard optimal control techniques.

4.2 A Model of Transit Firm Regulation

We saw that as long as organization matters, public transit subsidization should be treated as a regulation problem.[20] Organizational concern emerges in the public transit sector because of the following typical circumstances:

The transit firm maximizes its own rent while the regulator is concerned with social welfare. This latter circumstance is justified in that we are assuming the (normative) point of view of the regulator. That the transit firm maximizes its own monetary rent seems a good positive assumption at least for private companies. In the case of a public enterprise it could be intepreted as a typical managerial objective.

There is an asymmetry of information between the firm and the regulator in that:

a.   *The firm is better informed than the regulator about technology and about local demand conditions.* If we think of a regional authority in charge of subsidizing a multiplicity of local transit suppliers these circumstances seem quite plausible. There will be always some local specific features affecting technology and demand, that can not be properly detected by the regional authority.

b.   *The firm cost-reducing effort cannot be directly observed and quality standard is not easily verifiable by the regulator.* While the first point seems obvious the second is worth some comments. Quality of transit is difficult to check as long as it depends on local conditions (demographic, geographic, social, ...). Therefore even if quality could be observed,[21] in principle, it would be difficult to quantify and to include in a formal contract.

Given these circumstances, the regulatory problem appears quite complicated as long as it is one of two-dimensional adverse selection and two-dimensional moral hazard.

A very simplifying feature is given by the fact that quality of transit service can usually be observed by users before use. Therefore we might treat transit service as a typical *search* good. A general result in incentive theory is that, in the case of search good, the regulator might recreate the incentives of an unregulated firm to provide quality by rewarding the regulated firm on the basis of sales. This is not so in the case of *experience* goods, that is, those goods whose quality can be properly appreciated by users only after consumption. With experience goods incentives to cost reduction typically conflict with incentives to quality improvement, as long as the supply of quality is costly and not, even indirectly, observable.

Laffont and Tirole (1993, ch. 4), provide a thorough analysis of the regulatory problem in the precence of search goods. In the following we give a brief overview of their model.

The transit firm, which is a local monopoly, produces the service in quantity q with quality, which can be observed by users but not by regulator, s. Cost function is given by:

$$C = (\beta + s - e)q \tag{12.6}$$

where ß is the technological parameter and e is cost-reducing effort.
   The firm's rent is given by:

$$U = t - \psi(e) \tag{12.7}$$

Users derive from the consumption of the transit service a gross surplus:

$$S^g(q,s,\theta) = (A + ks - h\theta)q - \frac{B}{2}q^2 - \frac{(ks - h\theta)^2}{2} \tag{12.8}$$

where A, B, h and k are known positive constants and θ is a demand parameter.[22]

The users'/taxpayers' net surplus S^n, given by gross surplus net of individual expenditure and social cost of providing the service, is:

$$S^n = S^g - [pq + (1 + \lambda)(C - pq + t)] \tag{12.9}$$

Under complete information a utilitarian regulator maximizes the sum of consumer and producer surpluses under the constraint that the firm be willing to participate:

$$\underset{(q,s,e)}{\text{Max}} \quad \{W(q,s,e) = S^n + U\} \tag{12.10}$$

$$s.c. \, I \geq 0 \tag{12.11}$$

The solution to this programme[23] suggests that service should be produced up to the point where the Lerner index is equal to a Ramsey index times the inverse of elasticity of demand. The optimal level of quality equates the marginal gross surplus plus the shadow cost of public funds times the increase in revenue to the social marginal cost of quality. The firm is left with no rent and exerts the optimal level of effort, that is, that level that equates the marginal disutility of effort to its marginal utility.

When we take into account the asymmetry of information the regulator knows neither ß nor θ and cannot observe e and s. However he observes C, p and q. We assume that the regulator maximizes expected social welfare and has a prior cumulative distribution

$$F_1 \text{ on } \beta \in [\underline{\beta}, \bar{\beta}], F_2 \text{ on } \theta \in [\underline{\theta}, \bar{\theta}].$$

The firm knows ß and θ before contracting.

The regulator knows that users equate their marginal utility of service to the price:

$$p = A + ks - h\theta - Bq \tag{12.12}$$

By using equation (12.12) it is possible to eliminate the unobservable quality level s in the users' gross surplus (12.8), and in the cost function. By perfoming these substitutions it is possible to see that the adverse selection parameters ß and θ enter the cost function and the firm's objective function only through a linear combination $\gamma = ß + h\theta/k$. This feature, which holds also for the regulator's objective function, reduces the model to a one-dimensional adverse selection model. We note at this point that high (low) values of ß and θ which are due respectively to a low (high) cost efficiency and a low (high) demand, imply high (low) values of γ.

The regulator wishes to maximize social welfare. From the revelation principle we can restrict the problem to the analysis of direct and truthful revelation contracts. Thus the regulator designs the contract $[t(\gamma), c(\gamma), p(\gamma), q(\gamma)]$ that specifies for each value of γ announced by the firm a net transfer to the firm $t(\gamma)$, an average cost to realize $c(\gamma)$, a price to charge $p(\gamma)$ and a quantity to sell $q(\gamma)$, by solving the following optimal control problem:[24]

$$\max_{\{p(.), q(.), e(.), U(.)\}} \int_{\underline{\gamma}}^{\overline{\gamma}} \{W(p, q, e)\} dF(z) \tag{12.13}$$

under the individual rationality and the incentive compatibility constraints.[25]

It can be demonstrated that in the optimal allocation effort is decreasing in the firm's type. The same is true for the rent function. Therefore the less efficient types, those with a high cost inefficiency and low demand, exert a lower effort and receive a lower rent than the more efficient types, that is those with low cost inefficiency and high demand.[26] To implement the optimal regulatory contract the regulator must define an appropriate transfer $t(\gamma)$ offered to the firm in order to induce truthful behaviour. This transfer can be intepreted as a function $T(.)$ of the variable $z = C/q - (p - A - Bq)/k$. Laffont and Tirole demonstrate that the transfer is a decreasing function of z. Moreover it can be demonstrated (see Laffont and Tirole 1993, appendix A4.3) that the transfer as a function of z is also a convex function. Since $T(z)$ is convex it can be replaced by the family of its tangents. These tangents represent a menu of contracts that are linear in the observed value of z.

$$t(\gamma^{\circ}, z) = t^{*}(\gamma^{\circ}) + T'[z - z(\gamma^{\circ})] = t^{*}(\gamma^{\circ}) + \psi'(e^{*}(\gamma^{\circ}))[z(\gamma^{\circ}) - z] \tag{12.14}$$

where γ° is a firm's announcement and γ^{*} denotes solutions to the optimal regulatory contract. Thus the transfer function $t(\gamma)$ can be replaced by the menu of linear contracts:

$$t(\gamma, z) = a(\gamma) x + b(\gamma)[z(\gamma) - z] \tag{12.15}$$

where $z(\gamma)$ is the announced value of $C/q - [p - A + Bq]/k$, and z is the observed ex-post value. The transfer is therefore a function of a performance index that subtracts from the realized cost an approximation of the service quality inferred from market data. In other words, the firm is offered a choice in a menu of linear contracts and is rewarded or penalized according to deviations from an index aggregating cost data and service quality data inferred from observation of market price and quantity and from a priori knowledge of the demand induces truth telling and the optimal level of effort. It can be easily demonstrated that the regulator by asking the firm for its type, γ, and offering the menu of linear contracts (12.15) $t(z,\gamma)$ is able to induce the firm to implement the truthful value of $C/q-[p-A+Bq]/k$ and the right level of effort.[27]

Moreover it can be demonstrated (see Laffont and Tirole 1993) that:

1. The fixed payment $a(z)$ is a concave, increasing function of the parameters characterizing the power of the incentive schemes, b_1 and b_2.
2. The parameters characterizing the power of the incentive schemes b_1 and b_2, are positively correlated over the sample of types.

The more 'efficient' type faces a fixed price transfer, with $b_1=\Psi'(e^*(\gamma))/q=1/q$, $b_2=\psi'(e^*(\gamma))=1$ and a set at the highest level, and is therefore residual claimant for its cost savings and sales increases. The other types will face incentive contracts that are intermediate between the fixed price and the cost-plus contract.

5. INCENTIVE PROGRAMMES IN PRACTICE

In the last section we wish to provide some general guidelines for the adoption of incentive schemes in public transit subsidization. We will not deal with the difficult questions regarding the design of 'real' incentive contracts.[28] This is out of the scope of the chapter and might be the subject of further research. We prefer here just to define some requirements from the previous treatment of the incentive approach. These criteria might be useful to understand old and current experiments with performance based public transit subsidization.

5.1 General Rules for Incentive Contract in the Public Transit Sector

The publicly managed transit sector typically suffers from high deficits associated with low performance. It is thus quite obvious that incentive subsidization has been repeatedly advocated, and will be increasingly promoted, by local government in charge of financing these deficits. Therefore it is very important to understand, especially for the publicly managed transit firms, what makes an incentive subsidization scheme successful. As long as we are explicitly referring to the theory of incentives as a normative paradigm, we identify conditions for the success of such schemes with the assumptions and normative prescriptions of that theory.

In order to be successful, the contract set by a regulator must be voluntarily accepted by the regulated firm. Moreover the regulator should not be able to withdraw his initial offer once it is accepted by the firm. Once these conditions have been met, the regulator and the regulated firm enter a mechanism design game that can be solved in the way we showed in the previous section. The firm voluntarily accepts the contract as long as the regulator sets it in a way to leave her at least as well off as she would have been if she had not accepted it. In order to exclude renegotiation the regulator should have a reputation incentive, that is, it should be better for him not to reject the contract once accepted by the firm as long as he wishes to have the reputation for respecting agreements. Therefore, as a first set of prescriptions the theory suggests that the regulator:

- quantifies the firm's reservation level of utility and considers it carefully while defining the contract;
- invests in a reputation for respecting agreements. In this way the regulator will be commited to a non-renegotiation behaviour and will therefore be able to propose credible contracts, that is, contracts that may induce truthful revelation.

A second general guideline is to give each firm its own contract, that is, a contract properly tailored to the firm's information. Therefore there should be one contract for each firm. A properly defined contract induces truthful revelation, that is, solves problems due to asymmetry of information. This implies that it should have a particular structure. We have seen that it might be defined as a transfer, linear in the realized, observed performance index, with a target rent, or fixed price component, plus a penalty, or bonus component, for performance overruns. Moreover we have seen that each contract must be defined as a menu of linear transfers, so that each firm might choose its own incentive transfer out of a menu of such transfers. The firm selects the target fixed price and the corresponding reward (penalty) rate by announcing its performance target. If the regulator properly calibrates these two parameters both conditional on the performace target announced by the firm, he might induce the firm to self-select, that is, to announce the truthful performance target.

In relation to the specific regulation problem faced in the transit sector, we argue that a fundamental concern is quality. As long as transfers cannot be made to depend on quality, since it cannot be oserved by the regulator, we have seen that the regulation problem can be represented as a two dimensional moral hazard and two dimensional adverse selection model. However we have shown that as long as the service is a search good, that is, its quality is observed by users before use, this fairly complicated regulation problem might be solved quite easily. As long as the firm has the incentive to boost current sales, consumption is a signal of quality. In this situation, incentives to provide quality might be disconnected from those to reduce cost, if the firm is rewarded also on the basis of sales. We have seen therefore that an important role might be played by observed performance indicators directly linked to consumption. Moreover we have shown that the power of the incentive scheme should be determined by the regulator depending on the a priori probabilistic knowledge of unobservable cost and demand parameters. High powered schemes should be given to firms with lower productive inefficiency and high demand parameters. This implies that high powered schemes should be dependent on low cost and high sales announced performance. An important question[30] is to identify the more appropriate ex-post observable performance measures. An obvious choice would be to use only indicators that are easy to audit.[29] An alternative would be to introduce performance assessment on the basis of information provided by a third party (for example, a panel of users or a firm's input suppliers).

These general rules can be immediately applied by a regulator dealing with a private transit firm. On the other hand, some complications arise if the regulator wants to apply these rules to the design of performance based subsidization for a system of publicly owned transit firms. We will briefly discuss these problems after having presented some of these experiences.

5.2 Some Experiments with Performance Based Transit Subsidization

Fielding (1992) surveys some of the experiments with performance based transit subsidization carried out in the United States. All the cases he explicitly refers to were unsuccessful.

In Michigan the state transit authority calculated 47 indicators of transit performance. The mean, range and standard deviation for each indicator were calculated and each transit firm rewarded on the basis of its relative status in these rankings. The scheme failed because the use of so many indicators created confusion.

The state of Pennsylvania[30] was a very interesting example. Four indicators were calculated for each firm to cover the efficiency and effectiveness dimensions: cost per hour, revenue per hour, ridership per hour and the revenue-to-cost ratio. The state awarded 8.33 percent of the permissable deficit of each firm as a performance incentive, if the firm had maintained or improved performance over the previous year on the first three measures. To qualify for the incentive, a firm had to exceed a statewide revenue-to-cost ratio. The system, introduced in 1979, was later abandoned. Opposition arose because it was easier for smaller firms to qualify for the incentive reward.[31]

By referring to the theory of incentives, it is quite easy to see why these attempts failed: the regulator imposed the same contract on each firm. Therefore individual rationality and incentive compatibility constraints were not considered. This feature reveals that the underlying theory was still the standard welfarist approach, in that there was no concern for organizational aspects.

A slightly improved version of performance based transit subsidization has been recently introduced in Emilia-Romagna. In Italy each regional transit authority receives a transfer from the central government that must be allocated to local transit firms[32] to cover their deficits. Usually this is done by political negotiations on historical sharing quotas. At the beginning of 1995, Emilia-Romagna regional authority accomplished this task by stipulating, separately with each local transit firm, incentive contracts (Contratti di Servizio). These contracts have the above mentioned prescribed form, since they consist of a fixed payment plus a penalty, or bonus, component contingent on performance overruns.

Even if in theory this scheme is sound, in practice it suffers from at least three main drawbacks. (1) performance is evaluated on the basis of 10 indicators calculated with data provided by each firm; (2) the penalty rate is set at the same value for each firm; in fact, the regional authority negotiated assuming that each firm should have been rewarded on the basis of the same penalty rates; (3) the penalty rate is very low, only 1 percent of the total eligible subsidy. Thus the contracts are all fixed-price transfers.

The first failure is quite evident since firms may give false reports. The second is partly a consequence of the first: the penalty rate should not provide different incentives to false reporting. Finally the third drawback is a direct result of the second: if the penalty rate must be the same, then the firms collectively opt for the lowest one, that is for a fixed-price contract. This high powered contract allows the highest rent to be realized. From incentive theory we know that this contract induces the socially correct amount of effort in the most efficient type but may leave too high a rent to the less efficient ones. Therefore in the end this arrangement fails both in extracting rents and inducing effort at a socially desirable level. However it is still better than those surveyed by Fielding in that at least each firm deliberately signs its own contract.

5.3 Open Issues

According to the theory, all these experiences more or less failed to provide the proper incentives to the firms. This failure can be explained in two ways: (1) regulators do not know the incentives theory; (2) this theoretical test is much too demanding in that incentives theory does not account for all the complexities. Assuming that the answer lies somewhere in between, transport economists have two main tasks to accomplish: (1) to teach incentives theory to regulators and planners; (2) to improve it in order to correspond to reality. In this last case there are two main aspects of real transit subsidization schemes that must be carefully considered: dynamic contracting and endogeneity of reservation utility levels.

The first aspect, which is common to the subsidization of both private and public enterprises, emerges if we consider that subsidization is usually part of a multiperiod relationship. In this context it might be quite difficult to let the agent reveal its own private information as long as the regulatory contract could be renegotiated or stipulated year by year. In such a case truthful revelation today implies losing informational rents tomorrow.

The second issue may arise whenever subsidization involves a multiplicity of agents. The consistency of each menu of transfers might be undermined by an externality effect. The theory says that incentive contracts depend on the reservation level of utility, that is determined, for each agent, by his best alternative to signing the contract. It may be that this alternative depends on the number of agents that refuse to sign: the more agents refuse to sign the more easily they can cooperate in enforcing the regulator to implement a new more favourable subsidization scheme. Therefore reservation levels of utility may be influenced also by the extent of cooperation in refusing the contract and by the degree of rent extraction in itself.

6. CONCLUSIONS

The aim of this chapter was twofold. First of all we aimed to evaluate the theories of public transit subsidization. After an early abundance of contributions to the literature of public transit economics mainly inspired by welfare theory and public economics, in the last decade the issue of transit privatization determined a shift towards different theoretical paradigms. Transport economists debated about the opportunity of privatizing public transit firms by referring very frequently to the theory of industrial organization. This change has been implicitly determined by a shift from second-best to first-best arguments. Privatization might be an answer to the enormous costs of organizations in charge of achieving the second-best.

Actually the experiences of deregulation showed that regulation through competition does not alone imply socially desirable consequences in the transit market. Moreover deregulation does not necessarily mean that transit subsidies are completely eliminated. Even in a privatized transit market, a local government may decide to give public subsidies in return for a socially superior transit service. From this point of view, the second aim of this chapter was to suggest a new framework to define regulatory contracts that assign transfers to the transit firms according to the achievement of announced performance. The same reasoning is valid, a fortiori, in the case of a publicly owned transit firm. The theory of incentives might provide the appropriate framework for analysing such arrangements, that is, to give a third-best answer to public transit problems that also take into consideration organizational constraints.

REFERENCES

Berechman, J. (1993), *Public Transit Economics and Deregulation Policy*, Amsterdam: North-Holland.

Bly, P.H. and R.H. Oldfield (1986), 'The effects of public transport subsidies on demand supply', *Transportation Research A* **20**, pp. 415–27.

Bly, P.H. and R.H. Oldfield (1987), 'An analytic assessment of subsidies to bus services', in Glaister, S. (ed.), *Transport Subsidy,* Policy Journals, Bristol: Arrowsmith.

Bös, D. (1978), 'Distributional effects of maximizing passengers miles', *Journal of Transport Economics and Policy* **12**, pp. 322–29.

Bös, D. (1986), *Public Enterprise Economics*, Amsterdam: North-Holland.

Button, K. (1988), 'Subsidies, political control and costs of U.K. urban bus provision', *Transportation Research Record* **1012**, pp. 8–13.

De Borger, B. (1993), 'The behaviour of public enterprise offering scheduled services', paper presented at the 38th International Conference of The Applied Econometrics Association, Athens, 13–14 April.

De Borger, B., I. Meyers, S. Proost and S. Wouters (1993), *Social Cost Pricing of Urban Passenger Transport*, Public Economic Research Paper no. 34, CES, Leuven, Belgium: Katholieke Universiteit.

Dodgson, J.S. (1987), 'Benefits of changes in urban public transport subsidies in the major Australian cities', in Glaister, S. (ed.), *Transport Subsidy*, Policy Journals, Bristol: Arrowsmith.

Dodgson, J.S. and N. Topham, N (1987), 'Benefit-cost rules for urban transit subsidies', *Journal of Transport Economics and Policy* **21**, pp. 57–71.

Evans, A. (1985), 'Equalising grants for public transport subsidy', *Journal of Transport Economics and Policy* **19**, pp. 105–38.

Fielding, G.J. (1992), 'Transit performance evaluation in the U.S.A.', *Transportation Research A* **26**, pp. 483–491.

Fielding, G.J., T.T. Babitsky and M. Brenner, M. (1985), 'Performance evaluation for bus transit', *Transportation Research A* **19**, pp. 73–82.

Filippini, M., R.Maggi and P. Prioni, P. (1992), 'Inefficiency in a regulated industry: the case of the Swiss regional bus companies', *Annals of Public and Cooperative Economics* **63**, pp. 437–55.

Frankena, M. (1981), 'The effects of alternative urban transit subsidy formulas', *Journal of Public Economics* **15**, pp. 337–48.

Frankena, M. (1983), 'The efficiency of public transport objectives and subsidy formulas', *Journal of Transport Economics and Policy* **17**, pp. 67–76.

Fudenberg, D. and J. Tirole, (1991), *Game Theory*, Cambridge, Mass: MIT Press.

Glaister, S. (1987), 'The allocation of urban public transport subsidy', in Glaister, S. (ed.), *Transport Subsidy*, Policy Journals, Bristol: Arrowsmith.

Glaister, S. and J.J. Collings (1978), 'Theory and practice of maximizing passenger miles', *Journal of Transport Economics and Policy* **12**, pp. 304–21.

Glaister, S. and D.L. Lewis (1978), 'An integrated fares policy for transport in Greater London', *Journal of Public Economics* **9**, pp. 341–55.

Goodwin, P.B., J.M. Bailey, R.H. Brisbourne, M.I. Clarke, J.R. Donnison, T.E. Render and G.K. Whiteley (1983), *Subsidised Public Transport and the Demand for Travel*, Gower.

Gwilliam, K.M. (1987), 'Market failures, subsidy and welfare maximization', in Glaister, S. (ed.), *Transport Subsidy*, Policy Journals, Bristol: Arrowsmith.

Heseltine, P.M. and D.T. Silcock, (1990), 'The effects of bus deregulation on costs', *Journal of Transport Economics and Policy* **24**, pp. 239–54.

Laffont, J.J. and J. Tirole (1993), *A Theory of Incentives in Procurements and Regulation*, Cambridge, MA: MIT Press.

Miller, J.H. (1980), 'The use of performance-based methodologies for the allocation of transit operating funds', *Traffic Quarterly* **34**, pp. 555–85.

Nash, C.A. (1978), 'Management objectives, fares and service levels in bus transportation', *Journal of Transport Economics and Policy* **12**, pp. 70–85.

Pedersen, P.A. (1994), 'Regulating public transport company with private information about costs', *Journal of Transport Economics and Policy* **28**, pp. 307–18.

Pickrell, D.H. (1985), 'Rising deficits and the uses of transit subsidies in the United States', *Journal of Transport Economics and Policy* **19**, pp. 281–98.

Pucher, J., R. Markstedt and I. Hirschman (1983), 'Impacts of subsidies on the costs of public transport', *Journal of Transport Economics and Policy* **17**, pp. 155–76.

Rees, R. (1984), 'A positive theory of the public enterprise', in Marchand, Pestieau and Tulkens (eds), *The Performance of Public Enterprise: Concepts and Measurement*, Amsterdam: North-Holland.

Reichelstein, S. (1992), 'Constructing incentives schemes for government contracts: an application of agency theory', *The Accounting Review* **67**, pp. 712–31.

Searle, G. (1987), 'Value for money from rural public transport subsidies: a summary of the Lewes approach', in Glaister, S. (ed.), *Transport Subsidy*, Policy Journals, Bristol: Arrowsmith.

Spence, A.M. (1975), 'Monopoly, quality and regulation', *Bell Journal of Economics* **6**, pp. 417–29.

NOTES

1. If the tariff is initially set at marginal cost there is no space for increasing net social surplus. Otherwise if marginal cost is zero the increase in net social benefit will depend only on tariff elasticity of demand. Subsidizing a tariff reduction will be more welfare improving the more initial tariff exceeds marginal cost and demand is elastic to the tariff.

2. Spence (1975) realizes that this is the main problem faced by the regulator of a monopolist 'with quality'. The regulator should provide the *non-market* informations needed in order to evaluate total willingness to pay for quality improvements.

3. At this point the problem becomes transport-specific. In the generalized travel cost approach the problem is the building of behavioural models explaining the impact of quality of service on walking, waiting, boarding and travel time. The impact on these time requirements of the whole set of inframarginal consumers might then be translated into monetary terms by means of value of time coefficients. This is the approach followed by Dodgson (1987). He solves Equation (12.2) in terms of a relationship between vehicles-km and waiting-time.

4. See Evans (1985) for the definition of different equalization schemes in transit transfers. Dodgson (1987), by referring to a sample of Australian cities, suggested that an increase in vehicle-km would not be welfare improving in most of the towns. An improved version of this model has been made operational in England by Stephen Glaister (see Glaister 1987). METS (Model for Evaluating Transport Subsidies) was able to calculate Equations (12.1) and (12.2) by solving complicated local mobility simulation models. It considered a multiplicity of transport modes: car, bus, rail and metro. METS allowed the estimation of modal impacts produced by pricing and quality policies by measuring their effect on congestion reduction and other second-best concerns.

5. De Borger et al. (1993) recently applied an improved version of the Glaister and Lewis model of urban transport in Belgium. Their social cost includes congestion costs, environmental costs and accidents. Therefore the model provides an exhaustive treatment of second-best arguments for transit subsidy.

6. All the limits listed are escapable in theory. Dodgson and Topham (1987) introduced distributional elements in the cost-benefit calculus. Bly and

Oldfield (1987) extended the model in order to consider environmental impact, capacity optimization and optimal mixing of tariff reduction and quality improvement policies. However all these extensions would imply higher costs of model building.

7. Two examples of such approaches are the application of Activity Analysis to public transit subsidization provided by Goodwin et al. (1983) and that of the so-called Lewes Approach (see Searle 1987).

8. The narrowness of these theoretical results partially justify the relevance, in public transit economics, of a-theoretical approaches to performance analysis. See Fielding et al. (1985).

9. In other words, willingness to pay for quality improvement is assumed to be higher among users with a lower total willingness to pay.

10. In a previous paper (Frankena 1981), the author considered the effect of different subsidization schemes (lump sum, matching on cost and on passenger) on the performance of transit firms with different objective functions.

11. Potential objectives of public enterprise managers, suggested in the literature, are, among others, budget maximization, output or revenue maximization and even price stabilization or energy consumption minimization. See Bös (1986).

12. De Borger (1993) recently applied this framework to the case of the Belgian national railroad company. In his model the company does not minimize cost with respect to market prices of inputs but with respect to shadow prices generated by political constraint and the bargaining power of the labour union. Empirical estimation of the shadow cost function suggests that the shadow wage varies from 67 percent to 86 percent of observed wage and that this implies a misallocation of labour such that 4.4 percent more labour has been employed than stricly required.

13. Pucher et al. (1983) show that the impact on unitary costs is higher the further is the firm from the government agency subsidizing it. Similar results have been reached by Filippini et al. (1992). Bly and Oldfield (1986) by using regression with lagged variables provide some evidence on the causality links from subsidy to unitary cost increase.

14. Some analyses of the British bus deregulation experience confirm this prescription. Heseltine and Silcock (1990) for instance report that the newly privatized transit firm lowered quality, increased prices and reduced unitary costs by cutting labour, that is, by redefining productive mix.

15. Actually subsidization is not the only issue in public transit policy that can be usefully addressed with incentives theory. Several new issues have recently emerged in this field, for example contracting out and second sourcing strategies, auctioning and regulation through competition. See Berechman (1993) in this regard. All these policy options can be properly analysed within an incentives theory approach.

16. By convention $C_\beta > 0$, i.e. a high ß corresponds to an inefficient technology, and $C_e < 0$ and $C_{ee} > 0$, that is, effort reduces cost at a decreasing rate. Omitted variables in the cost function may be the vector of outputs $q_1, ... q_n$, of goods 1,..., n or the level of service quality, s.

17. In this case ex-post social welfare for a utilitarian regulator is given by:
$$S-(1+\lambda)(t+\beta-e)+t-\Psi(e)=S-(1+\lambda)[\beta-e+\Psi(e)]-U$$
where S is the consumer surplus due to the project. The crucial feature of this welfare function is that the regulator dislikes leaving a rent to the firm.

18. In this case the fixed fee is optimally set at the lowest level consistent with the firm's participation provided that the firm chooses the effort that minimizes $C+\Psi(e)$.

19. We refer here to the textbook treatment contained in Fudenberg and Tirole (1991), ch. 7.

20. See the paper by Pedersen (1994) for the first attempt, to my knowledge, in this direction.

21. This implies in any case high costs of monitoring and auditing.

22. Quantity and quality are net complements if k>1 and net substitutes if k<1. Quantity and quality are net complements if an increase in quality raises the net marginal willingness to pay, that is the difference between price and marginal cost.

23. For B large enough the program [(10), (11)] is concave and its interior maximum is fully characterized by the first-order conditions.

24. For A and B large enough the program is concave and the optimum is characterized by its first-order conditions (see Laffont and Tirole 1993, appendix A4.3.).

25. The welfare function W is obtained by substituting out quality from the social welfare function (16), and the cumulative distribution $F(\gamma)$ is the convolution of F_1 and F_2.

26. Type $\gamma=\bar{\gamma}$ will receive $U=0$ and exert low effort; type $\gamma=\underline{\gamma}$ will receive the maximum rent and will exert the effort e^* such that $\psi'(e^*)=q$.

27. It is interesting to note that the menu of linear contracts can be alternatively decomposed into a linear sharing of total cost overruns with a coefficient $b_1(\gamma)=\psi'(e^*(\gamma))/q^*(\gamma)$ and a linear sharing of overruns in the service quality index with coefficient $b_2(\gamma)=\psi'(e^*(\gamma))$, or:

$$t = a(\gamma) + b_1(\gamma)[C(\gamma) - C] + b_2(\gamma) \left[\frac{p + Bq}{k} - \frac{p(\gamma) + Bq(\gamma)}{k} \right]$$

28. See the paper by Reichelstein (1992) for a rare example of numerical computation of the incentive schemes for a government contract.

29. See Pedersen (1994) in this regard.

30. See Miller (1980).

31. More recently, Los Angeles county designed a similar subsidization scheme that had the same fate.

32. In Italy local transit firms are publicly owned.

13. Public Transport Efficiency and Effectiveness: Metro de Madrid

Álvaro Costa

1. INTRODUCTION

There has been a general trend to reduce economic regulation in Europe and the United States and the 'prevailing wisdom is now that intervention failures are often potentially more damaging than market imperfections' (Button 1993:251). This new economic climate has induced a movement to reorganize urban public transport systems in large metropolitan areas within Western Europe, even in cities with satisfactory operational results (for example, Hamburg – creation of new authority in 1996 – and London – privatization of bus companies in 1994).

The structures of organization chosen favour the coordination of public transport (for example, Madrid from 1985, Zurich from 1990) often with a simultaneous introduction of a degree of competition in the provision of the services (for example, London from 1985, Copenhagen from 1991, Gothenburg from 1993). This reflects the desire to have an effective public transport system achieved by the coordination of transport authorities and, in the case of tendered services, also an efficient system with the discipline of market forces driving operational costs down.

The main concern here is to evaluate urban public transport service performance over a short period, taking into consideration the need to evaluate the recent reorganizations undertaken in Western Europe.

Because an urban public transport operation is generally managed as a public service, in spite of the presence of a traded output, profitability cannot normally be used as the only measure of performance. Approaches using univariate performance indicators such as ratios of efficiency, effectiveness and quality of service give intuitive information, but it is not clear whether a change in value of any individual univariate ratio affects the overall performance of a transport operator (Henscher and DeMellow 1991). Given the dimension of the data sets Total Factor Productivity (TFP) methods also cannot easily be applied. In this chapter a different approach to evaluating performance is explored – the Efficiency/Effectiveness Matrix (EEM).

The chapter starts with a general characterization of the main functions of an urban public transport system in order to clarify the concept of the performance in this context. Since EEM is constructed with Data Envelopment Analysis (DEA) values the explanation of EEM is preceded by a presentation of the main theoretical concepts underlying DEA. The main difference between the two approaches is that DEA considers only one measure of performance and EEM considers two, supporting the view that 'public transport agencies cannot focus on a single objective function' (Fielding et al. 1985). The public transport system in Madrid underwent a major reorganization in 1985 and this gives the opportunity for the potential of the EEM method to be examined in the context of a performance evaluation of the operation of Metro de Madrid between 1981 and 1992.

2. THE URBAN PUBLIC TRANSPORT SERVICE

The evaluation of the performance of any urban public transport system involves consideration of two main functions: the production of the service and its utilization. Those functions are performed by different agents: the producers of the service are the operators and the users are a subset of potential passengers. Figure 13.1 offers a representation of the interrelationship between those functions with indicators showing inputs and outputs of those activities.

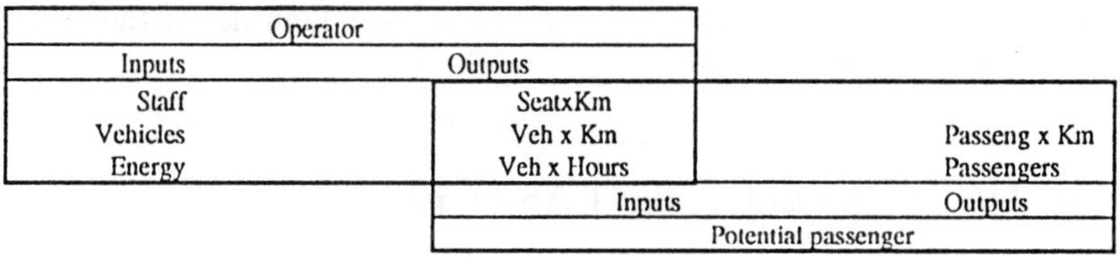

Operator		
Inputs	Outputs	
Staff Vehicles Energy	SeatxKm Veh x Km Veh x Hours	Passeng x Km Passengers
	Inputs	Outputs
	Potential passenger	

Figure 13.1   Inputs and outputs of an urban public transport system

The production of the transport service is a process of transforming inputs such as staff, vehicles and energy, into outputs such as distance covered by the fleet, distance covered by each seat in the fleet or hours of vehicle operation. In some ways the process of production is similar to many manufacturing companies but, unlike most of them, to be successful it is not enough to have a productive efficient unit. Because the service cannot be either stored or produced under client order, the service provided has to match instant client needs. The intimate presence of the clients during the process of production causes disturbance (for example, through congestion) and decreases the efficiency of the operator but, since they are the reason for the existence of the service and purpose behind its operation, they have to be handled.

A transport service is used by a subset of potential customers over the entire system – the passengers. The inputs of the utilization function include staff, vehicles and energy, and the outputs are the number of passengers or the distance covered by the passengers. For potential passengers to become actual passengers the vehicle must be available when they want to use it, in the place they want to use it, going to the destination where they want to go, arriving when they want to be there. This depends very much on matching the services offered to customers' needs.

To evaluate the performance of public transport operators both aspects – the production and the utilization of the service – need to be taken into consideration. The indicators of performance must also be related to objectives beyond the provision of public transport services. The performance of the operator – efficiency – is a measure of the success transforming inputs into outputs in the provision of the service. The performance of the system – effectiveness – is a measure of the delivery of the consumption of the resource inputs.

The purpose of creating transport commission authorities and the like in many metropolitan areas has been to balance those two, often conflicting, objectives (efficiency and effectiveness). Efficient production is better attained without congestion which corresponds to periods of low demand. Large numbers of passengers and congested transport networks cause disruptions to production. Effective production is better attained with high demand and this corresponds to congested periods.

3.   DATA DEVELOPMENT ANALYSIS

DEA was developed by Charnes et al. (1978) from initial work on efficiency measurement carried out by Farrell (1957). Charnes et al. (1978) solved the problem of evaluating efficiency of multiple inputs and multiple outputs producers and later Banker et al. (1984) related these efficiency evaluations obtained from observed data with the axiomatic formulations of Shephard's work (1970) which enables the consideration of variable returns to scale. This brings together the notions of efficiency and modern production theory.

DEA provides a relative measure of performance and is increasingly being used in evaluating the performance of public service industries (see Ganley and Cubbin 1992 for a general overview; Oum and Yu 1994, for an application in the transport sector; Weyman-Jones 1991 for an explanation of the method).

Figure 13.2, used by Farrell (1957) to explain the concept of efficiency, represents a firm employing two inputs to produce a single output under constant returns to scale.

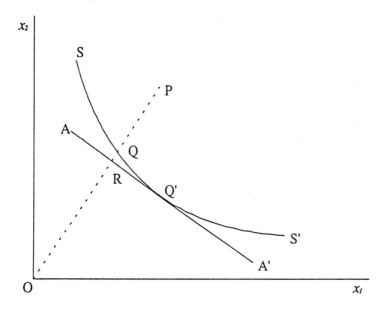

Figure 13.2   Farrell efficiency measures

Line SS' is the isoquant representing the various combinations of inputs x_1 and x_2 in the production of one unit of output for technically efficient firms. The slope of line AA' represents the relative factor prices and Q', the point of tangency between SS' and AA', represents an overall efficient producer – technically efficient and using the most economic combination of the factor inputs.

Point P represents a technically and allocatively inefficient firm. Point Q in the unit isoquant represents a firm using the same ratio of factors as P but only using part of each factor, given by the ratio of distances OQ/OP, to produce the same unit of output. Therefore, OQ/OP represents the technical efficiency value for the firm lying on point P. Though the firm represented by the point Q is technically efficient, it is allocatively inefficient because the firm represented by the point Q' incurs only part of the cost given by the ratio of the distances OR/OQ. Hence a firm lying on point Q is technically efficient because it lies on the unit isoquant but is allocatively inefficient. The allocatively efficiency value is OR/OQ.

The overall efficiency of a firm is the composition of allocative efficiency and technical efficiency and in the case of the firm represented by the point P is:

$$[\text{overall efficiency}]=[\text{allocative efficiency}]\times[\text{technical efficiency}]$$
$$[\overline{OR}/\overline{OP}]=[\overline{OR}/\overline{OQ}]\times[\overline{OQ}/\overline{OP}]$$

This concept of efficiency has subsequently been generalized to include, among other things, the case of multiple inputs and multiple outputs (Charnes et al. 1978) and to situations exhibiting different returns to scale (Banker et al. 1984).

Turning to multiproduct producers, we initially have raw data collected from observation. There are two forms of defining the production frontier from such a set of resource inputs used to produce a level of outputs: parametric and non-parametric approaches. In the parametric approach, the functional form of the production function is chosen, a distribution to the inefficiency terms is assumed and the function is adjusted to the data. In the non-parametric approach the frontier envelops all the units and no functional form is assumed.

DEA is a non-parametric approach and the efficiency measures derived are functions of distance to an empirical production frontier. There is no need to assume a functional form for the production function because the frontier is the observed best practice of the raw data set available. Assuming a specific functional form involves a strong a priori assumption about the underlying production technology; the revealed technology is, however, a closer estimate of the true, unknown technology underlying the data (Ganley and Cubbin 1992).

DEA allows one scalar overview of performance obtained with the inputs and outputs of each organization by calculating weights through the comparison of the performance of the organizations. This calculation is based on the standard Pareto efficiency concept.

DEA has recently been widely applied to evaluate the performance of public sector undertakings, but can also be applied to private sector suppliers. In the public sector, where the outputs are non-traded services, instead of defining shadow prices, with all the inherent problems involved, DEA offers a non-subjective weight formation. According to Lewin and Morey (1981), 'the procedure [DEA] is most appropriate for performing evaluations where administrators are not free to redirect resources to their programs because they are more "profitable", but where their mission is to maximize the outputs to be obtained from the resources and non controllable factors assigned to them'.

The input-minimization version of DEA programming is used in this study. It assumes that managers wish to minimize the inputs required for any given level of output. This need not be the case with all operators but as outputs are in general more prone to stochastic influences (Ganley and Cubbin 1992), and to reporting problems than inputs, the input minimization version is adopted here.

In this context, Charnes et al. (1978) propose the following model:

$$\max h_0 = \frac{\sum\limits_{r=1}^{s} u_r r_{r0}}{\sum\limits_{i=1}^{m} v_i x_{i0}}$$

$$(13.1)$$

subject to

$$\frac{\sum\limits_{r=1}^{s} u_r y_{rj}}{\sum\limits_{i=1}^{m} v_i x_{ij}} \leq 1 \qquad j = 1...n$$

$$u_r, v_i > 0 \qquad r = 1...s \quad i = 1...m$$

where

y_{ri} = output r of unit j

x_{ij} = input i of unit j

m = number of inputs

s = number of outputs

n = number of units

The fractional programming problem can be converted into a linear programming problem. This is done by imposing a unity value on the denominator of the objective h_0 and adding this as a constraint to maximize the new objective h_0'. The linear program can then be written as:

$$\max h'_0 = \sum_{r=1}^{s} u_r y_{r0} \tag{13.2}$$

subject to

$$\sum_{r=1}^{s} u_r y_{rj} - \sum_{i=1}^{m} v_i x_{ij} \leq 0 \quad j = 1...n$$

$$\sum_{i=1}^{m} v_i x_{i0} = 1$$

$$u_r' v_i > 0 \qquad r = 1...s \quad i = 1...m$$

The efficiency values are calculated by solving the dual program and the formulation becomes:

$$\min z_0 \tag{13.3}$$

subject to

$$\sum_{j=1}^{n} y_{rj} \lambda_j \geq y_{r0} \qquad r = 1...s$$

$$\sum_{j=1}^{n} x_{ij} \lambda_j \leq z_0 x_{i0} \quad i = 1...m$$

$$\lambda_j \geq 0; \; z_0 \text{ unconstrained}$$

4. EFFICIENCY/EFFECTIVENESS MATRIX

The Efficiency/Effectiveness Matrix (EEM) is a methodology proposed to evaluate the performance and resource allocation of a public transport operator.[1] Examination of the EEM is carried out in the context of performance evaluation of an operator over time, but the method can also be deployed to compare various operators over the same time period (variable returns to scale should be considered in this latter case). The EEM is constructed with DEA values measuring the relative efficiency of the operations and the relative effectiveness of the transport system. The same concept of technical efficiency explored by Farrell (1957) is applied to measure effectiveness.

The measure of the relative performance of any operator is defined as the 'efficiency-EEM' and the measure of relative performance of a transport system is the 'effectiveness-EEM'. The inputs used to calculate the relative efficiency-EEM value are those used by the transport operator in the production of the service – for example, staff, vehicles, energy – and environmental conditions – for example, network route length. The output is defined in terms of the distance covered by the fleet or the duration of its operation (see Figure 13.1). The inputs used to calculate the relative effectiveness-EEM value are also the inputs of the transport operator but the outputs measure the utilization of the service – that is, distance covered by the passengers.

Accepting that the application refers to a unit over a period of time, the formulation of the dual program becomes:

$$\min z_0 \tag{13.4}$$

subject to

$$\sum_{j=1}^{n} y_{rj} \lambda_j \geq y_{r0} \qquad r = 1...s$$

$$\sum_{j=1}^{n} x_{ij} \lambda_j \leq z_0 x_{i0} \qquad i = 1...m$$

$$\lambda_j \geq 0; \ z_0 \text{ unconstrained}$$

where

y_{rj} = output r of year j
x_{ij} = input i of year j
m = number of inputs
s = number of outputs
n = number of years

The relative efficiency-EEM value, therefore, provides information on the relative productivity of the operator in a particular year while the relative effectiveness-EEM value gives information on the relative patronage of the transport system in a particular year.

Figure 13.3 is a representation of the EEM. The relative efficiency-EEM value is plotted on the x-axis and effectiveness-EEM value on the y-axis. Points lying in quadrant I correspond to years of relatively efficient and effective operations. Because DEA gives relative measures of performance those points represent above average values in both efficiency-EEM and effectiveness-EEM values. Points lying in quadrant II correspond to years in which the operations were effective but the production was inefficient, meaning the operator could have produced more output with the resources available or could have produced the same output level using fewer inputs. Points lying in quadrant III correspond to inefficient and ineffective operations, meaning not only that the operator could have been more productive, but also that the level of utilization could have been higher with the resources available or the same level of utilization could have been obtained with less inputs. Points lying in quadrant IV correspond to efficient producers but low level of utilization of the service produced.

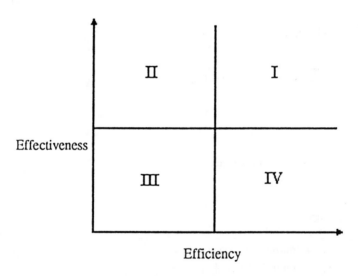

Figure 13.3 Efficiency/Effectiveness Matrix (EEM)

A successful undertaking may be managed efficiently or enjoy favourable environmental conditions and conversely an unsuccessful undertaking may be poorly managed or face unfavourable external conditions. The EEM provides a tool to distinguish those situations. The position of the operator in the matrix highlights the types of action needed to enhance the performance of the system. The evaluation of performance in an urban public transport service cannot normally be reduced simply to profitability or to a single measure of productivity given the nature of the service.

5.   CASE STUDY – MADRID

Madrid underwent a major reorganization in the urban public transport with the constitution in 1985 of Consorcio Regional de Transportes Públicos de Madrid, a public transport authority, which concentrates all the competencies related to the regular transport of passengers. Ayuntamento de Madrid decided to take part in the Consorcio in July 1985 and at the end of 1986 transferred the assets of Metro de Madrid to the ownership of Consorcio de Transportes. Figure 13.4 provides a representation of the organizational form of urban public transport in Madrid since 1985.

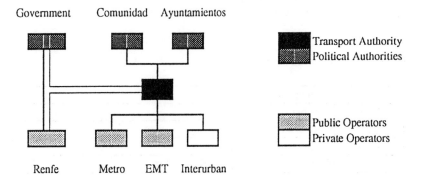

Figure 13.4   The organizational structure of the transport system in Madrid

Consorcio assumed the functions of planning the passenger transport infrastructure, the definition and coordination of programmes for exploiting all modes, the introduction of a common fare system and the creation of a coherent image for the transport system. It is also responsible for answering to the customer. The public (Renfe (railway operator), EMT (public bus operator) and Metro de Madrid) and private operators maintain legal independence, management autonomy and patrimony but follow the regulations set by the Consorcio in relation to transport service. Table 13.1 offers a description of some characteristics of the transport system coordinated by the Consorcio in 1992.

Table 13.1 The public transport system in the Comunidad de Madrid in 1992

	Number of companies	Network length (km)	Number of lines	Number of stations	Number of vehicles	Vehicle Km (10^6)	Place Km (10^6)
Metro	1	112.5	11	155	976	81.5	14263
Renfe	1	277.8	8	110	559	61.4	15534
EMT	1	1301.4	266	7054	1777	77.0	6160
Interurban	36	2996.0	174	6264	778	72.0	4752

Source: Consorcio Regional de Transportes Públicos de Madrid

The DEA and EEM methods can be applied to the operation of Metro de Madrid between 1981 and 1992 to evaluate the impact of the reorganization of its public transport system. The data employed is taken from the 1992 annual report of Metro de Madrid.

Table 13.2 shows the variables used in the evaluation of performance.

Table 13.2 Input and output variables

XSTA	Number of workers
XVEH	Number of vehicles
XROU	Network route length
YPAS	Number of passengers
YVKM	Distance covered by the fleet in km

The inputs considered to calculate the DEA value are the average number of staff (XSTA), the number of vehicles (XVEH), the energy in KWH (XENE) and the network route length (XROU) while the outputs are the distance in kilometres covered by the fleet (YVKM) and the number of passengers (YPAS). All the data is for a single year. The inputs used to calculate the relative efficiency-EEM value are the average number of staff (XSTA), the number of vehicles (XVEH), the energy in KWH (XENE) and the network route length (XROU) while the output is the distance in kilometres covered by the fleet (YVKM). The calculation of the relative effectiveness-EEM value is computed with the same inputs (staff, vehicles, energy and network route length) but the output is the number of passengers carried (YPAS) – see Table 13.3. A more accurate measure for the output would have been passenger kilometres but this data is not publicly available.

Table 13.3 Inputs and outputs of DEA and EEM values

	DEA	Efficiency-EEM	Effectiveness-EEM
Inputs			
XVEH	x	x	x
XSTA	x	x	x
XROU	x	x	x
Outputs			
YPAS	x		x
YVKM	x	x	

The respective relevance of the DEA and EEM methods can be seen in Table 13.4 which contains DEA, efficiency-EEM and effectiveness-EEM values related to the operations of Metro de Madrid. The DEA values obtained are in most cases larger than the EEM values because the performance measures are functions of distance to an empirical production frontier and, as the inputs and outputs used in computing DEA include all those used in EEM values, the distance is similar to one of the EEM values (the minimum distance to the frontier which gives the best performance value).

Table 13.4 DEA and EEM values for Metro de Madrid (1981–1992)

	DEA	Efficiency-EEM	Effectiveness-EEM
1981	1.000	1.000	1.000
1982	0.973	0.973	0.942
1983	0.911	0.911	0.846
1984	0.857	0.857	0.804
1985	0.829	0.829	0.784
1986	0.884	0.884	0.786
1987	0.896	0.896	0.798
1988	0.886	0.884	0.855
1989	0.938	0.882	0.934
1990	1.000	0.916	1.000
1991	0.995	0.924	0.995
1992	1.000	0.965	1.000

Figure 13.5 shows the relative DEA value taken from Table 13.4. The operation of Metro de Madrid shows a decreasing trend in efficiency between 1981 and 1985 with the efficiency value decreasing from 100 percent to 83 percent during the period. In 1986 this changed, and in the following two

years the efficiency value remained approximately the same – around 89 percent. In 1989 efficiency increased again and in 1990 it reached 100 percent which was maintained up to 1992.

   Figure 13.6 shows the EEM. This plots the relative efficiency-EEM value against the relative effectiveness-EEM value. Between 1981 and 1985 the relative efficiency and effectiveness-EEM values decreased. This is seen in the figure where the tracing of points moves towards the origin for each year up to 1985. In 1986 the relative efficiency improved compared to 1985 but the relative effectiveness remained unchanged. Between 1986 and 1990 effectiveness improved but the level of efficiency remained, with minor changes, similar to the 1986 value. This is represented in the figure by a vertical shift in the position of the points. From 1990 to 1992 relative efficiency increased and the relative effectiveness of the system remained constant. The results show that, in relative terms, 1981 was an efficient and effective year while 1990 and 1992 were also very effective years, but less efficient.

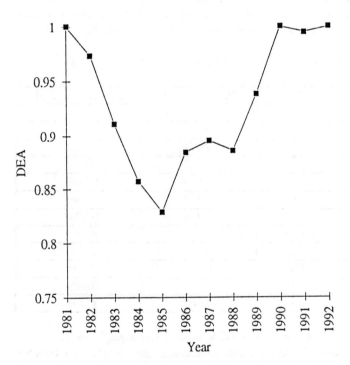

Figure 13.5   Relative efficiency DEA value for Metro de Madrid 1981–1992

The pattern which emerges in the figures can be explained by several events that occurred in the enterprise from 1981 to 1992.

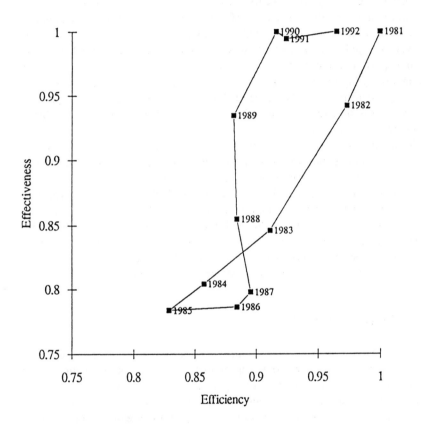

Figure 13.6   Metro de Madrid Efficiency/Effectiveness Matrix

Between 1981 and 1985 the number of passengers continued a downward trend from previous years which, combined with network expansions, acquisition of new vehicles and more staff, led to a significant decrease in the effectiveness of the service provided. These combined effects decreased overall performance. The creation, in 1985, of Consorcio Regional de Transportes Públicos de Madrid may have introduced more discipline into the management of Metro de Madrid. The following years correspond to the introduction of travel cards and a general increase in the number of passengers. It appears that much of the increase in the number of passengers was due to a lowering of transport fares resulting from intense utilization of the new travel cards and to probably also to better coordination of public transport modes. This corresponds to a general increase in the effectiveness of the enterprise until 1990. However, efficiency improvements were not experienced during those years. From 1990 onwards, there is a general increase in the relative efficiency of the enterprise due to a new agreement, between Metro de Madrid and Consorcio de Transportes, establishing the levels of supply and productivity that they should seek to achieve. During the same period, effectiveness remained constant mainly because it was abnormally high in 1990 due to a long strike at the bus operator that induced extra passengers to use Metro de Madrid. Further, an increase in the price of travel cards in 1992, the first since their introduction in 1987, probably deterred new passengers.

Two aspects seem to have affected the performance of Metro de Madrid. First, the introduction in 1987 of the travel cards and their subsequent rapid uptake (1195564 sold in 1987, 5264478 in 1990 and 7482778 in 1992) resulting from the decrease in the price of travel (the price of the travel card remained constant in nominal terms from 1987 to 1991) that led to increases in the number of passengers. Second, the contract established in 1990 with the transport authority with production targets created greater cost discipline. These two aspects cannot be identified in the DEA application (Figure 13.5) but can be clearly spotted in the EEM application (Figure 13.6).

6.   CONCLUSIONS

A new economic climate has induced a movement to reorganize public transport systems in Western European metropolitan areas. Evaluation of the impacts of the new structures of organization which have emerged on the operation and utilization of transport systems is not easy in part because profitability is not the only measure of the performance of a public service. Traditional approaches to evaluating performance based either on univariate ratios of performance or on single objective functions are therefore limited in their usefulness.

The EEM method used here can evaluate a transport system over a period of time and give relative information on the productivity and effectiveness of the transport service. This is highlighted in a case study involving two different applications to the operation of Metro de Madrid between 1981 and 1992 – a DEA and an EEM application. The results confirm an increase in the discretionary power of EEM methodology when compared with the DEA. EEM gives more information because it offers a mechanism for distinguishing between efficiency and effectiveness – productivity and level of utilization of the service – which in the public transport sector is important.

Changes in the organization and operation of the service had considerable repercussions to the performance of Metro de Madrid which experienced gains in efficiency and effectiveness. The creation of the transport authority with the introduction of a common and much cheaper fare system favoured gains in effectiveness and the introduction of contracts with specific production targets favoured gains in efficiency.

ACKNOWLEDGEMENTS

The author would like to acknowledge the financial support of Calouste Gulbenkian Foundation, Lisbon, and to express a special gratitude to Kenneth Button, Thomas Weyman-Jones and two unknown referees. The author would like to thank also Carlos Cristóbal Pinto from Consorcio Regional de Transportes Públicos de Madrid.

REFERENCES

Banker, R., A. Charnes and W. Cooper (1984), 'Some models for estimating technical and scale inefficiencies in data envelopment analysis', *Management Science* **30**, pp. 1078–92.

Boussofaine, A., R. Dyson and E. Thanassoulis (1991), 'Applied data envelopment analysis', *European Journal of Operational Research* **52**, pp. 1–15.

Button, K. (1993), *Transport Economics*, 2nd edition, Aldershot, UK: Edward Elgar.

Charnes, A., W. Cooper and E. Rhodes (1978), 'Measuring the efficiency of decision making units', *European Journal of Operational Research* **2**, pp. 429–44.

Chu, X., G. Fielding and B. Lamar (1992), 'Measuring transit performance using data envelopment analysis', *Transportation Research* **26A**, pp. 223–30.

Consorcio Regional de Transportes Públicos de Madrid, Memoria 92, Madrid, Spain.

Farrell, M. (1957), 'The measurement of productive efficiency', *Journal of the Royal Statistical Society*, (Series A) **120**, pp. 253–81.

Fielding, G., T. Babitsky and M. Brenner (1985), 'Performance evaluation for bus transit', *Transportation Research* **19A**, pp. 73–82.

Ganley, J. and J. Cubbin (1992), *Public Sector Efficiency Measurement: Applications of Data Envelopment Analysis*, Amsterdam, Netherlands: Elsevier.

Henscher, D. and I. DeMellow (1991), 'Performance evaluation in passenger transportation: what are relevant measures?', *Proceedings of the 2nd International Conference in Privatization and Deregulation in Passenger Transportation*, Tampere, Finland, pp. 23–38.

Lewin, A. and R. Morey (1981), 'Measuring the relative efficiency and output potential of public sector organizations: an application of data envelopment analysis', *International Journal of Policy Analysis and Information Systems* **5**, pp. 267–85.

Metro de Madrid, Cuentas anuales e informe de gestión 1992, Madrid, Spain.

Oum, T. and C. Yu (1994), 'Economic efficiency of railways and implications for public policy – a comparative study of the OECD countries' railways', *Journal of Transport Economics and Policy* **28**, pp. 121–38.

Shephard, R. (1970), *Theory of Cost and Production Functions*, Princeton, USA: Princeton University Press.

Weyman-Jones, T. (1991), 'Productive efficiency in a regulated industry – the area electricity boards of England and Wales', *Energy Economics*, April, pp. 116–22.

NOTE

1. For a similar methodology in the cases where profits are a good measure of performance evaluation see Boussofaine et al. (1991).

14. Network Impacts of Changes in the European Aviation Industry

Aisling J. Reynolds-Feighan and Joseph Berechman

1. INTRODUCTION

Air transport plays a vital role in facilitating the movement of goods and people, particularly over long distances. Within Europe, the air transport sector will have an important role in catering to the needs of the internal market as it becomes more integrated and interaction levels over all distances continue to increase. Air transport will also continue to play a pivotal role in linking Europe with the external world, contributing to the growth of traded goods and services. Fostering the growth and development of an efficient air transport system, which caters for the internal and external needs of the European market, requires a flexible and imaginative framework in which existing players and new players may operate to provide differentiated air services to passengers and shippers alike.

The recent European approach to air transport has been one of 'phased liberalization' as opposed to the more dramatic US-style deregulation which took place in the late 1970s. This approach in Europe has given airlines many new opportunities for growth and development. These airlines had until recently been constrained in the development of their networks, which lie at the heart of their operations. These networks represent at once the production plans and products of the carriers. Under the liberalized regime, market forces will influence the evolution of the industry in the expanding single market. The US experience, however, has shown that regulations governing new practices, products and networks need to be in place to ensure that there is a net benefit in this process. In this contribution, changes in Europe's air transport policies will be focused and the important network implications of these changes will be discussed in detail.

The 'third package' of air transport liberalization measures came into effect on January 1st 1993 for the 12 members of the European Union (EU). The main features of the third package are summarized in Section 2 of this chapter. In Section 3, the theoretical literature examining the implications of deregulation for airline network structure is reviewed. The effects of intensified 'hub and spoke' (HS) airline networks are discussed in this regard. Data on the current state of the European air transport sector are piecemeal and distinctive trends are not yet apparent. Section 4 of this chapter looks at the current state of air transport in Europe and tries to assess the competitive impacts of the third package so far. There are many limitations in the third package and significant barriers to competition remain. These barriers are outlined in this section as well. The impact of these barriers on the development of efficient air transport network structures is highlighted. When subsectors of the air transport industry are examined closely, additional difficulties in the form of constraints and barriers to competition become apparent. To highlight this fact, in Section 5 the air freight industry in Europe is examined and several of the constraints and barriers to competition in this subsector are revealed. In Section 6, the final section of the chapter, some general conclusions are drawn relating to network evolution and structure under the liberalized European regime.

2. THE THIRD PACKAGE OF AIR TRANSPORT LIBERALIZATION MEASURES

The EU took substantial steps towards liberalizing the internal European air transport market in July 1992 with the adoption of Council Regulations No. L240, the so called 'third package' relating to several key aspects of the industry's operation including access for community air carriers to intra-community air routes, licensing, and fares. The previous packages (the first package of 1987 and second package of 1989) represented more modest moves to liberalization and came in the wake of European Court of Justice rulings applying, for the first time, Articles 85 and 86 of the Treaty of Rome (relating to antitrust type restrictions) to air transport.[1] The first two packages were related only to scheduled passenger services. The adoption of the third package came at a time of crisis for the airline industry, with the sector in Europe and elsewhere coming to terms with the effects of the Gulf War and subsequent recession. The third package applied to the twelve member states from January 1st 1993 and also to Norway and Sweden from mid 1993 because of the unusual situation of cooperation between the three Scandinavian countries in international aviation. The second package of air transport liberalization measures (with more limited liberalization of passenger fares, full cargo pricing freedom, capacity restrictions (60/40) and some fifth freedom rights and public service obligations) was adopted in Austria, Finland and Iceland on January 1st 1994 with the third package to be adopted in 1995. Switzerland is expected to be included in the AEA air transport market from 1997. So by 1997, it is expected that 18 countries will be covered by the third package. This amounts to 20 percent of the global scheduled air transport passenger market in terms of revenue passenger kilometres (RPKs) (21 percent in terms of passengers carried) and 32 percent of global scheduled air freight RTKs (ICAO 1994).

The third package removed the distinction between scheduled and non-scheduled operations in air transport although it has to be noted that the distinctions were becoming more ill-defined over time as scheduled carriers had been offering increasing numbers of charter services or setting up subsidiary charter companies. The charter carriers for their part have been offering scheduled services on a limited number of North-South intra-European routes in recent years. Europe's charter industry accounted for over half of all intra-European passengers and about two-thirds of total intra-European RPKs. These shares have remained relatively constant for the last ten years (*Avmark Aviation Economist*, April 1994; Doganis 1994).

Council Regulations Nos. 2407/92 to 2411/92 cover a wide range of issues in the scheduled and non-scheduled passenger and cargo markets. Council Regulation 2407/92 deals with common licensing arrangements and the rights of community registered carriers to operate aircraft owned anywhere in the Community. The licensing regulation requires that the principal place of business and registered office be located in the state in which the carrier is registered, that the carrier carries insurance and that air transport is the main concern of the licensee. Licensed carriers are not required to own their own aircraft, but they must have at least one at their disposal. These aircraft must be registered in the state's aircraft register, although it is left to the discretion of the member state to issue a license to the carrier if the aircraft at their disposal are registered elsewhere in the EU.

Council Regulation 2408/92 covers access to intra-community air routes. This includes the abolition of capacity restrictions between member states, and the removal of restrictions concerning fifth-freedom[2] and multiple designation[3] rights along with a gradual phasing in of cabotage[4] rights. Full cabotage is not required before April 1997. Consecutive cabotage is permitted where a carrier uses less than 50 percent of its seasonal capacity on a service on which the cabotage segment is an extension or preliminary to an interstate route. This regulation also makes provision for the imposition of public service obligations and permits entry to be restricted on new routes between regional airports (these aspects are discussed in detail in Reynolds-Feighan 1995a and 1995b). Provision is made for member states to establish non-discriminatory rules for distributing air traffic between airports within an airport system (for example, the London or Paris airport systems). These regulations permit carriers to significantly extend their market areas and offer substantial opportunities for greater efficiency through scale and scope economies. On the demand side, greater product differentiation will have a significant effect on traffic volumes. The network implications of these forces will be discussed in Section 4.

Council Regulation No. 2409/92 grants freedom for EU carriers to set air fares and rates for services, except in specific limited circumstances. In Council Regulation 2410/92, the EU competition rules are formally extended to the air transport sector while amendments to certain categories of agreements and concerted practices in the air transport sector are made in Council Regulation No. 2411/92. Several of the negative outcomes associated with deregulation in the US are now subject to safeguard provisions in the European liberalization programme: computer reservation system ownership and bias, predatory pricing practices and slot allocation issues relating to hub airport dominance (see Van De Voorde 1992; Button and Swann 1992; Bjarnadottir 1994). These regulations will impact on the pattern of consumer demand, on carrier profitability and airline industry structure. The empirical and theoretical literature to emerge in the US after deregulation suggests the possible consequences of these forces for carrier network structure. This theoretical literature is reviewed in the next section.

3. AIRLINE DEREGULATION AND THE CHOICE OF NETWORK STRUCTURE: REVIEW OF THEORETICAL EXPLANATIONS

It has long been observed that, following the aviation deregulation in the USA in 1978, airlines have significantly intensified their use of hub and spoke (HS) network structure while increasing frequency of operations (Bailey et al. 1985; McShane and Windle 1989). These observations raise two interesting and interlaced analytical questions. First, what are the possible underlying explanations for the HS phenomenon? Second, why has this phenomenon intensified following the liberalization of aviation markets? In this section, the alternative explanations found in the economic literature are reviewed.

The overall theoretical explanations provided in the literature for airlines' choice of HS network structure can be grouped into three major types: cost side economies; demand side effects and market dominance. Each of these will be examined and then related to the present realities in the European aviation market. For illustrative purposes and in order to provide a common basis for the three interpretations given to the HS network structure, we make use of a simple network structure, composed of three nodes (cities) linked by three routes, as shown in Figure 14.1.[5]

I. Cost Economies: A number of authors (for example, Bailey et al. 1985; Morrison and Winston 1986; Keeler 1991; Brueckner and Spiller 1991; Hendricks et al. 1992) argue that cost considerations, mainly economies of aircraft size coupled with scope economies underlie the intensified use of HS networks. What this argument essentially implies is that the use of an HS network has two major effects: (a) it increases traffic density on each route served and, as a consequence, enforces aircraft size economies; (b) the use of a major hub, through which all traffic is funnelled, introduces conditions of joint production which, in turn, intensifies scope economies.

In terms of the above simple network, assuming the profit maximization objective,

$$\pi^{HS}(f_1, f_2) > \pi^{FC}f_1, f_2 f_3)$$

which, in turn, implies:

$$\sum_{i=1}^{2}[(y_i^{HS} * p_i^{HS})] - c(y_1^{HS}, y_2^{HS}) > \sum_{i=1}^{3}[(d_i^{FC} * p_i^{FC})] - \sum_{i=1}^{3} c(y_i^{FC})$$

The superscripts HS and FC are used to indicate that output, prices and costs under the HS network are distinct from those under the FC network. Thus, even if total revenue under the two network options are similar, cost savings from aircraft size economies and from scope economies will make the use of HS more profitable than the use of FC networks.

It should be emphasized that, from theoretical as well as empirical viewpoints, traffic density economies do not imply scope or scale economies. In fact, airline costs in some markets (for example, local or feeder services) can be explained on the basis of traffic density economies whereas costs in other markets (for example, trunk services) are strongly affected by scope and scale economies (Caves et al. 1984).

II. Demand Side Effects: Demand side effects is another argument advanced in the literature to explain the intensified use of HS networks following deregulation. Two types of explanations fall under this school of analysis: relative demand elasticity and product differentiation.

In general, passengers' utility from air travel is affected by two main factors, airfare and total travel time. The latter factor is composed of several components, the two main ones being wait time and actual (airborne and transfer) travel time.

Since demand elasticities relative to airfare and travel time components are disproportionate (in particular, for different types of passengers like business and non-business), then it is conceivable that the adoption of HS networks has a positive effect on demand by reinforcing those demand factors with higher relative elasticities. Specifying demand in utility terms the following expression characterizes air travel demand (see Berechman and Shy 1994):

$$U_i \cong x_i \bullet \Delta + \mu(y_i)^\gamma - (p_i)^\alpha > 0; \; y_i$$

where U_i is an individual utility function common to each passenger flying route i (only business and non-business passengers are differentiated); x_i is 1 if route i is served and 0 otherwise; Δ is the premium a traveller is willing to pay to fly direct (not via the hub); μ is the (monetary) value of time; γ ($0 < \gamma < 1$) is frequency elasticity (ACM per time unit), and α is fare elasticity.

Beginning with the airfare elasticity factor it has been observed that following the deregulation in the US, on most routes on which effective competition has developed, airfares have substantially declined (Morrison and Winston 1986; Borenstein 1989). A simple explanation might be that competition within markets (for example, within routes) which has evolved after deregulation, has brought down fares by eliminating (or reducing) previous monopolistic rents. In this case the decline in airfare does not in itself explain the HS phenomenon, but the decline in airfares is linked to the use of HS networks through the increase in competition which has ensued (see below). A related explanation is that in deregulated competitive aviation markets the use of HS networks which, in the presence of density and scope economies, result in lower average costs to the airline, will also result in lower airfares. With airfare elasticities of -0.378 and -0.180, for non-business and for business passengers, respectively, one can expect an increase in traffic from airfare decline with positive effects on overall profitability.

A major theoretical and empirical result from the use of HS relative to FC networks, is the significant increase in frequency, that is, in ACM per time unit (Morrison and Winston 1986; Barrett 1990; Oum et al. 1993; Berechman and Shy 1994). This effect, in turn, significantly reduces wait times (time between departures) and produces more favourable multiple departure times. Morrison and Winston report demand elasticity for wait time of −0.047 and −0.206, for non-business and business passengers which, in the case of the latter group, is larger than their travel time demand elasticity (−0.158). Under these conditions, the use of HS can be explained on the basis of increased revenue resulting from increased traffic, given the cost level. Berechman and Shy (1994) have shown that if the premium passengers are willing to pay to travel directly (Δ) is low enough, the airline firm will operate an HS network. One case where this might happen is when the demand elasticity with respect to frequency (γ), is sufficiently large to outweigh the effect of Δ.[8] Morrison and Winston (1986) estimate that doubling frequency will result in 21 percent demand increase by business travellers compared with 5 percent for non-business travellers.

Product differentiation is another line of argument found in the literature to explain aviation network restructuring. Encaoua et al. 1992, argue that this demand side effect has also a profound effect on network structure. Briefly stated, product differentiation implies that competing airlines have an incentive to make their services as unsubstitutable as possible (thus differentiated products) in order to retain a distinctive share of the market. They do so by having their own departure (frequency) schedules and price structure. In the first stage of the analysis consumers who face these divergent schedules (called network properties) incur extra waiting time costs. In order to capture more demand airline firms will then have an incentive to schedule their departure times closer which, in turn, will weaken their ability to charge differentiated prices. Based on these tradeoffs Encaoua et al. (1992) show that when carriers have the same network structure maximum differentiation in departure times is viable. It is interesting to note that this explanation notwithstanding, carriers tend to use flight amenities and frequent flier programmes to differentiate their services and, at the same time, to price discriminate between classes of passengers.

III. Market Dominance: The empirical literature suggests that airfares on routes which are served by more than one carrier are likely to be significantly lower than comparable routes served by a single carrier or by a carrier with a dominant position in that market (see Borenstein 1992, for a review). This observation raises the question of the potential relationships between competition in the aviation industry and the structure of aviation networks. In particular, if airlines aspire to maintain a dominant market position, can they use HS networks to that end and if so, how?

Several researchers have hypothesized such relationships by making the structure of the network an endogenous variable as well as a strategic means under the threat of entry (Berechman et al. 1994; Bittilingmayer 1990). To see this, in the above simple network model consider the case where prior to deregulation a monopoly airline decides to operate an HS network, namely routes 1 and 2 with services between cities A and C via the hub at B. Suppose now that following deregulation a potential entrant is threatening to provide direct service on route 3 (between A and C). If he is successful, the incumbent firm will face a decline in demand (thus profits) since the A-to-C passengers can now switch to the new entrant's market. Under what conditions can the incumbent retain his market share by deterring entry? Will he always attempt to deter entry or will he, under certain conditions, accommodate entry?

Berechman et al. (1994) have examined the conditions under which an incumbent airline firm will deter entry attempts by a new entrant following deregulation, or will choose to accommodate entry. The principal result from the analysis is that the HS network can serve as an entry deterrence (or accommodation) mechanism even in cases where the HS is more costly to operate. Key factors in this analysis are the nature of the deregulation policy (partial deregulation – one route only, or global deregulation – all routes); passengers' demand structure as characterized above; the airline's cost structure; and available aircraft capacity. Given the proper conditions relative to these factors, the analysis shows that when faced with the threat of entry the incumbent airline will operate an HS network, thus successfully obstructing entry. Profitable entry accommodation, on the other hand, will transpire if a certain group of passengers of sufficient size have high value of time relative to other groups (the Δ, μ parameters), so that the incumbent will find it profitable to split the market with the entrant, each serving a particular group of passengers.

While it is beyond our scope here to describe in detail the deterrence/accommodation mechanism there are two points worth mentioning regarding these results. First, the entry deterrence or accommodation market arrangements are not due to any possible asymmetry between the incumbent and entrant airlines but rather ensue from the heterogeneity of passengers relative to their value of time. The second point is the decisive effect of the type of aircraft available to the airline, on its market behaviour.[9] The overall results from the analysis are summarized in Table 14.1. Notice that FC operations under deregulation are associated with zero profits whereas HS operations are associated with strictly positive profits.

Obviously, an entrant needs to maintain slots at cities A and C, if he is to actually carry out his entry threat in market 3. Alternatively, if he wants to enter on markets 1 and 2, he needs to hold slots also at hub B. Hence, another useful entry deterrence approach is for the incumbent to exercise grandfather rights at airports thereby hindering new entrants from gaining slots. The importance of hub dominance was highlighted by Borenstein (1989), who showed that airlines which have a dominant position in hubs also charged much higher prices compared with cases where they did not have such a position.

In relating this discussion of the theoretical literature to the European experience, the role of entry barriers and capacity or slot constraints in particular must be emphasized again. The development of US style hub and spoke network systems would require that carriers have the ability to coordinate their schedules to allow for increased volumes of transfer passengers at hub airports. This requires that there is capacity available in the form of terminal and runway slots and that there are efficient ground handling services and air traffic management systems in place to facilitate reorganization or expansion of flight schedules. The capacity constraints at many of the large EU airports will limit the extent to which existing carriers may experiment with new network schedules and expand the scale of their operations. The scope for cost economies for some carriers may be limited.

Table 14.1 Entry deterrence/accommodation under different deregulation policies and aircraft capacity characteristics

Market Structure	High Aircraft Capacity	Low Aircraft Capacity
Partial Deregulation	Accommodation: HS ($\pi>0$) Deterrence: HS ($\pi>0$) FC ($\pi>0$)	Accommodation ($\pi>0$) Deterrence: FC ($\pi>0$)
Complete Deregulation	Accommodation: HS ($\pi>0$) Deterrence: HS ($\pi>0$)	Deterrence: FC ($\pi>0$)

Note: π is profits.

Effective free entry at all EU hub airports will also impact on the extent to which competition among carriers develops on individual routes and therefore the extent to which demand side effects can impact on network structures. As shown in Table 14.3, it is reported that 6 percent of intra-community routes had three or more carriers. Commentators like Doganis (1994) and Balfour (1994) suggested that so far in Europe, significant competition has not emerged. This situation is not independent of the capacity constraints discussed above, and will impact on carriers' ability to differentiate their services in the form of increased frequency. These factors may conspire to permit some carriers to continue dominating their home markets at least in the short to medium term.

The barriers to competition and to efficient network development discussed above apply to passenger carriers as well as cargo carriers. In the next section, the current state of the European scheduled air transport sector is reviewed.

4.   CURRENT STRUCTURE AND COMPETITIVE SITUATION IN EUROPEAN AIR TRANSPORT

The European air transport industry is dominated by the flag carriers of the member states. Table 14.2 shows the proportion of total scheduled air traffic for each EU state carried by the flag carrier. On average, 83 percent of total scheduled traffic (measured in revenue passenger kilometres) or 73 percent of total passenger numbers are carried by the flag carriers. The table also shows the proportion of each flag carrier's passenger and freight traffic carried on intra-European routes. Because of the short or medium haul nature of most European interstate routes the average proportion of revenue passenger kilometres (RPKs) on European routes is 34 percent while the average proportion of total passengers carried on these routes is 55 percent.

The current state of competition on European interstate routes was examined by using data from the UK Civil Aviation Authority (CAA) and the Association of European Airlines (AEA). Price data for routes with differing numbers of carriers were not available for assessment of monopoly or collusive behaviour. The number of carriers is used to give a broad indication of the level of competition on routes. These data are presented in Tables 14.2 and 14.3. Table 14.2 shows the twelve EU flag carriers with the total number of intra-EU routes (cross-state, as opposed to domestic routes) being given along with the number of single carrier routes. On average 36 percent of carriers' routes are single carrier routes.[10]

Table 14.3 looks at the breakdown of 'international EU routes' and domestic scheduled city pairs characterized by (i) single carrier routes (ii) routes with two carriers and (iii) routes with three or more carriers. The data from the CAA pertain to all intra-EU routes in 1994; the AEA data pertain to routes operated by AEA members only. According to the CAA data, 65 percent of all routes are single carrier routes, with a further 29 percent having just two carriers operating. The AEA data reflect to a greater degree the competitive situation for the flag carriers. They suggest that 47 percent of the routes are single carrier, while a further 41 percent are two carrier routes. For most of the two carrier routes, the flag carriers would have been subject to capacity and possibly revenue sharing agreements in the past. The extent to which competition has now developed between the carriers on these routes cannot be properly assessed at this stage, given the lack of adequate price data. The AEA data show that an additional 22 routes have been characterized by having three or more carriers competing since passage of the third package.

Table 14.2 Passenger traffic characteristics of European flag carriers, 1993

Carrier	Country	European as % of Total Scheduled		Domestic as % of Total Scheduled		ICAO Traffic per State, 1993		Number of Intra-European	
		RPKs 1993	Pax Carried 1993	RPKs 1993	Pax Carried 1993	RPKs	Pax Carried	Routes	% Single carrier
Aer Lingus	Ireland	44.2	80.9	1.4	8.0	4209	4650	28	16
Air France	France	13.2	50.5	16.4	12.0	59201	34472	64	16
Alitalia	Italy	23.2	45.4	7.4	33.5	29759	21803	48	2
Austrian Airlines	Austria	52.8	85.6	0.0	0.0	5629	3297	N/A	N/A
British Airways	UK	15.8	48.9	6.3	20.5	124882	50185	73	22
British Midland	UK	49.3	49.7	50.7	50.3	"	"	N/A	N/A
Finnair	Finland	38.6	52.6	11.4	35.6	5529	3947	N/A	N/A
Iberia	Spain	24.0	34.3	23.1	52.9	27105	22279	45	11
Icelandair	Iceland	39.8	45.0	3.2	31.0	1968	801	N/A	N/A
KLM	Netherlands	11.1	53.2	0.0	0.3	38544	11775	45	24
Lufthansa	Germany	18.9	38.9	9.3	42.8	52941	29363	127	49
Luxair	Luxembourg	100.0	100.0	0.0	0.0	290	471	23	19
Olympic Airways	Greece	34.3	29.8	11.8	58.2	7899	5478	27	10
Sabena	Belgium	34.5	80.5	0.0	0.0	6484	3651	40	16
SAS	Scandinavia	36.5	44.7	23.5	49.8	20583	25126	28	6
Swissair	Switzerland	23.3	65.7	0.6	7.8	17704	9887	N/A	N/A
TAP	Portugal	38.0	54.7	11.4	26.0	7917	4026	41	19

On the domestic routes, the CAA data suggest that 91 percent of routes are single carrier routes. This may reflect the fact that many domestic routes can only sustain one carrier, or that many routes are operated for social or regional development purposes. Only 2 percent of domestic routes have three or more carriers present. These domestic routes will not be subject to free access and price setting until at least 1997.

Table 14.3 State of competition on intra-European routes

(A) UK CAA – 1993 Data

	Intra-European Routes	Domestic Scheduled City Pairs
Total number of routes	636	763
One airline on route	411 (65%)	694 (91%)
Two airlines on route	187 (29%)	53 (7%)
Three or more airlines	38 (6%)	16 (2%)

(B) AEA Carriers Intra-European Routes

	December 1992	April 1994
Total number of routes	410	427
One airline on route	196 (48%)	201 (47%)
Two airlines on route	186 (45%)	176 (41%)
Three or more airlines	28 (7%)	50 (12%)

Source: Association of European Airlines 1994 Yearbook, AEA, Brussels

Some early predictions suggested that Europe's charter airlines would face significant competition from the scheduled sector, once the third package came into force. However the fact that Europe's charters operate in distinctive niche leisure markets and have substantially lower overall costs as well as having higher aircraft utilization rates than the scheduled carriers, means that they are in a strong position to continue as a significant market sector in Europe. The third package afforded the charter carriers the rights to offer new cargo services and to be treated equally on CRSs. The charter airlines are now offering seat only sales alongside inclusive package tours. There is still discrimination against charter carriers according to *Avmark* (April 1994), particularly in relation to ground handling services and facilities and access to airport slots, where scheduled operators have been treated more favourably particularly at congested airports. So far, the charter carriers have not ventured to compete with the scheduled carriers on non-leisure intra-European routes despite their relatively large presence in the intra-European market.[11] Within the charter sector, carriers have faced a very competitive market in Europe and there continues to be overcapacity in the subsector. As a result, several companies have failed financially and do not have state governments to bail them out. Entering scheduled markets would increase a charter carrier's costs and possibly make the carrier uncompetitive in their base market (*Avmark*, April 1994). Competing with a strong incumbent on a route requires provision of significant capacity and extensive marketing in order to attract customers. Several of Europe's flag carriers have shown a very aggressive response to entry by new carriers (for example, Aer Lingus on the London–Dublin route).

In assessing the current liberalized air transport regime in Europe, several significant barriers to entry and to competition remain in the industry which limit the extent to which a truly competitive market can evolve. Several recent papers detail these problems (Doganis 1994; Balfour 1994); Comité des sages 1994). As has been shown, Europe's air transport markets remain highly concentrated with the majority of routes being single carrier or two carrier routes. Doganis (1994) suggests that three specific factors indicate that the expected benefits and market changes associated with successful liberalization have not emerged in Europe. These are: (i) that no serious competition has emerged within Europe to challenge the dominance of existing flag carriers; (ii) there has been a growing concentration within the European airline industry due to mergers and share purchases among major carriers, along with the collapse of some smaller carriers and failure of new entrants; (iii) while limited competition has increased on some intra-European routes (most notably those out of London), and a wider range of fares has emerged on these routes, on the majority of routes which continue to be operated by two flag carriers, 'fare competition and innovation tend to be limited'. It has already been noted, however, that the European liberalization came at a time of recession in the industry and that comprehensive data which would help assess the short term impact of liberalization in Europe are not available as yet.

The Comité des sages report of 1994 showed great concern about capacity constraints at European airports and argued that 'slots will again become the crucial issue for achieving real liberalization of the market' (page 20). The Comité called for an increase in overall airport capacity as a matter of urgency. Balfour (1994) argues that in relation to the slot allocation rules which were adopted by the Commission in 1993 (Commission Regulation 95/93, OJ L141, 22.1.93) 'the Regulation as eventually adopted by the Council departs little from normal practice and creates few opportunities for new entrants, except by extending the "use it or lose it" rule to a certain degree'. Because of this, 'new entry, and hence competition, on many major routes remain virtually impossible'.

The Comité comprehensively reviewed the main problems facing the European industry. They demanded that state aid to national carriers be permitted only in limited circumstances and that carrier restructuring plans should ultimately lead to privatization. The Comité called, for the most part (there were two dissentions), for complete liberalization of ground handling services as soon as possible. With regard to external policy, the Comité felt that in order to reduce competitive imbalances currently existing between member states, a common external policy was vital. Without it, the process of improving the competitive position of the European industry was undermined. The slow pace with which problems were being addressed in the area of air traffic control came in for criticism as did the lack of development of a European airport system serving the internal market, rather than being left to local planning agencies. Removal of VAT on internal air transport was called for along with rejection of any carbon tax proposals. In relation to the environment, the Comité called for harmonization of the legal basis and procedures for planning and construction of airport facilities so as to reduce delays and costs associated with lengthy hearings on such cases. In summary, several key barriers to competition remain in the industry despite the significant liberalization in the third package.

These barriers to entry and to effective competition will have a significant impact on the extent to which carriers (both new and incumbents) will be able to reorganize and optimize their networks. Reynolds-Feighan (1994) has shown that the European flag carriers in 1990 organized their traffic flows around a single hub network. The extent to which schedules can be optimally coordinated in time and space is constrained by such factors as air traffic control delays and other difficulties and by airport slot availability. One of the most dramatic effects of US deregulation was the move by carriers to concentrate traffic and coordinate its flows through multiple interactive hub and spoke network systems. The reasons why this network system developed were discussed in the previous section. Empirical evidence for the US can be found in Borenstein (1992) and Hansen and Kanafani (1990). For the air cargo sector, these barriers to competition will constrain its development and its ability to organize carrier networks in an efficient manner. However in addition to many of the practical difficulties outlined above, the air cargo sector faces several additional constrains which restrain the development of an efficient and competitive air cargo sector in Europe. These issues will be explored in the next section.

5. COMPETITION AND NETWORK STRUCTURE IN THE EUROPEAN AIR FREIGHT SECTOR

In this section, the nature of network organization in the air freight sector is highlighted and several constraints on this subsector's development are presented. The outcomes of US deregulation of air cargo in 1977 and 1978 are briefly reviewed particularly in relation to carrier network structure. The main characteristics of Europe's air freight industry are then described for 1993, before the prospects for European air freight markets are examined.

US air cargo deregulation impacts: The major trends to emerge in global air freight have been influenced to a significant degree by the outcome of deregulation in the US domestic cargo market in 1977 and 1978. The impacts are discussed in Reynolds-Feighan (1994) and in terms of industry structure and organization can be summarized as follows:

(i) The number of all-cargo operators increased from 3 in 1977 to 19 in 1993 (including non-scheduled and express operators).

(ii) The market share of the total US domestic freight market carried by all-cargo operators increased from less than 17 percent in 1977 to 56.7 percent in 1993. (International traffic statistics were not available from the FAA for 1993).

(iii) The express or integrated carrier emerged as a significant new player in the deregulated market. Express carriers freight tons accounted for 80 percent of the all-cargo tonnage and for 45 percent of total US domestic freight in 1993. Federal Express, the largest of the express carriers, accounted for 72.6 percent of the all-cargo share of traffic and for 41 percent of total domestic freight tons in 1993. Federal Express merged in 1989 with Flying Tiger which at the time was the second largest US all-cargo carrier. The market is highly concentrated.

(iv) All-cargo carrier air networks are organized typically as single hub systems (unlike passenger carriers, where networks are typically multiple interactive hub and spoke networks). In the case of express carriers, the substantial surface transport operation is combined with these air networks to produce multimodal interactive hub and spoke networks.

(v) Express carriers have sought to significantly expand their networks internationally and develop new products such as warehousing/stock control, shipment tracking and logistics management which they package with their door to door freight services.

(vi) Express carriers have sought to have federal deregulation of certain aspects of surface transport, which until 1994 remained regulated at the state level. This constrained efficient operation of local level operations in many instances.

Table 14.4   Characteristics of Europe's air freight markets

Carrier	Country	% of State's RTKs	% Freight carried on Freight services		Total Europe freight as % of total scheduled		Total Nth Atlantic freight as % of total scheduled		Total Long Haul freight as % of total scheduled	
			RTKs	Tonnes	RTKs	Tonnes	RTKs	Tonnes	RTKs	Tonnes
Aer Lingus	Ireland	100.0	50.5	45.9	11.9	52.1	88.0	42.6	88.0	42.6
Air France	France	97.4	52.8	46.9	1.3	9.2	30.9	29.0	93.9	82.6
Alitalia	Italy	99.4	41.4	35.3	3.6	17.8	49.3	37.9	93.4	68.9
Austrian Airlines	Austria	66.9	0.0	0.0	22.8	63.7	46.7	18.7	66.9	26.0
British Airways	UK	50.6	5.0	2.6	2.9	17.3	44.7	42.2	90.3	73.6
Finnair	Finland	99.7	3.6	11.9	12.7	40.6	44.0	27.3	86.4	51.8
Iberia	Spain	98.2	19.1	24.3	8.1	22.7	30.0	17.4	80.4	41.3
Icelandair	Iceland	100.0	14.6	17.7	38.7	49.1	60.3	41.0	60.3	41.0
KLM	Netherlands	110.8	18.6	15.3	2.7	19.4	37.6	37.0	94.2	76.0
Lufthansa	Germany	99.9	49.8	43.8	3.1	17.5	37.6	30.6	90.0	65.7
Luxair	Luxembourg	90.0	0.0	0.0	100.0	100.0	0.0	0.0	0.0	0.0
Olympic Airways	Greece	100.0	0.0	0.0	31.9	36.5	22.8	5.8	56.7	14.1
Sabena	Belgium	100.0	0.0	0.0	4.6	24.2	50.4	40.8	92.9	71.8
SAS	Scandinavia	95.4	0.0	0.0	11.1	40.4	49.9	23.8	84.5	38.3
Swissair	Switzerland	99.6	0.0	0.0	5.4	30.6	43.6	32.2	90.6	59.6
TAP	Portugal	99.8	0.8	1.6	18.8	40.4	23.7	14.5	73.4	38.8

The US express carriers have sought to expand their US operations into Europe in the last decade. These efforts will be reviewed because they help to highlight several difficulties constraining the development of these kinds of operation in Europe.

European Developments: The third package relates to air freight carriers as well as passenger and combination carriers. Cargo services had not been dealt with in EU regulations until 1991, when third and fourth freedom rights were specified along with authorization of fifth freedom rights for carriage of freight by EU registered carriers within the EU and full pricing freedom (Bjarnadottir 1994; *Official Journal of the European Communities* L036/91). The data in Table 14.4 describe the main characteristics of European carriers' air freight traffic.

As with scheduled passenger services, air cargo is dominated by the national or flag carriers. Table 14.4 shows that on average, 94 percent of total revenue tonne kilometres (RTKs) are performed by the flag carrier. The main exception is the UK where BA perform about 51 percent of total RTKs. Europe's air freight is carried by passenger carriers and by combination passenger cargo carriers (such as Lufthansa and Air France). In Table 14.4, the proportion of freight carried on freight only services by the flag carriers is given. For Lufthansa, Air France, Aer Lingus and Alitalia only, over 40 percent of RTKs are performed on dedicated freighter services.

Air freight within Europe tends to account for a small proportion of carriers' total RTKs and tonnes carried. For the AEA carriers covered by the third package, intra-European traffic accounts for 17 percent of RTKs on average, and for 36 percent of freight tonnes. For many of the carriers, the North Atlantic is the most important market sector for freight, averaging 41 percent of total RTKs and 27.5 percent of freight tonnes carried. This reflects the significantly larger stage length on these long haul routes compared with intra-European routes. Long haul routes more generally (i.e. North, mid- and South Atlantic, sub-Saharan Africa, Far East/Australasia and other routes) account for an average of 78 percent of RTKs and 50 percent of freight tonnes. The breakdown for individual carriers is given in Table 14.4.

The proportion of freight carried on freighter only services is greater for the long haul routes than for short/medium haul routes, for those carriers offering freight only services. This reflects the fact that on longer haul routes, as distance increases, the cargo capacity of passenger aircraft becomes increasingly constrained by the weight of passengers, baggage and fuel (this is not the case for the B747-400 and B777 aircraft). Within Europe, competition from surface modes has a negative impact on air freight potential. The fact that passenger airlines have traditionally looked on cargo as a byproduct of their passenger operations (with the marginal cost of cargo considered close to zero) and priced accordingly, means that rates have been low relative to the economic costs of the services. Domestic markets account for a small share of the total RTKs (averaging less than 2 percent of RTKs) but a more substantial 10 percent of total freight tonnes.

Earlier it was stated that there has been air cargo pricing freedom in Europe since 1991, and access to intra-European routes. Because of the small geographical size of the European internal market (compared with the US domestic market), significant developments and growth in European carriers' air cargo traffic are expected to emerge in the long haul markets. The North Atlantic and Europe–Asia markets are expected to record 6.5–7 percent annual growth rates in RTKs according to Boeing. The forecast for intra-Europe growth is a more modest 2–3 percent per annum for the same period (1993–2013).

Policy implications for network development: The fact that the European Commission has not been able to adopt and implement a common external policy limits access on long haul international routes typically to the flag carrier designated in the bilaterals. This impediment to competition is much more significant in air cargo markets than in passenger markets because of the heavier reliance on long haul routes. European, US and other governments have shown less resistance to air cargo deregulation than to passenger deregulation in the past and perhaps this area will be first to experience more widespread liberalization beyond Europe.

In relation to slot allocations, particularly at congested airports, scheduled passenger operations have been prioritized until recently. While charter passenger carriers can expect more favourable treatment under the new regulations, cargo carriers will still face disadvantages. One alleviating factor arises because of the different preferences which cargo carriers face compared to passenger carriers – where passengers have a preference for daytime direct routings, shippers have a preference for early morning delivery with the elapsed business time between pickup and delivery being minimized. The carrier's routing is less important. However, noise regulations and airport curfews restrict the choice of airports for the cargo operators and in many instances will force cargo developments to be centred on secondary European hubs rather than the main hubs. This may impact to a significant degree on the development of dedicated all-cargo carrier networks and on the cost efficiencies which may be gained through network reorganization.

The aircraft noise legislation agreed by European ministers of transport related to two areas. These are (i) non-addition of 'Chapter 2' aircraft to EU aircraft registers after 1992, and (ii) a ban on Chapter 2 aircraft and engines after 1997. For some all-cargo operators, particularly express operators, low utilization rates make newer aircraft uneconomic. New entrants after 1997 will be competing for aircraft equipment purchases/leases as well as trying to compete in offering air services. Europe's air freight industry will rely on developments in the EU's external aviation policy in order to open up greater opportunities to competition. Europe's passenger carriers already offer low cost competition because of their cargo pricing procedures along with their advantages in having substantial access to the main European airports.

Policy issues for air courier operations: As was reported earlier, the US market saw very significant growth in the express carriers in the 1980s. Federal Express, UPS and DHL set up significant European operations during the 1980s. UPS continues to operate in Europe but has suffered losses in this segment. Federal Express suffered very substantial losses in their attempt to clone their US operation in Europe, eventually pulling out of Europe in 1992.[12] TNT (the Australian owned carrier) and DHL continue to operate in Europe but like UPS they have sought to ally themselves with European local distribution networks or European postal services. The failure of Federal Express in Europe suggests several further constraints on the development of courier operations and other air freight developments despite liberalization.

The size of the European express market is small relative to the US with US interstate express packages averaging three million per day while in Europe, the average daily traffic is estimated to be of the order of 120000 to 140000 per day (*Economist* 1993). Establishing a presence in the express market requires a significant air network and surface distribution system at local levels, with strong marketing of services. The entry costs are high. In Europe, the postal services have moved to compete with the private operators, unlike the US where it is estimated that the Post Office now carries about 10 percent of overnight mail. Some of Europe's post offices have sought to form alliances with air carriers (for example, TNT) in order to compete in the express market. Links with the national airlines and rail companies, which have been put in place on a small scale so far, may present formidable market presence and keep out new entrants as they expand. Rail-air links particularly may offer a significant advantage in meeting city centre to city centre time-definite delivery requirements. As in the US, regulations governing other surface transport modes as well as other activities (for example, postal services, telecommunications etc.) must be considered in parallel with air transport regulations.

6.   CONCLUSIONS

In this chapter, European air transport policy has been reviewed in some detail, with recent evidence suggesting that the market still faces significant barriers to competition. Entry to intra-European routes has been slow, and no significant new competitor has emerged. Because of capacity constraints at several major European airports, and state ownership of (and often state aid to) flag carriers, entry will continue to be difficult for new carriers in the short to medium term at least.

The theoretical literature on network structure in deregulated markets was reviewed and it was shown that three main sets of factors could explain the intensified use of hub and spoke networks after deregulation. These were (i) cost economies (of scale, scope and density) impacting on firms' operations; (ii) demand side effects (such as fare reductions or frequency increases); and (iii) market dominance, where hub and spoke network structures permitted carriers to achieve or maintain dominant positions. These factors were related to the European experience in terms of how barriers to competition could hinder the development of more efficient network structures.

This chapter then looked at the air freight sector where several additional constraints were identified which may significantly hinder network growth and development. In this sector globally, the forecasts suggest that growth will continue at a rate of 1–2 percent higher than that for passenger services. In Europe however, the air freight sector is faced with several constraints limiting its growth and development. Environmental constraints limiting airport operating hours and requiring fleet replacement for many carriers reduce the ability of the air freight sector to gain from liberalization. Slot constraints at several key hub airports (which will impact on all classes of carriers) will force some carriers to develop cargo hubs at secondary centres. For integrators, where city centre to city centre elapsed times are crucial, the further development of multimodal networks may be problematic. Rail-air links together with alliances with Europe's postal services are likely to continue offering formidable competition to private integrated or express carriers.

The European 'liberalization' rather than 'deregulation' approach attempts to dismantle a complex series of national, bilateral and multilateral regulations within a single European market context. Network structure under EU liberalization was to become a matter solely for carriers to determine. The liberalization should in theory lead to net benefits because of improved efficiency in the industry, lower fares and greater choice for consumers via flight frequency and product variety. At present, a vision of how the industry is to evolve at different scales or in different subsectors does not emerge. The major phases of EU air transport liberalization will be achieved by 1997. What is required at this juncture is a fine tuning of these and other policies in order to facilitate the efficient development of this key component of the EU's transport networks.

ABBREVIATIONS

AEA: Association of European Airlines
CAA: UK Civil Aviation Authority
CRS: Computer Reservation System
EU: European Union
ICAO: International Civil Aviation Organization
RPK: Revenue Passenger Kilometre (one paying passenger carried one kilometre)
RTK: Revenue Tonne Kilometre (one revenue tonne carried one kilometre)

REFERENCES

Avmark Aviation Economist, various editions, 1993 and 1994.

Bailey, E., D. Graham and D. Kaplan (1985), *Deregulating the Airlines*, Cambridge, MA: The MIT Press.

Balfour, J (1994) 'The changing role of regulation in European air transport liberalization', *Journal of Air Transport Management* **1** (1), pp. 27–36.

Barrett, S.D. (1990), 'Deregulating European aviation', *Transportation* **16**, pp. 311–27.

Barrett, S.D. (1991), *Transport Policy in Ireland in the 1990s*, Dublin: Gill & MacMillan.

Berechman, J., S. Poddar and O. Shy (1994), Network Structure and Entry in the Deregulated Airline Industry, Discussion Paper No. 9464, Center for Operations Research & Econometrics, Catholic University of Louvain.

Berechman, J. and O. Shy (1994), 'The structure of airline equilibrium networks', in Van der Bergh, J., Nijkamp, P. and P. Rietveld (eds), *Recent Advances in Spatial Equilibrium: Methodology and Applications: A Volume in Honor of T. Takayama*, Heidelberg: Springer-Verlag.

Bittilingmayer, G. (1990), 'Efficiency and entry in a simple airline network', *International Journal of Industrial Organization* **8**, pp. 245–57.

Bjarnadottir, V. (1994), *Air Transport in European Economic Integration: Effects of 1992 on the Services Sectors of the EFTA Countries*, Occasional Paper no. 49, European Free Trade Association, Economic Affairs Department, December 1994.

Borenstein, S. (1989), 'Hubs and high fares: dominance and market power in the U.S. airline industry', *Rand Journal of Economics* **20** (3), pp. 344–65.

Borenstein, S. (1992), 'The evolution of U.S. airline competition', *Journal of Economic Perspective*, **6** (2), pp. 45–73.

Brueckner J. and P. Spiller (1991), 'Competition and mergers in airlines network', *International Journal of Industrial Organization* **9** (3), pp. 323–42.

Button, K. (1990), 'Transport deregulation in advanced capitalist nations: the case of the USA', in Bell, P. and P. Cloke (eds), *Deregulation and Transport: Market Forces in the Modern World*, London: David Fullerton Publishers.

Button, K.J. and D. Swann (1992) 'Transatlantic lessons in aviation deregulation: EEC and US experiences', *Antitrust Bulletin*, **XXXVII** (1), pp. 207–55.

Caves, D., L. Christensen and M. Tretheway (1984), 'Economies of density versus economies of scale: why trunk and local airline costs differ', *Rand Journal of Economics* **15** pp. 471–89.

CEC, European Council (1992) *On the Evaluation of Aid Schemes Established in Favour of Community Air Carriers*, report to the Council and European Parliament, Brussels, March 1992.

CEC, Official Journal of the European Communities, various editions 1989–1993.

Comité des sages (1994), *Expanding Horizons*, report to the European Commission, Brussels, February 1994.

Doganis, R. (1994) 'The impact of liberalization on European airline strategies and operations', *Journal of Air Transport Management* **1** (1), pp. 15–26.

Economist, June 1993

Encaoua, D., M.A. Moreaux and Perrot (1992), *Demand-Side Network Effect in Airline Markets*, Working Paper, University of Paris, Center for Mathematical Economics.

Hansen, M. and A. Kanafani (1990), 'Airline hubbing and airline economics', *Transportation Research A* **24** (3), pp. 217–30.

Hendricks, K., M. Piccione and G. Tan (1992), *The Economics of Hubs: The Case of Monopoly*, Discussion Paper No. 92–09, Department of Economics, Vancouver, Canada: The University of British Columbia.

ICAO (1994), Civil Aviation Statistics of the World 1993, ICAO Statistical Yearbook (DOC 9180/19) International Civil Aviation Organisation, Montreal, September 1994.

Johnson, R.L. (1985), 'Networking and market entry in the airline industry', *Journal of Transport Economics and Policy* **19** (3), pp. 299–304.

Keeler, T.E. (1991), 'Airline deregulation and market performance: the economic basis for regulatory reform and lessons from the US experience', in Banister D. and K. Button (eds), *Transport in a Free Market Economy*, London: Macmillan, pp. 121–76.

Levine, M.E. (1987), 'Airline competition in deregulated markets: theory, firm strategy and public policy', *Yale Journal of Regulation* **4** (2), pp. 393–494.

McGowan, F. (1994), *The EEA Air Transport Industry and a Single European Air Transport Market*, Occasional Paper No. 47, European Free Trade Association, Economic Affairs Department, Geneva, July 1994.

McGowan, F. and P. Seabright (1989), 'Deregulating European airlines', *Economic Policy: A European Forum*, No. 9, pp. 283–344.

McShane S. and R. Windle (1989), 'The implications of the hub-and-spoke routing for airline costs and competitiveness', *The Logistics and Transportation Review* **25** (3), pp. 209–30.

Morrison, S. and C. Winston (1986), *The Economic Effects of Airline Deregulation*, Washington, DC: Brookings Institute.

Oum, T.H., A. Zhang and Y. Zhang (1993), 'Inter-firm rivalry and firm-specific price elasticities in deregulated airline markets', *Journal of Transport Economics and Policy* **27** (2), pp. 171–92.

Reynolds-Feighan, A.J. (1994), 'The EU and US air freight markets: network organisation in a deregulated environment', *Transport Reviews* **14** (3), pp. 193–217.

Reynolds-Feighan, A.J. (1995a), 'European air transport public service obligations: a periodic review', *Fiscal Studies* **16** (1), pp. 58–73.

Reynolds-Feighan, A.J. (1995b), 'EU air transport liberalisation: implications for small communities', *Transportation Research A* **29A** (6), pp. 467–83.

Van De Voorde, E.E. (1992), 'European air transport after 1992: deregulation or re-regulation?', *Antitrust Bulletin*, **37**, pp. 507–28.

NOTES

1. For a review of the legal and political progress towards the third package, see Button and Swann (1992); McGowan (1994).

2. A fifth-freedom right is the right to carry passengers and/or freight between two foreign countries on a route originating in or destined for the country of registration or ownership of the carrier.

3. Multiple designation is where multiple carriers are permitted to offer air services on an international route.

4. Cabotage is the right of a carrier of one state to carry traffic exclusively between two points within another state. Consecutive cabotage occurs when a carrier flies between two points within another state as a preliminary or continuation of a service to the home state.

5. The use of such a simplified network is a standard approach in the germane literature since the use of a more elaborate network with many nodes introduces mathematical complexity without any significant theoretical gains (see, for example, Morrison and Winston, 1986; Bittilingmayer, 1990; Berechman and Shy 1994).

6. Some authors (for example, Morrison and Winston 1986) have used 'number of passengers' to measure output. Yet, airlines actually provide capacity or number of flights per time unit which, given the demand, may or may not be fully utilized (load factors less than 100 percent). Furthermore, the use of ACM per time unit as a measure of output enables us to investigate the effect of deregulation on frequency of service.

7. In a more elaborate model we should have considered classes of passengers, e.g., business and non-business passengers. See Berechman and Shy (1994).

8. More specifically, for this result to hold it is necessary that the extra markup from passengers who are willing to pay the premium to fly directly is less than the extra markup from all other passengers. In most cases, the size of the former population is significantly smaller than that of the latter. In addition to frequency, the price that the airline firm can charge on each route is a critical factor. See the discussion below on entry deterrence.

9. It is certainly true that in the long run aircraft capacity is an endogenous choice variable. Here we treat it as an exogenous one mainly because entry attempts are essentially short run phenomena.

10. Many short haul low density routes are included in this total.

11. *Avmark* (April 1994) suggests that the charter carriers account for about 50 percent of total intra-European passengers and almost two-thirds of RPKs.

12. Recently they have established a small scale distribution network in Europe focusing on the main centres of population only.

15. Borders and Barriers and Changing Opportunities for Border Regional Development

Fabienne Corvers and Maria Giaoutzi

1. INTRODUCTION

Border regions constitute an interesting type of region which, due to their specific characteristics, comprise the most significant spatial discontinuities. In many cases the border *functions* as a barrier to communication, thereby disrupting the smooth flow of information in space. Since a considerable amount of interaction taking place among actors is concerned with information exchange, access to such networks is considered to reinforce the efficiency and competitiveness of the actors involved. Barriers to communication on the other hand can affect the intensity or even the existence of communication channels with serious implications for the development potential of each region. Border region barriers have induced a fragmentation of market areas, along with a duplication of services, resulting in diseconomies of scale and scope that reduce the region's development potential and efficiency (Suarez Villa et al. 1992).

The focus of this chapter will be on borders and barriers. Particular attention is given to the role of the border as a barrier to communication which has affected the cross-border diffusion of information and as a result the region's economic development potential. Section 2 starts with some theoretical approaches that can be found in spatial-economic research for the analysis of the effects of borders on the economic development of border regions. The increasing importance attached to innovation as a factor contributing to economic development and the crucial role of knowledge in innovation processes are considered in Section 3. In many cases, the border has been acting as a barrier to communication hindering the possibility for regional actors involved in innovation processes to get in touch, start linkages and set up networks with their counterparts just across the border. A typology of barriers to communication is drawn which enables the exploration of possible actions to overcome these barriers. The scope for government intervention, also at the regional level, to facilitate the cross-border diffusion of knowledge is explored in Section 4. Section 5, finally, concludes the chapter.

2   SOME THEORETICAL APPROACHES TO BORDERS AND BARRIERS

Theoretical approaches analysing the spatial effects of borders on determinants of economic development in border regions are few in number and of a very recent date (Von Malchus 1975; Corvers 1992, Corvers et al. 1994; Cappellin and Batey 1993; Ratti 1993; Suarez Villa et al. 1992; Nijkamp 1994). Within the existing literature on this research topic, two main views have been distinguished by Ratti (1993) (see Table 15.1):

• the 'border area' view, and
• the 'frontier limit' view

The *border area* view is the traditional view where the border is seen as a separating line between two or more countries, representing the legal limit of a nation state, and where border area is defined as the territory lying astride this fixed frontier line – in most cases institutional – inside which the socioeconomic effects resulting from the existence of a border are significantly felt (Hansen 1977). In his definition, Hansen considered only open or potentially open regions, excluding regions with a closed natural border situation, like mountainous regions, for example in the Alps.

Empirical studies have shown that many border regions face a poor or poorer economic development, due to their peripheral location within the nation state. Historically, border regions have rarely played an important role in the industrial development of a country. The few times industrialization occurred, it was because of their natural resources, for example coal (Mikus 1986). In most cases, border regions are economically less developed, because of the danger of a military conflict, the agglomeration tendency of industry elsewhere and the constraints in market expansion (Mikus 1986). Apart from their peripheral location, they can be often characterized by a lopsided production structure (either agriculture or declining industries) and lacking basic (let alone cross-border) infrastructure (Corvers 1992).

The *frontier limit* view refers to a border which functions less as a demarcation line, but more as a mobile external limit; border regions are seen as contact areas linking up two or more countries. The *frontier limit* approach links the study of barriers to communication with theories of spatial-economic integration (Peschel 1982). Every disappearance of obstacles to communication will influence, apart from the distance, the diffusion of material and immaterial goods (Ratti 1993:25), changing thereby the spatial economic integration of territories and economies.

Table 15.1 Two different views to evaluate the spatial impact of borders in a socioeconomic approach

Border Area view	Frontier Limit view
Definition: border = land near the dividing line between two countries	**Definition:** frontier = - a line that affects whoever or whatever is crossing it (refraction law) - limit of the land or of the country - place where marginal cost = price
Perspective: - border as fixed line - districts of physical territory	**Perspective:** - frontier as a mobile limit - discontinuity of the spatial impact accepted
Policy orientation: - regional development in a special context - infrastructure and location policy	**Policy orientation:** - enlarged area of diffusion and of economic integration - reduction in global cost of communication

Source: Ratti 1993:25

In an approach where the border is seen as a mobile frontier, barriers to communication are seen as temporary; obstacles to the diffusion of material and immaterial goods may disappear and lead to cost reduction and acceleration of diffusion processes, thereby promoting spatial economic integration. The removal of barriers to enhance the free movement of goods, services, labour and capital in the European Union, for example, offers border regions the opportunity to achieve economies of scale and improved efficiency through the joint planning, production and provision of public goods and services (for example, the linking up of missing infrastructure, the organization of common transport and communication systems, the joint promotion of industry and services).

Border area view
From the viewpoint of the *border area*, Ratti (1993) distinguishes four types of approaches which can be found in regional science literature:

- the functional activity approach;
- the core-periphery approach;
- the regional system approach and
- the strategic planning approach.

The *functional activity approach* places emphasis upon identifying and measuring the functions of the border and its impact upon the development of a border region. Three main paradigms have emerged within this approach.

Firstly, the *border-barrier* paradigm regards the border as a barrier which induces penalizing and discriminating effects in the areas adjacent to the border; an attempt is made to estimate the negative impact of the frontier on the flows. The hypothesis is that border regions have been hindered in their economic development, partly because of their peripheral location with respect to the economic centres of the country and partly because of the separation principle for which the central government awards a priority rank to its sectorial policies with respect to the regional and interregional socioeconomic relations (Hansen 1983).

The second paradigm interprets the *border* in its *filtering role* which acts as a discriminating mediator between two or more political–institutional and economic systems (House 1980). The introduction of an institutional barrier acts as a filter which modifies the economic space and results in differential rent (Ratti 1993), namely economic conditions for one or the other side of the border where the total outcome does not add up to zero. Within this paradigm an attempt is made to identify the discriminating effects (positive or negative) which result in differential incomes (for example, smuggling).

The third paradigm within the functional activity approach is the idea of the *open border* where the function of contact prevails over the separation function of the border between two or more political-institutional systems or socioeconomic subsystems (Courlet 1988). In this view, the economic development of border regions will no longer be determined by the political–institutional differential, but by the combination of the comparative advantages of the border area located at both sides of the borders. The *open border* view (Ratti and Baggi 1990) implies a transition from the economic concept of border areas (Hansen 1983) to that of the transborder economies.

The *core-periphery approach* is based on the core-periphery theory which implies a dualistic spatial segmentation into centre and outskirts. In many cases, border areas are not only outskirts in an institutional sense, but also in an economic sense (Giaoutzi and Stratigea 1989). The complex intra and interregional relationships provoke the need for proper insight into the problem of barriers which would enable the identification of the processes conditioning the structural transformations of border regions.

The *regional system approach* refers to a systemic interpretation of regional development patterns which can be considered as a spatial response to changes taking place in a dynamic, but contradictory economic system (Stillwell 1991). Borders in such a context may be identified as specific elements of a regional restructuring process which create instabilities in patterns of regional economic development. Instead of the divisory aspect of the border, the regional system approach emphasizes the contact function of the border, where transbordering relationships may arise from the encounter of diverse structures (Ratti 1993).

The *strategic planning approach* places emphasis on the role of borders for the individual subjective perception of economic agents and in particular on their strategic behaviour resulting from the presence of the border (Covin and Slevin 1989). 'The emphasis is upon individuals, upon their surrounding perception and upon their action space in the specific case of the border region. However, people do not act only following a subjective image of the space, but also following the function of external parameters, such as the economic situation, the internal and external politics of the bordering countries, and so on' (Reichman 1989).

Frontier limit view

The view of the *frontier limit* refers to a border which functions less as a demarcation line, but more as a mobile external limit. Under a political–economic profile, the *frontier limit* approach links the study of barriers to communication with the objective of spatial economic integration (Peschel 1982).

Ratti (1993) distinguishes four theoretical approaches within the *frontier limit* view in order to cope with the spatial impact of barriers to communication:

• the spatial microeconomic approach;
• the international trade theory approach;
• the spatial behaviourial approach and
• the spatial diffusion of innovation approach.

The *spatial microeconomic approach* (Hansen 1977) refers to the work of Lösch which gives one of the most interesting presentations of the border effect on the spatial economic organization. He distinguishes between political and economic borders which in rather diverse ways interrupt the network of market areas (Ratti 1993). The political borders have the role of interrupting the natural economic space, while the economic borders are defined as the places where the marginal costs equal the selling price. This border is determined by the distance, but above all by other barriers to communication, such as custom–fiscal, political–cultural, physical and so on (Ratti 1993).

Another classical author of the same school, Christaller (1933), claimed that the existence of barriers has the inconvenience of limiting the expansion area of commercialized services from central locations. However, the way Christaller introduces the element of time is interesting as he observes the way historical incidences condition the subsequent spatial organization. Both authors recognize that the negative effects – due to the existence of barriers – will determine the spatial effects of distortion and non-integration (Nijkamp 1994).

In the second approach the *theory of international trade* (Bröcker 1984) plays an important role in the study of communication barriers, since the question arising in this respect refers to the effects of economic integration on regional disparity at an aggregate level.

Thirdly, the *spatial behavioural approach* relates to the analysis of the spatial individual perception (Huriot and Perreur 1990). The concept of borders in this limited view has centred around the context of the geography of perception. Man perceives a specific territory where the border plays a role in the perception one has about space. Therefore, 'mental maps' can be an important tool to study the effects of the border on the level of perception, but also on the level of regional identity.

The fourth approach to studying the spatial impact of communication barriers is the one developed by theories of *spatial diffusion of innovations* (Brown 1981). The main paradigms developed in this context are:

• the epidemic paradigm;
• the hierarchical paradigm and
• the network paradigm.

The *epidemic paradigm* sees the diffusion of innovation taking place by contagion as a function of communication channels and inversely related to economic, sociological, cultural, and so on, obstacles and obstacles due to distance.

In the *hierarchical paradigm* the diffusion of innovations does not take place as a decreasing function of distance, but follows more precisely the urban hierarchy. The theory has been introduced mainly by geographers like Christaller and Hägerstrand, but economists have also contributed by offering arguments based on the theory of 'filtering down'.

The *network paradigm* places emphasis on the spatial differentiation in the selection environment as an important aspect of the origin and diffusion of new ideas and innovations. This is to a large extent determined by the network freedom and participation of actors. The analysis of the diffusion of innovations and, therefore, the analysis of barriers to communication is important for resolving the distortions and disparities in their spatial perspective. Table 15.2 summarizes the above mentioned theoretical approaches.

Table 15.2 Overview of theoretical approaches to borders and barriers

Border Area View:	Frontier Limit View:
Functional Activity approach	Spatial Microeconomic Approach
– Border as a Barrier	International Trade Approach
– Filtering Border	Spatial Individual Perception Approach
– Open Border	Spatial Diffusion of Innovations
Core-Periphery approach	– Epidemic paradigm
Regional System approach	– Hierarchical paradigm
Strategic Planning approach	– Network paradigm

3. TECHNOLOGICAL INNOVATION, REGIONAL DEVELOPMENT AND BARRIERS TO COMMUNICATION

The economic development potential of a region is a complicated interplay of the regional production structure and the regional production environment, something that is even more complicated in border regions since the border has cut these natural economic entities in half.

Technological innovation is increasingly considered to be an important promoter of economic growth as it is reflected in the innovative performance of firms. The innovative performance of firms is their capacity to create, diffuse, apply and adapt technological knowledge into new or improved products or production methods. Innovation is therefore not equal to Research and Development activities (R&D). The notion of (industrial) innovation has been explained in the Oslo Manual (OECD 1992:82) thus: 'Technological innovations comprise new products and processes and significant technical changes of products and processes. An innovation has been implemented if it has been introduced on the market (product innovation) or used within a production process (process innovation). Innovations therefore involve a series of scientific, technological, organizational, financial and commercial activities.'

According to this definition innovation, perceived as new or improved products or production methods, is the result of innovative activities. These cover R&D, but also tooling up and industrial engineering (for example, changes in production machinery, in tools, in production procedures), and the manufacturing start-up (for example, product or process modifications, training of staff with regard to new production methods or experimental production). The marketing for new products (for example, market tests, advertising or the adaption of the product to different markets) is also included as the acquisition of disembodied technology (for example, patents, non-patented inventions, licences) and the acquisition of embodied technology (for example, machinery and equipment relevant for a product or process innovation within an enterprise, hiring of highly qualified personnel). Design is also an essential innovative activity, since it comprises plans and drawings necessary to design, develop, manufacture and market new products or production methods.[1]

Finally, but by no means less important, the organizational change required to integrate the above mentioned activities is also an innovative activity in itself. The use of integrated development techniques which span the traditional division between R&D, production, marketing, and finance is one example to increase the internal interactive linkages between the different stages of the innovative process as well as to influence the composition of these linkages (Soete and Arundel 1993). Besides closer internal linkages between the various stages of the innovation process, firms have also sought to increase the external linkages within each stage, for example collaborative alliances between companies to share R&D expertise or R&D costs, or to investigate opportunities through the fusion of different technologies. Linkages or networks have also developed among and between public and privately funded R&D laboratories; alliances which act to increase the density of links within a particular stage (Soete and Arundel 1993:32). Tighter internal and external linkages between and within the different stages of an innovation process appear to have been partly undertaken by private firms in order to improve their competitiveness. Soete and Arundel (1993:33) have summarized several benefits to firms to organize innovation as described above. Table 15.3 gives an overview.

Network structures have received increasing attention in explaining spatial dynamics related to technology. The interaction and interrelations between different actors in a network involve communication that is made up of information flows and, more importantly, by the transfer of knowledge. Knowledge performs a crucial role in innovation processes since it encompasses the knowhow, skills and experience to innovate (Soete and Arundel 1993:35).

Although knowledge can be obtained from codified sources of information as well as from direct experience as a result of doing, the most effective means is often through direct contacts with knowledgeable individuals.

Since innovation encompasses more than R&D, these knowledgeable individuals can be scientists, engineers and technicians, but also marketing staff, accountants and financial experts, people who work at institutions involved in technical change such as production plants, research institutes, universities, as well as people who work at institutions facilitating technical change in the widest sense such as technology transfer agencies, innovation support organizations, banks and other capital providers, regional development organizations, public authorities, and so on.

Table 15.3 Expected competitive benefits to firms from closer internal and external linkages in the innovative process

---

1. Shorter development times for innovations.
2. Increase in the number and quality of innovations.
3. Reduction in costs and financial risks, due to the increasing complexity of R&D, through collaboration with other firms.
4. Increase in technological opportunities from linking several technologies to develop innovations based on 'technological fusion'.
5. Improved transfer of tacit knowledge and better user-producer relationships through networking.

Source: Soete and Arundel 1993:33

In border regions the possibility to interact with knowledgeable individuals has been hindered by the existence of the border that has functioned as a barrier to communication. Setting up and gaining access to cross-border networks could provide a means to promote regional economic development in border regions.

Since innovations are the product of a network of actors (Lecoq 1990), interregional differences are likely to occur as each region provides its own specific environment or 'milieu' in which R&D and innovation activities take place. Companies enter international competition by exploiting all the territorial resources of skills, knowhow and infrastructures of the places where they are located (Quévit 1991:236). In addition, although knowledge has become globally available due to new information and communication technologies, the region provides the entrance to this knowledge through its own resources and its external links with resources located outside the region.

Due to the specific characteristics of border regions – where nation states often treated border regions as peripheral areas – actors located in border regions became occupied with establishing links with the economic and administrative centres of the country. Exploiting the economic potential of their own border area was neglected, in some cases not even considered.

As a result, many sources of knowledge within border regions are still untapped: this refers not only to potential customers, but also to potential suppliers of capital goods, raw materials or semi-manufactured articles, competitors, employees, public and private research institutes, transfer organizations and other interface organizations (Corvers et al. 1994).

The advantages of these unexploited sources of knowledge can be grasped once the border barriers to communication are overcome. Barriers to communication may be interpreted as 'all obstacles in space or time that – apart from normal average distance friction costs in spatial communication – impede the smooth transfer or free movement of information related activities' (Nijkamp and Rietveld 1989, as quoted in Giaoutzi and Stratigea 1994:1).

With regard to communication barriers a distinction can be made between natural barriers (that is, not caused or created by mankind) and manmade barriers, for both of which the solution can be endogenous or exogenous to the region (Corvers 1992).

Natural barriers to communication are:

- barriers related to *different time zones*;
- *physical barriers* such as mountains (for example, France and Spain being separated by the Pyrenees) or seas (for example, between Great Britain and the rest of 'continental' Europe);
- *cost barriers* that relate to the costs that have to be made to overcome physical and time zone barriers.

Manmade barriers to communication are either caused (unintentionally) or created (intentionally or at least knowingly) by mankind and relate to:

- *language barriers*, often considered to be an important obstacle in border regions to start cross-border links. It is true that two different languages complicate the setting up of a joint database for example. Yet, it should also be considered that people in border regions often speak a dialect on both sides of the border that has more joint similarities than exist between their dialect and their respective national language;
- *cultural barriers* that exist between countries are often 'softer' in border regions due to the role of border regions as separation and contact zone at the same time;
- *political barriers* created by different political systems reflect the interest of national policies in their territories;

- *technical barriers* referring to different standards holding in different countries;
- the above mentioned barriers have also caused *network barriers* due to missing communication links between actors, limited capacity of the existing network or due to limited access to the network (Giaoutzi and Stratigea 1994).

The solution to these barriers can be either endogenous, that is actors (firms, public authorities, and so on) which have the possibility to solve these barriers through their own actions, or exogenous in the sense that the keyholders to the solution are located outside the region, at national or even international level.

Physical barriers can be overcome by developing infrastructure. In border regions cross-border roads, railways and bridges are often lacking or at a bare minimum. These problems can often be solved at a regional level. In some cases, for example in the case of the Channel Tunnel, the strategic impact of the project, however, is so large that it becomes a national and even international issue. Even in this latter case, where the solution to the problem lies outside the realm of the regional decision makers, regional actors still have an important role in raising awareness of the problem.

Language barriers, cultural barriers, political and technical barriers are particularly felt in border regions since this is the location where two nation states (with their distinctive language, culture, political system, economic system, and so on) meet. Regional actors can undertake actions to set up communication links, to enlarge the capacity of the existing network and to facilitate the access to the network. In that case, the border is perceived as a mobile frontier and opens up the possibility for spatial economic integration of the border region as a whole. The implications of this approach for public intervention will be described in the next section. Table 15.4 summarizes the various types of communication barriers in border regions.

Table 15.4 Tentative typology of barriers to communication in border regions

	natural	manmade
endogenous	– physical barriers (small infrastructure works) – related cost barriers	– network
exogenous	– physical barriers (large infrastructure works) – related cost barriers – time zone barriers	– language barriers – cultural barriers – technical barriers – political barriers

4.   POLICY OPTIONS TO FACILITATE CROSS-BORDER DIFFUSION PROCESSES

Regions can favour innovation processes within firms if they can supply firms with the knowledge they require either by producing this knowledge in the region or by exploiting links with sources of knowledge outside the region.

Regions can favour technological innovation if they can create conditions that favour the diffusion of knowledge between the actors within the various stages of the innovation process.

Communication is a key issue in the process of knowledge diffusion. Barriers to communication, such as national borders, may hinder the flow of information and thereby cause serious implications for the development potential of the region.

Given the existence of unexploited sources of knowledge, the economic development potential of border regions can be stimulated by setting up cross-border networks that favour the diffusion of knowledge. Research done by Corvers et al. (1994) on cross-border networking in Dutch border regions showed that firms undertaking many cross-border activities and having a high technology capacity show a better economic performance in terms of development in turnover than firms without or with only one of these two assets.

The major goal of public intervention – by public and semi public authorities at the regional level in the first instance – should be to take away network barriers by giving information on how to get access to sources of knowledge, by favouring a process that enables actors to start linkages, by increasing the number of linkages through which information can be diffused and by advertising the full exploitation of these linkages.

However, the possibility to organize such a cross-border network is not equally available in all border regions. It depends on the economic fabric of the region, the margin of manoeuvre of the various actors, not only public authorities (devolution of power), but also firms (branch plant or headquarters), the composition of the training system (universities, polytechnics), research organizations, transfer organizations, and support services available to firms, for example, whether such a strategy is viable.

The following examples are to illustrate how public intervention at a regional level could stimulate cross-border networks that favour the diffusion of information and knowledge.

Firms are interested in receiving information that is accurate and up to date on aspects such as export opportunities on the other side of the border, potential suppliers, useful research institutes and possibilities of cooperation with complementary firms.

Intermediary organizations such as Chambers of Commerce, Regional Development Corporations and employers' organizations can try to favour the day-to-day relationships between firms and their customers and suppliers (the two most important sources for technological ideas for firms). Some have already taken up this role of network facilitator by organizing industrial fora, contact days for firms in specific sectors or branches, partner match conferences, workshops and information gatherings (for example on the use of a specific technology).

Another possibility to enhance cross-border knowledge diffusion is to concentrate on sectors where opportunities for networking are likely to exist, because firms in these sectors can complement each other (in terms of supply, sales, distribution, R&D cooperation).

Some border regions are well endowed with a knowledge infrastructure and stimulating cross-border contacts between universities, their transfer agencies and research centres on either side of the border seems almost natural. Yet, the training system could receive more attention, particularly where it concerns cross-border cooperation between firms and education institutes. Since knowledge is by definition linked to persons, cross-border technology transfer can be effectively supported by stimulating the exchange of students and cross-border apprenticeships; this gives the firm a relatively easy entrance into universities and polytechnics. Other activities could be exchanges among schools (secondary level), cross-border vocational training, profession oriented language courses for employees and stimulating students to take courses at other universities in the border region (and certifying them).

5. CONCLUSION

This chapter has argued that the economic development potential of border regions has been affected by the existence of the border. In its function as a barrier to communication the border has hindered the cross-border diffusion of information.

Innovation theories stress the importance of information flows for the innovation capacity of firms, particularly the transfer of knowledge between different actors in different stages of the innovation process.

Network structures have increasingly received attention as a place of origin of new ideas and a means to diffuse information and knowledge due to the interaction of and interrelationships between different actors. Given the existence of unexploited sources of knowledge in border regions, setting up and gaining access to cross-border networks that favour the communication between knowledgeable individuals is recommended in this chapter as one potential route to foster border regional development.

In the perception of the border as a barrier to communication, we have stressed the barrier effect of the border on the cross-border diffusion of knowledge. We do not address, however, the effect of the border on the creation of knowledge in border regions.

The border can also provide incentives to create knowledge as it protects firms from their competitors just across the border. Since the border limits the immediate diffusion of knowledge, firms can reap the benefits of their new ideas, inventions and innovations first, which provides those firms with the incentive to continue their work. As a result, barriers to communication, whether linguistic, technical, administrative or political, are sometimes erected deliberately to stop or slow down the diffusion of knowledge.

The challenge for border regional development seems to be to find the right balance between the dynamics of knowledge creation and the statics of knowledge diffusion.

REFERENCES

Bröcker, J. (1984), *How Do International Trade Barriers Affect International Trade? Regional and Industrial Development Theories, Models and Empirical Evidence*. Amsterdam: Elsevier Science Publishers B.V., pp. 134–47.

Brown, L. (1981), *Innovation Diffusion*. London/New York: Methuen.

Cappellin, R. and P. Batey (eds), (1993), *Regional Networks, Border Regions and European Integration. European Research in Regional Science 3*. London: Pion Limited.

Christaller, W. (1933), *Die zentralen Orte in Süddeutschland*, Darmstadt: Wissenschaftliche Buchgesellschaft (reprinted 1980).

Corvers, F.B.J.A. (1992), *Grensregionale samenwerking als institutioneel arrangement. De Nederlandse grensregio Euregio Maas-Rijn als voorbeeld*, MA thesis, University of Leiden, Faculty of Social Sciences, Department of Public Administration.

Corvers, F., B. Dankbaar and R. Hassink (1994), *Nieuwe kansen voor bedrijven in grensregio's*, Eindrapport, Den Haag: COB/SER.

Courlet, C. (1988), 'La frontière: couture ou coupure?', *Economie et Humanisme* **301**, pp. 5–12.

Covin, J. and P. Slevin (1989), 'Strategic management of small firms in hostile and benign environments', *Strategic Management Journal* **10** (1), pp. 75–87.

Giaoutzi, M. and A. Stratigea (1989), 'Barriers to communication: the case of border areas', paper presented at the 29th European RSA Congress, Cambridge.

Giaoutzi, M. and A. Stratigea (1994), *Barriers to Network Performance in Border Areas*.

Hansen, N. (1977), 'Border regions: a critique of spatial theory and a European case study', *Annals of Regional Science* **11** pp. 1–14.

Hansen, N. (1983), 'International cooperation in border regions: an overview and a research agenda', *International Regional Science Review* **8** (3), pp. 255–70.

House, J. (1980), 'The frontier zone: a conceptual problem for policy-makers', *International Regional Science Review* **1** (4), pp. 456–77.

Huriot, J. and J. Perreur (1990), 'Distance, espace et representations', *Revue d'Economie Regionale et Urbaine* **2**, pp. 197–237.

Lecoq, B. (1990), 'Industrial organization, technological change and regional developments: a network approach', paper presented at the 30th European Congress of the Regional Science Association, Istanbul.

Mikus, W. (1986), 'Industrial systems and change in the economies of border regions: cross-cultural comparisons', in Hamilton, F. (ed.), *Industrialization in Developing and Peripheral Regions*, London/Sydney/Dover: Croom Helm.

Nijkamp, P. (1994), 'Borders and barriers: bottlenecks or potential? A prologue', in Nijkamp, P. (ed.), *New Borders and Old Barriers in Spatial Development*, Aldershot: Avebury.

Nijkamp, P. and P. Rietveld (1989), 'Barriers to communication: conceptual issues', paper presented at the NECTAR meeting on Barriers to Communication. Zürich.

OECD (1992), *OECD Proposed Guidelines for Collecting and Interpreting Technological Innovation Data – Oslo manual*, Paris: OECD.

Peschel, K. (1982), 'International trade, integration and industrial location', *Regional Science and Urban Economics* **12**, pp. 247–69.

Quévit, M. (1991), *Regional Development Trajectories and the Attainment of the European Internal Market*, Louvain-La-Neuve: GREMI.

Ratti, R. (1993), 'Spatial and economic effects of frontiers: overview of traditional and new approaches and theories of border area development', in Ratti, R. and S. Reichman (eds), *Theory and Practice of Transborder Cooperation*, Basel/Frankfurt am Main: Helbing und Lichtenhahn.

Ratti, R. and M. Baggi (1990), 'Strategies to overcome barriers: theoretical elements and empirical evidence', paper presented at the NECTAR meeting, Lund.

Reichman, S. (1989), 'Barriers and strategic planning: a tentative research formulation', paper presented at the NECTAR meeting Zürich.

Soete, L. and A. Arundl (eds), (1993), *An Integrated Approach to European Innovation and Technology Diffusion Policy: a Maastricht Memorandum*, Brussels/Luxembourg: CEC/SPRINT.

Stillwell, F. (1991), 'Regional economic development: an analytical framework', *Revue d'Economie Regionale et Urbaine* **1**, pp. 107–15.

Suarez Villa, L., M. Giaoutzi and A. Stratigea (1992), 'Territorial and border barriers in information and communication networks: a conceptual exploration', in *Tijdschrift voor Economische en Sociale Geografie* (Journal of Economic and Social Geography) **1** XXXIII 2. Amsterdam.

Von Malchus, V. (1975), *Partnerschaft an Europäischen Grenzen. Integration durch grenzüberschreitende Zusammenarbeit. Europäische Geschriften des Instituts für Europäische Politik*, Band 39/40, Bonn: Europa Union Verlag GmbH.

NOTE

1. This paragraph is based upon the draft version of the 'Manual on the Regional Dimension of R&D and Innovation Statistics' by EUROSTAT, version March 1995, 7–8.

16. Design and Assessment of Long Term Sustainable Transport System Scenarios

Peter Nijkamp, Sytze A. Rienstra and Jaap M. Vleugel

1. INTRODUCTION

The Common European transport policy has three main objectives (Commission of the EC 1993a; Nijkamp et al. 1994). In the first place, the development of Trans European Networks should be stimulated, a policy which should also favour the development of peripheral regions. Second, the transport markets should be liberalized to the maximum extent possible; market regulations should be equal in each member state and product markets would have to be opened for agents of each country. Finally, the transport sector should also aim at achieving sustainable mobility.

Fusing the economic needs with ecological constraints may, however, be fraught with many difficulties. Transport causes several externalities, such as noise, stench and visual annoyance, segmentation of landscapes, local and global air pollution. In the last few decades the externalities caused by the transport system have significantly increased because of several societal driving forces (Nijkamp 1994). Therefore, it is widely acknowledged that current trends should not continue in the medium and long term. For example, a large survey among Dutch transportation experts (see also Section 4) demonstrated that some 80 percent of the respondents were of the opinion that current trends cannot continue when a sustainable transport system should be achieved.

In practice however, sustainability goals are often not a main operational policy aim in complex and conflicting policy choices. One may wonder why this is the case, since formally a sustainable development is advocated and accepted in many countries. It appears that especially the car – as a modern 'sacred cow', but also as the most polluting mode (apart from the aeroplane) – is so popular that measures aimed at reducing car use are not appealing to

307

politicians. In this case, there appears to be a wide gap between the attitudes and wishes of individuals, and collective needs and behaviour when a policy is actually introduced (the so called 'social dilemma'). Therefore, the advocated policy during election times is usually more oriented towards sustainability than the actual policy afterwards (Rietveld 1997).

It may be clear, however, that large scale changes are necessary in order to reduce externalities caused by the transport sector. The nature of such changes may be quite diverse. Therefore, one of the main goals of this chapter is to analyse where policies may interfere in order to achieve a more sustainable transport system.

The chapter is therefore set out as follows. First, an analysis is made of prevailing trends in transport. Next, underlying factors and trends of spatial, institutional, economic and social psychological natures are discussed. Then an investigation is made of expert opinions by means of an expected and desired expert-based scenario experiment for future transport systems with a view on sustainable development. The expert opinions have been examined by means of a survey among Dutch transportation experts and scientists, complemented with expert opinions from various European countries. Finally, some conclusions are drawn about feasible, likely and desired government policies.

We restrict ourselves to passenger transport in Western Europe. The selected time horizon is 2030. For a more detailed overview as well as a description and underpinning of the questionnaire we refer to Nijkamp et al. (forthcoming).[1]

2.   CURRENT MAJOR TRENDS IN TRANSPORT

Several megatrends are important for creating a possible future outlook of the transport system. In the first place this holds for the mobility level itself, but also for changes in the modal split, since the modes differ largely in terms of their contribution to externalities (see Section 3). In this section, an analysis of the trends and expectations regarding mobility growth and modal split is presented.

2.1   Mobility Growth

The last three decades are characterized by a strong growth in surface transport in all West European countries (see Figure 16.1). The mobility growth was especially high in Southern European countries like Italy, Portugal and Spain, which may be explained by a backlog effect. Their economic development was lagging behind the other countries and their mobility level was relatively low in 1965. Therefore, the mobility growth rate in these countries is relatively high in the period considered here.

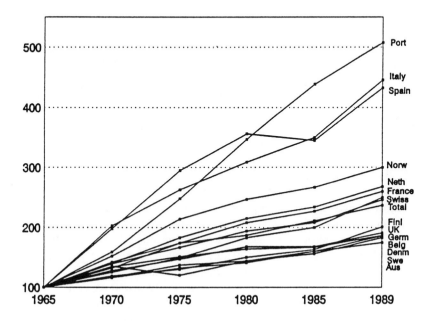

Notes: 1. Western Europe excluding Luxembourg, Greece and Ireland (because of lack of data).
　　　　2. Only passenger kilometres by private car, rail and bus are taken into account.

Source: Own calculations based on ECMT 1993

Figure 16.1　*Mobility growth in land transport in Western Europe[1,2] (index million passenger kilometres, 1965 = 100)*

When mobility growth in distinct periods is analysed, we observe that the growth rate in Europe declined between 1965 and 1985, whereas after 1985 this growth rate returned to its former growth pace. It also appears that the discrepancies in the mobility growth rates between countries were especially high in the beginning of the period under review, whereas nowadays the growth rates in Europe seem to have converged to a large extent.

Although mobility growth is expected to continue, this may occur at lower growth rates than was the case in the past decades. A main reason is that population growth may largely come to a standstill, which may reduce total mobility growth. Also the capacity of infrastructure is limited, while unlimited expansion seems infeasible because it leaves a great many externalities unsolved. Another reason may be that the individual travelling time budget is limited, while also car ownership levels may stabilize in the next decades.

An example of a gradual decline in mobility growth can be found in the Netherlands. Between 1965 and 1989 the mobility growth was about 4 percent a year, while – without policy measures (that is, 'business as usual') – the average growth in the period 1986–2015 is expected to be 2.15 percent a year (the current transport policy aims at reducing this rate to about 1 percent a year) (Ministry of Transport 1990). However, the mobility growth may still be significant, and as a result, the transport system may move further away from sustainability.

2.2 The Modal Split

The growth in mobility in Europe was very unequal for the distinct transport modes in the same period 1965–1989 (see Table 16.1). The highest mobility growth by far can clearly be found in air transport; this rise stabilized largely between 1980 and 1985, but grew rapidly again after 1985. This growth was largely achieved in very long distance (intercontinental) transport.

Also private car use increased, while the use of collective modes grew much less. Thus, the modal split changed in favour of the modes which contributed most to the negative external effects.[2] The modal split for train, car and bus in Western Europe changed from 14, 73 and 13 percent in 1965 towards 7, 85 and 7 percent in 1989 (based on ECMT 1993). The lowest share for the private car is found in the Southern European countries (75–79 percent), Austria (72 percent) and Denmark (79 percent), whereas in the Netherlands, Norway and the UK this share is the highest (86, 87 and 88 percent, respectively). The share of rail transport is decreasing in every country; its share is the highest in Austria (11 percent) and Switzerland (12 percent), while the by far lowest share is found in the UK (5 percent).

For air transport, the Commission of the EC (1993a) mentions a rise in modal share from 2.2 percent in 1970 to 5.6 percent in 1990. So it may be concluded that, besides a general mobility growth, also a modal shift occurred towards the most polluting modes.

One of the objectives of public policy in many countries is to achieve a modal shift towards more environmentally benign collective modes. In this respect it is interesting to analyse the extent to which such a shift is possible. It appears that this objective is very difficult to achieve. For example, according to calculations of the Commission of the EC (1993b), the construction of a complete High Speed Train Network may result in a reduction of the modal share of the car by only 2.5 percent in 2015 (car from 83.5 to 81 percent; rail from 8.5 to 12 percent), while the modal share of the car still increases (1987: 78 percent).

Table 16.1 Transport growth[1] and CO_2 emissions[2] by mode in Western Europe[3]

	1965	1970	1975	1980	1985	1989	CO_2[4]
Car	100	151	184	218	237	287	201
Train	100	104	115	121	126	133	71[5]
Bus	100	110	126	135	132	138	159
Air[6]	100	177	288	432	477	702	176

Notes:
1. Index 1965 = 100.
2. Grams/pass.km.; index, tram/metro = 100.
3. The same countries as in Figure 16.1.
4. In the figures about CO_2 emissions there may be an uncertainty margin of 25% or more, depending on the assumptions regarding seat occupation, technology used, vehicle use etc.
5. Electric trains only.
6. As a proxy for air traffic the number of passenger kilometres flown by the main European carriers is used.

Source: Transport growth: own calculations based on ECMT 1993 (car, train, bus) and Eurostat, several years (air); CO_2 emissions: Netherlands Railways

In order to understand this phenomenon it is necessary to analyse the travel motives for car as well as public transport use. Some illustrative figures for the Netherlands from 1992 are presented in Figure 16.2.

The private car is used mainly for commuting, business and visiting trips; public transport for commuting, visits and education. The main differences between car and public transport are found in business traffic and education. In the first category public transport is seldom used; for education this holds true for the private car, probably because school children and students often use public transport (and seldom use a car). When demographic trends are taken into account, it seems plausible that the number of children and students will decrease in the future, while the number of business trips (by middle-aged people) may increase. The commuting travel patterns – and to a lesser extent the visiting travel pattern – may be largely dependent on the spatial organization of living and working areas. It may be concluded, however, that a priori a negative impact of future changes in travelling motives on the modal share of public transport may be expected, because of demographic trends.

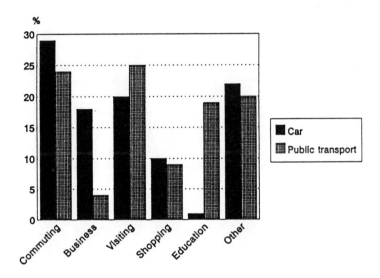

Note: Car: drivers only

Source: Own calculations based on CBS 1992

Figure 16.2   *Travel motives of Dutch car and public transport travellers (1992, %)*

An interesting contribution on the backgrounds and size of the future modal split is found in Grübler and Nakicenovic (1991). They use a dynamic theory in which every mode has its specific life cycle. A new mode may rapidly become dominant following its market introduction. After some time, however, a new mode is introduced, and the old mode loses its dominant market share. The new mode always causes a jump in mobility, and hence this rise is exponential. In a certain period at least three modes may coexist: the growing, dominating and declining one. At the moment we are living in a period in which road transport is dominating, while rail traffic is declining and air traffic is growing. According to this theory air traffic will increase its modal share, but around the year 2000 a new mode is likely to be introduced, which will start growing very fast (the authors think that maybe high speed trains and/or Maglev may be such new modes).

2.3   Environmental Impacts

It may be concluded that the past major trends indicate a continuing rise in mobility levels as well as a modal shift towards the private car and the aeroplane. These modes are the most polluting in terms of emissions of harmful gases (Martin and Michaelis 1992; see also Table 16.1). At the same time, however, new technologies like the catalytic converter and fuels of a more benign composition have been introduced. As a result, most emissions of gases like CO, particulates and SO_x have decreased, although the energy consumption by transport has largely increased (Gwilliam and Geerlings 1994; OECD 1993). At the same time however, the CO_2 emissions did largely increase.[3] At an aggregate level the transport sector appears to be the only one which has increased its CO_2 emissions, compared to industry and other sectors (see Figure 16.3).

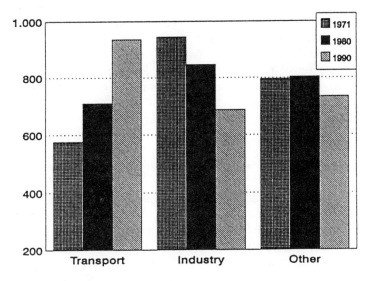

Source: OECD 1993

Figure 16.3   *CO_2 emissions in European OECD countries by sector (million tonnes)*

In light of the above observations it may be concluded that especially reductions of CO_2 emissions may be hard to achieve. An indication for the necessary reductions may be the targets in the Toronto declaration, which indicate a 50 percent reduction at a global level by 2025 (WMO 1988). For Western countries this would probably imply a reduction of 80–90 percent to compensate also for the expected emission increase in developing countries.

Solutions may inter alia be achieved by technological improvements, a modal shift towards cleaner modes and reductions in the mobility level. It is important to keep in mind, however, that transport is a derived activity; it is a means to facilitate other human activities. Therefore it is important to analyse underlying forces, which influence the growth of mobility and the modal split. This will be elaborated in the next section.

3.   DRIVING FACTORS OF SPATIAL MOBILITY

Future developments in transport may not only be analysed by investigating past trends, but also by mapping out developments in various scientific fields, which may largely influence the future of transport and the introduction of new technologies (see also Rienstra et al. 1996). In this respect it is important that technical developments and the introduction of new modes are influenced by several force fields, which may be of a spatial, institutional, economic and social psychological nature. In this section an overview will be given of trends and expected developments in these fields, in order to identify in which way such processes may affect the future of transport.

3.1 Spatial Trends

Three main spatial trends may be distinguished over the last few decades:

- centrally located regions in Europe – the so called core zone – tend to be more industrialized and economically more successful than predominantly agricultural regions in the European periphery. In this core zone the highest level of surface transport and the largest airports are found (Masser et al. 1992);
- metropolitan areas continue to be more productive and more innovative than rural regions, while at the same time the spatial area covered by large metropolises has increased (Davelaar and Nijkamp 1990). In addition, some smaller city regions outside metropolitan areas have developed innovative economic activities;
- regions in which the industrialization was built upon raw materials or heavy industry still suffer from the decline of their major industries (for example, north west England and the German Ruhr region).

To map out the future, appropriate spatial models may be constructed which take account of the level of concentration (or density) of population and economic activities and the level of functional homogeneity (or specialization). Two examples of extreme models – developed by the Dutch RPD (1991) – are the specialization and concentration model versus the chains and zones model. Their characteristics have been summarized in Table 16.2.

Table 16.2 Future spatial models at the European level

Features	Specialization and Concentration	Chains and Zones
Process	Specialization and concentration in large urban centres	Spread over urban regions (possibly some degree of self-support)
Structure	Hierarchy of functions and hierarchy of cities	Flat structure based on footloose activities
Traffic Pattern	Hierarchical radial	Crisscross relations

Also at the urban level two extreme patterns may be distinguished. During the last few decades a suburbanization of living areas has occurred, which has inter alia led to a diffusion of the spatial pattern of urban areas. In the future two extreme developments may be possible: the diffuse city in which the above mentioned trend is reinforced, as well as the compact city in which a concentration of living and working occurs in the city centre and some subcentres (Breheny 1994).

For regional European development also several futures can be imagined, which depend again on the underlying spatial model. Such developments may range from an improvement in the relative position of the European core zone, to an economic shift to the rural and peripheral regions (Masser et al. 1992).

3.2 Institutional and Economic Trends

The problem of the institutional environment is that long term trends are seldom observed. Several trends may be distinguished, however, at both the EU and national levels. A main trend is the European integration process, which should lead to increased coordination between countries in many policy areas. One of the main trends in this context is the development of the European Economic and Monetary Union (EMU). To become a participant in the EMU, countries have to meet several conditions, which concern amongst other things inflation, national debt and budgetary deficits, which reduce policy freedom at the national level. Other trends, which will not be discussed in length, are (see also Fokkema and Nijkamp 1994):

- a decreasing use of the subsidy instrument;
- a deregulation of many regulated sectors;
- a privatization of tasks and financing in many fields;
- an occurrence of a flatter organization in public policy with more sweeping contract management and self-management;
- a growth of an agreement culture between governments, and governments and groups in society;
- an occurrence of administrative shifts towards the regional level and the European level;
- an increasing social resistance to new infrastructure plans.

In general, these trends may reduce the influence of (especially national) governments in the economy and society, while an eventual intervention takes place in an indirect (market oriented) way. Also the transport market will be largely liberalized in the EU. This also holds in many cases for public transport, which has gained attention for increasing market incentives and for service provision by private instead of public companies (see also Nijkamp and Rienstra 1995). This may, however, have a negative impact on the quality and coverage of the provision of public transport, since unprofitable links may be closed.

The economic development of industrialized countries can be investigated by modelling experiments and scenario analysis. The Dutch CPB (1992) characterizes the European economy as follows:

- most stress is placed on coordination instead of free market principles;
- there is extensive paternalism in numerous fields of government policy;
- economic policy places strong emphasis on income distribution;
- there is a strong drive towards risk and uncertainty reduction, which causes many rigidities, weakens incentives and hampers individual adaptability.

Despite such background observations, it is still uncertain what and how the future economic development will be. This is analysed by the CPB by means of four scenarios for the world economy; varying from 'Global Crisis' to 'Balanced Growth', with a relatively stable and cohesive economic development. It is interesting in these scenarios that the one with the highest GDP growth leads to the lowest CO_2 emissions, because of worldwide taxes and cooperation while there is little free rider behaviour of national states.

3.3 Social Psychological Trends

Important factors determining individual travel mode options and travel needs include among other things: composition of the household, place of residence, occupation, lifestyle, income and activity pattern. When alterations take place with respect to one or more of these factors, travel behaviour may eventually change. Several future trends may be distinguished, which may have a significant impact on the future travel demand, motives and modal split:

- increase in leisure time, because of trends leading towards reducing working hours per week, which may be assumed to continue for the next few decades;
- ageing leading to a larger number of elderly people;
- individualization leading to major changes in lifestyles for example, because of a smaller size of households and an increasing population in the working force. Also the activities of people may be affected by these trends;
- globalization, which is reinforced by increasing telecommunication possibilities; it may be found in the economy, policy making, science, technology and tourism. In general, this trend may increase the demand for long distance transport (for example, air transport);
- levelling of social classes has been a major policy target in the past few decades, because of a strong emphasis on equity. In the past few years, however, a reversal of this trend may be observed in many countries.

It may be concluded that most trends in the social psychological field may lead to an increasing emphasis on individual modes of transport.

3.4 Conclusions

It is clear that past trends in transport may lead to a rising mobility level and towards a modal shift towards individual – most polluting – modes. Also the travelling motives and trends in connection with a set of different driving forces may lead to a reinforcement of these trends. Therefore, it may be concluded that without changes in behaviour and policy the transport system may move further away from sustainability criteria, an evaluation which might make radical changes necessary. Scenarios are a very useful tool for analysing such changes and policy options.

4. EXPERT BASED SCENARIOS

4.1 Introduction to Scenario Construction

An interesting and promising methodology for analysing possible futures and possible policy options under a high degree of uncertainty is constructing scenarios. This holds especially in the case of unstructured decision problems with uncertain outcomes, as is the case for transport. Interesting scenarios may be constructed by means of expert opinions, since these may have the best view on future (im)possibilities, as well as on the effectiveness of certain policy measures. Therefore, in the next section we will outline a way of constructing scenarios based on expert opinion.

There are several ways of constructing scenarios: they may be intuitive, a literary product (mostly historic), idealistic, qualitative expert assessments or an instrument for quantitative forecasts (Svidén 1989). Several distinctions between scenarios can be made (Nijkamp and Blaas 1994):

- scenarios may be either descriptive or normative. Normative scenarios include questions about, for example, the desirability of a development or choice. Normative scenarios may be constructed by means of majorities of respondents, but also by using small minority opinions;
- scenarios may be projective (based on forecasting in which the future picture is based upon the present situation and future paths leading to it) or it may be prospective (based on backcasting in which first the future picture is given, while next the paths leading to it are described);
- there are trend and extreme (reference) scenarios; the first are extrapolations of current trends, while the latter ones suppose a shock or break, leading to an entirely different future.

In the remainder of this chapter we will construct two types of scenarios – a desired and an expected one – based on a survey questionnaire which has been sent to hundreds of Dutch transportation experts and researchers who were participants in the Colloquium Vervoersplanologisch Speurwerk. These experts have various backgrounds: economy, planning, traffic engineering, geography, etc. The research population consists of scientists, consultants, policy makers of both national and regional authorities, etc. The survey contained an array of questions about the various key fields covered by the constituents of scenarios, as well as the viability and desirability of several new modes which are at present under development. The response rate of the survey was 36 percent (n = 271).

The questions were consistently subdivided into 'expected' and 'desired' answers, in order to separate factual information and subjective value statements of these experts. This allows us to identify the tension between reality and desire. Rather than describing the statistical results of this menu driven scenario experiment, we will depict here the resulting spatial, societal and transport patterns in the future by way of interpretative analysis.

It should be noted that we only present an aggregate interpretative picture; these results may be somewhat different for each subgroup of respondents (depending on age, gender, scientific background or current profession).

The methodology used for the scenario construction is the so called Spider model, which will be discussed in the next section.

4.2   The Methodology Used: The Spider Model

As shown in Section 3, many driving factors are important for the future of transport, which may relate in particular to spatial, institutional, economic and social psychological aspects represented in one of the four quadrants of Figure 16.4. In the designed scenarios the resulting future transport system is supposed to be the result of forces and developments in these fields. The most important future developments may be studied by using a multicriteria analysis, which is visualized by means of a Spider model (see Figure 16.4).

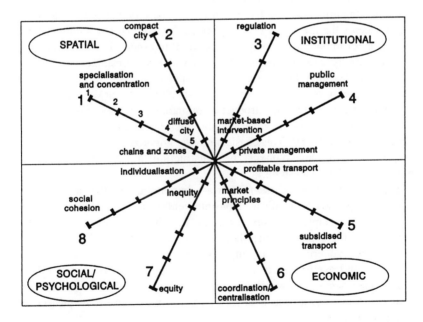

Figure 16.4 The Spider model for depicting the driving forces of future transport systems

For each of the four relevant scientific fields distinguished in our study, two axes are drawn in the Spider, which represent the most important factors influencing the future of transport and the transportation technologies used. We will now first turn to the left upper corner, which contains the spatial aspects influencing transport systems. On the first axis, possible developments in the future European *spatial organization* are mapped. At the one extreme (interior) side of this axis we find the chains and zones model vs. the specialization and concentration model. The second axis in the spatial organization is mainly concerned with urban patterns; it describes the diffuse and the compact city (as a result of explicit urban policy efforts) (see also Section 3).

In the *institutional part* (axes 3 and 4) we investigate the controlling and managerial systems for sustainable mobility. On the third axis the degree of government intervention is depicted; the contrasting ways are regulation versus market based measures. The management of transport modes and infrastructure is found on the next axis, where the two extreme ways in which this may be organized – purely public or private – are presented. In this context, public transport means that the ownership as well as the operation of the transport companies are the sole responsibility of the government (or governmental agencies).

Another important driving force stems from the *economic field*. The fifth axis concerns the feasibility of transport, as the required profitability of the system is an important factor for the future of transport. The main question in this case is whether the government wants to subsidize transport or whether modes should be operated on a commercial basis; in this way also private financing of infrastructure may be attractive. The next extremes – to be found on axis 6 – are the introduction of market principles in the economy versus coordination by the government (which may lead to some form of a centralized government). This consideration is important for future economic growth, regional development, the construction of infrastructure towards peripheral regions, and so on.

Finally, *sociopsychological factors* are important. On the seventh axis equity is opposed to inequity. Non-intervention may favour inequity in society (for example, an uneven income distribution, uneven chances for individuals, for example, travelling, education), while on the other hand much public governance may emphasize equity measures (social security, discounts on travelling costs, and so on). The eighth and final axis reflects individualization versus social cohesion, including related developments (for example, demographic, educational), which may again have consequences for transport (see Section 3).

In theory, all axes are entirely independent of each other; in the scenario construction, different variables have been used for each axis to determine the scores. Despite this, it is obvious that several developments are interrelated in the view of experts.

Scenarios can be constructed now by combining the eight points on the successive axes. When this is carried out a comprehensive picture of the future is shown and a scenario can be described. Some remarks have to be made regarding the interpretation of these axes:

- the information on the axes is only qualitative;
- the size of the resulting area has no meaning;
- technologies used in the resulting transport system are a result of developments on the axes.

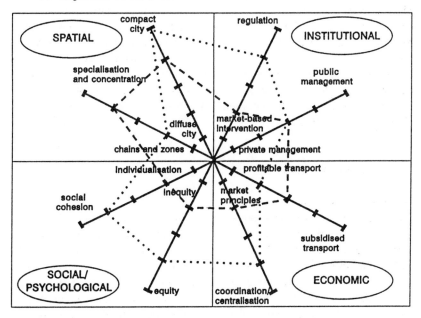

Legend - - - - expected developments
.... desired developments

Figure 16.5   The expert based scenarios

The order of items on each of the eight axes is such that the interior points are associated with less intervention (market forces and liberal attitudes when necessary combined with market based measures), which may lead to a transport system which is dominated by individual modes (for example, powered by alternative fuels; the market based scenario). The exterior points reflect the result of regulatory interventions (for example, land use planning, control strategies, and so on), in which the transport system is dominated by collective modes (the regulatory scenario) (see for a description Nijkamp et al. forthcoming).

Now we will discuss in more detail the way Dutch transportation experts expect and desire the above discussed trends and underlying factors to develop. The resulting scenarios in the Spider model based on the survey are presented in Figure 16.5.

In general, it appears that the expected scenario shows many intermediate developments in combination with a strict spatial concentration policy. The desired scenario is in general more in favour of the regulatory side of the Spider model, with two exceptions. First, the European spatial organization should develop towards a more diffuse pattern and the transport system should become more profitable than expected. Both are interesting views, but it should be emphasized that, because of the expert menu driven methodology, the consistency issue is not at stake here. We will now interpret these results for each of the four major driving forces in more detail. To construct scenarios which show the relationship between the distinct axes and developments, some developments are also mentioned briefly in the description of other fields.

4.3   Spatial Factors

Expected developments
The spatial policy is mainly expected to focus on concentrating activities and population in large urban areas in order to increase the competitiveness of collective modes, which may result in lower externalities. The suburbanization trend will largely be reversed. Especially richer groups however, do not want to move towards the cities; they prefer to stay in the more suburban and rural areas. Therefore, a moderate concentration occurs, especially in the core regions where economic and population growth is the highest.

Several metropolises appear to be very attractive for living and working. The spatial policy will not be entirely successful, however; therefore several economic activities will remain in other – medium sized – cities. In almost every country at least one so called Europolis will probably be found.

Cities also tend to develop towards a moderate compact spatial structure as a result of the public policy pursued. The people will mainly be living in centres and several subcentres of cities, because only there is affordable housing available. Several housing problems may occur however, because of the smaller size of households and because of the high prices of scarce space. Therefore, also a large share of the population lives in old living quarters outside the city centres. People who can afford it tend to move from the city centres to green suburbs. Therefore, the compact urban spatial policy is not likely to become entirely successful.

Desired developments

Next we turn to desired future images. When the desired developments – as expressed by transport experts – are analysed, it appears that in Europe a policy should be established in which an equitable regional economic development is a main objective. As a result activities and population should shift out of the core zone into more peripheral and rural regions.

In long distance transport, the policy should focus on a modal shift towards collective modes, despite the above discussed deconcentration. Activities and population should therefore be concentrated around nodes of the collective transport system. Especially the main regional cities will then become much more important. In this way a spatial organization may emerge like the chains and zones model, with a somewhat higher concentration in cities.

Also at the urban level, public policy should aim at a modal shift towards collective modes. Therefore, the compact city policy should proceed, with a strong concentration around the main nodes of the collective transport system.

4.4 Institutional Factors

Expected developments

In general, the devolution trends will tend to continue, although the influence of the government is still rather significant, especially in the spatial and land use field. Most policies, however, will be aiming at measures to keep the national economy competitive with other European countries, with other trade blocks and with the 'low wage countries'. As a result the integration of the European Union may largely stop. In several fields where cooperation is favourable for all countries (trade policy, environment), the EU is expected to gain more influence, however.

Transport will also remain the main responsibility of national governments. At the European level, strict standards for emission levels of private cars will be introduced, while the same holds for telematics standards.

Railway companies will become more independent from national governments, although the latter will still be mainly responsible for the construction of both road and rail infrastructure.

Desired developments

When the desired future developments are analysed, an entirely different future picture is found. In general, the influence of the government in many areas of society and economy should be increased in order to redress social and environmental externalities of transport, while the EU should develop as the most important authority in this area. It should introduce more compulsory standards and targets, while also the regional and local support programmes should be extended. Likewise, regional and local authorities should become much more important because of the subsidiarity principle accepted nowadays in Europe.

Because of the political emphasis on equity, regulation should be accepted as the best way for reducing externalities. A strict environmental policy may thus be introduced, implemented and respected at the European level. In the transport system many standards and regulations should be introduced, which make a shift towards environmentally benign collective modes possible. The EU should become the most important authority for transport, while urban and regional authorities should be mainly responsible for the regional and urban modes. The EU should also initiate a large scale investment programme in collective transport mode infrastructure.

Railway companies should become more independent of government influence, although the infrastructure may still be publicly owned. This may be possible if there is a separation between ownership and operation, while the government takes the responsibility for the infrastructure and its costs.

4.5 Economic Factors

Expected developments
European countries will have largely integrated their markets by the year 2030, and further cooperation is not likely to be achieved. The competition between countries and trade blocks tends to have a negative impact on mutual coordination; environmental policies, for example, are probably not centrally introduced and accepted because of frequent 'free rider' behaviour of various countries in the large European space.

European funds for rural and peripheral regions will largely be abolished, while at the same time a shift towards the core zone of individual countries will be fairly probable. Therefore, the core regions may develop relatively favourably, while peripheral and rural regions will face a relative decline.

The government is expected largely to withdraw from the transport market, in particular from longer distance transport. The trend towards resistance in society against closing public transport links increases, but – in view of equity principles – the regional and urban transport system may still be subsidized to a large degree.

Profitability of railway companies will be rather high for long distance transport. For other segments however, profitability is fairly low, so that the railway system is still largely subsidized. The same holds largely for car transport, as user charge principles like road pricing are not likely to be introduced on a large scale, but only on the most congested links of transport networks.

Desired developments
The desired economic organization in the year 2030 contains much more coordination and centralization in the European society and economy, which may however have a negative impact on economic growth. This should be accepted, because of equity reasons (both regional and individual). As a result, however, the European position in the world economy may become relatively less important.

Because of regional support and the policy to achieve equal regional development, a shift from core regions towards surrounding regions is needed and has to be encouraged. As a result the economic position of regions will converge.

In the desired scenario, the government should also intervene more in the transport market and should oblige railway companies to cover all transport links. At the same time large price increases should be avoided in order to stimulate public transport use. Profitability of the rail sector should increase drastically, because of the policy measures to make car use more expensive which stimulates the modal shift. Road pricing may be introduced to a large extent, so that investments in road infrastructure will also become profitable. The efficiency of railway companies should largely be increased by a shift from a bureaucratic organization to a commercial service oriented corporation. As a result, the transport sector as a whole should be operated on a cost covering basis.

4.6 Social Psychological Factors

Expected developments
The individualization trend in society is expected to continue at the current pace. As a result, a society with more and smaller households is likely to occur. This may increase evasion behaviour and obstruct spatial policy; consequently, behaviourial changes will not be sufficient to change the transport system dramatically.

At the same time social security systems may have to be abolished; the same will hold for many subsidies, for example, in public transport. Also taxes will be lowered to improve the competitiveness of national economies.

Three main income classes may be distinguished. The class of rich people (approximately 15 percent of the population) can afford to live outside the cities and in green suburbs. They will own a private car used for most transport needs.

About 75 percent belongs to the middle class, which mainly lives in the centres and subcentres of cities. They own a private car, powered by conventional fuels or by electricity. Collective modes will be more attractive on dense transport links for this class, which is often the case between compact city centres, because of the lower prices and the high quality of the transport service offered.

The lowest income class will eventually probably account for about 10 percent of the population. This class will mainly live in the old living quarters, where housing is cheap but of low quality. They often will not be able to afford a private car. High quality nodes and terminals of the collective transport system (HST and main train stations) may be rather remote. Thus, the mobility possibilities of this less privileged group tend to be significantly lower.

Desired developments

A desired trend as seen by Dutch transport experts is that society should increasingly accept that individualization and its impacts cannot continue, because of the great many negative consequences for the environment and the well-being of individuals; therefore, this trend should be reversed. It should be widely accepted, however, that environmental measures are necessary, while equity may become a main objective of public policy. As a result, regional support has to be increased, while also the social security systems should not be abolished.

The income classes should differ largely from the expected situation, since the middle class is much larger, while the other classes are smaller. The rich people (some 10 percent of the population) can still afford to live outside the compact cities in 'green areas'. They own a car, powered by new fuels or electricity, which is often used for reaching nodes and terminals of the collective transport system.

About 85 percent of the population belongs to the middle class, which lives mainly in compact city centres. They often do not own a private car, because of its high costs and the scarce space in these centres. When they need a car, it can easily be rented.

The lowest class (approximately 5 percent of the population) lives mostly in the older living quarters of cities. These areas can only be reached by relatively low quality modes like bus or tram, upon which they are dependent. These services should be guaranteed by the government.

Next, we will discuss the resulting transport system, also based on expert opinions investigated by means of the questionnaire.

5. LONG DISTANCE AND URBAN TRANSPORT SYSTEMS

5.1 The Long Distance Transport System

The expected system
In general, by the year 2030 a radial transport system is likely to emerge with rather high density links between the various metropolises, mutually and between the metropolises and Europolises. High quality HST trains are expected to offer a frequent service on these links; they will be mainly used for transport between (compact) city centres.

Most people will use private cars for transport, driven by conventional fuels. The engines have become much more economical and therefore the emission of harmful gases is significantly reduced. On (very) long distances, aeroplanes will offer a regular service. Their use will become rather expensive due to tax increases, while the HST will become an important competitor.

For connections with smaller cities in Europe slower trains will also be in operation; the same holds for the main regional links. On these links the private car is also the dominant mode, however.

Mobility growth will largely continue, although it will be lower than in the 1990s because of the changes in the spatial organization. Infrastructure investments will not rise dramatically. Road infrastructure capacity tends to be increased by using telematics.

The modal split at longer distances will remain in favour of the private car, which will account for about 70 percent of transport demand. Collective modes will account for some 30 percent of the modal split; their modal share between metropolises and Europolises will, however, be relatively high with a share of about 50 percent.

The desired system
The desired system is dominated by collective modes, while the transport system should cover many crisscross links between the larger cities. These links are covered by an extensive network of HST and fast train links. Private car use should be largely reduced on long distances. Cars driving on new fuels might be used only on low density links. Road pricing has to be introduced on the main transport links. Very long distance links (where no HST connections are available) may be covered by LH_2 airplanes (powered by liquid hydrogen).

Also the main regional links should be served by trains and for smaller distances by metro/light rail systems. Here again cars may be used for low density links and also to reach public transport nodes (especially by the richest class).

Mobility growth should be negative after the introduction of the measures aimed at a reduction of car use. Mobility may grow again when much new infrastructure will be constructed for collective modes, mainly because of the more diffuse spatial organization of society.

Collective modes may account for some 75 percent of travel demand. Especially because of the relatively high share in regional traffic, the private car (driving on new fuels) may have a total market share of some 20 percent, while the LH_2 aeroplane may have a share of about 5 percent. This pattern is clearly different from the one offered by the expected scenario.

5.2 The Urban Transport System

The expected system
The urban and short distance transport system is also important for the future of transport. For example, about 40 percent of car trips are shorter than five kilometres in the Netherlands, which is an indication for the importance of this system. Another indication for possible problems is that for public transport this figure is about 16 percent, which indicates the poor competitive position of collective modes on short distances (for example, due to the waiting times) (own calculations based on CBS 1994). In this section therefore, the expected and desired urban system for 2030 will be elaborated.

A radial transport system will likely be established at the urban level like that at the European level, where the main links will be formed between the city centre and various subcentres as a result of the moderate compact spatial structure. These links will largely be served by metro and light rail connections as well as by cars, which also cover the lower density links. Also buses and trams will still be in operation, especially on links to the old living quarters. In most cases however, electric and conventionally fuelled cars will be used, especially when destinations are not within easy reach of high quality collective modes.

Mobility growth in cities is expected to be rather low because of the new spatial structures. A continuing population growth, however, may cause some new mobility growth. About 60 percent of the modal share will be covered by the private car (approximately 30 percent conventional and 30 percent electric), while 40 percent will be served by collective modes.

The desired system
In the desired future, the view is expressed that a radial transport system should come into being, with high density links between a compact city centre and its subcentres. These links are served by metro and light rail systems, which should form the backbone of the urban transport system instead of individual modes.

For short distances, walking and cycling should strongly be encouraged, because collective modes are not efficient on short distances. Sometimes, however, people-movers may offer a high quality service on very high density links.

From the nodes (terminals) of the metro/light rail systems to the final destination trams and buses may offer a complementary service. At the terminals, nodes of metro systems parking places should be constructed, which may also be used by the richer classes living outside the urban areas.

Mobility growth should become negative, as soon as car use is restricted. Later on, however, the mobility level may start rising again, because of the accompanying economic growth. About 75 percent of transport should be covered by collective modes in the year 2030, while 25 percent may be covered by the private car (using new fuels or electricity).

So it may be concluded that both scenarios lead to entirely different transport systems. An interesting question is how and to what extent policies may help to reach sustainability objectives.

6. STRATEGIC POLICY REFLECTIONS

In this section we will offer some retrospective remarks of a strategic nature and explore whether dedicated policy strategies may influence the future of transport systems and whether this development is to be expected or desired.

From the scenario results it becomes clear that human action space is structurally broadening. There seems to be a long term megatrend from a low mobility society in the past (where only nomads, scientists, artists, soldiers, tradesmen and missionaries were geographically mobile) to a mass mobility society (in which not a happy few, but society at large is exhibiting a geographical drift). In contrast to the English expression 'my home is my castle' we observe nowadays a trend where 'the globe is our home'. Transport is the trademark of a mobile society.

Policies to cope with the resulting externalities cannot yet boast a high degree of success. Regulatory systems often failed because of too ambitious target levels, an insufficient use of instruments or lack of insight into behaviourial responses. As a result, a broad spectrum of government failures in the transport sector arose, which did not contribute to the development of environmentally sustainable transport systems.

Several of the above observations were directly or indirectly also addressed in our scenario experiments. When the *expected scenario* is analysed it appears that the trends and underlying factors which are discussed in Sections 2 and 3 will not change to a large extent. For example no large scale changes are expected for individual citizens, who are not expected to change their behaviour greatly in order to reduce the externalities caused by transport. The same holds for the government, whose policy is not expected to be sufficient. Especially future spatial developments appeared to be a focal point of attention of the various transportation experts in the panel. In the *desired scenario* a clear choice is made for a collective transport system. Therefore large scale changes are necessary in the behaviour of individuals, as well as in the institutional and economic environment.

It may be concluded that the relation between *spatial organization* and the transport system was widely acknowledged. Spatial policy is therefore of major importance for the future of transport. Also other factors, like living conditions (large versus small dwellings; green suburbs versus multistorey buildings) and regional development play a major role in this policy field. Societal trends such as individualization impact also on the preferred living conditions. A concentrated and compact spatial development may be an important success factor for a shift towards collective modes, although in the desired scenario this option is combined with a moderate diffuse spatial organization. It is also important that the planning of the transport system is a major variable in decisions concerning the planning of new living quarters and working areas.

From an *institutional angle* a tradeoff has to be made between efficiency and equity, which may lead to an entirely different future transport system. In the last decade, there was a clear trend towards privatization and deregulation in the transport sector. Such policies, however, may change over time, because views on the role of the government may change compared to the past. A stable institutional environment, however, is important because then uncertainty is reduced, which may stimulate private investments in sustainable transport options. It appears that the current devolution trends may lead to a more market oriented transport system, which is mainly individually oriented.

In *economic policy* a choice seems to be inevitable between coordination/centralization and deregulation, which has a big impact on transport. Economic growth, the social security system, societal views etc. may be more important for such a decision than the resulting transport system, however. Society also has to decide on the necessary profitability of transport, and on the extent to which it wishes to earmark scarce funds for transport and for the mobility possibilities of individuals.

Governments may of course also try to steer underlying *social developments*, but it is questionable whether a significant impact from these policies may be expected. Governments in democratic countries are dependent on their citizens and may therefore largely follow these trends instead of trying to bend them. It is clear, however, that the societal view on many elements of a transport system and of the organization of space is very important for public policy in other fields.

It may be concluded, therefore, that achieving a more environmentally benign transport system is possible but hard to achieve; such a system may lead to major changes in society, which may affect the lives of individuals to a great extent.

REFERENCES

Breheny, M. (1994), 'Counterurbanisation and sustainable urban forms', in Brotchie, J., M. Batty, P. Hall and P. Newton (eds), *Cities in Competition: The Emergence of Productive and Sustainable Cities for the 21st Century*, Melbourne: Longman Cheshire.

CBS (Central Bureau of Statistics) (1992), *Statistiek van het Personenvervoer*, CBS No. N15, Voorburg/Heerlen.

CBS (1994), *De Mobiliteit van de Nederlandse Bevolking 1993*, CBS-no. N8, Voorburg/Heerlen.

Commission of the EC (European Communities) (1993a), *The Future Development of the Common Transport Policy, a Broad Approach for the Establishment of a Community Framework for Sustainable Mobility*, Brussels/Luxembourg: ECSC–EEC–Euratom.

Commission of the EC (1993b), *European High Speed Rail Network: A Socio-economic Impact Study*, Brussels/Luxembourg.

CPB (Central Planning Bureau) (1992), *Scanning the Future*, The Hague.

Davelaar, E.J. and P. Nijkamp (1990), 'Operational models on industrial innovation and spatial development: a case study for the Netherlands', *Journal of Scientific and Industrial Research*, **51**, pp. 273–84.

ECMT (European Conference of Ministers of Transport) (1993), *Annual Trends in Transport 1965–1989*, Paris.

Eurostat, (several editions), *Basisstatistieken van de Gemeenschap*, Brussels/Luxembourg.

Fokkema, T. and P. Nijkamp (1994), 'The changing role of governments: the end of planning history?', *International Journal of Transport Economics* **21** (2), pp. 127–45.

Grübler, A. and N. Nakicenovic (1991), *Evolution of Transport Systems: Past and Future*, IIASA-report RR–91–8, Laxenburg.

Gwilliam, K.M. and H. Geerlings (1994), 'New technologies and their potential to reduce the environmental impact of transportation', *Transportation Research* **28A** (4), pp. 307–19.

Martin, D.J. and L.A. Michaelis (1992), *Research and Technology Strategy to Help Overcome the Environmental Problems in Relation to Transport: Global Pollution Study*, Sast Project No. 3, Monitor – SAST Activity, EUR–14713–EN, Luxembourg: EC.

Masser, I., O. Svidén and M. Wegener (1992), *The Geography of Europe's Futures*, London: Belhaven Press.

Ministry of Transport and Public Works (1990), *Tweede Structuurschema Verkeer en Vervoer, Deel d: Regeringsbeslissing*, Tweede Kamer, 1989–1990, 20 922, (15–16), The Hague.

Nijkamp, P. (1994), 'Roads toward environmentally sustainable transport', *Transportation Research* **28A** (4), pp. 261–71.

Nijkamp, P. and E. Blaas, (1994), *Impact Assessment and Evaluation in Transportation Planning*, Dordrecht: Kluwer.

Nijkamp, P. and S.A. Rienstra (1995), 'Private sector involvement in financing and operating transport infrastructure', *Annals of Regional Science*, **29** (2), pp. 221–35.

Nijkamp, P., J.M. Vleugel, R. Maggi and I. Masser (1994), *Missing Transport Networks in Europe*, Aldershot: Avebury.

Nijkamp, P., S.A. Rienstra and J.M. Vleugel, *Transportation Planning and the Future*, Cheshire: John Wiley (forthcoming).

OECD (Organisation for Economic Cooperation and Development) (1993), *OECD Environmental Data Compendium 1993*, Paris.

Rienstra, S.A., J.M. Vleugel and P. Nijkamp (1996), 'Options for sustainable transport: an assessment of policy choices', *Transportation Planning and Technology* **19**, pp. 221–33.

Rietveld, P. (1997), 'Political economy issues of environmentally friendly transport policies', *International Journal of Environment and Technology*.

RPD (National Physical Planning Agency) (1991), *Perspectives in Europe: Exploring Options for a European Spatial Policy for North-Western Europe*, Ministry of Housing, Physical Planning and Environment (VROM), The Hague.

Svidén, O. (1989), *Scenarios: On Expert Generated Scenarios for Long Range Infrastructure Planning of Transportation and Energy Systems*, Linköping Studies in Management and Economics, dissertation no. 19, Linköping.

WMO (1988), World Conference on the Changing Atmosphere Implications for Global Security, *Proceedings Toronto 1988*, WMO–report no. 710, Geneva.

NOTES

1. The research project was carried out in cooperation with Marina van Geenhuizen (FUA Amsterdam), Edith van der Heijden and Ton Rooijers (VSC Groningen), Richard Smokers (ECN Petten) and Johan Visser (OTB Delft).

2. Air transport is also the main contributor to NO_x emissions.

3. In short, the NO_x emissions also largely increased. The emissions in the stratosphere have largely diminished because of the introduction of the catalytic converter in cars. At the tropospheric level however, emissions have strongly increased because of the increase in aeroplane kilometres.

17. Transport at the Edge of Mobility and Sustainability

Kenneth Button and Erik T. Verhoef

1. INTRODUCTION

Although the notion of 'sustainable development' has become a key concept in environmental economics and in popular political jargon, rigorous analytical support and unambiguous interpretation of its features are lacking. This is especially so in fields closely related to, but not at the core of environmental economics. An example is transport economics. The last decades have witnessed a stream of economic studies in the field of transport and environment, which typically rely on the neoclassical concept of external costs, and are performed in a static, partial equilibrium setting (Verhoef 1994). While the results of such studies may underpin the urge to develop a more stringent line of transport policies embracing the environment, they leave many crucial issues untouched. Apart from difficulties of coming to a satisfactory mapping between external cost approaches and the paradigm of sustainability, a partial approach to transport related phenomena overlooks the fact that most transport demand is derived, usually depending on spatial patterns of economic activity, and spatial and modal patterns of infrastructure supply. Therefore, 'optimal' levels of transport and 'optimal' Pigouvian transport taxes may suffer from second-best biases, since they are not derived in the context of a first-best world.

This chapter aims to shed light on a more comprehensive concept of 'sustainable transport'. It focuses on interdependencies between transport, spatial economy and the environment in the context of policies designed to achieve a global environmental target. The spatial price equilibrium (SPE) approach is adapted to analyse the environmental sustainability of spatioeconomic development, and to evaluate first-best and second-best policies. A small scale SPE model is used to perform a number of numerical simulations, investigating market based versus sustainable spatioeconomic configurations with first-best and second-best policies.

Section 2 of the chapter discusses some issues that become relevant when studying the environmental impacts of transport from a sustainability rather than an externality perspective. In the subsequent sections, these ideas are translated into a spatial price equilibrium model. Section 3 focuses on the optimal sustainable spatioeconomic system and compares it with the market based configuration. In Section 4, second-best transport policies are considered, namely the case where the transport regulator has no control over regulation in other sectors. Section 5 contains the conclusions.

2. SUSTAINABLE TRANSPORT: A CONCEPTUAL FRAMEWORK

'Sustainable development' is usually interpreted in terms of the commitment of the present generation to act consistently with future as well as present needs. After the publication of the Brundtland Report (World Commission on Environment and Development 1987), the concept has received much attention and some political support. The concept itself, however, has challenged and still challenges economic environmental analysis in several ways.

Starting from the treatment of environmental degradation in the neoclassical context of externalities, it is clear that a consistent consideration of 'future needs' in terms of intertemporal externalities and efficiency is bound to be hampered by numerous practical and theoretical obstacles. Among these are issues concerning discount rates, consumer sovereignty, and uncertainty (Pezzey 1993). Consequently, any satisfactory incorporation of the concept of sustainable development within the neoclassical framework, where the valuation of the intertemporal environmental spillovers should be based on future willingness to pay for avoiding these effects, seems beyond reach. Rather, in addition to allocative efficiency, the concept of sustainability seems to call for a scale dimension when considering environmental regulation from the economic perspective (Daly 1989). A possible approach to the operationalization of this scale dimension has been put forward by Siebert (1982) and Opschoor (1992), who suggest application of the 'Environmental Utilization Space' as a restriction on the extent to which a generation should be allowed to use natural resources (see also Opschoor and Weterings 1994). The specification of a set of upper bounds to a generation's allowable environmental claims could be based on ecological phenomena such as carrying and regenerative capacities of ecosystems, and would be the domain of biology and ecology rather than economics.

Furthermore, through its focus on the long run and system wide issues, the paradigm of sustainability embraces a much 'broader' connotation than does the notion of externalities. In terms of modelling characteristics, this points towards the application of dynamic general – rather than static partial – analyses. Whereas the consideration of dynamics in relation to sustainability is often cast in terms of aggregate macroeconomic growth models (Toman et al. 1994), a more disaggregate systems analysis becomes relevant when studying the sustainability of an open system such as a region or a sector (van den Bergh and Nijkamp 1994). Therefore, we do not explicitly consider dynamic processes, but focus on economy wide and spatial interactions. This reflects some steady state view of spatial sustainable development. It allows us to concentrate on the consequences of the interactions between transport, the economy and the environment in a spatial context when comparing market based and sustainable systems. Both sectoral and spatial disaggregation will, thus, be accounted for.

As the goal of sustainability reflects an orientation towards the long run behaviour of a well defined, closed system, some complications arise in interpreting 'sustainable transport'. In particular, it is not straightforward how sustainability should or could be defined for a subsystem because of interdependencies with other subsystems. The virtue and stability of regional or sectoral 'sustainability' are questionable when the overall system to which this region or sector belongs does not behave in a sustainable manner. Besides, environmental claims from different, economically related regions or sectors often infringe on the same global environmental goals (such as emissions of greenhouse gases). As a consequence, regulation on the level of a subsystem may often, indirectly, either benefit from synergetic side effects, or suffer from counterproductive compensatory effects in related subsystems. It is important to investigate the potential impacts of such interdependencies upon the effectiveness of environmental regulation aiming at global targets.

Consequently, sustainability as such seems to be a concept much more applicable to closed, full systems than to open subsystems. Hence, when considered on the level of a subsystem, sustainability calls for analyses allowing for consideration of all sorts of feedback effects with the 'macro' system. A necessary condition for a transport system to qualify as 'sustainable' can then be that its operation should not be inconsistent with overall sustainability. Overall sustainability refers to a sustainable level of overall activity, a sustainable spatial organization of these activities, and a supporting infrastructure network which is able to serve the transport flows resulting from this organization without conflicting with sustainability criteria. The crucial issue is, therefore, not a quest for 'sustainable transport' as some independently defined goal. Rather, the relevant ultimate target is overall sustainability, implying certain necessary features of transport. The policy issue is the attainment of sustainability, given the policy instruments available, and taking account of possibly counteracting individual behaviour.

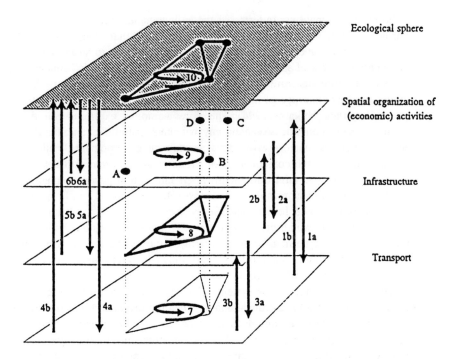

Figure 17.1   Transport, spatial economy and the global environment in a multilayer representation

Figure 17.1 serves to illustrate such a comprehensive approach. Four different, but closely related and interacting layers are distinguished. As a start, consider the second layer, which represents the spatial organization of (economic) activities. The parentheses indicate that a broad definition of the term 'economic' is used, including all possible kinds of productive and consumptive activities. It is assumed that these activities are concentrated in various nodes (labelled A–D). At this level of abstraction, one of the nodes may be taken to represent a more spacious 'node' such as the agricultural sector. Due to specialization of these nodes (fed by comparative advantages, scale economies or agglomeration economics), the nodes are not self-sufficient: the bundle of goods and factors supplied within a node is not the same as the bundle demanded at prevailing local market prices, and, therefore, internodal trade takes place. This trade is made possible by means of the presence of infrastructure (the third layer) and gives rise to all sorts of transport activities (the fourth layer). Finally, the upper layer represents the ecological sphere.

The arrows indicate various interactions that may occur in the system. The arrows on the right hand side describe issues which are traditionally at the heart of regional and transport economics. From the right to the left: (1a) indicates that the demand for transport is a derived demand, following from the spatial organization of economic activities. Conversely, (1b) represents the effect of transport on the spatial distribution of activities. Arrows (2a) and (2b) show that the construction of infrastructure depends on the spatial distribution of economic activities, but that the supply of infrastructure may in turn affect the development of the economic system. Next, (3a) represents the restrictions that the existing infrastructure pose upon transport activities, whereas (3b) indicates that an increasing demand for transport may eventually result in the construction of additional infrastructure.

The arrows on the left hand side represent the additional interactions involved when considering the question of ecological sustainability. The three ascending arrows (4b)–(6b) indicate the environmental degradation resulting from transport activities, the existence of infrastructure, and other economic activities. These effects will, to some extent, be localized. This is represented by the reprint of the spatial structure of the other layers in the ecological sphere. Other environmental externalities will be non-localized, and this is represented by the shading of the ecological layer. The three descending arrows (4a)–(6a) indicate that the state of the environment may in turn affect the other three layers. In particular, environmental degradation may affect both productivity and utility in the second layer. Additionally, the productivity in the transport sector, and the quality of and possibilities for infrastructure supply may depend on environmental characteristics.

Finally, interactions may occur within each layer. The curved arrows may for instance represent: congestion effects in transport (7); inter and intramodal network dependencies in infrastructure (8); any form of economic interdependencies (9); and physical interactions within the ecosystem (10).

It is now clear that a serious consideration of the issue of sustainable transport results in the adoption of a quite complex system of multilateral interdependent spatiodynamic interactions. Traditional economic approaches regarding the relation between transport and environment, in contrast, usually concentrate exclusively on the outer left arrow (4b) and only on its static, non-localized component. A first step to broaden such analyses to a more comprehensive one, allowing for consideration of the above issues, was presented in Verhoef and van den Bergh (1995). In that paper, a general modelling framework was discussed, based on the spatial price equilibrium (SPE) approach. One needs not be an expert in mathematics to understand that such a formal representation of the spatioeconomic system represented in Figure 17.1 leads to highly complex sets of equations, which can only be solved analytically up to the level of first order conditions. In order to get a grasp of the full comparative static properties of this model, the same starting point was taken in Verhoef, van den Bergh and Button (1995), when considering regulation in a full, closed, small scale spatioeconomic system with a global environmental restriction. This exogenous restriction represents the environmental utilization space, taken as a necessary prerequisite for overall sustainability. It is important, however, to stress that the analysis could refer to any global environmental target, be it sustainability or any other less ambitious goal. In the sequel, some results and policy implications of this latter model will be presented. Readers interested in the analytical backgrounds may consult the two above mentioned papers.

First, however, a few words on the SPE methodology should be said. This methodology, introduced by Samuelson (1952) and further developed by Takayama and others (Takayama and Judge 1971; Takayama and Labys 1986), has the property that equilibrating transport flows between two nodes come into existence as soon as the difference between nodal prices exceed transport costs. Both nodes benefit from such trade, and overall efficiency increases. Usually, SPE models are used to analyse spatial interactions in terms of commodity flows, with flexible prices clearing spatial excess demands and supplies for given transport cost structures and local demand and supply structures (hence, the spatial patterns of consumption, production, and prices are endogenous). A more general interpretation of SPE can embrace flows of production factors and intermediates, and even passenger transport. An advantage of the SPE approach in the present context is its close relation to traditional welfare economic modelling, thus lending itself to formulations in terms of welfare maximization, and derivations of associated optimal policies in a spatioeconomic equilibrium setting. The SPE approach is apt for studying questions relating to transport and the global environment, as it allows inclusion of each of the layers and possible interactions indicated in Figure 17.1. The following sections will present some simulation results obtained with a small scale SPE model based on the conceptual model presented in Figure 17.1.

3. SPATIAL SUSTAINABILITY VERSUS MARKET OUTCOMES

For the simulation model, a number of simplifying assumptions are made: the model is restricted to one good, two nodes, and one uncongested transport mode with a given level of infrastructural capacity. Furthermore, only the impact of emissions on one common global environmental target (the environmental utilization space) is considered. Although this model could obviously be criticized for the assumed simplicity of the spatioeconomic system (2 regions, 1 good, 1 transport mode, and a one dimensional environmental utilization space), we think it is more fair to judge the model as an extension of existing, even more simple models of externality regulation in transport, in which interactions with the spatioeconomic system are ignored altogether. The model is nothing more than a tool to point out and a illustrate a number of crucial issues in the environmental regulation of transport that are too often ignored. Simulation results, although having limited meaning in terms of the absolute values produced, are very useful for investigating questions of what could happen in reality, and especially why and when. In this section, some simulation results obtained with this model are presented, comparing market outcomes versus first-best sustainable spatioeconomic configurations. Before turning to these, we briefly discuss the 'base case'.

The two demand functions for the good (one for each node) are assumed to be linear and identical for both nodes (R=A,B), with intercepts $d_R=80$ and slopes $a_R=-0.5$. The production side of the two nodes are both linear but different, with intercepts $s_A=25$ and $s_B=5$; and slopes $b_A=1.5$ and $b_B=0.5$: production is more efficient in node B than it is in node A. Transport costs are equal to 5, which is smaller than the autarky price difference, and hence equilibrating transport flows will exist. As expected, in the trade equilibrium, B will be the net exporter with exports $F_B=30$, which exactly compensates for the nodal imbalances implied by $Q_A^T=20$ and $Y_A^T=50$ at the after trade nodal price $P_A^T=55$; and $Q_B^T=90$ and $Y_B^T=60$ at the after trade nodal price $P_B^T=50$ (Q denotes production, and Y consumption). In comparison with the autarky situation, total welfare in node A increases from 756.25 to 925, and in node B from 2812.5 to 2925.[1] Both nodes, therefore, benefit from trade; as they would with voluntary trade. By setting emission factors for production at $e_A=e_B=10$, and for transport at $e_T=15$, total emissions of 1550 result in the unregulated trade equilibrium: $E_A=200$; $E_B=900$ and $E_T=450$. Transport thus accounts for $\pm30\%$ of the emissions. The environmental utilization space E^* is set at 1000.

To illustrate the SPE methodology, in combination with the environmental model, in the first simulation the two production structures are gradually interchanged. On the right hand side of Figure 17.2, the base case is found; on the left hand side, $s_A=5$ and $b_A=0.5$, and $s_B=25$ and $b_B=1.5$. Moving right, s_A (s_B) is increased (decreased) by 1 each step; and b_A (b_B) is increased (decreased) by 0.05 each step. The simultaneous variation of the four parameters is summarized along the horizontal axis by showing their impact on the autarky price difference $P_A^A-P_B^A$ (the autarky prices being the nodal prices that would arise in absence of trade). Given the identical demand structures, this simulation yields symmetric results, with completely identical nodes (as reflected by $P_A{}^A-P_B{}^A=0$) in the centre.

Figure 17.2 focuses on environmental issues. From the curvature of the non-intervention emissions (NIE), it is clear that the more the two nodes differ, the higher emissions will be, due to the induced transport flows. Alternatively, when the two nodes are identical, in the centre of the figure, NIE fall within the environmental utilization space E^* and the shadow price of sustainability λ_E is zero. The basic relation between NIE, E^*, and emissions and λ_E under integral activity regulation (IAR) is illustrated. As long as NIE<E^*, no regulation is needed, and emissions under IAR are equal to NIE. As soon as NIE>E^*, regulation becomes necessary in order to prevent emissions to exceed E^*. This is reflected in a positive shadow price of sustainability λ_E. The larger the difference between NIE and E^*, the higher this value of λ_E.

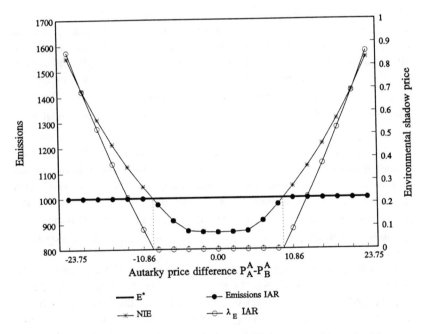

Figure 17.2 Emissions in the market based and the optimal sustainable spatial equilibrium and the shadow price of sustainability

The spatioeconomic impacts of regulation, as well as some typical SPE characteristics, are shown in Figure 17.3. First, with identical nodes and autarky prices, no trade takes place; when the autarky price difference exceeds the transport costs, the node with the lower autarky price becomes the net exporter. When NEI exceed E*, free market activity levels are excessive. Figure 17.3 shows that the more different the nodes are, the larger the discrepancy between non-intervention and sustainable levels of trade and nodal specialization. For the optimal sustainable spatial configuration, production and transport have to be increasingly restricted. Given the identical demand structures, this implies a relatively stronger restriction in production in the exporting node than in the importing node, as can be seen on both ends of Figure 17.3.

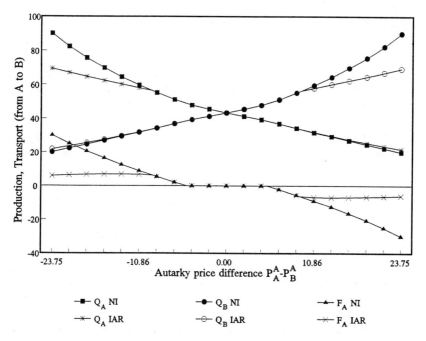

Figure 17.3   Production and transport in the market based and the optimal sustainable spatial equilibrium

4.   SECOND-BEST TRANSPORT VOLUME REGULATION

The same modelling framework can be used to evaluate various second-best policies. Second-best regulation of road transport, in particular in case of congestion, has received quite some attention over the last years. See, for instance, Wilson (1983) and d'Ouville and McDonald (1990) on optimal road capacity supply with suboptimal congestion pricing; Braid (1989) and Arnott et al. (1990) on uniform versus stepwise pricing of a bottleneck; Arnott (1979), Sullivan (1983) and Fujita (1989) on congestion policies through urban land use policies; Arnott et al. (1991), Glazer and Niskanen (1992) and Verhoef, Nijkamp and Rietveld (1995b) on regulatory parking policies; and Verhoef, Nijkamp and Rietveld (1994) on congestion pricing with an untolled alternative. Second-best regulation of environmental externalities of road transport has been dealt with in Verhoef, Nijkamp and Rietveld (1995c).

Except for the studies focusing on the dependencies between congestion and urban land use, the above analyses typically consider transport in isolation from other economic activities. This partial equilibrium approach to transport ignores the fact that transport demand is often a derived demand, depending on issues such as spatial patterns of economic activity, and spatial and modal patterns of infrastructure supply. Therefore, 'optimal' levels of transport and 'optimal' Pigouvian transport taxes derived in such analyses may suffer from considerable second-best biases. Indeed, considering transport in isolation is equivalent to assuming first-best conditions to apply for the entire spatioeconomic system. A main advantage of the above SPE model is that it offers an analytical framework for investigating these issues, and the associated complexities of different sectors infringing on the same global environmental targets.

We consider the second-best case where the regulator is capable of regulating the transport sector only, and has no influence over regulation in the production sectors. This could correspond to the situation of a relatively small transit region, concerned with the impact of its 'through-put' on some global environmental amenity, but unable to directly influence environmental policies in the nodes of origin and destination. The Netherlands are a good example. Although such a regulator cannot directly affect production and consumption, its transport policies will indirectly do so. The optimal second-best taxes in such cases were presented in Verhoef and van den Bergh (1995). These taxes trade off, in the most efficient way, the three impacts of (a) directly reducing emissions from transport; (b) indirectly reducing the emissions from production in the node of origin, due to reduced exports; and, conversely, stimulating production and hence emissions in the node of destination, due to induced local production. In the simulations to be discussed below, the focus is on how the underlying spatioeconomic system might affect the efficiency and effectiveness of such second-best transport policies in comparison with the first-best situation where the regulator can set an optimal policy mix of transport and production taxes.

Figure 17.4 considers emissions and shadow prices of sustainability under both policies. Along the horizontal axis, the emission coefficient in the node of destination e_A is raised from 0 to 45; in comparison with the base case, e_T is set at 5 rather than 15. Furthermore, production taxes are set at zero. The underlying spatioeconomic structure has a decisive impact on the performance and potential of second-best regulation. On the left hand side, this structure is relatively favourable for such policies. Not only does second-best transport volume regulation (TVR) have a favourable direct impact on emissions of transport itself, it also induces a shift from consumption of imported goods towards the purchase of locally produced goods in node A, which are produced in a relatively environmentally friendly way compared to node B. When moving right, however, this favourable indirect effect of transport policies is gradually eroded. Up to the point where $e_A=9$, this shows in an increasing discrepancy between in the shadow prices of sustainability λ_E for both policies. This shadow price, therefore, not only depends on the extent to which NIE exceed E^*, as illustrated by the gradual increase of λ_E for IAR. In addition, this shadow price also depends on the efficiency and effectiveness of regulation itself.

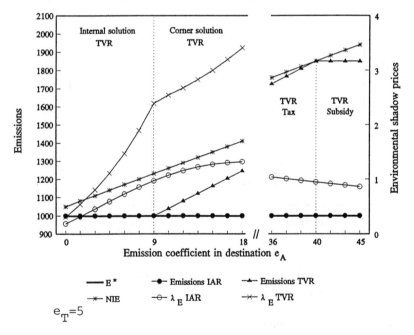

Figure 17.4 Emissions and shadow prices of sustainability under integral activity regulation and transport volume regulation

When e_A exceeds the value of 9, the outcome is in the range where TVR is
no longer capable of meeting the sustainability constraint. In this regime,
'optimal' TVR consists of the corner solution of prohibitive taxation with
zero transport (Figure 17.5). Here, λ_E for TVR should no longer be referred
to as the 'shadow price of sustainability', but rather as the 'shadow price of
reducing emissions as much as possible'. The efficiency of TVR increasingly
falls short of those of IAR, as shown by the increasing difference of
emissions and λ_E for both policies in Figure 17.4. With prohibitive
transport taxation, total regulatory tax revenues will be zero. With IAR,
internal solutions will generally result, implying positive tax revenues for
the regulator (Figure 17.5).

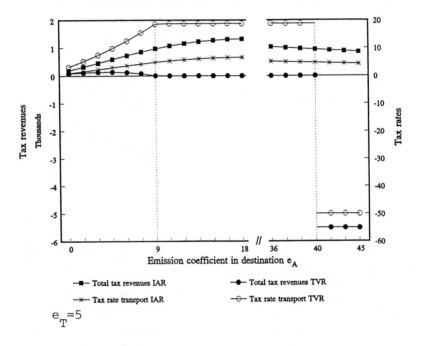

*Figure 17.5 Regulatory tax rates and revenues under integral activity
regulation and transport volume regulation*

When e_A increases further, a point will be reached where TVR becomes
completely inefficient. In this simulation, $e_A=40$ creates that particular
unfavourable combination of parameters where transport regulation has no
effect whatsoever on total emissions. Here, the direct environmental impacts

on emissions from transport are completely compensated for by additional emissions from increased local production in the node of destination; an increase induced by the transport policy itself. Here, λ_E for TVR approaches infinity.

When moving beyond this point, we end up in a third regime, where second-best TVR is in the form of transport subsidization rather than taxation. Transport taxation would be counterproductive, as it induces more emissions from production in the node of destination than it reduces transport emissions. As shown in Figure 17.5, the best thing the TVR regulator can do is to subsidize transport in such a way that local production in node A is completely reduced to zero (in this case, TVR transport subsidies should be direction specific, which is never the case for transport taxes). Simulation results not depicted graphically here show that under this regime, narrow welfare under TVR falls considerably, and even goes below welfare under IAR (even though the sustainability constraint is not met with TVR). Such TVR subsidization creates severe distortions in the spatioeconomic system.

The curvature of λ_E under IAR deserves some attention. The fact that it is rising on the left hand side of Figure 17.4 reflects that the economy as a whole becomes more polluting due to the increase of e_A. In that light, the flattening of the curve's slope on the left hand side, and its decline on the right hand side, may seem perverse. The explanation lies in the fact that the shadow price λ_E is attached to the factors e_i in the optimal tax rules. The increase in e_A, therefore, in itself has a deflating impact on λ_E. The observed pattern arises from the combination of both effects.

Although one might argue that this situation of TVR subsidization is quite extreme and unrealistic because one would not expect a transport regulator in the sort of transit region considered to actually subsidize transport for environmental reasons, the simulation has important implications also for a less ambitious transport regulator. The underlying spatioeconomic equilibrium processes leading to the pattern seen in Figure 17.4 cannot be ignored, and will affect the effectiveness of any form of transport regulation. This is illustrated in Figure 17.6, where the impact of four different levels of transport taxes ($\tau=-4$, $\tau=-2$, $\tau=2$ and $\tau=4$) on total emissions is seen for various levels of e_A. On the left hand side, taxes have a favourable impact on total emissions because of their direct effect on transport, as well as the indirect impact of stimulating a production shift from node B to A; the impact naturally being greater the higher the tax. With an increasing emission coefficient, however, these impacts decline, and beyond $e_A=40$, the transport regulator would find total emissions increasing more, the higher the transport tax charged. Transport subsidization is necessary if TVR is to reduce total emissions. If he is not inclined to subsidize transport, the best thing a regulator can do is to keep transport taxes at zero.

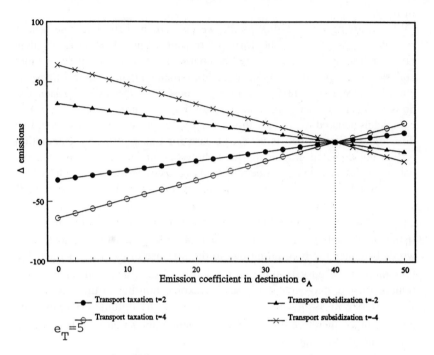

Figure 17.6   The effectiveness of transport volume regulation in a spatioeconomic setting

These simulations clearly demonstrate the sometimes unexpected effects of regulation when considered in the context of a full spatioeconomic setting, including the interdependencies between the transport sector and the spatial pattern of economic activities.

5.   CONCLUSION

In the foregoing analysis, interdependencies between transport, spatial economy and environment were investigated in the context of regulatory environmental policies aimed at a global environmental target, defined in terms of the environmental utilization space as a prerequisite for global sustainability. The results from the simulation model provide comparative static insights into issues that are important in the formulation of environmental and transport policies when considered from the viewpoint of global sustainability rather than from the more narrow perspective of a partial equilibrium externalities approach.

A binding environmental utilization space results in a positive, system wide social 'shadow price of sustainability'. This can be interpreted as a counterpart to the concept of marginal external costs in more traditional economic approaches to environmental policy. The level of this shadow price not only depends on the extent to which non-intervention emissions exceed the global environmental target, but is, in addition, inversely related to the quality of the environmental policies pursued.

Application of system wide marginal tax rules based on this shadow price leads to the most cost-effective way of achieving global environmental targets. However, in many cases, such first-best policies cannot or will not be applied. In such instances, one needs to derive the optimal second-best policies within a model that takes account of the likely sectoral and spatial spillovers that such policies may induce. In particular, environmental transport policies conducted in isolation have indirect side effects. These side effects may be advantageous, since a reduction in transport will generally lead to a reduction in overall trade and production. In some instances, however, notably if the local production sector in the importing node is relatively polluting, induced production shifts may partly or even completely offset the envisaged positive impacts of transport regulation. The analytical model used presents a framework for investigating such interdependencies.

Consequently, for the realization of global environmental targets, the formulation of isolated transport policies is not as straightforward as is sometimes believed. One would prefer to apply a first-best policy mix in which all sectors can simultaneously be regulated. If this is not possible, the transport regulator should give close consideration to the environmental implications associated with the induced shifts in the spatioeconomic structure due to the transport policies considered. The analysis thus unambiguously demonstrated the need to coordinate transport policies, spatioeconomic policies and environmental policies. Coordination failures will otherwise unnecessarily drive up the 'shadow price of sustainability', implying excessive social costs in the attainment of environmental goals.

The analysis, because of its level of generality, has relevance for transport policies at any spatial level, varying from urban to global. It therefore also has important implications for transport policies within the European Union. Due to the rapid unification of markets, intra-community transport is increasingly seen not only as a crucial supporting mechanism for integration, but also as an increasing threat to the environment. The European Commission's concern with the environmental impacts of transport, and the wish to come to a 'sustainable' European transport system, is reflected in various reports (EC 1992a, 1992b). The results presented in this chapter strongly suggest that such EU strategies towards the realization of a more environmentally friendly transport system cannot and should not be formulated in isolation from a spatial policy, which should be consistent with these transport policies, and should stimulate the spatial changes supporting the realization of a sustainable transport system.

It should be clear, though, that some of these changes are contrary to the goal of economic integration. In contrast, sustainable transport often requires enhanced spatial self-sufficiency. In other words, economic integration on such a large spatial scale may be excessive from the viewpoint of environmental sustainability, not only because of induced production and consumption, but in particular because of the induced transport flows. This does not mean that integration as such is inconsistent with the goal of environmental sustainability. However, it does imply that integration generally poses threats to this goal, and should therefore only be strived for in cases where the benefits outweigh the associated environmental costs, be they expressed in external costs or in terms of the shadow price of sustainability. Environmental policies based on economic principles should leave the problem of deciding when and where this is the case to the market, and may therefore lead to considerable social cost savings and a generally lower shadow price of sustainability. Whether such policies should be designed in terms of regulatory taxes, or in terms of socially more feasible instruments such as tradable permits, is an important question that deserves careful further analysis (see, for instance, Verhoef, Nijkamp and Rietveld 1995d, 1995e).

REFERENCES

Arnott, R.J. (1979), 'Unpriced transport congestion', *Journal of Economic Theory* **21**, pp. 294–316.

Arnott, R., A. de Palma and R. Lindsey (1990), 'Economics of a bottleneck', *Journal of Urban Economics* **27**, pp. 11–30.

Arnott, R., A. de Palma and R. Lindsey (1991), 'A temporal and spatial equilibrium analysis of commuter parking', *Journal of Public Economics* **45**, pp. 301–35.

Bergh, J.C.J.M. van den and P. Nijkamp (eds), (1994), *Annals of Regional Science* **28** (1), Special issue on 'Sustainability, Resources and Region'.

Braid, R.M. (1989), 'Uniform versus peak-load pricing of a bottleneck with elastic demand', *Journal of Urban Economics* **26**, pp. 320–27.

Daly, H.E. (1989), 'Steady-state and growth concepts for the next century', in Archibugi, F. and P. Nijkamp (eds), *Economy and Ecology: Towards Sustainable Development*, Dordrecht: Kluwer, pp. 73–87.

EC (Commission of the European Communities) (1992a), *White Paper on The Future Development of the Common Transport Policy: A Global Approach to the Construction of a Community Framework for Sustainable Mobility*, Brussels.

EC (Commission of the European Communities) (1992b), *Green Paper on The Impact of Transport on the Environment: A Community Strategy for Sustainable Development*, Brussels: DGVII.

Fujita, M. (1989), *Urban Economic Theory: Land Use and City Size*, Cambridge: Cambridge University Press.

Glazer, A. and E. Niskanen (1992), 'Parking fees and congestion', *Regional Science and Urban Economics* 22, pp. 123–32.

Opschoor, J.B. (1992), 'Sustainable development, the economic process and economic analysis', in Opschoor, J.B. (ed.), *Environment, Economy and Sustainable Development*, Groningen: Wolters-Noordhoff, pp. 25–52.

Opschoor, J.B. and R. Weterings (eds), *Milieu* 9 (5) Special Issue on 'Environmental Utilisation Space'.

d'Ouville, E.L. and J.F. McDonald (1990), 'Optimal road capacity with a suboptimal congestion toll', *Journal of Urban Economics* 28, pp. 34–49.

Pezzey, J. (1993). 'Sustainability: an interdisciplinary guide', *Environmental Values* 1, pp. 321–62.

Samuelson, P.A. (1952), 'Spatial price equilibrium and linear programming', *American Economic Review* 42, pp. 283–303.

Siebert, H. (1982), 'Nature as a life support system: renewable resources and environmental disruption', *Journal of Economics* 42 (2), pp. 133–42.

Sullivan, A.M. (1983), 'Second-best policies for congestion externalities', *Journal of Urban Economics* 14, pp. 105–23.

Takayama, T. and G.G. Judge (1971), *Spatial and Temporal Price and Allocation Models*, Contributions to Economic Analysis 73, Amsterdam: North-Holland.

Takayama, T. and W.C. Labys (1986), 'Spatial equilibrium analysis', in Nijkamp, P. (ed.), *Handbook of Regional and Urban Economics* 1, Amsterdam: Elsevier Science Publishers.

Toman, M.A., J. Pezzey and J. Krautkraemer (1994), 'Neoclassical economic growth theory and 'sustainability', in Bromley, D. (ed.), *Handbook of Environmental Economics*, Oxford: Blackwell, pp. 39–65.

Verhoef, E.T. (1994), 'External effects and social costs of road transport', *Transportation Research A* 28A (4), pp. 273–87.

Verhoef, E.T. and J.C.J.M. van den Bergh (1995), 'A spatial price equilibrium model for environmental policy analysis of mobile and immobile sources of pollution', in Bergh, J.C.J.M. van den, P. Nijkamp and P. Rietveld (eds), *Recent Advances in Spatial Equilibrium Modelling: Methodology and Applications*. Heidelberg: Springer-Verlag.

Verhoef, E.T., P. Nijkamp and P. Rietveld (1994), 'Second-best congestion pricing: the case of an untolled alternative', TRACE discussion paper TI

94–129, Amsterdam–Rotterdam: Tinbergen Institute. Forthcoming in *Journal of Urban Economics*.

Verhoef, E.T., J.C.J.M. van den Bergh, and K.J. Button (1995a), *Transport, Spatial Economy and Global Sustainability*, Working paper, Amsterdam: Free University.

Verhoef, E.T., P. Nijkamp and P. Rietveld (1995b), 'The economics of regulatory parking policies: the (im-)possibilities of parking policies in traffic regulation', *Transportation Research A* **29A** (2), pp. 141–56.

Verhoef, E.T., P. Nijkamp and P. Rietveld (1995c), 'Second-best regulation of road transport externalities', *Journal of Transport Economics and Policy* **29** (2), pp. 147–67.

Verhoef, E.T., P. Nijkamp and P. Rietveld (1995d), 'The trade-off between efficiency, effectiveness and social feasibility of regulating road transport externalities', TRACE discussion paper TI 95–11, Amsterdam–Rotterdam: Tinbergen Institute. Forthcoming in *Transportation Planning and Technology*.

Verhoef, E.T., P. Nijkamp and P. Rietveld (1995e), *Tradable Permits: Their Potentials in Regulating Road Transport Externalities*, Draft, Amsterdam: Free University.

Wilson, J.D. (1983), 'Optimal road capacity in the presence of unpriced congestion', *Journal of Urban Economics* **13**, pp. 337–57.

World Commission on Environment and Development (1987), *Our Common Future*, Oxford/New York: Oxford University Press.

NOTE

1. Welfare is here a narrowly defined concept, measured as the sum of consumer and producer surpluses, and does not include environmental values because environment is treated as a constraint rather than as a temporal externality.

Index